The FBI's Pre-9/11 Vulgar Betrayal

THE FBI'S PRE-9/11 VULGAR BETRAYAL

The True Story of the FBI's Negligent Closing
of the FBI Terrorism Investigation
That Could Have Prevented 9/11

VOLUME 2

FBI SPECIAL AGENT ROBERT G. WRIGHT JR.

The FBI's Pre-9/11 Vulgar Betrayal

© 2025 Robert G. Wright Jr.

All rights reserved. No part of this publication may be reproduced, distributed, or transmitted in any form or by any means, including photocopying, recording, or other electronic or mechanical methods, or by any information storage and retrieval system without the prior written permission of the publisher, except with very brief quotations embodied in critical reviews and certain other noncommercial uses permitted by copyright law.

The information provided within this book is for general informational purposes only. This work depicts actual events, locales, and conversations as truthfully as possible, recalled from personal memories and government documents. Although every effort has been made to ensure that information in this book was correct at press time, the author does not assume, and hereby disclaims, any liability to any party for any loss, damage, or disruption caused by errors or omissions, whether such errors or omissions result from negligence, accident, or any other cause. Some names have been changed to protect privacy.

No generative artificial intelligence (AI) was used in the writing of this book. The author and publisher expressly prohibit any entity from using this publication for purposes of training AI technologies to generate text, including without limitation technologies that are capable of generating works in the same style of genre as this publication. The author and publisher reserve all rights to license use of this work for generative AI training and development of machine learning language models.

Book Interior Design: Creative Publishing Book Design, California
Book Cover Design: Marko Markovic, 5 Media Design, Serbia
Copy Editor: Lisa Cowley, New York

ISBN 979-8-9909444-6-6 (paperback)
ISBN 979-8-9909444-7-3 (hardcover)
ISBN 979-8-9909444-8-0 (ebook)
ISBN 979-8-9909444-9-7 (audiobook)

Published by VB Publishing, LLC
Contact the author at Robert.Wright@VulgarBetrayal.com

Printed in the United States of America.

CONTENTS

	Foreword	vii
	Acronyms	ix
22	The First Trip to Israel	1
23	The Unpredictability of Agent Reed	11
24	"A Muslim Does Not Record Another Muslim!"	25
25	Why Middle East Peace Failed During the 1990s – Part 1	65
26	Why Middle East Peace Failed During the 1990s – Part 2	87
27	The Second Trip to Israel	117
28	The EEO Complaint	135
29	Vulgar Betrayal's Arrest of A HAMAS Terrorist	163
30	The Closing of Agent Reed's Case	181
31	The Retaliation of Morally Bankrupt Agent Reed	195
32	The FBI's Punished Until Proven Innocent Policy	207
33	SAC McChesney Kills Vulgar Betrayal	227
34	The Double Standard of FBI Management	251
35	The FBIHQ OPR Decision	301
36	The OPR Appeal and My Meeting With SAC McChesney	317
37	Mr. Schipper's Confession	331
38	The FBIHQ OPR Appeal Board's Decision	357

39	September 2001	389
40	Afterword	407
	Appendix A	471
	About the Author	487

FOREWORD

John Vincent
FBI Special Agent (retired)

The FBI failed the American people. This is the story of Robert Wright's and my attempt to thwart terrorist attacks before the 9/11 attacks. I was his partner in the FBI and supported our efforts that often fell on deaf ears.

I anguished over whether I should come forward and attempt to awaken the American people and their elected representatives about the FBI's terrorism failures. I was a loyal agent of the FBI and expected to retire as a loyal FBI agent, which I did. I regret needing to share the truth about the FBI before and after the terrorist attacks on 9/11/2001. A former fellow agent asked me how I "could bite the hand that fed me." As did Bob.

Given our direct knowledge of the FBI's terrorism failures, how could we not? How could we allow the FBI to continue its deadly failures? I prided myself on knowing that dissention is not the same as disloyalty. On that premise, I will continue to voice my concerns and my dissent.

I had worked counter terrorism since 1994, and although I had three of the five most important HAMAS cases in Chicago, I gave them up. I gave them up because I wanted to help Robert Wright pursue the Vulgar Betrayal case, which I believed could thwart financial support to Middle Eastern terrorists from within the United States.

Since 1995, Bob and I worked to alter the FBI's failing approach to the war on terrorism. Many within the FBI fought our successful criminal efforts to pursue Middle Eastern terrorists operating in America. I brought my concerns to FBI Director Louie Freeh, explaining that there were forces within the FBI that did not want our criminal prosecutions of terrorists to succeed. All our efforts to prevent future terrorist attacks were negligently shut down by FBI management in August 1999, two years before 9/11.

The most disappointing event I have struggled with since 9/11 is the fact we could not awaken the American people or their elected representatives with the truth about the FBI's lack of terrorism efforts. The most serious offense to the American public are the steps, after 9/11, that the FBI had taken to silence Robert Wright and me from telling you the truth about their negligible antiterrorism efforts.

Much needed changes after 9/11 failed to materialize.

I commend this book to you. Finally—the truth of what Bob and I tried to do is being told.

Why should you read *Vulgar Betrayal?* Inside are the raw facts the FBI has hidden from you—no lies, no spin, or cover-ups. Form your own opinion; then, communicate your feelings about not trusting the FBI to protect you, your family, and your fellow Americans from international terrorism.

ACRONYMS

AD	Assistant Director
AOT	Act of Terrorism
A/SAC	Associate Special Agent in Charge
ASAC	Special Agent in Charge
AUSA	Assistant United States Attorney
BMI	Bait ul-Mal Incorporate
CT	Counter Terrorism
CT-1	Counter Terrorism Squad One
DOJ	Department of Justice
EEO	Equal Employment Opportunity
FBI	Federal Bureau of Investigation
FBIHQ	Federal Bureau of Investigation Headquarters
FD-302	FBI Document Summarizing an Interview
HAMAS	Harakat al-Muqawama al-Islamiyya
INS	Immigration and Naturalization Service
IT	International Terrorism
ITU	International Terrorism Unit
JTTF	Joint Terrorism Task Force
OPR	Office of Professional Responsibility

The FBI's Pre-9/11 Vulgar Betrayal

QLI	Quranic Literacy Institute
RICO	Racketeer Influenced and Corrupt Organizations Act
SA	Special Agent
SAC	Special Agent in Charge
SRA	South Resident Agency Office
SSA	Supervisory Special Agent
UBL	Usama Bin Laden
UC	Under Cover
US	United States
VB	Vulgar Betrayal (FBI Terrorism Investigation)

Author's Note: This is volume 2 in the four-volume Vulgar Betrayal series. You will want to read the first volume first, and then continue the story here. Endnotes and appendix material appear on the website www.VulgarBetrayal.com.

CHAPTER 22
THE FIRST TRIP TO ISRAEL

The purpose of the trip to Israel was to interview Jamil Sarsour, a Palestinian American HAMAS member, regarding his role as a US-based financier of HAMAS terrorists in Palestine. We would inspect the physical evidence that he and the two terrorists, Adel and Imad Awadallah, had with them when they were killed. During the trip, Milwaukee gathered intelligence for the FBI intelligence case. The role of the Chicago personnel was to collect evidence to assist with the VB criminal investigation, with particular emphasis on Sarsour's activities related to providing material support in aid of terrorism to known terrorists in the West Bank and Gaza, for whom Mohammad Salah also provided financial, material support in 1992 and 1993.

The flight from New York to Israel took approximately eleven hours. After landing, our delegation was driven to a hotel near the US embassy in Tel Aviv. As I stood on the balcony overlooking the city, the size of the city surprised me. I understood what Anwar Sadat meant decades earlier when he said, "Israel has become an accomplished fact recognized by the entire world and superpowers." I thought to myself, "What is HAMAS thinking? They are hurting their people by continuing to commit random terrorist attacks against Israel. Their attacks will not prevent the State of Israel from existing."

Later that evening, the attorneys and FBI agents gathered in the hotel's small dining room to eat appetizers and discuss our schedule for the next five days. While waiting for Assistant United States Attorney (AUSA) Mark Flessner to arrive, Milwaukee AUSA Shannon Kern began reminiscing with DOJ Attorney Tony Murphy about their twenty-year friendship. I had already decided Murphy had an ulterior motive for requesting Kern travel on this trip. I suspected that after his unsuccessful attempts to prevent the Chicago United States Attorney's Office from conducting the $1.4 million seizure of HAMAS assets, he was now seeking the assistance of Kern, his close friend, to pursue a Milwaukee criminal case against Sarsour. By utilizing the Milwaukee AUSA and Milwaukee FBI office, he would eliminate having to deal with anyone in the Chicago FBI and US Attorney's offices.

When AUSA Flessner arrived in the dining room, I again warned him about my suspicions regarding Murphy plotting to break away the Sarsour criminal portion of the VB case to pursue a separate speedy material support indictment of Sarsour. In the past, Murphy expressed his desire to be the first attorney to prosecute a material support case under the 1996 Terrorism statute. Because of my past dealings with this man, I believed he would do whatever he could to get his way regarding Sarsour, even if it meant interfering with and harming the VB investigation. Flessner strongly disagreed with me and again told me such a thing could not happen.

During our first meeting with Israeli officials, Agent Cybil Reed and I sat on opposite ends on the same side of the table with Reed's supervisor and the three DOJ attorneys between us. The host country's

The First Trip to Israel

officials sat at a table six feet across from our table. Although I was displeased with Murphy's past interference with the $1.4 million seizure, I assumed that he possessed knowledge regarding HAMAS, particularly the mindset of its extremist members.

At the beginning of the meeting, Murphy said he would like to offer a Palestinian HAMAS terrorist a deal for his cooperation. This took both Reed and me by surprise. I was so impressed that I thought, "This guy came with a game plan. He wants to hurry things along. This is great!"

My excitement was short-lived after Murphy said the name of the HAMAS terrorist. In a state of bafflement because of his absurd suggestion, Reed and I simultaneously blurted out, "What?" Upon hearing each other's response, we leaned back in our seats, shaking our heads in disbelief while looking at each other. This terrorist had spent most of his adult life in prison, spoke no English, had never traveled abroad, was in his thirties or forties, lived with his mother, and had no immediate family in America. Murphy suggested to the host country's officials he wanted to offer this terrorist protection in the US in exchange for his cooperation against his fellow HAMAS brothers.

By making such a ridiculous suggestion, Murphy let our counterparts know he knew nothing about HAMAS and the difficulties in gaining members' cooperation. The head foreign official from the host country chuckled at him and jokingly said, "Sure, no problem. We will even pay for his ticket to America." As FBI agents who understood HAMAS and who were familiar with this terrorist, Reed and I knew no matter what, if he cooperated with the US government and hid in America, HAMAS would find and kill him. Although he would never accept such an offer, I thought to myself, "This is just what

America needs: a trained HAMAS terrorist intentionally moved to America by the United States Department of Justice."

During a break, Reed and I asked Murphy why he did not run this idea by us before the meeting. He deemed it a legal issue, requiring no further explanation. Reed and I attempted to explain the overall situation to him and the other attorneys. We asked them to listen to our suggestions on addressing these matters, especially if Sarsour agreed to be interviewed during our trip. We said that the attorneys should not treat a terrorist as an ordinary criminal, as their terrorist activities did not compare to a typical criminal case. Throughout the day, the attorneys refused to consider our recommendations.

That evening, we made plans for the FBI agents and three DOJ attorneys to travel to Jerusalem, for the next phase of our visit. Out of frustration with the three attorneys' refusal to acknowledge, listen to, or include us in their discussions, Agent Reed and I remained behind for the evening while the others left for Jerusalem. We walked around Tel Aviv and had dinner at a restaurant near the hotel. We talked about feeling sorry for Milwaukee Supervisory Special Agent (SSA) Brad Ford, Reed's supervisor, since he had to travel ahead to Jerusalem with the three attorneys.

Reed and I traveled to Jerusalem in a taxi the following morning. When we arrived at the Hilton Hotel, Ford met us. He told us he had spoken to the attorneys about our frustrations and believed things would be better in the future. He asked us to forget about the previous day, declaring, "This is a new beginning." Reed and I were looking forward to a better relationship with the attorneys. We all took a tour of Old Jerusalem together.

During the tour, we noticed a young man with a camel offering paid rides. Kern and Flessner took a ride together. After they finished,

The First Trip to Israel

Reed and I rode the camel together while the others took pictures. After the rides, we spent several hours touring the old city. What surprised me was the city's incredible history, particularly the number of times Old Jerusalem had been leveled and rebuilt. During the tour, our relationships with the attorneys improved significantly.

However, once work resumed the following day, things reverted to how they had been on the first day. Again, the attorneys refused to accept our recommendations and did not allow us to give any input regarding their decisions. For example, during our meeting with the attorneys regarding how best to gain Sarsour's cooperation, I recommended that the US government use President Bill Clinton's Executive Order to freeze Sarsour's assets in America. The FBI could freeze his many business and personal bank accounts, using them as leverage to convince him to cooperate. In fact, "He [Jamil Sarsour] does own nine mostly commercial properties in the central city [of Milwaukee], city records show. One is a W. Vliet St. property that houses Best Quality Furniture, run by one of Sarsour's brothers, 28-year-old Salah Sarsour."[1]

After Murphy ignored my recommendation, I asked why he was not willing to use such a powerful tool to fight the terrorists. He claimed that President Clinton's Executive Order was not legal and that he did not believe it would be upheld in a court of law.

"It worked well against Mohammad Salah. Why not use it and let the courts decide if it is illegal or not?" I asked.

"We are not going to pursue your avenue!" he yelled.

During another meeting between the attorneys and FBI agents, Reed became upset with one attorney and stated, "I would like to slap your face." Following moments of silence and confusion as to whom Reed was speaking, Flessner asked if she was directing her statement toward him, and if so, why. Reed confirmed it was directed at him for a statement he had made about her. Flessner denied making the alleged statement. After further discussions between the two, Reed became upset and walked out of the meeting. None of us heard anyone make the alleged comment Reed accused Flessner of making.

After the meeting I went to Reed's room to discuss what had occurred. When she answered the door, she was crying. While talking, she calmed down and began laughing about the whole situation. She confessed that she was an emotional person and had difficulty controlling her emotions.

Because of the repeated incidents between the attorneys and us, we had limited contact with the attorneys and spent a lot of time sightseeing and working together. Fortunately, Reed's supervisor continued communicating with the attorneys and informed us about what was happening.

During our second evening in Jerusalem, she and I met in my room to draft questions in anticipation of the Sarsour interview. We worked well together and enjoyed one another's company, something neither of us expected would happen. She confessed she was not pleased when she learned I was coming along on the trip. She thought I wouldn't be fun because I took things too seriously. I admitted I felt the same, and we agreed it was nice we were wrong about each other.

We discovered we shared the same work ethic and opinions about problems within the FBI and had the same terrorism concerns. Both of us grew up in Indiana, and we talked about our aspirations to move to the Indianapolis FBI office someday. After realizing I was interested in moving to Indianapolis, she offered, "I could set you up with some friends I have in Indianapolis."

"No, thanks. I can find someone on my own," I said.

The First Trip to Israel

I told her I wouldn't commit to a relationship during the Vulgar Betrayal investigation because of its demands. My planned investigation's duration made me doubt any relationship's survival. She stated during the evening, "I cannot believe how much alike we are. It is scary how well we are getting along." I agreed.

The following evening, while working on some paperwork, we discussed our families and parents and where we grew up in Indiana. I asked her how she and her husband met. She said they were just friends when, one day, he approached her and asked if she would go on a date with him. They later married and had three children, two boys and a girl. Her daughter was the youngest and had been born within the past eight months.

Knowing our parents were worried about us traveling to the Middle East, we took a break to call and let them know we were safe. She even spoke to my mother; likewise, I talked to her mother to assure her we were fine. At least something positive came from the frustration caused by the attorneys; she and I got to know one another and discovered we enjoyed working together and were becoming friends.

The following evening, she and I began working on some paperwork. Ford periodically entered the room during the evening to discuss the continuing problems between the attorneys and us. We jokingly informed him we were still waiting for "the new beginning" he had promised us when we first arrived in Jerusalem. During the evening, she kept repeating how scary it was that she and I were so much alike. After she left the room to retrieve some documents, Brad said, "Bob, I am so happy to see you both getting along so well. She has a tough time dealing well with others. Collaboration between you two is excellent."

The following afternoon, while the others were interviewing someone, Brad and I had lunch at the Hilton Hotel. During lunch,

I explained why I had begun the VB case, the complications caused by the ignorance and misunderstandings of others within the FBI, the case goals and my plans for achieving them. After about thirty minutes of my explanations, he leaned back in his chair and stated, "Oh my God! You know what you are talking about. You know what you are doing!" Confused by his exclamation, I asked why he would make such statements.

He said, before departing for the trip, SSA Barney Clinton had informed him I was "out-of-control, did not know what I was doing, and was conducting an out-of-control fishing expedition." It was very disappointing to discover that Clinton, who could help the VB criminal investigation move forward, continued to make defamatory statements regarding VB and my investigative efforts to locate and neutralize Middle Eastern terrorists living and operating within America.

I said, "Brad, before this trip, Clinton said to me, 'Bob, to be honest with you, I have no idea what your Vulgar Betrayal criminal investigation is about myself. I do not understand it.'"

I also informed him that I discovered Clinton had made the same slanderous statements to SSA Timothy Gossfeld in December 1997, when Clinton learned Gossfeld was the new supervisor of the Chicago Joint Terrorism Task Force (JTTF).

I said, "Tim and I recently agreed, with all that had occurred during the past year, Clinton could no longer justify making such statements about me or the Vulgar Betrayal investigation. We were wrong."

I realized how it could take just one incompetent FBI Headquarters (FBIHQ) supervisor, such as Clinton, to destroy any FBI investigation, no matter how critical the investigation is to the national security of the United States. I then knew why Vulgar Betrayal had received no support from the International Terrorism Unit (ITU).

The First Trip to Israel

Clinton, who admitted to me he did not know what it was about and did not understand the case, had been intentionally sabotaging my efforts by lying to other FBI managers about me and my investigation. Unfortunately, there was nothing a street agent could do to have these matters resolved. By then, three FBI supervisors had each told me how Clinton had slandered me and the Vulgar Betrayal case.

The next day, attorneys and agents met Sarsour. He required time before deciding whether to speak. Again, I told Murphy that he would likely cooperate if he used President Clinton's Executive Order to seize Sarsour's US assets. Murphy again dismissed my recommendation.

The following evening, we learned Sarsour had refused to meet with us for a second meeting. The attorneys traveled back to America. The attorneys assumed Ford, Reed, and I would fly back to America with them. However, Reed and I remained for another day to review further evidence. Ford advised he had contacted one of the host country's officials, who was upset over the sudden departure of the DOJ attorneys without the courtesy of a meeting to explain their findings and plans. Therefore, he remained behind with us.

The following morning, we met with the host country's officials, who assisted us during the visit. The officials advised they intended to file a formal protest against the visit of Murphy. They were upset over his unexpected departure and did not extend the courtesy of a meeting to explain his findings and plans. We did our best to cover the DOJ attorney's back and helped to prevent the formal protest from being filed against him.

Before leaving the hotel to travel to the airport that evening, I telephoned my supervisor to brief him about the trip. Aware Gossfeld was not a fan of Reed, I stated, "I have some news. Cybil and I are getting along. It looks as if we are going to work well together."

"If it helps the case, this is great news," he remarked.

At the airport, Reed suggested she and I sit together on the return flight if possible, and I agreed. A few hours into the flight, we fell asleep. In the morning, when we awoke, had breakfast, and prepared for the landing, Reed stated, "Now I understand why some people have affairs."

"Excuse me," I said.

"Now I understand why some people have affairs," she repeated.

I did not ask her to explain, as I figured she was referring to our enjoyable time together in Israel. I thought it was nice that we worked well together and became friends, but I had no interest or intentions of being anything other than friends.

When I arrived home from the trip to Israel, I purchased a flagpole and an American flag. The following morning, I installed the flagpole in the front yard of my home. Until I traveled abroad, I did not realize nor appreciate how lucky I was to be an American citizen.

During my first day back in the Chicago office, while talking to Agent John Vincent, I said, "John, so many Americans take what we have here in America for granted. Until my Middle East trip, I also took it for granted. I wish every American could take such a trip overseas and discover how lucky they are to be living in America."

"I agree," he said.

CHAPTER 23

THE UNPREDICTABILITY OF AGENT REED

Upon returning from Israel, I informed SSA Gossfeld about the problems between the agents and attorneys during our trip. I told him I was considering leaving the FBI and would take the week off to contemplate whether I wanted to remain with the FBI. He asked me to take home my FBI laptop computer, necessary VB files, and my FBI vehicle.

His request that I take items home ensured my return. He explained. "Take the computer and files with you; when you get bored, review the material to see what you will give up. I hope you realize unless you stay and finish this case, the case will die, and the terrorists will win."

I did as he requested and took the computer, necessary files, and car home with me for the next week.

During the first week of February 1999, I completed home improvement projects, including installing a new water heater. I began reviewing the criminal files and databases on the second day of my week off. Although some of the databases were several years old, no one, including myself, had ever taken the time to analyze all the information within them to identify the overall structure of the HAMAS criminal enterprise within the US. After thirty minutes of reviewing the timeline database, I noticed some significant financial links I had never seen before. However, still frustrated with HQ, I stopped looking at the material and thought, "The hell with it. If no one else cares what these terrorists are doing to America, why should I?" I went back to working on my home improvement projects.

Later that evening I thought about the dedication and support of Agent Vincent, other Chicago agents as well as others around the country, and the three assistant US attorneys who had dedicated significant time to the success of the VB investigation. I did not want to let them down after they had helped move it forward despite the ITU's intentional lack of support over protecting the terrorism subjects of their unproductive intelligence case files.

The following morning, I again looked at the VB timeline database and continued linking more significant pieces of the international HAMAS puzzle. With no distractions from phone calls and noisy office space, I found more pieces of it. I realized I needed to organize a tremendous amount of information to identify the size of the organization in America.

I gathered two four-foot-by-four-foot marker boards and several smaller boards from my basement and placed them around the dining room. Each board contained a specific category for individuals, organizations, and financial transactions. When I developed information regarding each category, I marked the information on the boards in chronological order.

During the rest of my week off, I worked from home day and night, reviewing all the information. When I discovered something

The Unpredictability of Agent Reed

significant about HAMAS, I called Gossfeld, the AUSAs, and Vincent to share the discoveries. I made fifty-six phone calls to my coworkers in Chicago during that week.

Through further review of the VB timeline database, I identified many individuals and organizations in the US and many other countries responsible for assisting with the creation of the US-based HAMAS terrorist organization. I also identified the leadership, those who provided material support to aid Middle East terrorism, and additional terrorists.

I could identify each of the US-based HAMAS terrorist training camps, the names of each terrorist attendee, the camp instructors, and the speakers. I recognized many more unknown US-based front organizations. I created another dozen full-color charts to present my findings to others in an understandable, chronological, and coherent manner.

Realizing the significance of the databases, I stayed with the FBI. Leaving at that point would have meant that the past five years of my life were a complete waste of time. I knew the FBI would eventually kill the VB investigation. Gossfeld and I discussed many times that should I leave the case, they would close the case and return the seized $1.4 million back to the terrorists. I believed the best way to defeat the terrorists, save American and Israeli lives, and protect the national and economic security of the US was to remain with the FBI and continue working on the case.

The Chicago and Milwaukee FBI and US Attorney's offices convened a meeting in Chicago on February 25, 1999. Before the meeting began, Ford approached me and mentioned how Reed had expressed to him many times how happy she was to be working with me since the trip to Israel. According to him, she often mentioned how she could not believe how much we were alike. He again expressed his happiness over how well we got along. I told him that I, too, was surprised at how well we were getting along and that I was happy to work with her.

With Reed present, Brad presented me with a T-shirt. He had a photograph of her and me riding the camel in Jerusalem transposed onto the T-shirt. He superimposed his head over the camel handler's head, creating the illusion that he was holding the camel. Under the photo, he had "To a New Beginning" printed on the T-shirt. The wording was an inside joke between the three of us regarding our difficulties with the attorneys during the recent Middle East trip.

The shirt Brad made depicting Reed and me on a camel.

To avoid duplication of efforts by the VB criminal agents in Chicago and the intelligence agents in Milwaukee, we decided to hold bi-weekly meetings between the two divisions for information sharing. Reed and I would take turns traveling to and from Chicago and Milwaukee to compare notes regarding our investigations.

Realizing these trips might require an overnight stay, she stated several times to me, "You had better not abandon me after five o'clock when I come down to Chicago." She suggested I avoid going home after work and instead join her during her Chicago visit. I agreed and told her I would enjoy hanging out with her since I rarely did anything downtown after work. She also stated, "When you come up to Milwaukee, you need to come over to my house and have dinner with my family." It was nice, we were becoming friends.

The Unpredictability of Agent Reed

After the meeting on February 25, 1999, there were no indications of impending issues between the Chicago and Milwaukee offices. Both the Chicago FBI and the United States Attorney's offices believed Milwaukee was handling the FBI's intelligence investigation of Sarsour and the Chicago division was handling the FBI's Act of Terrorism (AOT) criminal investigation.

However, the first sign of a severe problem between Chicago and Milwaukee occurred on March 1, 1999. In an unexpected turn of events, my suspicions about DOJ Attorney Murphy using Milwaukee to further his selfish goal of pursuing Sarsour independently of the FBI's VB criminal investigation were proven right. After calling me into his office, Gossfeld handed me a communication he had received from Reed. He asked me to read it before leaving his office. Her communication requested copies of all pertinent VB criminal investigation documents. In addition, she asked for a copy of the analysis completed to date regarding all financial records received. Turn over my entire Vulgar Betrayal work product for the past three years to her.

"What's this, Tim?" I laughed, questioning. "Does she think we are working full-time on Sarsour? We have not even begun analyzing his records. She is working on an intelligence case. She does not need our criminal analysis."

"Bob, look closer. You missed something," said Tim.

While reviewing the communication a second time, it hit me like a ton of bricks. She had opened a duplicate VB criminal investigation.

"What is this? How in the hell does she think she will get away with this? I warned all of you that this would happen, and none of you listened to me," I said.

Chicago and Milwaukee were now simultaneously conducting the same criminal investigation on Jamil Sarsour. On the first day of her new criminal case, Reed requested the VB work product to aid Murphy in pursuing a rapid indictment of Sarsour for providing material support to HAMAS.

The Chicago FBI and US Attorney's offices were concerned that an indictment of Sarsour by Milwaukee would jeopardize the entire VB investigation. The concern was that such an indictment by Milwaukee would open the whole three-year VB investigation up to discovery by Sarsour's attorney. Most importantly, Sarsour's recent activities established the two criminal counts required within the past five years to allow the prosecution of many other HAMAS members under the Racketeer Influenced and Corrupt Organizations Act (RICO) criminal statute. VB was not seeking quick indictments for statistical reasons, as most agents do. It was working to identify the entire HAMAS membership, organizations, those responsible for training, financing, and ordering deadly terrorist attacks against innocent civilians. The plan was to take out as much of the HAMAS criminal enterprise as possible simultaneously, not in the usual piecemeal fashion in which FBI cases are usually worked.

In addition, there were concerns that Milwaukee would waste investigative time by duplicating Chicago's three years of investigative efforts. As Murphy stated after the VB I Conference held in Chicago on January 28, 1998, this duplication of a portion of the VB case should not occur.

Murphy's motivation had nothing to do with what was in the best interest of the US government, nor was he concerned about the negative effect his actions would have on the VB investigation. His concerns were personal in that he wanted credit for being instrumental in the first indictment and conviction by the US Department of Justice against a terrorist under the US Anti-Terrorism Statute 2339(b), passed by Congress in 1996.

To prevent Milwaukee from conducting a duplicate investigation, I spent several days and valuable investigative time preparing charts to establish the potential harm such an investigation would cause in advancing VB's goals. Unfortunately, neither Clinton nor anyone else at FBIHQ would do their job. When I finished the charts, I presented them to the Chicago AUSAs for their review before the next bi-weekly meeting between Milwaukee and Chicago. The charts, comprising fifteen pages, aided those present at the meeting in baby-stepping through Sarsour's connections with many HAMAS members identified through the VB investigation.

On March 5, 1999, we held a conference in Chicago to discuss Milwaukee's decision to open a duplicate criminal investigation of Sarsour. Murphy flew in from Washington, DC, to attend the meeting to protect his selfish pursuit of Sarsour. Using the fifteen charts, I showed how a separate criminal investigation by Milwaukee into the same criminal activity already being investigated through VB would cause a massive duplication of Chicago's three-year investigation of the HAMAS Enterprise. I further warned that, if Milwaukee continued with its criminal investigation, it would overlap the VB investigation in many areas, harming the planned future arrest and indictments of HAMAS members throughout the US and overseas.

I then reminded Murphy about his strong recommendation in January 1998 against splitting apart any part of the VB case. He was now splitting an essential and critical piece to seek a material support indictment against Sarsour. He said he was not concerned about the adverse effects the split would have on the investigation.

Murphy then had the nerve to blame the problems I had outlined squarely on members of the United States Congress. He said he was under tremendous pressure from members of Congress to prosecute someone under the Material Support Statute 2339(b). He, for the first time, announced his true intentions. I glanced at the Chicago AUSAs and exclaimed, "There it is! I told you what he was up to, and you ignored me. You thought I was paranoid, stating this could never happen." Chicago argued unsuccessfully with Murphy that to indict this one person would jeopardize the entire three-year investigation.

To avoid overlapping problems of duplicate criminal investigations, the Milwaukee FBI and US Attorney's offices agreed not to request any records outside the State of Wisconsin and they limited their criminal investigation to matters occurring within the state. Reed received copies of all requested documents related to the Milwaukee division from Chicago. The Milwaukee FBI and US Attorney's offices requested Chicago forward copies of all future records obtained concerning residents of the Milwaukee division. All parties expressed satisfaction with this agreement and believed it would help avoid interference and duplication of the VB investigation.

On March 17, 1999, Kathleen L. McChesney, the new Chicago Special Agent in Charge (SAC), arrived in the Chicago division. SAC McChesney appeared supportive of the VB efforts, which was welcome news to Gossfeld, Vincent, and me.

On March 26, 1999, another bi-weekly meeting occurred in Milwaukee. During the meeting, FBIHQ announced we would return to Israel to attempt another interview with Sarsour. Before departing Milwaukee, while standing beside her desk, Reed showed me pictures of her three children and husband. She also gave me several FBI Milwaukee souvenir pens.

The Unpredictability of Agent Reed

After returning to Chicago, I discovered she had issued duplicate subpoenas to financial institutions, from which I had already subpoenaed the identical records. On the same day, the two out-of-state financial institutions called me. They questioned why they needed to reproduce the duplicate financial records they provided to Chicago for the Milwaukee office. This is one example of the many problems that we expected. However, to make it more frustrating, Reed failed to mention anything about issuing these subpoenas after we agreed that the two offices would work together. I contacted one of the Chicago AUSAs to advise him of Milwaukee's duplication efforts. He would now have to address this matter with the Milwaukee AUSA.

Since March 26, 1999, dealing with Reed had become increasingly difficult. She began accusing Chicago agents of withholding requested records. She was told there were only three agents assigned to VB, and we were working on many complicated avenues of a complex investigation. We informed her that the Chicago agents were not focusing 100 percent of our efforts on Sarsour.

She then accused Chicago of not considering Sarsour vital since we were not investigating him full-time. I said that for the VB investigation to work appropriately, the Chicago agents must simultaneously work on various facets of the investigation. We could not drop the hundreds of other VB targets to focus on Jamil Sarsour full-time.

In addition, I said there was only so much Chicago could do until we received the subpoenaed documents regarding Sarsour and entered them into the VB databases. Then, we would review the databases and connect Sarsour's HAMAS-related activities with all other HAMAS members. I added I was sure of my actions, requesting her patience. She was told Chicago management would not provide any support employees to assist with the massive reproduction of such a large volume of VB records being received by Chicago daily.

After March 26, complicating matters further, Reed complained to her supervisor every time I spoke to her on the phone if I did not meet her immediate demands for VB documentation. Although the phone conversations were cordial and pleasant, she would tell her supervisor I had just upset her during our call. Within minutes of my calls with her, her supervisor would call Gossfeld and inform him I had upset Reed. When Gossfeld questioned me, her allegations would genuinely confuse me, since there was no hint of any anger or hostility between us during our conversations.

After she repeated similar allegations following our next two conversations, I asked her to tell me if anything I said during our phone conversations upset her. I said that I did not want my supervisor to receive calls from her supervisor saying there was a problem when I had no sign any problem existed between us. She promised future feedback regarding my actions and words that displeased her.

Unfortunately, Reed continued to make similar complaints to her supervisor after we talked. Not only after our telephone conversations but also over innocent voicemail messages. Ultimately, calls from the Milwaukee SAC and ASAC were even being placed to Chicago management complaining about how I was upsetting her during our conversations. Reed's complaining became so predictable that, following every conversation I had with her, I would immediately brief Gossfeld about the details of our discussion before the calls started coming in from Milwaukee management. Sometimes, the Milwaukee supervisor called Gossfeld while I was briefing him about the call. The entire situation with her was mind-boggling for both Gossfeld and me. At one point, I said, "Tim, I am confident no agent has ever asked this question before, but can I please have

The Unpredictability of Agent Reed

permission to record my conversations with Agent Reed? This will reveal her serious mental problems. It's unconventional, I admit, but I see no alternative."

"Recording your conversations with her is serious, let's hold off on recording your conversations," said Tim.

This situation was so bad that, on one occasion, after leaving a message in her voicemail box, I sat at my desk thinking about the message I had just left. Vincent noticed something was wrong with me and asked, "What is wrong?"

"Nothing. I recorded a message for Agent Reed, and now I'm considering how she could misinterpret my message," I said.

I called and left a second message that ensured her understanding of the first message. Within an hour, Reed's supervisor called Gossfeld regarding the two messages. This time, though, her supervisor listened to both messages to understand why Reed was so upset.

Gossfeld said the Milwaukee supervisor said he received a "frantic call" from Reed, stating, "He is doing it again! He is doing it again!" She demanded that her supervisor listen to the messages I had left on her voicemail and provided him with her numeric code to retrieve my messages. He listened to the first message I left, felt there was nothing wrong with the message, and failed to understand why she was upset. He then realized I had left a second message and suspected this was the message she was frantically upset over. He questioned why I recorded a second message after he listened to it, since there was nothing wrong with the first message.

On April 8, 1999, the fourth meeting between Milwaukee and Chicago occurred in Chicago. Since Reed could not attend the conference, I approached her supervisor, Brad Ford, and expressed my concerns over her making false allegations regarding my intentional withholding of records from Milwaukee. In addition, I expressed my concern over her constant misinterpretations of conversations and her complaints to Milwaukee management.

Brad mentioned the frantic call he had received concerning the two messages I had left on her voicemail.

"Bob, I found nothing wrong with your messages on her voice mailbox. I cannot understand why she became so upset. Did the message contain a hidden meaning that only you two could comprehend?"

"No. Brad, I believe she has some serious problems. We are trying to investigate a serious matter, and all she has done is cause grief, anger, and loss of investigative time for me and the other two Vulgar Betrayal agents."

Brad then asked, "Why did you call back and leave the second message?"

"I left the second message in her voicemail to prevent any misinterpretation of my first message. Brad, after we get off the phone or I leave a message for her, I replay our conversation or the message I left in my head. I do this each time I talk to her to figure out if there was any possibility of her misinterpreting what I said."

"When did this start?" he asked.

"Since she started complaining after every conversation we have on the phone. Brad, I am so confused over her constant complaining and misinterpretation of our conversations. I am hesitant to call or speak to her since each time we speak, no matter the subject we discuss, she misinterprets our conversations and complains about me to Milwaukee management. Then your office calls Chicago, complaining to my supervisors."

"Bob, I'm speechless. You need to work together. Please try to work with her," said Brad.

The Unpredictability of Agent Reed

"I am sorry, Brad. I cannot do such a thing now. I have enough issues to deal with regarding the Vulgar Betrayal investigation. I cannot continue dealing with her issues. It's so bad that, following each phone call with her, I now immediately advise Tim that I have just finished a phone call with her and provide him with the accurate details of the call. I must warn him before any Milwaukee managers reach out to him," I explained.

"Did someone call after you briefed Tim?"

"Brad, there were times I was briefing Tim when you called. I have reached a point where I no longer want to talk to her. She has some serious issues. It has become so frustrating. I requested permission from Tim to start recording my telephone conversations with her."

"Bob, please stay in contact with her. I will talk to her; I assure you, things will get better."

"This entire problem wouldn't even exist if someone at headquarters would simply do their job, step in, and announce which office handles the criminal investigation of Sarsour," I said.

Also present at the April 8 meeting was a new supervisor from FBIHQ, SSA Michael Resnick. Resnick said that he was now responsible for handling the ITU's criminal investigations of suspected terrorists. I provided him with an overview of the entire VB criminal investigation and shared the problems between Chicago and Milwaukee. He said that his role was to evaluate the FBI's criminal cases of terrorist subjects and organizations, identify any issues, and resolve them in a manner that was in the best interest of the FBI as an organization, not by the individual interest or desires of a particular FBI office.

Although this sounded good, the tone and manner in which he made his statement left me with the impression that Clinton had spoken to him about VB and me. I am confident Clinton told Resnick the same things he told Tim, Brad, and others.

I would have to convince Resnick that I knew what I was doing, that VB was a complicated and exceptional criminal investigation, and that, with help from him as the FBIHQ supervisor, VB could help save lives. He needed to understand that VB had realistic goals geared toward preventing HAMAS from committing future terrorist attacks in Israel by stopping their significant financial support network within the United States.

Near concluding this meeting, Milwaukee agreed to send support personnel to Chicago to help copy all records in Chicago's possession needed by their office. One of the Chicago AUSAs assigned to the investigation agreed that the Chicago US Attorney's Office would copy and forward all future Wisconsin-related records to Milwaukee, since the Chicago FBI management was unwilling to provide an FBI employee to perform this task. They made this agreement to ease Reed's concerns about Chicago, promptly sending future records to Milwaukee.

CHAPTER 24

A MUSLIM DOES NOT RECORD ANOTHER MUSLIM!

"The vast majority of Muslims are honorable, decent people. But US interests are in danger from Middle East terrorism. You have to say that without fear of being called a bigot."[1]
 –Steve Pomerantz, Former FBI Counterterrorism Chief

This chapter concerns the FBI's investigation, or lack thereof, of the Bait ul-Mal Incorporate (BMI), aka House of Money and Kadi International,[2] which has been operating in the US and financed by known international terrorists and financial supporters of known US-designated terrorists since the 1980s. "BMI's investor list reads like a who's who of US-designated terrorists and Islamic extremist investors in BMI, including, [but not limited to]" the following:[3]

Soliman Biheiri   The head of BMI and the US banker for the Muslim Brotherhood, a banned Egyptian militant group.[4]

Abdullah Awad bin Laden	A nephew of Osama bin Laden, he invested half-a-million dollars in the BMI real estate ventures. Heads a Saudi charity called World Assembly of Muslim Youth (WAMY).[5]
Mousa Abu Marzook	He has identified himself as a top leader of Hamas. The US declared him a terrorist in 1995.[6]
Yassin al-Qadi (Kadi)	A Saudi multimillionaire. His lawyers will later claim he only has a passing involvement and liquidated his investment in it in 1996. However, another company operating from the same office as BMI is called Kadi International Inc. and lists its president as al-Qadi [Kadi]. Al-Qadi [Kadi] is also a major investor in the suspected computer company P-Tech.[7]
Tarek Swaidan	He is a Kuwaiti, an associate of al-Qadi [Kadi], and a leading member of the Kuwaiti branch of the Muslim Brotherhood.[8]
Saleh Kamel	BMI allegedly receives $500,000 investment from the Dallah Al-Baraka banking conglomerate, which is headed by Kamel. Kamel founded a Sudanese Islamic bank which housed accounts for senior Al-Qaeda operatives. He is a multi-billionaire heavily involved in promoting Islam, and his name appears on the Golden Chain, a list of early Al-Qaeda supporters.[9]
Abdurahman Alamoudi	For many years, he ran the American Muslim Council, a lobby group funded by a top Muslim Brotherhood figure. He also is in the [Muslim] Brotherhood, with ties to Hamas.[10]
Nur and Iman bin Laden	Two female relatives of Osama bin Laden. Neither has been accused of any knowing connections to terrorist financing.[11]

A Muslim Does Not Record Another Muslim!

During early March 1999, information identified BMI as a significant financial link to many Middle Eastern terrorist groups and was one of the three Muslim organizations I suspected of sending funds overseas to finance terrorist attacks against the United States. Terrorist attacks like the US embassy bombings in Kenya and Tanzania on August 7, 1998. A federal grand jury in Chicago issued two subpoenas to Soliman Biheiri, President of BMI, and his vice president. The federal grand jury awaits these men.

On March 16, 1999, while qualifying at the Chicago FBI gun range, I received a call from Dallas FBI Agent Gamal Abdel-Hafiz, the Muslim FBI agent who helped us during the review of the Dallas intelligence files in December 1998. Abdel-Hafiz said he needed to talk to me about a matter concerning the VB investigation. He said, "Bob, before I tell you what happened, I need to inform you that the person I am about to refer to is someone I listed as a reference on my FBI application when I applied for my FBI agent position." He then said he and the accountant for BMI, Abu Abu, were good friends.[12] According to him, Abu contacted him and asked him to meet privately to discuss a problem with Abu's BMI employment. Shortly after, Gamal traveled to Washington, DC, and met with Abu at his home.

According to Abdel-Hafiz, during the meeting, Abu expressed his concern over a federal grand jury investigation in Chicago focusing on BMI. Abu informed him of the subpoenas of BMI's president and vice president. Abu asked if he should quit his employment with BMI, as a criminal investigation was underway. Abu told Abdel-Hafiz he feared the investigation of BMI may harm his chances of being hired by the FBI; he had a pending FBI employment application at FBIHQ. For the record, Abu was not the HAMAS member VB identified as having filed an FBI agent application.

Abdel-Hafiz said that, following his meeting with the BMI accountant, he returned to the Dallas office and retrieved and reviewed the Chicago VB case files available there. He said he reviewed the VB documentation to learn to what extent BMI was involved in the VB investigation. After reading the files and confirming BMI's status within the investigation, he then decided to contact me.

To this day, I still find it disturbing that Gamal went through the VB files to determine the extent of the FBI's investigation of the terrorist-linked organization BMI, of which his friend was the accountant, before calling me. I believe he should have called the Chicago FBI office to relay Abu Abu's request for the meeting before visiting with him. Not doing this, he had an obligation to contact Chicago after meeting with Abu at his home. He had no right to review any VB files to discover to what extent his friend might have been involved with criminal activities associated with BMI.

During our conversation, I informed him that, through the course of the VB investigation, I learned BMI had a close association with well-known terrorists, such as Mousa Abu Marzook.[13] I also informed him of Mohammad Salah, Yassin Kadi, the Quranic Literacy Institute (QLI), and others' financial connections to BMI, which are linked to international terrorism.

Although I was concerned about Abu, I had made no preconceived judgments about Abdel-Hafiz's close personal relationship with him.

I said to him, "Gamal, to protect yourself in the future, should we discover your friend is involved in terrorism activities, you need to write an EC detailing your meeting with the BMI accountant and forward the EC to the Chicago Vulgar Betrayal case file. Include in the EC how you know Abu Abu and everything you discussed with him."

"I will write the EC," he said.

"Gamal, listen to me; this may be hard, but you must avoid further contact with Abu. We are investigating a serious matter about BMI and its international financial links to terrorism. Abu may be involved being the BMI accountant. Do not talk to him until we determine his role within BMI," I said.

"All right," he agreed.

On March 22, 1999, Gamal sent the following FBI communication to Chicago's VB file regarding his contact with Abu:

FEDERAL BUREAU OF INVESTIGATION
Precedence: ROUTINE   Date: 03/22/1999
To: National Security
             Chicago
From: Dallas JTTF/IT
Drafted By: Contact: Dallas FBI Agent
Case ID #:   265C-CG-101942 (Pending)
Title: VULGAR BETRAYAL
             OO: CHICAGO
Synopsis: To advise Chicago of a conversation between writer and a contact in Falls Church, Virginia.

Administrative: Express promises of confidentiality, both limited and unlimited, have been granted to the individual Abu Abu (Not real name, the FBI blacked the real name out).

Reference: Telephone conversation between SA Dallas Agent and SA Robert G. Wright on 03/16/1999.

Details: Per the telephone conversation between Dallas FBI Agent and SA Robert G. Wright, neither the FBI nor the AUSA (Assistant United States Attorney) will reveal that Abu Abu came forward with this information to the FBI nor should it be revealed that he expressed his willingness to testify if he was subpoenaed. Revealing this information may jeopardize Abu Abu's life or safety. It may also jeopardize his chances of obtaining employment connected to the Arab community. [Note: The Dallas Agent omitted Abu Abu, had a pending employment application with FBIHQ in this communication.] Should the FBI decide to use Abu Abu's assistance in this case, they need to subpoena him without revealing his prior contact with SA Gamal Abdel-Hafiz.

On 3/12/1999, while SA Abdel-Hafiz was returning to Dallas, Texas from an in-service at the FBI Academy, he met a longtime friend, Abu Abu who resides [in Virginia], who is an accountant for a company called BMI and currently handles [responsibilities] for same. Abu Abu advised SA Abdel-Hafiz that his boss [Soliman Biheiri] was subpoenaed to testify before a Federal Grand Jury in Chicago. Abu Abu was concerned for several reasons: [Note: The FBI blacked out the next two full paragraphs.]

Abu Abu advised SA Abdel-Hafiz of his uneasy feeling with the situation and asked if he should resign. SA Abdel-Hafiz advised Abu Abu that he (Agent Abdel-Hafiz) is not aware of any investigation regarding either of those individuals nor the companies he (Abu Abu) mentioned. SA Abdel-Hafiz advised Abu Abu to remain with his employment as long as he desired and there should not be any reason to be alarmed. SA Abel-Hafiz also advised Abu Abu to continue carrying out his duties as usual.

Abu Abu advised that if he is questioned or subpoenaed by the FBI, he will appear and tell the truth regarding inquires.[14]

Also on March 16, 1999, following Abdel-Hafiz's call, I informed AUSA Mark Flessner about the BMI accountant's contact with

A Muslim Does Not Record Another Muslim!

Abdel-Hafiz. I said that the BMI accountant was concerned about the federal grand jury subpoena we served on Soliman Biheiri, ordering him to appear in Chicago.[15] Flessner asked if the FBI, through the VB investigation, had gathered any information about BMI and its employees.

I said, "Yes, but I cannot recall the information gathered to date. However, the good news is that a year ago, Agent Leonard Brat, an accountant, was assigned to the VB investigation. He's focused solely on BMI this past year. He should be able to answer any questions you have regarding BMI."

Flessner requested I return to his office in one hour with Agent Brat.

Although Agent Brat had been assigned to the VB case on April 18, 1998, he continuously bragged about not conducting any work on BMI, the only assignment he was tasked to investigate during the past eleven months. Instead, he placed an eight-inch-by-ten-inch mirror on his desk to pretend to be working when he noticed FBI management approaching from behind. He continually lowered the morale of other agents assisting with the VB investigation. He did this by telling other agents the VB case was unrealistic and a complete waste of time, and he continually distracted others working it. Although he did little work on the case, he received about $100,000 in FBI pay while assigned to VB.

After returning to the JTTF squad room, I informed agents Vincent and Brat that we needed to attend a meeting regarding BMI in Flessner's office. Brat questioned why he needed to participate in the meeting. I told him he was the only agent assigned to investigate BMI, and Flessner requested he attend.

After Brat left the room, Vincent asked, "Bob, should I attend this meeting?"

I replied, "John, this meeting will not go well. Brat cannot answer any of Flessner's questions during this meeting. Flessner will fully expose Brat's dereliction of duty over the past year, and when he does, the meeting will turn ugly. I don't want it to be my word against Brat's. I need you to attend this meeting to inform FBI management what occurred during this meeting."

"I understand. I'll be there," said John.

John, Brat, and I met with Flessner in his office an hour later. Flessner summarized his concerns regarding BMI and Abu's meeting with Abdel-Hafiz.

"There is something up with BMI. I want to learn more about BMI and those running the organization. Agent Brat, what can you tell me about BMI?" asked Flessner.

Brat asked, "What information do you seek?"

"How was BMI established? Was it set up as a corporation or non-profit organization?" asked Flessner.

"I cannot recall," said Brat.

"Ok, tell me about the history of BMI's president and vice president," said Flessner.

"I cannot recall," said Brat.

Sensing a problem, Flessner asked, "Agent Brat, can you tell me the names of BMI's president and vice president?"

"No," said Brat.

"Is your work product in the case file?" asked Flessner.

"Yes," said Brat.

"Okay, we're going to take a break while you grab the files and bring them back to my office," said Flessner.

"You are not my supervisor! I do not answer to you, and I do not have to show you my files!" Brat yelled at Flessner.

Brat's outburst took us all by surprise. Perplexed by Brat's demeanor, Flessner turned to me and asked, "Bob, what is this? What is going on here?"

"Do not ask me. I am not his supervisor either. His sole assignment for the last eleven months has been BMI," I remarked.

Although BMI was a priority aspect of the VB investigation, after he spent a year of no investigative work on BMI, someone finally exposed Brat's willful dereliction of duty. The meeting ended with nothing accomplished. John and I believed this incident with Flessner would force FBI management to remove Brat from the VB case and replace him with another agent willing to perform their duties. Unfortunately, Gossfeld's absence delayed addressing Brat's situation.

Brat met with Gossfeld the following morning before I arrived in the office. John and I discovered he portrayed himself as the victim during his version of the meeting with Flessner. John and I told Tim that Brat became defensive and disrespectful toward Flessner simply because Brat had no work product to show for the past eleven months. We asked Tim to remove him from the VB case. We also pleaded with Tim to move Brat from the north end of the squad room to the south end near Tim's office. When Tim asked why we wanted him moved, we informed him Brat was a constant distraction to others.

After further discussions between the three AUSAs, Tim, and I regarding Brat, it was recommended Agent Brat be replaced. However, Chicago FBI management believed Brat deserved a second chance to redeem himself. He had four weeks to complete the investigative analysis of the BMI records the FBI got over a year ago. I informed Tim that Brat had intentionally failed to perform his investigative duties during the past year. Therefore, I was against giving him a second chance to redeem himself. Tim said Chicago management's decision was final, and we needed to wait four weeks to determine if Brat could conduct the required investigation of BMI.

On April 5, 1999, "Investigative Case Management List of Vulgar Betrayal Case Subfiles" showed the VB investigation, less than three years old, contained 642 subfiles.[16] I opened a subfile for each Muslim for-profit and non-profit organization, business, and individual with links to known international terrorists.

On April 6, 1999, Flessner requested AUSA James Robertson meet with Brat to assess Brat's progress. Later that afternoon, Flessner called me and asked if Gossfeld and I could come to his office for a short meeting. This was an unprecedented meeting request from Flessner. We met in a conference room across from his office. When Tim and I arrived, all three AUSAs met us. Their demeanor was serious, and it was apparent there was a problem.

They informed us there was a severe problem with the lack of work product produced by Brat during the past year. Robertson said that, during his meeting with Brat hours earlier, he concluded Brat could not provide sufficient information regarding BMI since he had failed to perform his required investigative duties as requested two weeks earlier. The AUSAs unanimously agreed Brat must be removed from the VB investigation and replaced with an FBI agent capable of reviewing BMI's records. Tim informed them that he would consider their recommendation and get back to them the following morning. When Tim and I arrived in the JTTF squad area, Brat had already left for the day. Tim said he would speak to him in the morning.

When I arrived in the office the following morning, JTTF agents informed me that Gossfeld wanted to see me immediately. After I entered his office, Tim said he had met with Brat to discuss his meeting with Robertson the previous afternoon. According to Tim,

Brat claimed Robertson did not know what he was doing and that the entire VB investigation was a bogus case, which the FBI should not investigate.

His words to Tim were ill-advised.

Tim exclaimed, "Bob, without Robertson, the seizure would not have occurred. How dare Brat say Robertson does not know what he is talking about!"

Tim, John, and I respected Robertson and credited him with accomplishing the $1.4 million seizure in 1998. He was the attorney who wrote the thirty-seven-page affidavit I had signed to justify the seizure.

Upset with the negative comments Brat made regarding Robertson, Tim informed him that, effective immediately, Brat was no longer assigned to the VB investigation. In addition, Tim instructed him to move his desk from the VB work area to the front of the room. Tim said he was replacing him with Agent Smith, who was looking forward to doing the job. John and I were pleased to see Brat removed from the case and moved as far away from us as possible. It had been frustrating to watch an agent conduct no work for an entire year and face no disciplinary action.

On April 12, 1999, I received a second call from Agent Gamal Abdel-Hafiz regarding his additional contacts with Abu Abu, the BMI accountant. According to Abdel-Hafiz, during one of these contacts, Abu told him that Soliman Biheiri, the BMI president, was aware of his relationship with Abdel-Hafiz.[17] Biheiri inquired if Abu could arrange a meeting between him and Abdel-Hafiz regarding the "Chicago [VB] investigation."[18] Abu also mentioned that he was concerned about the tens of thousands of dollars a month he was told to transfer to specific overseas bank accounts.[19] In addition, Abu recounted other unusual events following the receipt of the Chicago subpoenas.

One event, which was unusual to Abu, involved a friend of his who traveled from the Middle East to meet in secret with Biheiri and his vice president concerning the Chicago investigation. Abu expressed his concern about the possibility of the wire transfers he had been sending to specific overseas accounts being linked to the US embassy bombings in Africa during the summer of 1998.[20]

After hearing this, I said, "Gamal, the US embassy bombings are one reason we are looking into BMI!"

US investigators established a financial link between BMI and an Islamic charity named Mercy International. A Nairobi, Kenya, branch of that charity helped support the embassy bombings.[21] Following the US embassy bombings in Kenya and Tanzania, investigators searched Mercy International's offices in Africa.

Abdel-Hafiz asked, "Bob, do you want me to meet with the BMI president?"

"Yes, I will update the AUSAs regarding this situation," I said.

Just before ending the call, I mentioned, "Remember we need to record your meeting."

Following the telephone call, I informed Tim about the call with Abdel-Hafiz. I left his office and went to the United States Attorney's Office to notify the three AUSAs. They were pleased about the pending meeting.

Tim summoned me to his office after my meeting with the AUSAs. As I walked into his office, he informed me that Abdel-Hafiz was unwilling to wear a wire. In a state of disbelief, I inquired about Abdel-Hafiz's reasoning for not recording his meeting with a terrorist target who wanted to meet with Gamal to discuss the Chicago VB investigation.

"Don't worry about it. Gamal won't meet and record his conversation with BMI's president," Tim said.

A Muslim Does Not Record Another Muslim!

"What do you mean he won't?" I asked.

"Just forget about it. He will not do it," repeated Tim.

I knew the AUSAs would not like this, especially since there was no rational explanation for how an FBI agent could justifiably refuse to conduct a recording against someone running a terrorist-financed organization. Especially since the target was requesting to meet with Gamal, through the BMI accountant, to discuss the FBI's VB investigation.

The following morning, John and I attended a scheduled meeting with the three AUSAs in Flessner's office. When we arrived, Flessner asked, "When will the meeting between Agent Abdel-Hafiz and the BMI president occur?"

Feeling embarrassed, I glanced at John and mumbled, "It will not happen. Just forget I even mentioned anything about it."

Flessner demanded to know why the meeting would not occur. I glanced at John again, saying, "You tell them. I cannot say it. The premier law enforcement agency, my ass."

"Agent Abdel-Hafiz refuses to record any meeting with the BMI president; therefore, the meeting will not occur," said John.

The AUSAs demanded a further explanation. Unable to provide them with a justifiable reason, John suggested Flessner call Abdel-Hafiz and ask him. Flessner wished to include us in a conference call. I told Flessner I needed to seek permission from Gossfeld before John and I could take part in the call.

I called Tim and asked for approval. He approved our participation in the conference call. Flessner called from the speakerphone in his office to the FBI Dallas office and reached Abdel-Hafiz and his supervisor. Abdel-Hafiz's supervisor and I were in the same FBI Academy New Agents Class, 90-15, in 1990.

During this conference call, Flessner informed Abdel-Hafiz and his supervisor that the three AUSAs, John, and I were present. Flessner started by expressing the importance of the VB terrorism investigation and the benefits to the US government's case a recording of the BMI president would bring.

Abdel-Hafiz told us he would only wear the wire if he could tell Biheiri the FBI was recording their conversation. With looks of disbelief on their faces, the three attorneys looked at one another. It was hard to comprehend an FBI agent had just demanded to be allowed to inform a terrorism target he was being secretly recorded by the FBI.

One of the AUSAs proposed arranging the meeting in a pre-wired location, such as a hotel room or an apartment, if Abdel-Hafiz felt uncomfortable wearing the wire. Abdel-Hafiz again refused, insisting he needed to inform Biheiri that the room was bugged.

Flessner explained to Abdel-Hafiz the significance of the contact made by Biheiri through Abu and the potential importance of a contact with Abdel-Hafiz as yielding: (1) possible evidence of specific intent or knowledge of wrongdoing, and (2) lines of inquiry that would constitute possible obstruction of justice. Abdel-Hafiz was told the recording would protect him and provide the best evidence for the US government's case. Flessner again asked whether Abdel-Hafiz would meet with Biheiri and secretly record the conversation. Abdel-Hafiz could not answer the question.

Abdel-Hafiz then proposed placing a tape recorder on a table between himself and Biheiri during their meeting.

He said, "This way, he will know the FBI is recording him."

When the AUSAs deemed this unacceptable, Abdel-Hafiz recommended he meet with the target and report the meeting in writing as he had done before in response to a similar request a few months earlier.

A Muslim Does Not Record Another Muslim!

Flessner advised him that they did not want to reduce the conversation to writing instead of a recording. The attorneys asked what the difference was between him writing a summary of the conversation and recording it. Abdel-Hafiz had no response to this question.

They then inquired further as to the root of his objection. Abdel-Hafiz told us he feared for his safety. When told the FBI would protect him, he said, "I do not trust the FBI to protect me!"

Understanding why he was really refusing to record the meeting, I was upset over his excuse about not trusting the FBI to protect him. I started yelling at him for using that as an excuse not to perform his sworn duty as an FBI agent. The AUSAs calmed me down so they could continue talking to him.

To find an acceptable reason for his refusal to record the conversation, Flessner asked him again how the recording differed from writing and testifying about the conversation. Abdel-Hafiz said, "It is a cultural matter you would not understand."

John and I looked at one another and knowingly smiled because we knew why Gamal was refusing to record a meeting with the Muslim BMI president.

Noticing the smile John and I exchanged, Flessner placed the call on hold. "What is going on here, guys? Why is he refusing to do this? You know why, don't you?"

"Yes, but we won't say it out loud. It would be best if you forced him to tell you," I said.

"How do I get him to tell me?" Flessner asked.

"Get into a yelling match with him, keep pushing him hard to make him angry. He may blurt it out," I suggested.

Flessner continued with the conference call. A few minutes into his heated conversation with Abdel-Hafiz, he asked, "Why will you not wear a recording device or meet the subject in a pre-wired room? The wire's location in the room will remain unknown to you."

"You would not understand!" yelled Abdel-Hafiz.

Angry over his refusal to explain, Flessner slammed his fist onto his desk and yelled back, "Explain it to us so that we will understand!"

"A Muslim does not record another Muslim!" Abdel-Hafiz yelled back.

The room fell silent for a full minute. Disbelief was clear on all their faces. No one in Chicago could believe his words, including John and me. Although we knew this was his reason before he said it, we did not believe Gamal would say it aloud.

After the initial shock of hearing what he yelled wore off, when Flessner began asking another question, Abdel-Hafiz's supervisor cut him off. The Dallas supervisor concluded the conference call, preventing further questioning. The Dallas supervisor told Abdel-Hafiz to return to his desk.

After Abdel-Hafiz left his office, the Dallas supervisor stated, "Listen to me. We all heard the same thing. I can do nothing on my end. Please address this matter from your end."

He implied he could do nothing in Dallas because Dallas management would protect Abdel-Hafiz. He wanted Chicago to pursue Abdel-Hafiz's refusal to record the terrorism target based on religious grounds.

I later spoke to the Dallas supervisor and asked why he could not pursue Abdel-Hafiz's refusal to record a fellow Muslim. He shared how Abdel-Hafiz would accompany the FBI director each time the FBI director traveled to the Middle East. He further shared Dallas management would back Abdel-Hafiz's decision and protect him. He

A Muslim Does Not Record Another Muslim!

informed me he would suffer retaliation from Dallas management if he tried to file a dereliction of duty complaint against Abdel-Hafiz. What concerned the Dallas supervisor was how Abdel-Hafiz, having no conversation with him or anyone else in FBI Dallas management, decided on his own to refuse, for religious reasons, to conduct the secret recording with an FBI terrorist target. A terrorism target who was reaching out to Abdel-Hafiz to discuss VB.

Immediately following the conference call, the three AUSAs went to the United States Attorney and informed him about what had transpired. Meanwhile, John and I returned to the FBI office. We told Tim about Abdel-Hafiz's refusal on religious grounds. Tim instructed me to call SSA Clinton at FBIHQ to inform him about Abdel-Hafiz's refusal to record a Muslim terrorist subject.

When I called Clinton, he said, "Well, Bob, you have to understand where he is coming from."

"No, no, no, no! I understand where I am coming from! This FBI agent took the same damn oath I took to protect this country against all enemies, foreign and domestic, and he just said no, no way in hell! It is inexcusable for him to refuse to record a conversation with someone financially linked to many US-designated terrorists, especially when Abu himself suspects BMI may have helped finance the bombings in Africa. There's no way in hell I need to understand where he's coming from," I said sternly.

"You have a good point," said Clinton.

I realized I was wasting my time talking to Clinton and ended the call.

Later that afternoon, I received a call from Agent Reed. I informed her about the whole Abdel-Hafiz development.

Reed was upset that he refused to perform his duty and compared the situation to one in Milwaukee years earlier. According to her, a Catholic Milwaukee FBI agent received orders to help guard an abortion clinic and make necessary arrests of protesters who violated federal law. The FBI agent told his supervisor he was Catholic, and abortions were against his religious beliefs. He then refused to work at the abortion clinic based on religious grounds. The agent was told to report to the abortion clinic, to perform his sworn duty, or turn in his FBI property and resign from the FBI. After being told that, the FBI agent took part in the operation.

While Reed and I were on the phone, after being briefed about the conference call with Agent Abdel-Hafiz, the United States Attorney for the Northern District of Illinois telephoned FBI Chicago SAC Kathleen McChesney. Following that call, McChesney called Gossfeld and me into her office to discuss her conversation with the US Attorney.

At the end of our meeting, McChesney directed me to draft a communication to Dallas SAC Danny Defenbaugh and the FBIHQ National Security Unit. The communication was to include the background information regarding BMI, the purpose of the VB investigation, and the significance of the recording between Agent Abdel-Hafiz and the BMI president. She instructed me to conclude the communication with, "The Chicago SAC and US Attorney agree the covert recording should take place."

On April 16, 1999, I completed the communication for Defenbaugh and the National Security Unit. The following is, in part, contained in the seven-page communication:

A Muslim Does Not Record Another Muslim!

FEDERAL BUREAU OF INVESTIGATION
Precedence: PRIORITY   Date: 04/16/1999
To: Dallas
             National Security
From: Chicago CT-1
Contact: SA Robert Wright, Jr.
Drafted By: Wright, Robert Jr.
Case ID #:   265C-CG-101942 (Pending)
Title: VULGAR BETRAYAL
             AOT-IT (MONEY LAUNDERING)
Synopsis: To request Dallas Division assistance in the Vulgar Betrayal Investigation.

Details: The mission of the Vulgar Betrayal investigation is for the FBI to identify and neutralize, through criminal process the HAMAS terrorist support organization located within the United States.

The investigation has uncovered clear & convincing evidence of a RICO-like criminal enterprise, which has been operating within the United States since 1987. The FBI's goal is to neutralize the HAMAS RICO enterprise by means of criminal prosecution, and criminal and civil seizures of its assets. In pursuit of this mission, the FBI is continuously striving to collect the best evidence possible to accomplish the goal of neutralizing the HAMAS RICO enterprise. To date the FBI criminal investigation has identified the following:

1: The source of the funds to create the [US-based] HAMAS RICO enterprise.
2: The profit and not-for-profit organizations established in the United States by HAMAS.
3: [The FBI blacked out this information.]

4: Individuals taking money from the US to HAMAS members in the Middle East for support of terrorism.

5: Over [FBI blacked out the number of] bank accounts in [FBI blacked out the number of] countries used by HAMAS to launder international funds in support of terrorism.

6: Linked funds from the US-based HAMAS RICO enterprise to… [FBI blacked out the rest of this paragraph].

Twenty HAMAS incorporated organizations, two of which are linked to a US Specially Designated Terrorist and founder of the US HAMAS RICO enterprise. The investment of money into a land development project [by HAMAS] and used the profits to fund HAMAS military training and activities.

[The FBI partially blacked out this paragraph] Fearing all of the funds would soon be transferred, the FBI executed the first-ever use of the civil forfeiture laws in a terrorism-related matter to seize the remaining funds ($1.4 million), a vehicle used by the QLI ($24,000) and the home of [a terrorist] ($200,000), which was paid for with terrorist funds.

[The FBI blacked the next six paragraphs out. These paragraphs focused on the BMI's links to known terrorists and terrorist front organizations.]

BMI was one of the very first organizations in which the HAMAS RICO enterprise had invested money. Following the creation of BMI, the same principles incorporated nineteen additional companies with the Secretary of State's Office. Two of these companies included Mostan International Inc. and Kadi International Inc. The top three contributors to the financing of BMI and its other subsidiaries include Mousa Abu Marzook, a US-Designated Terrorist and Founder of the US HAMAS RICO enterprise: Yassin Kadi, Saudi Arabia, leader of the Muwafaq and financial supporter of HAMAS, US-Designated Terrorist Mohammad Salah; and two siblings of Osama bin Laden.

Mohammad Salah, a US-Designated Terrorist, was the International Military Commander of HAMAS, while claiming to be an employee of the QLI, a non-profit Muslim organization. HAMAS used the US generated funds to finance military training, travel, & living expenses. Between the time of Salah's arrest in Israel in January 1993 and his release from prison in 1997, there was little activity regarding the $820,000 and the $600,000 in profits earned from the investment. However, upon Salah's return to the US, over $200,000 was transferred from the accounts. Fearing the remaining funds would soon be transferred as well, Chicago conducted the first-ever use of civil forfeiture laws to seize the remaining funds and the home of Mohammad Salah, which had been paid off with terrorist funds.

On 2/25/99, the FBI served a Federal Grand Jury Subpoena on the BMI president and vice president.

An interesting development occurred on 3/12/1999, when SA [Abdel-Hafiz] of the Dallas Division met with the [BMI accountant] following an In-Service that SA [Abdel-Hafiz] attended at Quantico. The [BMI accountant] told SA [Abdel-Hafiz] that [his boss] had been subpoenaed before a Federal Grand Jury in Chicago. The [BMI accountant] told SA [Abdel-Hafiz] that he was worried for the following reasons:

    1: [The FBI blacked out a name] …would not elaborate on the nature of the matter.

    2: [Name blacked out a name] did not tell him that, [Name blacked out] the same grand jury had also subpoenaed another [BMI] accountant.

3: [The FBI blacked out the entire paragraph.]
4: [The FBI blacked out the entire paragraph.]
5: [The FBI blacked out the entire paragraph.]

[The BMI accountant] asked SA Abdel-Hafiz if he should quit his job at [BMI]. SA Abdel-Hafiz told [the BMI accountant] that he was not aware of any investigation regarding the [BMI] & the other employees. [Upon his] return to Dallas, SA Abdel-Hafiz obtained some Vulgar Betrayal information from [Dallas PD Detective Willis] (Dallas JTTF) and discovered [BMI] was a target of the Vulgar Betrayal investigation.

On 3/16/99, SA Abdel-Hafiz telephoned SA Robert Wright regarding the above contact. SA Abdel-Hafiz advised that he has known [the BMI accountant] for many years and he had listed him as a reference on his application for employment with the FBI. In addition, [the BMI accountant] is applying for a Language Specialist position with the FBI.

On 4/12/99, SA Abdel-Hafiz telephoned SA Wright to advise [the BMI accountant] telephoned him over the weekend of April 10-11. [The BMI accountant] advised SA Abdel-Hafiz that [the BMI president] asked him if he thought it would be appropriate for him (BMI president) to contact the FBI agent [Abdel-Hafiz] in Dallas regarding the Chicago Federal Grand Jury. The [BMI accountant] told him the agent [Abdel-Hafiz] may not talk to him about the matter.

SA Abdel-Hafiz asked SA Wright if he wanted him to meet with [the BMI president]. SA Abdel-Hafiz was told that he should meet with him, however he would have to record the conversation since this person is the subject of a major criminal investigation. SA Wright met with the AUSA [Flessner], US Attorney's Office for the Northern District of Illinois, who concurred with the decision to have SA Abdel-Hafiz meet with [the BMI president].

On 4/14/99, SSA Gossfeld had a conference call with SA Abdel-Hafiz & [his supervisor] regarding a future meeting between SA Abdel-Hafiz & Vulgar Betrayal Target [BMI president]. The call concluded with SA Abdel-Hafiz deciding not to pursue a meeting with [the BMI president].

On 4/15/99, SA John Vincent and SA Robert Wright met with the [three] AUSAs to ...discuss the Vulgar Betrayal investigation. During the meeting, AUSA Flessner asked about the Dallas agent's future contact with [the BMI president]. The AUSAs were informed SA Abdel-Hafiz did not want to pursue this matter since there was a need to record the meeting. At 10:00 a.m., a conference call was made to SSA [Gamal's supervisor] and SA Abdel-Hafiz to clarify why SA Abdel-Hafiz was not willing to meet with [the BMI president]. SA Abdel-Hafiz related:

Since the 3/12/99 encounter in Washington DC with [the BMI accountant], the [BMI accountant] has telephoned SA Abdel-Hafiz on numerous occasions. The calls from [the BMI accountant] raised two issues. (1) The concerns of [the BMI president], in particular about his scheduled grand jury appearance, and (2) [BMI president] [The FBI blacked out the first two lines.]. The [BMI accountant] called on Sunday, April 11, 1999, and stated that [the BMI president] was getting scared about his upcoming grand jury appearance. The [BMI accountant] asked SA Abdel-Hafiz whether it would be appropriate and possible for the [BMI president] to contact SA Abdel-Hafiz to give [BMI president] some advice regarding his grand jury appearance.

AUSA [Flessner] said the significance of the contacts made by [the BMI accountant] and the potential significance of a contact with [the BMI president] as yielding: (1) possible evidence of mens rea, or knowledge, of wrongdoing, and (2) lines of inquiry that would possibly constitute an obstruction of justice violation. The Chicago AUSA asked SA Abdel-Hafiz whether he would meet with [the BMI president] and record the conversation by wearing a body recorder. SA Abdel-Hafiz was told the recording would protect him and provide the best possible evidence for the case.

SA Abdel-Hafiz related that he would meet with [the BMI president] or anybody else but that he did not want to wear a body recorder or consent to any other type of consensual recording. When the AUSA's asked for an explanation, SA Abdel-Hafiz stated that the recording would be subject to discovery at a later time and that it could possibly be learned in the Muslim community in Dallas and elsewhere that he had done this [secretly recorded a conversation with another Muslim]. He expressed that [such a] disclosure would create a grave safety issue for himself and his family. When AUSA [Flessner] told SA Abdel-Hafiz that the FBI would address any safety risks, SA Abdel-Hafiz responded that he did not trust the FBI to protect him or his family.

When asked by AUSA Flessner why he thought he would face safety risk, SA Abdel-Hafiz responded that the secret recording of a conversation between Muslims is regarded in the Muslim culture as the ultimate act of betrayal. When AUSA Flessner asked, why it was any different from reducing a conversation with a criminal subject to an FD-302 (FBI document summarizing an interview) and testifying about the conversation, SA Abdel-Hafiz related it was a cultural matter we would not understand.

A Muslim Does Not Record Another Muslim!

[NOTE: Following the last sentence above, I included another sentence that said Agent Abdel-Hafiz yelled out, "A Muslim does not record another Muslim!" However, Chicago SAC McChesney said, "It is not appropriate" to include this in the communication and instructed me to remove the sentence.]

SA Abdel-Hafiz asked why it was necessary to record a conversation with [the BMI president]. AUSA Flessner said that it was necessary to protect the agent, to assure that any false representations about what the agent said during the conversation could be disproved.

Following a 3:30 p.m. telephone conference call between the Chicago AUSA's and SSA Gossfeld, regarding the same subject as the 10:00 a.m. call, Scott R. Lassar, United States Attorney for the Northern District of Illinois, was briefed about the reluctance of SA Abdel-Hafiz to record a meeting that he might have with a prime target of the Vulgar Betrayal matter. USA Lassar then contacted Chicago SAC Kathleen McChesney to further discuss the situation. Both the USA Lassar and SAC McChesney agreed the FBI should pursue the effort to obtain this evidence.

LEAD: Set Lead 1: DALLAS AT DALLAS, TEXAS

The Dallas Division is requested to have SA GAMAL ABDEL-HAFIZ inform [the BMI accountant] to tell [the BMI president] that ABDEL-HAFIZ is willing to meet with [the BMI president] regarding the Chicago grand jury and its investigation. It is further requested that SA ABDEL-HAFIZ meet with [the BMI president] in Dallas and consensually monitor the meeting.

Should [the BMI president] prefer to conduct the conversation with SA ABDEL-HAFIZ on the telephone, Chicago request [the BMI president] be called at his residence after hours and that the conversation also be consensually recorded.[22] [NOTE: The FBI blacked out four and a half pages of this seven-page document.]

A few days later, while speaking to an FBI agent assigned to the Washington, DC, Field Office (WFO) regarding another matter, I shared how Abdel-Hafiz refused to wear a wire against an essential subject near the WFO. The WFO agent told me his office had had severe issues with Abdel-Hafiz in the past as well. He shared how the WFO's concerns about Abdel-Hafiz were serious enough that his office had drafted a communication and sent it to the Dallas SAC. According to the agent, the communication expressed concerns regarding Abdel-Hafiz's unreported contacts with terrorism subjects of WFO investigations.

He said, "Bob, you need to call Tampa Agent Barry Carmody. He can provide you with more information about Agent Abdel-Hafiz."

After ending my call with the WFO agent, I called the Tampa FBI office and spoke to Carmody. He was a fellow international terrorism investigator whom I had known and respected for years. In 1997, I traveled to Tampa to help Carmody and his co-case agent identify possible criminal charges against Sami-Al-Arian. After I shared my situation regarding Abdel-Hafiz, Barry informed me about an identical problem that had occurred ten months earlier between Abdel-Hafiz and himself.

Carmody explained how, in June 1998, University of South Florida Professor Sami Al-Arian, a Muslim and subject of an FBI criminal investigation, reached out to Abdel-Hafiz to discuss the Tampa investigation of Al-Arian.[23] Abdel-Hafiz agreed to meet with the subject; however, he refused to wear a recording device after Barry requested him to do so. After arguing about his refusal to record the conversation, Carmody agreed to allow Abdel-Hafiz to meet with Al-Arian and reduce their conversation to writing through an FD-302, only because it was better than nothing.

"Barry, I am currently in the same situation. I am thinking about allowing Abdel-Hafiz to meet with our target and reduce the conversation to writing. I guess it is better than nothing," I said.

"Bob, don't do it! It was a horrible mistake!" exclaimed Barry.

Curious about his statement, I inquired, "How could it be a mistake? Anything the subject says could only hurt him and not harm the case, right?"

He explained, "Bob, it turned out to be a serious mistake! He claimed the terrorist allegedly made several self-serving statements, statements critical of me and my motivation for investigating the terrorist. He then reduced the alleged self-serving statements of the terrorist to writing in an FD-302."

Then he added, "Bob, I will fax you a copy of Abdel-Hafiz's 302. Read it, and you will understand why I am telling you not to make the same mistake I made."

Within minutes, I received the faxed copy of the FD-302 drafted by Dallas Agent Abdel-Hafiz regarding his "chance meeting" with the Tampa terrorist in Virginia. Abdel-Hafiz's FD-302 reads the following:

FD-302   FEDERAL BUREAU OF INVESTIGATION
                Date of Transcription 6/30/98

On 6/26/1998, during the American Muslim Council convention [in Virginia], Professor Sami Al-Arian, introduced himself to Dallas Special Agent (SA) Gamal Abdel-Hafiz of the Federal Bureau of Investigation (FBI) as the same person who called him earlier this month from Florida. SA Abdel-Hafiz advised Professor Al-Arian that he had attempted to call him (Professor Al-Arian) on Wednesday 6/24/1998, but he did not find him at his office and was told he (Professor Al-Arian) is expected back in his office on Monday 6/29/1998. Professor Al-Arian advised SA Abdel-Hafiz that he did not receive this message. SA Abdel-Hafiz advised Professor Al-Arian that he could call him when he returned to his office next week.

Professor Al-Arian asked if SA Abdel-Hafiz could find anyone at the FBI who could talk to Professor Al-Arian. SA Abdel-Hafiz advised Professor Al-Arian that he could not find anyone who will confirm or deny Professor Al-Arian's claim because this is the FBI's policy. Professor Al-Arian thanked SA Abdel-Hafiz for trying to assist in this matter.

On 6/26/1998, during a dinner which was attended by SA Abdel-Hafiz and Professor Al-Arian, Professor Al-Arian asked SA Abdel-Hafiz why would an FBI Agent attempt to meet with him alone without his attorney. Professor Al-Arian went on stating that SA Barry Carmody of the Tampa-Clearwater FBI office approached an acquaintance of Professor Al-Arian and requested that the acquaintance arrange a meeting between SA Carmody and him without his attorney being present.

Professor Al-Arian also advised that a person from the Tampa FBI office advised him that he and SA Carmody have always worked interstate theft violations and he (SA Carmody) does not understand anything about a terrorism case. Professor Al-Arian also advised that the same person from the Tampa FBI office told him that SA Carmody should have retired two years ago but was granted extensions because of the terrorism case and SA Carmody may be exaggerating the facts about this terrorism case to remain with the FBI as long as he can.

Professor Al-Arian also asked SA Abdel-Hafiz if the FBI would fabricate evidence against anyone. SA Abdel-Hafiz advised Professor Al-Arian that he had never heard of the FBI fabricating any evidence since he joined the bureau.

Professor Al-Arian also advised that the FBI approached one of his former students who worked at a computer company and asked him to cooperate with them against Professor Al-Arian in exchange for a permanent residence card (i.e., the green card) and a job with IBM (International Business Machines Corp.). When the person refused the offer, he was arrested a week later and processed for deportation.[24]

After reading this FD-302, which had many self-serving statements favorable to the terrorist and derogatory statements regarding Agent Carmody, I notified my supervisor and the three AUSAs that I would never allow Abdel-Hafiz to meet with Biheiri without recording the conversation covertly. John and I had serious concerns about Abdel-Hafiz writing an FD-302 following a future meeting with the BMI president. Recording the conversation without the subject's knowledge is how the FBI has always handled criminal investigations of this magnitude. I would never allow Abdel-Hafiz to document in a FD-302, any meeting with any target connected to the VB terrorism investigation.

On April 21, 1999, Abdel-Hafiz wrote an FBI communication to Chicago in response to my April 16, 1999, communication to Dallas. In his communication, he falsely claimed the Dallas SAC was the one who decided he would not meet and covertly record a conversation with Biheiri. His communication reads in part:

FEDERAL BUREAU OF INVESTIGATION
Precedence: ROUTINE Date: 04/21/1999
To: Chicago
           National Security
           WMFO
From: Dallas
           JTTF/IT
Contact: SA Gamal Abdel-Hafiz
Approved By: [FBI blacked out name.]
Drafted By: Abdel-Hafiz Gamal: gah.
Case ID #: 265C-CG-101942 (Pending)
Title: VULGAR BETRAYAL
          AOT-IT (MONEY LAUNDERING)
Synopsis: Response to Chicago's request for Dallas Division's assistance in captioned investigation.
Reference: 265C-CG-101942 Serial 747 and SAC Dallas and Chicago's telcall on 4/22/1999.

Details: Referenced communication requested SA Gamal Abdel-Hafiz meet with a Vulgar Betrayal target. [The Vulgar Betrayal target] has been subpoenaed to appear before the Federal Grand Jury in Chicago. SA Abdel-Hafiz has been requested to wear a recording device and record the conversation that takes place between himself and [the Vulgar Betrayal target].

Referenced communication does not completely reflect the conversations which took place via telephone on 04/14/1999, between SA Abdel-Hafiz, SSA Dallas Supervisor and SSA Chicago Supervisor [SSA Gossfeld] or the subsequent conversation which took place on 04/15/1999, between SA Abdel-Hafiz, SSA Dallas Supervisor, SA Wright, SA Vincent

A Muslim Does Not Record Another Muslim!

and [three] Chicago Assistant US Attorneys. The following reflect the facts as to Dallas' recollection:

1. [Abu Abu] is a friend of the whole [FBI blacked out name] family. [Abu Abu] grew up in the same neighborhood in Cairo, Egypt as the [FBI blacked out name] family. [Note: Abdel-Hafiz grew up in Cairo, Egypt.]

2. After the original conversation with [Abu Abu] on 3/12/1999, the reason SA Abdel-Hafiz's attention was directed toward the Vulgar Betrayal case was that [Abu Abu] mentioned that [the grand jury testimony] was going to be in Chicago.

3. [Abu Abu] called SA Abdel-Hafiz on Sunday April 11, 1999, to discuss a few items. During [the] conversation, [Abu Abu] stated that [his boss] was getting scared and appeared very concerned about his upcoming grand jury appearance. [His boss] asked [Abu Abu] if [Abu Abu] thought whether SA Abdel-Hafiz knew about the issue [of the VB criminal investigation]. [Abu Abu] told [his boss] he did not know, but that SA Abdel-Hafiz might know about the matter since there "aren't many Arab agents within the FBI." [The boss] asked [Abu Abu] if he thought it might be appropriate to call SA Abdel-Hafiz and seek his advice about his [Vulgar Betrayal grand jury] situation. [Abu Abu] told [his boss] that he did not think it would be good since [Abu Abu] knew SA Abdel-Hafiz did not like to talk about his work with others. [Abu Abu] asked SA Abdel-Hafiz if he gave [his boss] the proper answer. SA Abdel-Hafiz advised [Abu Abu] that he answered correctly. [Abu Abu] never attempted to broker a meeting between SA Abdel-Hafiz and [his boss] as previously mentioned in the Chicago EC to Dallas.

[NOTE: The last sentence above is an absolute lie. Agent Abdel-Hafiz specifically asked me, "Do you want me to meet with the BMI President?" If he had not asked me this, I would not have had any justification to ask him to meet and record the meeting with the BMI President. Also, Abdel-Hafiz never denied the BMI president was seeking a meeting with him during the Chicago AUSAs conference call.]

4. Regarding 04/14/1999, tell call to discuss the possibility of SA Abdel-Hafiz consensually monitoring the meeting with [Abu Abu's boss] it was made clear that SA Abdel-Hafiz had no personal reason to meet with [Abu Abu's boss]. It was also said that there existed an enormous potential for SA Abdel-Hafiz to lose his ability to gather intelligence from the Arab community if it were known to the [Arab] community that he had recorded a conversation between himself and another Muslim seeking advice. SSA Chicago (Gossfeld) concurred with both SSA Dallas and SA Abdel-Hafiz and [SSA Gossfeld] advised SA Abdel-Hafiz not to meet with [Abu Abu's boss] at all. [Note: Chicago SSA Gossfeld informed Agent Vincent and me he did not say this to Agent Abdel-Hafiz.]

5. During the teleconference on 4/15/1999, between Chicago Agents and AUSA's, and Dallas Agent Abdel-Hafiz and his supervisor, the fact of the potential loss of SA Abdel-Hafiz's ability to assist the remaining fifty-five FBI field offices in gathering intelligence regarding their investigations was not addressed. SA Abdel-Hafiz also expressed that disclosure of the recording could create a grave safety issue for himself and his family because of previous threats.

In referenced telcall, SAC concurred with SA Abdel-Hafiz that the potential loss of his ability to work within the Muslim community and his security concerns was far too great to pursue the covert recording of any conversation that might take place between SA Abdel-Hafiz and [Abu Abu's boss].

However, SAC Dallas approves of the meeting if it is overtly recorded with the subject's agreement to the recording.

Dallas SA Abdel-Hafiz will coordinate with Chicago and WMFO (Washington (DC) Metro Field Office) to travel to WMFO and interview [Abu Abu's boss].[25]

At the time Abdel-Hafiz's above communication arrived in Chicago, I was in the Middle East preparing for an interview with a jailed HAMAS terrorism financier from Milwaukee. Agent John Vincent received Abdel-Hafiz's communication and became upset over Defenbaugh's refusal to instruct Abdel-Hafiz to meet and covertly record the meeting with Biheiri. With Gossfeld's consent, John drafted a reply to Abdel-Hafiz's communication.

Tim read Abdel-Hafiz's communication and determined that his comment regarding the conference call between him, Defenbaugh, and Abdel-Hafiz on April 14, 1999, was inaccurate. Tim drafted a comment clarifying what had occurred during their conference call. He then instructed John to incorporate this comment into Chicago's reply to Abdel-Hafiz's communication. John's FBI communication, in part, reads:

```
         FEDERAL BUREAU OF INVESTIGATION
Precedence: ROUTINE Date: 05/17/1999
To: National Security Att.: NS-3B; SSA [Name B.O.]
Dallas Att.: ASAC [Name B.O.]
Att.:        SA Gamal Abdel-Hafiz
From:        Chicago
             CT-1
Contact:     SA John Vincent
Approved By: SSA Gossfeld
Drafted By:  SA John Vincent
```

Case ID #:   265C-CG-101942 (Pending)
Title: VULGAR BETRAYAL
   AOT-IT (MONEY LAUNDERING)
Synopsis: Dallas division is requested not to proceed with consensual monitoring assistance to Chicago unless such recording is done covertly [without the target's knowledge].
Reference: 1. 265C-CG-101942 Serial 737
   2. 265C-CG-101942 Serial 758

Details: In #2 referenced communication, SA Abdel-Hafiz expressed his recollection of circumstances and telephonic discussions regarding [Abu Abu's boss] (currently under subpoena to testify before a Chicago grand jury), and Abu Abu, a personal friend of SA Abdel-Hafiz. The conclusion of #2 stated that SAC Dallas approved the meeting with [Abu Abu's boss] under the condition that the meeting be overtly recorded with the approval of the subject. [The FBI blacked out the second paragraph of this document.]

The Chicago division and the US Attorney's Office for the Northern District of Illinois are both of the opinion that an overtly recorded meeting between SA Abdel-Hafiz and [Abu Abu's boss] would be unproductive and, in fact, possibly detrimental to the Vulgar Betrayal investigation. The possibility exists that such a meeting would provide an open forum for [Abu Abu's boss] to make entirely self-serving statements which could subsequently be presented to the court in his defense. Therefore, Chicago opposes any overtly recorded future contact between SA Abdel-Hafiz and [Abu Abu's boss].

Based upon the suspicious activity linking [Abu Abu's employer to US-designated terrorists and other known terrorists] being investigated in the Vulgar Betrayal matter, Chicago suspects that a covertly [secretly] recorded interview of [Abu Abu's boss] could be productive from an investigative standpoint. Dallas is requested to re-consider proceeding with the covert [secret] recording, if, at any time in the future, the perceived problem of consensually monitoring a Muslim seeking advice regarding a major US government criminal investigation is overcome. [Note: This last sentence was added by Agent Vincent to address Abdel-Hafiz's 4/15/1999, conference call statement, "A Muslim does not record another Muslim!"]

Chicago would like to clarify paragraph four of [SA Abdel-Hafiz's] communication #2 [dated 4/21/1999]. It was the recollection of SSA [Gossfeld] that during the 4/14/1999 conversation, SSA [Gossfeld] expressed his respect for SSA [Dallas] and SA Abdel-Hafiz's opinion and their request that SA Abdel-Hafiz not meet with [Abu Abu's boss], but that he [SSA Gossfeld] did not specifically direct or advise SA Abdel-Hafiz to not meet with [Abu Abu's boss].[26]

As a side note, three years later, they would identify Dallas SAC Defenbaugh as the FBI agent who withheld over 3,000 documents from Timothy McVeigh's defense attorney. This caused a delay in the execution of McVeigh for the Oklahoma City federal building bombing. During questioning by the Senate Judiciary Committee to explain why he waited until May 2001 to notify FBI higher-ups about the 3,000 documents, "Defenbaugh said he wanted to be completely sure what the problem was and how bad it was"[27] before he brought it to higher ranking FBI executives. He seemed to take offense at the questioning by members of the committee, according to a source who said, "He was affronted."[28]

Meanwhile, we continued moving forward with the VB investigation. In mid-April 1999, as I was investigating the arrested Milwaukee resident's connection to terrorism in Israel, I discovered why no one could get any sources within HAMAS. It became apparent that HAMAS members have connections through blood or marriage. It was like the Italian crime families in America. There was one significant key difference between the HAMAS and mob families. The difference was money.

Money means nothing to a HAMAS member. Their motivation is religion. Therefore, the US and other intelligence organizations worldwide could not infiltrate them. However, I planned to identify most members worldwide with the aid of the VB databases and a family tree computer program. Unfortunately, even after the seizure of $1.4 million from HAMAS ten months earlier, the FBI refused to provide me with $69 to purchase a family tree program to aid the VB investigation.

Gossfeld and I discussed how embarrassing it was that the FBI would not pay $69 for the program. When I suggested I would buy the program myself, Tim said, "Bob, you should. Imagine the FBI's embarrassment if it came to light that you had to pay for computer programs to carry out your terrorism responsibilities."

"I don't have a choice, Tim. This is one key to locating all of them, tracing the money, and predicting who will probably become future terrorists, or make terrorist attacks before they occur. I must buy the program."

On April 17, 1999, I purchased a family tree program at Best Buy to aid in the investigative efforts.

During the last two weeks of April 1999, the Chicago office was undergoing an inspection by managers from FBIHQ. They conduct division inspections every three years to isolate problems within each field office. During the two-week inspection, they interviewed every FBI agent regarding their work assignment. The inspection staff conducted ten to fifteen-minute interviews with the agents, asking them if there were any problems they should know about.

During Agent Brat's interview, John noticed he had been in the interview room for an extended time. John made me aware he'd been in for over forty-five minutes.

I said, "I don't care. Brat's no longer assigned to the Vulgar Betrayal case. However, what is the reason for his prolonged stay without having done any work in the previous year?"

Thinking the worst, I then asked, "John, do you think he is dumb enough to be in there bad-mouthing Vulgar Betrayal?"

"I'm not sure, but if he is, he's making a huge mistake," said John.

An hour after he had entered the interview room, we watched the door open and noticed Brat walking out. He immediately left the squad room. Within seconds, the inspector rushed into Gossfeld's office and closed the door.

I piped up, "Well, John, here we go. Brat just tried to screw us over. While we have worked our asses off for the past year, and he has done nothing."

"Maybe they were talking about something else," VB Agent McDonald offered.

"What do you think, John?" I asked.

He replied, "Seeing how fast the inspector walked into Tim's office and shut the door, I would have to agree with Bob. Brat just tried to screw us over."

Five minutes later, Tim walked out of his office and came to my desk.

"Bob, the inspector is requesting to meet with AUSA Flessner right now. Can you call Flessner to find out if he is available?"

"Yes," I said.

While dialing the number, I looked at Tim and asked, "Brat just tried to screw us over, didn't he?"

"Yes, I cannot believe he did this. I will not forget this," said Tim.

I remarked, "After you supported him and gave him a second chance, he did this. How pathetic. At least we did nothing wrong. We will be okay. It is disheartening to see someone who did virtually nothing for an entire year cause problems for those of us doing our jobs."

I reached Flessner and informed him the FBI inspector had just completed his interview with Brat and had requested an immediate interview with the lead AUSA assigned to the Vulgar Betrayal investigation. Following their meeting, the inspector gave the VB investigation a highly favorable review.

A few days later, while discussing the VB case with one of the FBIHQ inspectors, I mentioned I had another upcoming trip back to Israel in a week or two. I also mentioned DOJ Attorney Murphy's name.

The inspector asked, "Are you talking about Tony Murphy?"

"Yes, do you know him?" I asked.

"That man should be indicted for aiding terrorists!" the inspector said.

"You do know him! I've been expressing the same thing about him. The terrorists should pay him for what he has done for them," I said.

The inspector and I shared stories about the many problems Murphy had caused us during our investigations of international terrorists.

A Muslim Does Not Record Another Muslim!

On April 26, 1999, I received my annual performance appraisal. I received an overall rating of "Exceptional." Each category was virtually identical to the comments made in my April 1998 performance appraisal written by Gossfeld.[29]

> "To accomplish the FBI's mission, we must identify and follow core values. They all relate to uncompromising integrity. The public expects the FBI to do its utmost to protect the people and their rights."[30]
>
> — Louis J. Freeh, FBI Director

CHAPTER 25

WHY MIDDLE EAST PEACE FAILED DURING THE 1990S

Part 1
1989–1995

"The threat of terrorism is both real at home and abroad. Today Americans engaged in activities as routine as working in an office building, commuting to and from work, or visiting museums and historical sites in foreign lands, can become random victims in a deadly game acted out by international terrorists. America's democratic tradition and global presence make United States citizens and interests targets for opportunists who are willing to shed the blood of innocents for their causes."[31]

— Louis J. Freeh, The FBI Director

The Vulgar Betrayal investigation primarily centered on money laundering between the US-based HAMAS and HAMAS elements in the West Bank and Gaza Strip. Simultaneously, VB was intensely investigating the recruitment and training of HAMAS members, as well as the purchase of weapons and explosives overseas with funding from the United States. By the summer of 1999, the focus was to link Milwaukee HAMAS member Jamil Sarsour to terrorism-related activities of the past five years, with the activities of other known US-based members such as Mousa Abu Marzook, Mohammad Salah, and many others since the creation of HAMAS in 1987.

Establishing this connection would allow the US government to pursue Racketeer Influenced and Corrupt Organizations Act (RICO) violations against US-based HAMAS members and financiers. The RICO statute carries a ten-year statute of limitations rather than the usual five years held by many of the criminal violations HAMAS leaders and financial supporters have committed. By providing material support, they have assisted their counterparts in the Occupied Territories (OT) with carrying out acts of terrorism in Israel, which led to the loss of innocent lives including both Israeli and American citizens.

If the FBI had conducted a proper and thorough investigation into the activities of Chicago resident Mohammad Salah and his US-based HAMAS superiors following his 1993 arrest, they could have prevented many of the terrorist attacks that occurred in Israel after January 1993.

Unfortunately, the failures of the management of the FBI's Counter Terrorism Unit allowed deadly suicide missions to continue with uninterrupted financing from the US. The financial support of HAMAS suicide missions ultimately led to the deaths of hundreds. Eventually, these attacks derailed the Middle East peace process during the 1990s, which was their goal.

Although some of the following information is in previous chapters, this chapter and chapter 26 will chronologically summarize

Why Middle East Peace Failed During the 1990s – Part 1

HAMAS' US-based creation and the establishment of its criminal enterprise within the US. In addition, this chapter will detail many deadly results achieved by HAMAS terrorists in the OT with support of the US-based HAMAS leaders and their financial support.

In 1989, Marzook and other Islamic radicals in the US set up the United Association for Studies and Research (UASR) in Chicago, Illinois.[32] The UASR would serve as the command headquarters for the US-based HAMAS enterprise.

In June 1989, a Palestinian uprising in the OT caused the arrest of Palestinian HAMAS founder and leader Sheik Yassin and many of his followers. Marzook and a delegation of Palestinian Americans traveled to the OT in order to assess the damage inflicted upon HAMAS and rebuild its structure. One member of the delegation, Mohammad Salah, a naturalized US citizen and allegedly a used-car dealer from Chicago, joined the mission.

Salah said, "I started out with the Muslim Brotherhood in 1978, with Sheikh Jamal Said, who serves as [the] Sheikh of the Mosque of the Arab community in Chicago."[33] About his Palestine visit with Marzook in 1989, he said, "The enemy [Israel] knows nothing apart from the fact that I came to visit my family in 1989 when I met Abu Abada. This was on the initiative of Brother Mousa Abu Marzook."[34] Salah also said, "We [Abu Abada, Marzook, and himself] also discussed a [HAMAS] leaflet and the contact with Jordan, and the uncovering of the armed [terrorism] squad in Hebron. The enemy [Israel] knew nothing about the [purpose of our] visit."[35]

Sheikh Mohammed Taher (aka Mohammed Abu Tair) was "described in the media as a leading HAMAS activist in Gaza."[36] He "was active in the operations of HAMAS within different prisons and even aided HAMAS activists that were released from jail to return to

[HAMAS terrorism] operations."[37] To finance his HAMAS activities, Abu Tair "met over three periods with a HAMAS activist, a US resident, by the name of Jamil Tzartzur [aka Jamil Sarsour], and received from him $10,000 US, $5,000 US, and $3,000 US (dollars) accordingly."[38] Mohammad Salah described Sarsour as someone who ran "a number of grocery and furniture stores, mostly in Milwaukee's central city."[39]

In 1990, HAMAS held a conference in Kansas City, Missouri, sponsored by HAMAS' Islamic Association for Palestine (IAP) organization.

"During these [US] conferences, it is not uncommon to hear Islamic militants praise terrorists and terrorist attacks, [verbally] attack the United States and the West, or call for the death of Jews and the destruction of the United States. For the most part, these incendiary lectures, almost invariably in Arabic, are not illegal . . . unless a specific act of violence is advocated, and falls under protected speech."[40]

During this particular conference, "secret meetings were held with a pre-selected 'class' of [US-based] future HAMAS terrorists who were taught car-bombings and other terrorist warfare. Meanwhile, at IAP's 'plenary' sessions—held in the Kansas City Convention center—several notorious militants and leaders of HAMAS gave fiery speeches praising attacks by HAMAS and other Islamic fundamentalist groups in language and rhetoric more familiar to HAMAS rallies in the Middle East rather than Kansas City. One of the most electrifying moments came when a costume-draped HAMAS leader of the Izzadin Al-Qassem death squads—the military arm of HAMAS—delivered a rousing account of the specific violent terrorist attacks carried out by HAMAS."[41]

Regarding another trip to Palestine in 1990, Salah stated, "On the initiative of Brother Mousa Abu Marzook, in 1990, there was

Why Middle East Peace Failed During the 1990s – Part 1

a similar visit. But the focus was on separating the West Bank from Gaza and the need for a [HAMAS] security apparatus in the West Bank and Gaza. In Gaza, I met brothers who were tired of the little military [terrorist] action, and [they] gave me a letter threatening that if the brothers abroad [in the US] did not help us, we would do what we like. This was after brother Musamah gave them instructions to carry out an action [terrorist attack] again. The only one, who was in the picture from America, was Mousa Abu Marzook."[42]

After returning, Salah reported to Mousa Abu Marzook regarding the frustrations of HAMAS members in Palestine, particularly their threats to abandon HAMAS if they did not receive more financial support. Marzook then tasked Salah to collect the names of HAMAS brothers from Palestine, who were currently living in America and attending US colleges/universities. He would contact them and tell them to attend the first US-based HAMAS terrorism training. He carried out this activity under the name of "The Security Committee." Salah said, "About 27 names [of US-based HAMAS members] were sorted, according to their expertise in chemical materials, toxins, physics, military education and knowledge of computers."[43] Among those selected were "Sherif Alwan and Razick Abdelrazick [from Chicago.]"[44]

Salah claimed he conducted several military training sessions in Chicago, Kansas City, and Wisconsin as the military commander of HAMAS. However, once the Gulf War started in 1991, HAMAS suspended all military training in the US. Their leaders feared US authorities would learn about their terrorism training on US soil. Instead of focusing on training terrorists in the US, they would focus on generating income to continue building its US-based enterprise and provide financial assistance to the members living in Palestine.

Also, in 1990, the UASR, the US-based HAMAS headquarters, printed a tribute to HAMAS founder and leader Sheikh Yassin entitled "Ahmed Yassin: The Phenomenon, the Miracle, and the Legend of the Challenge." The tribute contained odes of praise and letters extolling the imminent victory of HAMAS over the Jews, such as this letter from a HAMAS activist in Chicago to the HAMAS fighters in Palestine: "Greetings to you from here in America, from over the seas, that you may know that we are your sons of the era, the era of Allah, the era of Islam, the era of Palestine, the era of Jihad, the era of HAMAS, until complete liberation of all Palestine from the river to the sea!"[45]

In 1992, upon orders from Marzook, Salah traveled from Chicago to Boston to meet with HAMAS leaders visiting from Jordan. During the meeting, the Jordanians requested he take responsibility for the Holy War (Jihad) by becoming the military commander of the entire HAMAS terrorism wing. Salah agreed; however, he later realized it would be challenging to work full-time to support his family in Chicago on top of assuming the top HAMAS military position. Acknowledging his legitimate concerns, he claimed employment with the Quranic Literacy Institute (QLI), a non-profit Muslim organization. In addition, the QLI was used to establish a land development project in Woodridge, Illinois, "to generate [tax free] income for HAMAS activities," specifically his [Salah's] terrorist activities.[46]

The QLI land development scheme to finance his activities called for a $820,000 international wire transfer to be sent indirectly to the QLI. The QLI would also serve as his new employment front to conceal his role as the commander of the military wing. The QLI would invest the $820,000 into a for-profit land development project and forward the proceeds to Salah via international wire transfers to conceal themselves. Salah used the funds to finance the military (terrorist) activities, travel, and training of US-based HAMAS military members.

Eventually, the US-based HAMAS members responsible for physically transferring financial support from the US to the terrorist leaders in the OT began facing security concerns. HAMAS searched for a safer method to transfer financial support from America to fellow members in the OT. With the help of Jamil Sarsour, "Together with his brother Tzalah, they opened a 'special bank account' in the United States to deposit within the account money, of which he [Jamil] could transfer; through checks, to the Palestinian region to HAMAS activist [terrorist], Adel Awadallah. The accused [Jamil] and Tzalah would deposit different amounts from time to time, and Jamil Sarsour transferred the money to [HAMAS terrorist] Adel Awadallah."47

As a side note, through Vulgar Betrayal I discovered that Sarsour opened a "special bank account" under the name of an American citizen with mental disabilities. The Sarsours had tricked the American into allowing them to open the bank account in his name by falsely claiming it was an investment account for the mentally disabled man. They used the bank account to move money from America to the Middle East under the name of the American with mental disabilities.

In August 1992, after HAMAS Leader Abu Abada left the West Bank for the West, he and Marzook met with Mohammad Salah in Washington, DC. During the meeting, Salah was told the HAMAS "military situation in the West Bank is frozen and it has to be revived by means of the following people, Adel Awadallah, Ramallah—Salah Arouri, Hebron/Ramallah—Najah Afana, Jerusalem, Al-Zaatari, Bethlehem."48 Mousa Abu Marzook tasked Salah with traveling to Israel to reestablish the terrorist branches of HAMAS in the West Bank.49 Salah was instructed to contact Adel Awadallah and Salah Al-Arouri in order to check with them about the possibility of establishing terrorism units by means of their HAMAS squads. In addition, he was asked to meet with someone from Gaza, Abu Ali, and tell him the HAMAS unit in Gaza was operating well.[50]

In August 1992, following the meeting in Washington, DC, Salah arrived in Israel to meet with Palestinian HAMAS members. Regarding his first meeting with Salah Arouri, he said, "I passed him a message from Abu Abada, which served as a code."[51] He then said that he was there to talk to him about the military affairs of HAMAS.

He met with HAMAS terrorist Adel Awadallah just days after Awadallah's release from an Israeli prison, to inquire about his HAMAS terrorism unit. He said Awadallah told him "that after his arrest, he sent someone to his house to burn the [HAMAS terrorist cell] documents and that he now needs two or three months in order to formulate the situation [building a new terrorism squad] anew."[52]

Awadallah asked Salah to consult with Marzook about assassinating Seri Nouseiba. HAMAS considered Nouseiba the "brain" of the Middle East peace talks. Salah later raised the suggested assassination with Mousa Abu Marzook, who expressed enthusiasm over the assassination of Seri Nouseiba by a HAMAS terrorism unit.[53]

Regarding Awadallah and Salah's second meeting, Salah stated, "We discussed the situation in the [Israeli] prisons and the despair of the boys [HAMAS members] who feel they are not doing anything valuable while they are in prison. He [Awadallah] complained that the [HAMAS] leadership had no plans for the future, neither in the political sphere nor in the military sphere, and he asked me to pass on this description of the situation."[54]

To help finance the terrorist activities of Awadallah, Salah said, "We agreed to send him [Awadallah] money by means of the Sarsour family."55 Awadallah told him that he intended to flee Israel in the future. Salah gave him his Chicago telephone number in case he needed to contact him. During one of Salah's taped interviews following his arrest regarding the Sarsour family, he stated, "The Sarsour family is famous in America (Milwaukee, WI). They still have businesses here [in Palestine]."56 He did not like the Sarsour family "because many know the Sarsour family sells alcoholic drinks and pork."57

Regarding his meeting with Al-Arouri at Hebron University, Salah said, "After I passed him [Arouri] a message from Abu Abada which served as a code. I told him about the idea of reviving military [terrorist] activity, and he told me that there were many people who were ready to act, but he needed money to buy weapons, vehicles, and other things. I gave him $100,000 on the basis of a weapons deal offered him. It was noted that $45,000 was meant for this [weapons] deal, and the rest was for weapons or other items on sale. I gave him my [Chicago] telephone number."58

A third member Salah met was Abu Saab. Regarding meeting Saab, Salah said, "He said to me the situation regarding the [terrorism] squads in Gaza, and told me that he had 53 people ready for action."59 He also said, "Abu Saab told me that his men had killed a woman who had recruited 70 [Palestinian] people to [assist] the Israeli Intelligence. He also told me that his men had killed and murdered an Israeli soldier. This attack had been much publicized on television and papers."60

According to Salah, Abu Saab's "[terrorism] squad intended to carry out an attack on the beach in Gaza against Israeli soldiers and police officers who came regularly to bathe there and leave someone to guard their weapons. The plan was that the guard would be liquidated [killed], the weapons stolen, and the perpetrators escape from the site."[61] He said Abu Saab asked for $48,000 to fund the attack.

He shared, "In the meetings with Abu Saab he asked me to install a fax machine in Rahat for communicating with Abu Abada abroad regarding (HAMAS) military activity, transferring reports, and receiving (orders for military) missions."[62]

The HAMAS fax machine was to be set up in Dr. Mahud Rumhi's medical office. (See Appendix A–5.)

After meeting Abu Saab, Salah departed the Middle East and returned to the United States. Regarding his written report of his mission in Palestine, he said, "I handed the written report over to Mousa Abu Marzook. I think the trip failed because I did not organize matters in Bethlehem, Jerusalem, and Ramallah. Because brother Adel [Awadallah] needed a great deal of time [to establish his military group]. The only hope [for a terrorist attack] was brother Salah Al-Arouri."[63] According to Salah, Marzook wanted one of two HAMAS trainees, Sharif Alwan or Rizak Salah [Abdel Razick], both Chicago residents, to travel from the US to Palestine to replace terrorist Adel Awadallah. "Up to now the emphasis has been that these two brothers would arrive here (Israel) and stay here. This was decided at the beginning of February 1992."[64] The training of Alwan and Abdel Razick secretly continued under the instruction/training of the US-based HAMAS organization. Eventually, the terrorism training of these two called for them to receive training in the Middle East. Regarding them, Salah stated, "Those are two of my favorite names. My connection to them is personal. I mean they think of me as their father. They trust me, and they want to fight a holy war, they want to fight."[65]

Salah "admitted to directly financing domestic and international travel and terrorism training for new HAMAS members. Airline records obtained by the FBI show that he purchased airline tickets for travel between the United States and the Middle East for himself and other suspected HAMAS terrorists, including Shareef Alwan and Razick Saleh Abdel Razick, both of whom flew from the United States to Syria in September of 1992. Additionally, he acknowledged to Israeli authorities that these trips were taken for receiving training in preparation for HAMAS military and terrorist operations in Israel."[66]

Salah sent the two trainees to Syria for terrorism training sessions with the Hezbollah terrorist organization. After returning from this trip, Alwan and Razick briefed Salah about their training. A week later, he told them that Mousa Abu Marzook was not satisfied with the training they received in Syria. They then traveled to Lebanon for another training session with the Hezbollah terrorist organization on November 26, 1992. (See Appendix A–4.)

In October 1992, HAMAS terrorist cells in Palestine were firing shots "from a speeding car at an Israeli Defense Force observation post near the Cave of the Patriarchs in Hebron."[67] Killing one Israeli soldier, Shmuel Geresh, and wounding another. HAMAS terrorists carried out many more attacks against Israel throughout December 1992. These attacks caused Israel to arrest many HAMAS leaders in Gaza and the West Bank.

With the Israeli arrests of so many HAMAS military leaders, HAMAS devised another plan to transfer financial support to military members in the OT. The new plan had HAMAS military terrorists paying a visit to the older mother of one of the arrested HAMAS leaders. During the visit, the terrorist would request a specific amount of financial support to carry out more terrorist attacks. The older woman would then visit someone else who would send the financial request to Sarsour. Milwaukee resident Jamil Sarsour would visit El Bireh (Palestine) frequently, bringing with him bank checks drawn from the bank account in the name of the mentally disabled American man, which he cashed and transferred to Adel Awadallah via the older woman. The older woman was the mother of HAMAS leader Sheikh Mohammed Abu Tair, who was in prison during that period.[68] [Note: HAMAS leader Sheikh Mohammed Abu Tair was the person to whom Murphy wanted to offer protection in the US for his cooperation against HAMAS.]

In December 1992, HAMAS waged a series of terrorist attacks with weapons bought from the financial support of the $48,000 Mohammad Salah provided to Abu Saab during his September 1992 visit. One attack was in retaliation for Israel's arrest of HAMAS senior leaders, Sheikh Abu Tair and Dr. Ramahieh.

For the retaliation, HAMAS members kidnapped two Israeli soldiers, one of whom was Sgt. Major Nissim Toledano. HAMAS held twenty-nine-year-old Toledano hostage and killed the second soldier, Sa'adon, and hid his body.

HAMAS abducted "him (Toledano) Sunday… as he walked to work in the central Israeli city of Lod. HAMAS demanded the release of its leader, Sheik Ahmed Yassin, who is serving a life term in an Israeli prison on a manslaughter conviction."[69]

Instead of negotiating with Israel for the return of Toledano, HAMAS killed Toledano. "The stabbed and bound body of an Israeli border police officer (Sgt. Maj. Toledano) was found alongside a highway near a Jewish settlement outside Jerusalem, two days after Islamic militants had kidnapped him. The killing of Sgt. Maj. Toledano, 29, sent waves of anti-Arab anger rolling across Israel."[70] Toledano was the sixth Israeli soldier to be killed in eight days by HAMAS terrorists.

Why Middle East Peace Failed During the 1990s – Part 1

"Prime Minister Yitzhak Rabin told a stunned and angry nation that he will 'strike pitilessly' against Muslim fundamentalists who kidnapped and killed an Israeli soldier."[71]

"'We intend to continue to strike, within the law, against the (HAMAS) organization, its supporters and helpers,' said Rabin. 'Toledano was killed despite the readiness of the State of Israel to talk with his captors.' Rabin said the killing would not goad Israel into pulling out of the peace talks."[72]

Israel then retaliated against HAMAS by rounding up and evicting 415 members from the OT. The Israelis' actions not only destroyed the HAMAS infrastructure within the OT but also sparked international media attention and criticism from the global community. (See Appendix A–6.)

When Marzook learned of the 415 deportations, he telephoned Salah in Chicago. He instructed Salah to travel to the OT to appoint new leaders and distribute $790,000 in financial support to the terrorists and their families.[73] The QLI, Salah's alleged employer, received instructions to liquidate the remaining balance of the $820,000 investment in the Woodridge, Illinois, land development deal, which amounted to $790,000. "The QLI was to provide the $790,000 to Salah for delivery to the OT. Ahmad Zaki, the QLI president, told the owner of the Woodridge land development business to liquidate the business and return the QLI's money because it is needed for 'a mission above all else.'"[74] However, the owner of the Woodridge land development business could not liquidate the business within such short notice. "Shortly after these events, close associates of Abu Marzook initiated a series of wire transfers directly into Salah's La Salle Bank checking account, totaling $985,000."[75]

Before traveling to Israel in January 1993, Salah first traveled to Washington, DC, to meet with Marzook and another HAMAS member to discuss the situation in Palestine. During the meeting, Marzook provided Salah with a sketch of the hidden burial location of the body of Israeli soldier Sa'adon. Marzook instructed him to use Sa'adon's body as leverage in Israel.[76]

Salah left America on January 17, 1993, and traveled to the OT to carry out his HAMAS mission. Additionally, he had the task of "meeting other HAMAS operatives to coordinate, among other things, a terrorist attack against Israel." After arriving in Israel, Salah accomplished his mission by telephoning his wife in Chicago and instructing her to wire transfer $200,000 from their joint checking account into a Chicago bank account owned by Rihbe Abdel Rahman, a Palestinian money-changer living in the OT.[77] The $200,000 was transferred from Chicago to Israel, and Salah received it from the money-changer.

"I gave Marwan Hawajah [of Jerusalem] $60,000 for Adel [Awadallah]. Hawajah gave me the number of a bank account of Imad Musa in the US so that I could deposit money in Imad's account so that (the money) would reach Marwan Hawajah for Adel Awadallah. Adel was to distribute the money among the needy, among the families of [HAMAS] deportees and HAMAS activists [terrorists] in the area," said Salah.[78] On January 25, Israeli authorities apprehended Salah for his involvement in aiding HAMAS terrorism. "At the time of his arrest, he was found in possession of extensive notes he compiled from his meetings with over 40 HAMAS operatives over the preceding 11 days."[79] They charged Salah with being the military commander of HAMAS.

During his interviews with Israeli authorities, Salah said, "I would like to note that in the US, there are about 32 Muslim charity organizations whose role is to collect funds from Muslim citizens of the US and distribute them in areas where Muslims are in distress. Recently, these organizations collected funds for the (415) deportees. In the US there are also publications related to HAMAS: 1. A-Zaitana—in Texas, 2. Ala Falastin—in Texas. These periodicals are published by HAMAS activists."[80] Regarding HAMAS leaders, he stated, "Musa Abu Marzook is the political leader of HAMAS in the US."[81] Regarding the funds placed into his Chicago bank accounts, he stated, "I will have to face problems when I return to America and it is possible that the rest of the money will be confiscated, if we do not prove it comes from a charity organization."[82]

The 1993 "arrest of Mohammad Salah, Mohammad Jarad [a Chicago resident], and Nasser Hidmi, [a student at Kansas State University], by the Israeli authorities marked an important turning point in the investigation of Hamas. What was relevant because of the interrogations and confessions of these individuals was the importance of the United States as an operational base for Hamas. Under the leadership of Mousa Abu Marzook, the Hamas headquarters in the United States could operate virtually unimpeded from the intense scrutiny of authorities."[83]

"Nasser Hidmi, a Palestinian youth arrested in Israel for attempting to detonate a bomb, exposed the role of the Hamas military wing in the United States and how this wing recruited new Hamas activists/terrorists within the United States [colleges]. In his statements to the Israeli authorities, Hidmi described the role of Islamic conferences in the United States for training HAMAS activists/terrorists. Both sponsored these conferences, the Islamic Association for Palestine (IAP) and the Muslim Arab Youth Association (MAYA)."[84]

Hidmi said that while "at a conference in Kansas City [in 1989], Mohammad Salah gathered about twenty young men, including

Hidmi, for a secret meeting of the activists of HAMAS in a meeting hall at one of the hotels. At this meeting was Mohammad Salah, and Ibrahim Al-Muzain, an officer of the Holy Land Foundation for Relief and Development (HLFRD), lectured to us."[85]

Hidmi said, "They informed us that all the young men present were chosen for the secret meeting because they were from the Occupied Territories and were selected according to forms they filled out in the refugee camps. This was done in order that they will take part in [terrorist] activities that will support and strengthen the Intifada [struggle] within the framework of HAMAS."[86]

On September 13, 1993, "The Oslo negotiations paved the way for the signing of a peace accord between Israel and the PLO. It proposed a Palestinian self-rule to be phased in over several years in the West Bank and Gaza Strip."[87] For their efforts, Israeli leaders Shimon Peres and Rabin, and PLO's Yasser Arafat won the Nobel Peace Prize. These developments outraged HAMAS, which claimed it would commit acts of terrorism to disrupt any land for a peace deal between Yasser Arafat and the Israelis.

On May 4, 1994, "Israel and the PLO signed an agreement in Cairo on the final status of Jericho and the Gaza Strip. Israel completed its withdrawal of troops from the two regions. The Palestinian Authority (PA) led by Yasser Arafat assumed control of civil matters and set up a Palestinian police force to maintain internal security in Palestine."[88]

Shortly after that, Arafat's government was responsible for preventing HAMAS members from launching terrorist attacks against Israel from within Palestinian territories.

On October 26, 1994, Israeli Prime Minister Rabin and Jordanian King Hussein signed a peace treaty between their two countries. HAMAS carried out a terrorist attack on November 9, 1994, at the

Nahlat Shiv'a Mall in Jerusalem. The attack killed two and injured eighteen others.

On November 10, 1994, Hezbollah's Al-Manar TV interviewed Marzook in Lebanon. He stated, "Death is the goal of every Muslim, and every fighter wants to die on Palestine land. This is not the first time that the Izz AL-Din AL-Qassam heroes [HAMAS terrorists] carried out suicide and terrorism actions. We are doing them for a much higher aim, and they are steps on the way for a full restitution of the rights of the Palestinian people."[89]

Salah Sarsour, Jamil Sarsour's brother, traveled from the US to Israel. After his arrival, Israel arrested him. "Tzalah [Salah Sarsour] and Edal [Adel Awadallah] shared the same prison cell in Ramallah."[90] Suspecting a blood or marital relationship between Sarsour and Adel Awadallah, we searched the VB investigation databases and discovered that Adel Awadallah was married to a sister of the Sarsour brothers.

"On July 27, 1995, while Israeli authorities incarcerated Salah, the United States Treasury Department's Office of Foreign Assets Control added Mohammad Salah to the list of (US) Specially Designated terrorists because of his facilitation of terrorist activities in the Middle East."[91]

Under President Clinton's authority, Mohammad Salah became the first US citizen to be designated a terrorist by the United States Government. The United States Government froze Salah's assets. He had completed the second of his five-year Israeli prison sentence. My assignment, as Salah's intelligence file case agent, was to travel to the Treasury Department's Office of Foreign Assets Control (OFAC) to assist with the paperwork and expedite the freezing of Salah's assets.

Also, in July 1995, after being expelled from Jordan by King Hussien for his terrorist-related activities, Mousa Abu Marzook traveled to Iran and Syria. On July 5, 1995, authorities arrested Marzook at New York's JFK Airport when he attempted to re-enter the US. At the time of his arrest, he held permanent resident alien status in the US. On August 16, OFAC, believing Marzook had been acting on behalf of HAMAS, added his name to the "Specially Designated Terrorist List."

By August 1995, for peace in the Middle East to succeed, Palestine needed financial assistance to develop a modern infrastructure that would help to provide a self-sustaining economy. Furthermore, Israel and Palestine needed to jointly address security concerns to prevent HAMAS terrorist attacks against Israel.

Of course, this would have been much easier had the FBI's International Terrorism Unit (ITU) done its job and investigated the US-based HAMAS enterprise following Mohammad Salah's 1993 arrest. The failure of the FBI ITU to do so allowed the US-based HAMAS leaders to continue financing international terrorist attacks against Israel, which also cost the lives of innocent American citizens visiting Israel.

Instead of conducting logical investigations of known and suspected international terrorists who visited or lived in the United States, FBI leadership handcuffed its street agents from performing even the most basic investigative tool: interviews of the terrorists and their associates. Even worse, management instructed agents to ignore the criminal activities of money laundering, bank fraud, and many more criminal acts being committed by the US-based members of HAMAS, who were subjects of classified intelligence case files.

Although the FBI will lie about my serious allegations, a simple review by Congress of the FBI's intelligence files during the 1990s will prove my claims are valid. During August 1995, I was still fighting with

Why Middle East Peace Failed During the 1990s – Part 1

the Chicago office and Headquarters to allow me to conduct interviews of Mohammad Salah's associates and open a criminal investigation of the known criminal activities of the US-based terrorism network.

On August 2, 1995, Assistant US Secretary of State Robert H. Pelletreau addressed the US House International Relations Committee, discussing what was needed to bring peace to the Middle East. Pelletreau stated, in part, the below quotes:

> Since signing the Declaration of Principles in September 1993, Israel and Palestinians have concluded a series of important implementation agreements. They are now engaged in an intensive effort to reach an agreement on the implementation of phase 2 of the Declaration of Principles. The United States supports these negotiations and commends both parties for their determination to reach an agreement, despite the efforts of the enemies of peace [HAMAS] to undermine the negotiations.[92]
>
> The current negotiations focus on the issues of security and the redeployment of Israeli forces, the further transfer of authority to the Palestinian Authority, and future [Palestinian] elections. The parties are working hard to outline a framework for Israeli redeployment in the West Bank and arrangements for maintaining security and public order.[93]
>
> Redeployment will set in motion a process for elections for the Palestinian Council. Meanwhile, (HAMAS) terrorist incidents such as the July 24 bus bombing in Ramat Gan, a Tel Aviv suburb, and the murder of two Israeli hitchhikers in Wadi Kelt serve as a reminder of the challenge Israel and Palestinians must deal with.
>
> We note Chairman Arafat's strong condemnation of the terrorist bombing. For its part, the Palestinian Authority has

taken important steps to prevent violence and to punish those responsible for terrorism. The Palestinian Authority has also undertaken more meaningful measures to crack down on those that plan and carry out attacks. Cooperation and coordination with Israeli security forces continue to improve. If measures such as these are sustained, and they must be sustained, they will have a lasting effect on security stability.

As President Clinton has repeatedly emphasized, the enemies of peace cannot and will not prevail. This was amply demonstrated by the Israeli-Palestinian agreement to resume talks this week and to not allow terrorists to derail the process.

The United States will play a central role in mobilizing the political and economic support for the accord, as we have since 1993. For that reason, we look forward to continuing our dialog with the Congress on the terms of short-term and long-term extensions of the Middle East Peace Facilitation Act. Our own bilateral aid program is on track. US Aid has obligated $130 million of our total $150 million authority for fiscal years 1994 and 1995.[94]

Looking ahead to the donors' meetings, we intend to focus on four key issues: infrastructure development, particularly in the West Bank; continued support for start-up costs for the Palestinian Authority; housing; and industrial zones. In every case, the conviction will guide us that our aid program should complement the Palestinian Authority's effort to create effective institutions of self-government and promote enterprise necessary to promote long-term economic development.

Finally, cooperation on security matters remains a high priority. As an example, we are actively considering a request from the Government of Israel for the provisional arrest of Mousa Mohammed Abu Marzook under Article XI of our

1962 bilateral extradition treaty. Mr. Abu Marzook is the head of the political bureau of HAMAS, one of the organizations listed in the President's January 24, 1995, Executive Order "Prohibiting Transactions with Terrorists who Threaten to Disrupt the Middle East Peace Process."[95]

On August 21, 1995, the Israelis captured Abdel Nasser Issa, a HAMAS terrorist responsible for masterminding two suicide bombings that killed 12 people. While in custody, Issa kept quiet about the bombing he had orchestrated, set to occur shortly after his arrest. Issa had dropped off the suicide bomber in Tel Aviv shortly before his arrest. Issa had directed the suicide bomber to pick a bus at random for the bombing. The suicide bomber boarded a bus, detonated the bomb, and killed five people. One of the five killed was US citizen Joan Davenny, an American teacher from Connecticut.[96]

During a subsequent search of Issa's apartment and property, the Israelis found vats filled with chemicals, bomb materials, a car packed with explosives, and a videotape from the suicide bomber who killed Joan Davenny and four others.[97] HAMAS was committing terrorist attacks against Israel to sabotage the peace talks between Arafat and Israel. They believed, if their terrorist attacks continued to be launched from within Palestinian territory, the Israelis would lose faith in Arafat and his government's ability to prevent attacks. HAMAS leaders hoped the friction between Arafat and Israel would subsequently cause the Middle East peace process to fail.

Yahya Ayyash, also known as "The Engineer," had trained Issa in bomb-making. He masterminded six suicide bombings in Israel, which killed seventy-six innocent people during 1994 and 1995. He earned the title of the number one terrorist on Israel's Most Wanted

List because of these six bombings.⁹⁸ Issa and Ayyash were close associates of Adel Awadallah and Mouhidin Al-Sharif. Each earned the nickname "Engineer" because of their bomb-making skills and ability to engineer deadly terrorist attacks against Israel.

On September 25, 1995, Israel filed a formal request seeking the extradition of Marzook from the US to Israel. The Israeli government wanted Marzook to answer for his role in orchestrating and financing many terrorist attacks, which resulted in hundreds of deaths and injuries. Following Marzook's arrest, Khaled Mishal of Amman, Jordan, replaced him as the leader of HAMAS.

On November 4, 1995, one year after Israeli Prime Minister Rabin had received the Nobel Peace Prize, an Israeli student "who opposed the peace process assassinated Prime Minister Rabin at a peace rally in Tel Aviv."⁹⁹ Following the assassination, Shimon Peres, another major player in the peace process, became the Prime Minister of Israel.

On November 13, 1995, Israeli troops pulled out of six cities in the West Bank as agreed to in the Oslo Accords. The Palestinians were now given autonomy in the six cities. However, the many terrorist attacks orchestrated by Ayyash were threatening the entire peace process. Realizing his activities were a threat to the peace process, "Yasser Arafat's police force also joined the [Israeli] hunt to track down Ayyash (Engineer #1)."¹⁰⁰

CHAPTER 26

WHY MIDDLE EAST PEACE FAILED DURING THE 1990S

Part 2
1996–1999

After Israeli intelligence learned Yahya Ayyash was seeking a new cell phone, Israel's internal security service, Shin Bet, devised a spectacular plan to eliminate him. Shin Bet agents "packed a cell phone with 50 grams of explosives"[101] and had the phone delivered to him by the uncle of a friend. On the morning of January 5, 1996, while he was using the bomb-laden cell phone, Shin Bet agents were nearby monitoring the phone call. When they verified he was the person using the cell phone, they used a remote-control device to detonate the cell phone while it was being held up to his head.[102] (See Appendix A–9.)

When HAMAS leaders in Jordan learned of Ayyash's death, "they ordered Mohammed Deif, their HAMAS military wing leader in the Gaza Strip, to prepare an explosive device" and blow the bomb up next to Ayyash's body "to show that Ayyash (Engineer #1) was killed while preparing a bomb."[103] The purpose of the second explosion would be to cover up the fact top HAMAS military personnel were so vulnerable that Israeli Shin Bet agents could infiltrate them. However, HAMAS members in the OT strongly rejected this idea. They believed Ayyash was a hero, and they strongly opposed further mutilating his body.

The assassination of Ayyash by the Israelis caused a political nightmare for Yasser Arafat. Officials had scheduled Palestinian elections, the first since 1948, three weeks later. The Palestinian population became outraged over Ayyash's assassination by Israel. During the funeral, over 100,000 Palestinians swarmed through the streets of Gaza, carrying his coffin, screaming, "Death to Israel. We are all Yahya Ayyash the Engineer. We are all Ezzadin Qassem (HAMAS military)." HAMAS members passed out leaflets during the funeral, promising a new Jihad against Israel shortly.

With the Palestinian elections only weeks away, Arafat had no choice but to praise Ayyash and criticize the Israeli assassination. During a visit with the Ayyash family, Arafat declared him to be a "holy martyr" and ordered a twenty-one-gun salute. Arafat's acts outraged the Israeli government, and they accused him of aiding terrorists. He won the presidency of the Palestinian Authority on January 20, receiving over 80 percent of the vote.

Israel braced for another wave of suicide bombings by HAMAS, fearing retaliation for the assassination. With his death, HAMAS split its military cells in two. Adel Awadallah and Muhi al-Din Al-Sharif led the West Bank cell. The senior leader of the Gaza cell was Mohammed Deif. Awadallah, who met with Mohammad Salah and received funding from the Sarsour family in Milwaukee, together with Sharif, planned and coordinated multiple suicide bombings against Israel. Between February 25 and March 6, 1996, HAMAS committed four retaliation bombings against Israel, killing fifty-five people.

The first bombing occurred at 6:46 a.m. on February 25, when a Palestinian suicide bomber, disguised as an Israeli, boarded a public commuter bus in Jerusalem carrying a twenty-two-pound bomb packed with ball bearings and nails. When the bomb detonated, it scattered the roof and bus contents into the air. The ball bearings and nails shredded the flesh of the passengers and made identification difficult. Twenty-three passengers lost their lives, and forty-nine others suffered serious injuries.

Among the twenty-three dead "were two US citizens, Matt Eisenfeld, 25, of Hartford, CT, a student at the Jewish Theological Seminary in Jerusalem, and his girlfriend, Sarah Duker, 22, of Teaneck, NJ, a student at Jerusalem's Hebrew University."[104] On April 9, 1995, a suicide bomber drove a car bomb into a bus in the Gaza Strip, killing Alisa Flatow, twenty years old, a former high school classmate of Duker's from New Jersey, during her visit to Israel. Within hours of their son's brutal murder by HAMAS, the Eisenfeld family in America stated that "it was their hope that the peace process continues and succeeds, so that what happened to Matt never happens to anyone else in the future."[105]

Fifty minutes after the bus bombing occurred in Jerusalem, a second Palestinian suicide bomber exploded an eleven-pound bomb near a bus stop in Ashkelon, Israel. The suicide bomber disguised himself as an Israeli youngster and blended in with the rest of the waiting passengers. The bomb killed two, injuring many more.[106]

HAMAS made two claims of responsibility for the two bombings during a telephone call and a faxed communication to Israel radio.

During the call, "a man speaking Arabic claimed responsibility for the bombings on behalf of the Izzedine al-Qassam, the military wing of HAMAS, which has led opposition to peacemaking with Israel."[107] The faxed communication signed by "Students of The Engineer," read, "The cells of 'The Engineer' Yahya Ayyash announce their responsibility for the two explosive operations that occurred Sunday morning 25 February 1996 in the heart of occupied Jerusalem and in Ashkelon."[108]

Following news of the two bombings, the international community expressed its outrage. President Clinton said, "These brutal acts of terror offend the conscience of the world. They must not only be condemned; they must be brought to an end."[109] He referred to the HAMAS suicide bombers as "'enemies of peace.' Their dark vision is of the past, not the present; of violence, not hope for a better future."[110] US Secretary of State Warren Christopher referred to the bombings as "the desperate efforts of those enemies of peace whose only purpose is to kill the promise of peace and to destroy the chance of a better future for Israelis and Palestinians."[111]

"This is not a military operation. This is a terrorist operation. I condemn it completely. It is not against only civilians but against the whole peace process,"[112] Yasser Arafat told reporters. Israeli Prime Minister Shimon Peres expressed Israel's desire to continue with the peace process and said, "Terrorism, however painful, will not determine our fate."[113]

"Pope John Paul II joined those and others in other countries in denouncing the [HAMAS] attacks. The Pope said, 'I express firm condemnation for the new, cruel recourse to violence.'"[114] Israel called for action by Arafat against those responsible for the attacks. Arafat's security branch "arrested, tried, and convicted 12 HAMAS activists, including one of its founders, Ibrahim Yazouri, and another leader, Mohsen Abu Aita, all within 48 hours [of the bombings]."[115]

Less than a week later, on Sunday, March 3, 1996, a twenty-four-year-old HAMAS suicide bomber, Islam Abu Abed, from Hebron, boarded a commuter bus on one of Jerusalem's busiest streets. When he detonated the bomb strapped to his body, the explosion ripped apart the commuter bus, killing nineteen. Glass and shrapnel covered the streets and sidewalks. At the center of the scene was the bus's burned and twisted metal frame, surrounded by bodies. "A young man was lying amidst the debris, his head thrown back as if he were taking a nap. The lower half of his body lay next to him. One rabbinical student who was picking up body parts from the street held up a charred piece of human flesh and said, 'See, this proves you cannot trust Arabs!'"[116] The bus contained the same number and was along the same route as the bus blown up by HAMAS on February 25. HAMAS claimed responsibility for this attack. "The Israeli government declared 'all out-war' against HAMAS, saying tough steps will be taken against the families of Islamic suicide bombers." [117]

Prime Minister Peres said, "This is a total war, and even if it is painful, we will fight it. We will not refrain from any actions; we will not refrain from any measures. We've decided to give this war the very top, single-minded priority in terms of manpower and resources." Peres said all the Israelis, the government, and he are "determined to bring down HAMAS to its very foundations."[118] He launched "emergency measures in what he called a 'total war against HAMAS and other terrorist organizations.'"[119]

President Clinton re-emphasized his determination to do everything possible to be supportive of the effort against terrorism. He praised Arafat for his prompt actions following the bombing and said he would encourage Arafat to do more.

He said, "I do believe Chairman Arafat has made efforts, and I think that he will make more."[120]

He further said, "We have to build the capacity of all the forces in the Middle East, including the Palestinian authorities, to promote law and order to stand against terrorism."[121]

On the same day, HAMAS issued a statement claiming, "We will halt our military activities starting from this morning, in order to give the Israeli government and HAMAS' political leadership inside [the West Bank and Gaza] the chance to reach a truce through the Palestinian Authority within the coming three months."

The New Students of Yahya Ayyash, the same group that claimed responsibility for the two earlier bombings on February 25, issued the statement.

However, the following day, the fourth HAMAS terrorist bombing to hit Israel within nine days occurred when another HAMAS suicide bomber blew himself up, killing ten and wounding another thirty-five in the central downtown shopping area of Tel Aviv. Witnesses placed the HAMAS suicide bomber next to a line of people waiting near a cash machine. The victims included children in costumes for the Purim holiday. "'I saw children here in costumes bleeding profusely. It's a heart rendering site,' said Yigal Raviv, a reporter for Israel radio."[122] (See Appendix A–10.)

On March 8, 1996, while Yasser Arafat was meeting with senior CIA officials in Gaza to discuss ways to strengthen security against Muslim militants operating within Palestine, HAMAS circulated a flier claiming there would be more attacks.

Why Middle East Peace Failed During the 1990s – Part 2

The flier said, "The General Command of the Qassam [terrorist] units have studied the situation seriously and objectively and has decided to resume its suicide operation."

The flier also criticized the international terrorism summit scheduled for Egypt the following week. President Clinton, Yasser Arafat, Israeli Prime Minister Peres, Russian President Boris Yeltsin, and heads of state from European and Middle Eastern countries would attend the summit.

On May 8, 1996, US District Court Judge Kevin Duffy granted permission for Mousa Abu Marzook to be expedited to Israel for trial on charges of murder, attempted murder, and conspiracy connected to several shootings and bombings. Marzook contended he was not technically in the United States when arrested at the JFK Airport on July 25, 1995.

In addition, Marzook claimed there was no evidence of criminal liability against him under New York law, and the crimes Israel accused him of were not extraditable offenses. He further claimed that international extradition law should consider him exempt from extradition to Israel as he fell under the "political offense exception." He claimed he was being targeted because of his admitted role as head of the political wing of HAMAS.

Judge Duffy rejected all of his arguments, saying, "The conspiracy charge leveled against Marzook was grounds enough for his extradition."[123] He concluded that Marzook's involvement in ten terrorist attacks from 1990 to 1994, through which forty-seven people were killed and another 148 injured, was reason enough for his extradition.

"On May 13, 1996, 17-year-old David Boim, an American, was standing at a bus stop in the West Bank with fellow yeshiva students when two Palestinian (HAMAS) terrorists drove by in a car, shot him in the head, and killed him."[124] Although the two terrorists avoided capture following the murder of Boim, his killing would come back to haunt HAMAS in the future. On May 12, 2000, the parents of David Boim filed "a $600 million civil lawsuit in Chicago federal court against several US-based HAMAS front organizations."[125] The Boims' lawsuit sought the $1.4 million assets of US-based HAMAS organizations seized through the VB investigation.

On August 27, 1996, the new Israeli prime minister, Benjamin Netanyahu, lifted the four-year freeze on Jewish settlement construction in Palestinian territories by permitting the expansion of the Kiryat Sefer Settlement. The building angered Arabs and put the peace process into a dire situation.[126]

In early September 1996, while Milwaukee business owner Jamil Sarsour was in El-Beera, Palestine, he claimed to have received a sealed note from an unknown messenger. "The note was sent to the defendant [Jamil Sarsour] by Adel Awadallah [Engineer #2], a wanted senior HAMAS official, whom the accused [Sarsour] knew. In the note Adel informed the accused [Sarsour] that he was wanted by Israel and the Palestinian Authority and asked the accused [Sarsour] to transfer to him money through the family of Sheik Mahamad Abu-Tier, a HAMAS senior activist."[127]

The Israeli government wanted Adel Awadallah because of recent terrorist attacks he had masterminded. In addition, Yasser Arafat's government had banned Adel Awadallah from the Palestinian territory. Before returning to the US near the end of September, Sarsour "went to [Sheikh Abu Taher's] family home. There he met the Sheik's mother to whom he gave an envelope containing US $3,000 and a note and asked her (Sheik Abu Taher's mother) if she could get the letter to Adel Awadallah (Engineer #2). After receiving confirmation, Jamil left the note with the Sheik's mother and left."[128]

After returning to the US, Sarsour "together with his brother Tzalah [Salah Sarsour], opened a 'special bank account' in the United States in order to deposit within it, money, of which he could transfer later [through] checks to the region to the HAMAS activist, Adel Awadallah. The accused [Jamil Sarsour] and Tzalah [Salah Sarsour] would deposit different amounts from time to time, and Jamil then transferred the money to Adel Awadallah."[129] This was the "special bank account," opened under the name of a mentally disabled American citizen the Sarsours tricked.

On November 10, 1996, the American embassy in Amman, Jordan, received a terrorist threat regarding the United States' extradition of Marzook to Israel. The threat said, "We demand that you immediately release Dr. Mousa Abu Marzook and urge you not to hand him over to the Zionist enemy. We warn you that if you do not release Dr. Mousa Abu Marzook, and if you hand him over to the Jews, we will turn the ground upside down over your heads in Amman, Jerusalem, and the rest of the Arab countries. You will lament your dead just as we did to you in Lebanon in 1982 when we destroyed the Marine House with a booby-trapped car, and there are plenty of cars in our country. You will also still remember the oil tanker with which we blew up your soldiers in Saudi Arabia."[130]

On January 16, 1997, "after over 30 years of occupation, Israeli troops withdraw from the West Bank town of Hebron the day after an agreement is signed with the Palestinian Authority."[131] Although HAMAS had committed many recent terrorist attacks, Israel remained committed to pursuing peace with the Palestinians.

On February 3, 1997, after I discovered documents showing links between Sarsour and US-based HAMAS non-profit organizations,

I requested the opening of the Jamil Sarsour subfile. I recommended opening this subfile to investigate his activities in Milwaukee. I knew nothing about his HAMAS-related activities in Palestine, but I had found a connection. There were many subfiles opened on others connected to HAMAS.

Unfortunately, the FBI refused to assign more agents and support employees to the VB investigation that following year. I was the only agent assigned to VB. At the time, there was not enough information entered within the VB databases to yield sufficient information to justify my expanding investigating to Sarsour. However, VB gained vital financial records from him. When these records arrived, I entered the data on these checks into the VB financial database for future reference should his name reappear.

During February 1997, while again visiting the OT, Sheikh Abu Tair's mother, acting on behalf of Adel Awadallah, met with Sarsour. Abu Tair's mother gave Sarsour a letter from Adel Awadallah. "In the letter, Adel requested $10,000 and a passport from the accused [Jamil] and told him that he wished to leave the [Palestine] area."[132]

"Two days later, Jamil Sarsour would travel to the home of Abu Taher and passed to the mother of Mahmad Abu Taher an envelope, which contained $10,000 and a letter for Adel [Engineer #2] in which, he (Jamil) states he cannot obtain a passport for him."[133] Adel Awadallah needed to escape the area because of his planning and execution of several recent terrorist attacks. His terrorist attacks killed dozens of innocent Israeli citizens and two American citizens.

On March 20, 1997, the next HAMAS suicide attack occurred after Mouhidin Al-Sharif tasked Musa Ghneimat to take two bags, loaded with explosives and nails, into the Apropo Coffee House, a Tel Aviv café. When the bombs detonated, four Israeli citizens lost their lives.

People throughout Tel Aviv could hear the explosion. Israeli citizens were celebrating the Purim holiday by dressing in costumes. The bombs killed one male and three women and injured many others. "Among the injured was a 6-month-old baby, who was burned over a large portion of his body. The bomb was studded with nails for more deadliness."[134] Television pictures around the world showed an Israeli policewoman, Ziona, frantically searching for the parents of a baby she was cradling, Shani Winter, who was dressed in a small clown costume. Unfortunately, the child's mother was one of the three women killed by the HAMAS bomb.

HAMAS claimed responsibility for the attack. However, there was something unusual about this suicide bomber. Ghneimat did not fit the profile of a HAMAS suicide bomber. "Ghneimat, age 28, was from the village of Sourif, near Hebron, the West Bank strong–hold of HAMAS. He had a wife, two sons, and two daughters."[135] HAMAS "suicide bombers are almost inevitably young bachelors who rarely blow themselves up while in possession of their [real name] identity card."[136] Therefore, there was a suspicion that Ghneimat did not intend to commit suicide.

Israeli authorities suspected someone informed Ghneimat to set a timer on the bombs, giving him ample time to evacuate the area before the bombs exploded. However, as he attempted to set the timer, either he made a mistake, or someone misled him about the timer, leading to his death. Through their investigation, the Israeli authorities determined Ghneimat did not intend to commit suicide. Because of his death and discovered identity, the Israelis and Palestinians arrested four HAMAS members responsible for killing eleven Israelis and injuring forty-eight others.

Adel Awadallah became extremely upset with Al-Sharif for tasking Ghneimat. He was close friends with Ghneimat and questioned

Al-Sharif's judgment and motive for sending him. He suspected Al-Sharif had tricked Ghneimat into killing himself, which led to intense arguments between the two engineers. Each man claimed to be the leader of the same HAMAS military cell. Each claimed that getting approval from the other prior to executing HAMAS terrorist attacks was not required.

Meanwhile, as Marzook remained locked up in New York, continuing to fight his extradition to Israel, he received news about the café bombing. He realized the last thing the Israeli government needed was to deport him back to Israel following the bombing. He realized his extradition to Israel at that time would spark many HAMAS suicide bombings against the citizens of Israel. Therefore, he gave up his fight against extradition in anticipation that the Israeli government would withdraw its extradition request. On April 30, 1997, Israel did just that.

The US government now had to charge Marzook with a criminal violation or release him. Meanwhile, they detained him because of a pending immigration matter until they identified a criminal charge.

The FBI agent working the Marzook case in New York telephoned me to inquire about my VB criminal investigation of HAMAS. The agent said he was trying to identify a criminal violation Marzook had made. I told him that, based on the documents I had reviewed to date, there appeared to be many violations of the international money laundering statute. I sent VB documents to the New York office revealing the criminal acts committed by Marzook.

Unfortunately, the Department of Justice decided not to pursue international money laundering criminal violations. Instead, the US government agreed to release Marzook. They now needed to find another country willing to take him and allow him to live in their country.

Jordanian King Hussein informed President Clinton that Jordan would accept, "on humanitarian grounds," Marzook as a refuge in Jordan. On May 4, 1997, Marzook entered into an agreement with the Immigration and Naturalization Service in which he entered a plea of nolo contendere and did not contest exclusion charges. The exclusion charges said that he was an alien engaged in terrorist activities or that the US Attorney General knew or had reasonable grounds to believe he was likely to engage in terrorist activity.

On May 5, 1997, upon Marzook's arrival in Jordan, King Hussein said to him, "You are welcome in Jordan. I want you to feel secure. This is your family; this is your country."

"'That's all I heard...and I'm hoping to hear those words again,' Abu Marzook said."[137] He was then with his replacement, Khaled Misha'al. He had lost a year and a half of his life because of the imprisonment. Those truly familiar with HAMAS realized its leadership in Jordan, Marzook and Misha'al, would plan a retaliation attack against Israel in the future for their seeking Marzook's extradition.

Within twenty-four hours of his arrival in Jordan, Marzook "vowed to resume his own struggle against what he termed Israel's occupation of Palestinian territories. 'I have a long way to go in serving my people and helping them achieve their hopes and aspirations.' He was quoted as saying, he believed that Israel decided it had no evidence to support its charges that he helped orchestrate terrorist attacks that killed 47 people. Marzook (claimed) he was only a political leader and fundraiser for HAMAS, and his US detention was politically motivated."[138] (See Appendix A-11.)

On May 6, 1997, during the US State Department's daily briefing, John Dinger said, "I have a brief statement on the release of Mousa Abu Marzook. The Immigration and Naturalization Service (INS) yesterday excluded and deported Mousa Abu Marzook to Jordan under an agreement entered into by Abu Marzook and the Immigration service."[139]

A reporter asked, "Have people in this building or elsewhere in the government seen his (Marzook's) latest statements? He apparently has not changed his mind about war against Israel. Is there anybody—is it actionable in any way or is he out of . . . the machinery of the US Government?"[140]

Dinger said, "I have not seen those statements. We excluded him under a law, as I just described, that applies to an alien who is engaged in terrorist activity, or we believe we have reasonable grounds, [and] is likely after entry to engage in terrorist activity. So, if that applies to your question, I guess that would be my reaction to that."[141]

On May 13, 1997, FBI Director Louis J. Freeh appeared before the US Senate Appropriations Committee to provide a statement about the counterterrorism efforts of the FBI. He said, "The protection of our nation and its people against the threat of terrorism by individuals and groups operating from home and abroad is one of the highest priorities of the administration. As a nation, we must stand firm in our resolve against terrorism. We must not allow those who would resort to acts of terrorism to succeed in influencing the policies and actions of our government and tearing apart the very fabric of American society." [142]

He added, "Based upon policy of treating terrorists as criminals and applying the rule of law, the United States is one of the most visible and effective forces in identifying, locating, and apprehending terrorists here and overseas. This policy invites the possibility of reprisal." [143]

He further said, "The second major international terrorist threat to the United States is posed by formalized extremist groups. These autonomous organizations have their own infrastructures, personnel,

Why Middle East Peace Failed During the 1990s – Part 2

financial arrangements, and training facilities. They can plan and mount terrorist campaigns overseas and support terrorist operations inside the United States. Extremist groups such as Hezbollah, al-Gamat al-Islamiyya, and Hamas have placed supporters inside the United States who could be used to support an act of terrorism here."[144]

In mid-1997, Jamil Sarsour departed the US for Israel. He again received "a sealed envelope from activist Adel Awadallah [Engineer #2],"[145] from Sheikh Abu Tair's mother once he arrived in Israel. In the letter, Adel Awadallah again confided he was seeking a way to escape from the region before being captured. He was still seeking the assistance of Sarsour "to find a way to leave the region and requests help to obtain a passport and tools to change his appearance."[146] "After a few days, Jamil Sarsour traveled to the home of Abu Taher and gave the Sheik's mother an envelope for Adel containing $3,000 and a note."[147]

During this mid-1997 trip from America to Palestine, Jamil Sarsour gave $13,000 to Adel Awadallah. With the money from Jamil Sarsour, Adel Awadallah was planning to mastermind two HAMAS suicide bombings in Jerusalem. "The orders for [the] suicide bombings came from HAMAS leaders. The local HAMAS [Engineer #2] was responsible for all planning and coordination [of the suicide attacks]."[148]

On July 30, 1997, the first bombing since the March 21 bombing of the Tel Aviv café, occurred when two HAMAS suicide bombers detonated two bombs in the Mahane Yehuda Market in West Jerusalem, killing eighteen people and injuring over 100. The suicide bombers were standing near fruit stands crowded with lunchtime customers when the two bombs exploded within seconds of one another.

"Witnesses described a fireball and body parts 'flying through the air.' Blood covered the ground, where it mixed with the debris of fruit and vegetables. One witness told Israeli Radio that he was in a shop during the explosions. 'I was blown over, there was dust everywhere. Anybody who was between two walls was saved; anybody who poked his head out was killed.' Another witness, storekeeper David Boneh, said he heard two explosions three seconds apart. 'Suddenly everything went black,' he said."[149] This attack claimed the most lives since Prime Minister Netanyahu's election.

HAMAS intended to harm the peace process further by timing this bombing. It occurred on the eve before the planned visit to the region by US Middle East envoy Dennis Ross to revive stalled peace talks between Israel and the Palestinian Authority. Unfortunately, Arafat resisted pressure to round up HAMAS activists following the bombing. Instead, he met with and embraced leaders of HAMAS during "national unity" talks.

In August 1997, Mousa Abu Marzook, after "being expelled from the United States," called on the Palestinian people "to turn the lives of Jewish settlers 'into an unbearable hell.' Mousa Abu Marzook, whose comments were published in the United Arab Emirates, also told a magazine, 'We call on our people in Palestine to stalk the herds of these spiteful settlers.'"[150]

On September 4, 1997, the second wave of revenge bombings occurred when three HAMAS suicide bombers, one dressed as a woman, detonated bombs they were wearing during the afternoon hours in the crowded Ben Yehduha Pedestrian Mall in East Jerusalem. The trio blew themselves up within seconds of one another. The explosion scattered body parts over the sidewalks, windows, and business buildings. Five people were killed, and over 192 injured, including many children. After the attacks, HAMAS claimed responsibility for the bombings. Netanyahu warned there would be no peace process as long as Israelis continued to be blown up in the streets.

Why Middle East Peace Failed During the 1990s – Part 2

A "senior Israeli intelligence source said Adel Awadallah [Engineer #2] is thought to have planned the two recent suicide bombings at Jerusalem's Mahaneh Yehuda market and Rehov Ben-Yehuda mall, which killed 20 people and wounded hundreds. Adel Awadallah was in charge of a recently uncovered Beit Sahour bomb factory and probably made the five bombs used in the Jerusalem attacks."[151]

Netanyahu expressed the belief that this attack originated from within Palestine and declared that Israel would take action against HAMAS if the PA did not pursue those responsible. Arafat condemned the bombings as acts of terrorism aimed at harming the peace process between Israel and Palestine. He said he believed the attacks were being masterminded by HAMAS leaders abroad. Hours later, Israeli security forces rounded up sixty-nine Palestinians for questioning. Israel decided it must neutralize those responsible for masterminding the bombings to prevent any future attacks. Israel decided it would assassinate Khalid Misha'al, a founder of HAMAS and the president of the HAMAS Political Bureau. Misha'al lived in Amman, Jordan, with Marzook.

On September 25, 1997, two Israeli Mossad agents approached Misha'al as he was walking to work in Amman with his bodyguards. One of the Mossad agents pushed a syringe into Misha'al's neck and began injecting poison. "The assassination attempt failed when Mishaal's bodyguards chased and arrested the Mossad agents."[152] "King Hussein of Jordan asked for a US specialist to come to Amman and supervise the medical care that is being accorded to Misha'al."[153]

When news spread of the assassination attempt on Misha'al, HAMAS threatened to avenge the failed assassination. Their supporters injured two Israeli embassy guards in Jordan during an attack. Besides the international scrutiny and embarrassment Israel would suffer, they again had to fear deadly suicide bombings by HAMAS within their borders.

Jordan agreed to return the two Mossad agents to Israel in exchange for the release of Sheikh Ahmad Yassin, the HAMAS founder arrested in 1989 and sentenced to life in prison plus fifteen years for establishing HAMAS, inciting others to kidnap and murder Israeli soldiers, and establishing HAMAS military cells. The Israelis agreed to the exchange and released him on October 1, 1997.[154] (See Appendix A-12.)

On October 4, 1997, in an interview following his release, Sheikh Yassin said, "I say this one more time so that everyone understands. We do not hate the Jews as Jews. We do not fight the Jews as Jews. We are fighting [people] who take our rights and our land, and our homes and our houses. We are fighting those who kill us. We want truth. We are not aggressors against anyone. We do not oppress anyone. The Palestinian people want to return to their homes. For that reason, we are prepared to live with the Jews in the best possible circumstances, in brotherhood and a spirit of cooperation. But they must not infringe on our rights. If my Muslim brother, of the same mother and father, took my land, I would fight him. I would fight my brother, though he was from the same mother and father."[155]

In December 1997, Israel "arrested the director of the Holy Land Foundation (HLF) in Israel. Mohammed Antai, 26, [was] charged with membership in and [conducting] activity on behalf of the HLF, an illegal [HAMAS] organization in Israel. He is suspected of providing families of HAMAS suicide bombers and jailed terrorists with money raised by the American branch of the HLF (based in Richardson, Texas)."[156] The American branch of the HLF is a HAMAS front organization established and funded by Marzook with a portion of the initial $10 million he received in the 1980s while attending college in Rustin, Louisiana, to establish a US HAMAS base.

Why Middle East Peace Failed During the 1990s – Part 2

In addition, the HLF in Israel received funds from the Palestine Relief and Development Fund in England and the Committee for Help and Solidarity with Palestine organization based in France. Therefore, "the Israeli Government issued a decree banning three organizations that it contends supplied financial aid to support HAMAS. The ban authorizes the Israeli Government to seize assets, and any money found in Israel belonging to the Holy Land Foundation for Relief and Development, the England-based Palestine Relief and Development Fund, and the France-based Committee for Help and Solidarity with Palestine."[157]

Also, in December 1997, "Israel uncovered the HAMAS [terrorism] cell responsible for at least 10 [terrorist] attacks on Israeli targets, including the two [July and September] 1997 suicide bombings in Jerusalem that killed 22 Israeli civilians."[158] Israel intensified its manhunt for "Adel Awadallah [Engineer #2], his brother, Imad Awadallah [Engineer #4], and Al-Sharif [Engineer #3] for masterminding these terrorist attacks. The PA (Palestinian Authority) police arrested eight members of HAMAS's military wing, Izzadin Kassam, a Palestinian source in Ramallah said. The source said the arrests were linked to the manhunt for Adel Awadallah."[159]

Following the assassination attempt on Misha'al in Jordan, Adel Awadallah received orders for suicide bombings from the HAMAS headquarters in Damascus, Syria. The execution of these terrorist attacks would cause a grave problem for HAMAS in the coming months because of an excessive internal struggle between Adel Awadallah, his brother Imad, and Al-Sharif.

There are allegations that Al-Sharif [Engineer #3] refused to carry out attacks because of concern with the strict security measures put in place by Israel. The risk of being caught was too significant, in his opinion. Allegedly, Adel Awadallah [Engineer #2] decided he would pursue the attacks without the help of Al-Sharif. This decision led to heated disputes between the two since each believed he was in charge of the other. Adel Awadallah, with the aid of his brother Imad, spent the next several months planning and preparing for future terrorist attacks against Israel.

On February 1, 1998, the Israeli authorities released Sheikh Abu Tair from prison after he served time for the activities he conducted in 1996. Upon his release, he held a very senior position within the leadership of the military wing. Among his "responsibilities within the HAMAS Command, the accused [Sheikh Abu Taher] transferred funds between the HAMAS organization and Adel Awadallah. Sheikh Abu Taher met three [times] with a HAMAS activist, a US resident by the name of Jamil Sarsour, and received from him $10,000 US, $5,000 US, and $3,000 US accordingly. The Sheikh [gave $15,000] to Mahmad Natshe, and from him [Natshe] [the money went] to Adel Awadallah. The [Sheikh] kept for himself the last amount [$3,000]."[160]

One evening in March 1998, at 6:00 p.m., Sheikh Abu Tair's relative, Ghassan Adassi, drove Al-Sharif to a warehouse in the industrial zone in the Palestinian-controlled area of Ramallah. He used the warehouse as a hideout to prepare HAMAS bombs. After dropping Al-Sharif off at the warehouse, Adassi allegedly drove away. Later that evening, an explosion occurred at the warehouse. The Palestinian security service personnel arrived at the warehouse and discovered a body. The Palestinian preventive security then rounded up several suspects, including Adassi and his two brothers. Despite releasing his two brothers, the security personnel held Adassi in custody because of his suspicious behavior.

Why Middle East Peace Failed During the 1990s – Part 2

The initial Palestinian reports showed they found a dead man in the warehouse following the explosion. Authorities initially believed the man accidentally killed himself when the bomb he was building accidentally exploded. "A number of documents found at the warehouse by the Palestinian security personnel identified the dead man as Nadim Abu Sneineh. The Palestinians relayed the information to the Israeli General Security Services, who told them Nadim Abu Sneineh was the [alias] of Al-Sharif [Engineer #3]."[161] Al-Sharif was a thirty-two-year-old electrical engineer blamed for rigging bombs responsible for the deaths of seventy-three Israelis.

On April 1, 1998, the Palestinian Authority confirmed the identity of the bombing victim as Al-Sharif. They announced that he had been shot three times, twice in the chest and once in the leg, before the explosion. They shared he had been dead for at least three hours before the bomb exploded. This announcement outraged all parties, and the blame game began. Most, including his family, blamed the Israeli government for his cold-blooded murder. Following verification of the body, a family member said, "Ayyash was Engineer (#1). Israel killed him, but over 100 of his allies came to replace him. Now our son is killed, and we guess thousands will replace him."

On the day of the funeral, sporadic fighting broke out between Palestinian youths and Israeli troops. Most schools in East Jerusalem closed, and workers declared a commercial strike to mourn Al-Sharif's death. Senior officials from Palestine, who spoke during the funeral, held Israel responsible for the killing. Major Palestinian groups called on Arafat to cease all contact with Israel for their role in this assassination.

HAMAS claimed Israel, with the help of the PA, sent Israeli secret service agents into Ramallah to shoot Al-Sharif and later detonate a car bomb after placing his dead body inside a car. "'Israel has in practice violated an undeclared, seven-month cease-fire with HAMAS and thus has made a retaliatory suicide attack almost inevitable,' said a senior HAMAS member in Gaza on Friday."[162] HAMAS compared the assassination to that of Ayyash's, after which they had committed four suicide bombings within eight days.

"HAMAS is always ready,"[163] said Rabhi Rantisi, a relative of HAMAS leader Dr. Abdul Aziz Rantisi. "Israel has violated the cease-fire just as it did back in 1996 when its agents assassinated Yahya Ayyash [Engineer #1], the former top bomb-maker in HAMAS, who was killed... when explosives in his cellular phone were detonated."[164]

Israeli Prime Minister Netanyahu issued a statement denying Israel was involved in the killing. Concerned about suicide bombings, Israeli sources blamed the murder on the Palestinian government. They accused the Palestinian government of trying to cover up their killing to rid themselves of responsibility for any future HAMAS suicide attacks against Israel. Israel was skeptical of the PA investigation of the murder and demanded Arafat release information before Israel suffered the consequences of another attack.

"President Arafat directly called on HAMAS not to retaliate for Sharif's death; US officials also said they believe the Palestinian government is working to prevent any retaliatory attacks against Israel."[165] "Israel's General Security Head, Ami Ayalon, met with Palestinian President Yasser Arafat on Thursday and heard from him details about the Palestinian investigation into last Sunday's car blast in Ramallah where the body of Sharif was found riddled with three bullets."[166]

"Israeli sources admitted Friday that US officials have told Israel that the Palestinian government is doing its best to prevent an [HAMAS] attack, 'because of the dangerous impact it will have on the already stalled peace process.'"[167] "The Palestinian government's ultimatum to HAMAS was released in Ramallah following earlier revelations that fellow members of HAMAS's top leaders were the ones who shot dead... Muhyiddin Sharif [Engineer #3], before they [HAMAS] detonated his body in a stolen car in Ramallah."[168] The public release of his death details would embarrass HAMAS.

On Sunday, April 5, as rumors began circulating that Adel Awadallah had murdered him, Israeli radio stations reported that Al-Sharif was killed over an internal HAMAS power struggle. He had wanted to take over the HAMAS military wing, Izzedine al-Qassam, but met resistance from other group members. Adel Awadallah was then considered the primary subject of the murder.

"On Friday (April 12), the Palestinian police shut down the Reuters [news agency] office in Gaza after the agency had shown a videotape of Imad Awadallah's brother Adel, also a fugitive, who warned HAMAS 'would bring sorrow into every Israeli home.' (Adel) Awadallah also accused [Yasser Arafat's] Preventive Security Chief, Jabril Rajoub, of collaborating with Israel in Sharif's [Engineer #3's] death."[169] Adel Awadallah denied that the murder was over a HAMAS power struggle for leadership of the military wing and demanded his brother, Imad, who the PA had arrested, be released immediately.

Following the release of Adel Awadallah's videotape, "the head of the Palestinian General Intelligence (PGI), Brig.-Gen. Tawfik Tirawi reported to PA [Chairperson] Yasser Arafat on the preliminary investigation findings of (Imad) Awadallah [Engineer #4].

"Palestinian General Intelligence officials arrested Imad Awadallah [Engineer #4], a Hamas fugitive, in Ramallah yesterday morning and said he had confessed to killing Hamas bomb-maker Muhi Sharif [Engineer #3] two weeks ago."[170] "Security officials said the report in *The Jerusalem Post* last Sunday based on an interview with Rantisi, who hinted that the Palestinian Preventive Security Service was behind Sharif's [Engineer #3] death, forced the PA to go public with their information regarding an internal HAMAS rivalry."[171]

The following are the main events included in the Palestinian police report of Abdul Rahim, "which relied on the findings of the investigation and testimonies given by the prime suspect in the affair, Ghassan Adassi. Sharif [Engineer #3 was assassinated by Imad Awadallah [Engineer #4], brother of Adel Awadallah [Engineer #2], who is the commander of Hamas' military wing in the West Bank. The killing was perpetrated in the wake of a dispute within the military wing of Hamas."[172]

"Three members of the Hamas cell agreed to meet at a warehouse owned by the Adassi family in the industrial zone in Ramallah on March 30 [1998] at 19:00 hrs. (7:00 p.m.). Sharif (Engineer #3) had rented the warehouse from the Adassi family some months beforehand and had used it as his hideout, using a different identity under the name of Nadim Abu Sneineh. The three Hamas members who met at the warehouse were Engineer #3, Imad Awadallah (Engineer #4), and Ghassan Adassi, the son of the warehouse's owner."[173]

"Shortly after the three gathered at the warehouse, a dispute broke out between Engineer #3 and Engineer #4. They traded accusations and challenged each other on who was in charge and who was or was not authorized to act on behalf of Hamas's military wing."[174] "PA sources said the feud between Imad Awadallah (Engineer #4) and Sharif (Engineer #3 was) over leadership of the Izzadin Kassam [terrorism cell], and an $800,000 stipend from Hamas abroad, and allegations that Sharif (Engineer #3) collaborated with Israel."[175] "Suddenly, Engineer #4 strode toward a Fiat Uno that was on the scene, pulled out a gun, and shot three shots at Engineer #3. Two of the bullets hit Engineer #3 in the chest, and the third hit him in the leg. Engineer #3 died on the spot."[176]

"After the murder, Awadallah [Engineer #4] ordered Adassi to prepare an explosive device and to set the timer to go off at 20:50 hrs. (8:50 p.m.). Engineer #4 wanted to distort evidence at the crime scene. Adassi prepared a five-kilo device, known to Hamas military activists as 'white snow,' and then went to the mosque to pray. Engineer #4, on his part, left the warehouse and went to an apartment some 120 meters away to watch the blast when it happened and to make sure everything had gone as planned."[177] (See Appendix A–13.)

"The claim that Muhi a-Din Sharif [Engineer #3] was murdered by his HAMAS colleagues sounds so imaginative that there is only one claim that, on the face of it, sounds even more refutable: that he was murdered by his senior partner in HAMAS terrorism, Adel Awadallah [Engineer #2]. The reason: no information on violent internal struggles within HAMAS's military arm [over money and a power struggle] has been uncovered until today."[178]

Meanwhile, in America, the Sarsours and relatives of Adel Awadallah were making plans to aid him in escaping from Palestine before being captured or killed. Jamil Sarsour was traveling to Palestine in May 1998 to assist Adel in escaping before being captured by Israel. Sarsour "bought [in Chicago, IL] four wigs [and other items] for Adel Awadallah."[179] The wigs, mustaches, and other items were to be used by Awadallah to change his appearance and assist in his escape.

"At the end of April 1998, days before the accused [Jamil Sarsour] traveled from the United States to the region [Palestine], an unknown male [Jamil's brother Salah Sarsour] arrived at his [Jamil's] home and told him that he wanted him to take a note to the HAMAS wanted activist Adel Awadallah. He also told Jamil that in the note was written how Adel could obtain a passport with which he could flee the region."[180]

On May 5, 1998, Jamil Sarsour departed the US for Israel to assist Awadallah in escaping from Palestine. Before boarding his flight, he "swallowed the note at the airport, which was rolled and wrapped in a tube [capsule]."[181]

After arriving in Palestine, Jamil retrieved the letter he had swallowed after it "discharged in the bathroom."[182] He then "returned to the home of Sheik Abu-Taher and, through his mother, gave the Sheik the wigs and the sum of $5,000 plus the sealed note. Jamil requested that all the particles be given to Adel Awadallah, which the Sheik did through the senior HAMAS activist Mahmad Jeral Natshe."[183] Adel Awadalla wrote a note to Jamil after receiving the items, requesting help to get documents to aid in his leaving the area.

"After receiving the note, the accused [Jamil Sarsour] traveled to the home of [Sheik] Abu Tair and gave him the sum of another $3,000. Jamil said to the Sheik that he should give the money to Adel Awadallah. He also gave the Sheikh a note for Adel [Awadallah], in which Jamil wrote that he is trying to obtain the other things he asked for which would help Adel escape from the Israeli defense forces."[184]

Knowing he could not escape the region, Awadallah prepared for future terrorist attacks against Israel. "In June 1998, the accused [Sheikh Abu Tair] assisted [Engineer #2] in the purchase of explosives [from an] arms dealer on the West Bank and HAMAS. Sheikh Abu Tair transferred the sum of $5,000 US and 5000 Jordanian Dinars to the arms dealer, and the arms dealer transferred [sold] in exchange Kalashnikov rifles, M-16 rifles, and pistols to a messenger."[185]

Why Middle East Peace Failed During the 1990s – Part 2

Sheikh Abu Tair, around July 1998, learned, "El Wahidi was interested in selling an Uzi. . . .The accused [Sheikh Abu Tair] got the firearm [Uzi] and appropriate magazines, and gave them to Mahmad Natshe, who then gave them to Adel Awadallah."[186] By August 1998, with the financial aid of Jamil Sarsour and the assistance of Sheikh Abu Tair, Awadallah was well-armed. "Hamas leader Awadallah had been planning to detonate five consecutive terrorist bombs in Israel."[187]

On August 15, 1998, Imad Awadallah escaped the Palestinian-controlled prison in Jericho. After learning of the escape, "the Palestinian Government imposed a curfew on Jericho on Sunday, the first time since 1994, in which the police have imposed a curfew on a region under their control."[188] The government ordered businesses to close and told civilians to return home. Palestinian police patrolled the streets and conducted house-to-house searches for him. Israeli troops joined the manhunt by setting up roadblocks on all roads leading out of Jericho.

Palestinian forces also sealed off his family's property and prevented anyone from entering or leaving. The Palestinian troops did this to force the Awadallah brothers to turn themselves in to the authorities. The intensive search efforts did not produce the Awadallah brothers.

HAMAS issued a statement, "We hold the Palestinian Authority fully responsible for [Imad] Awadallah's safety, who had been arrested for several months without any solid evidence."[189] HAMAS continued to blame Israel for the murder of Al-Sharif and accused the PA of forcing Imad to endure extreme torture, forcing him to confess to a murder he did not commit. In addition, they claimed the PA tortured Imad into identifying their organizational structure and the whereabouts of their leaders abroad.[190]

On September 10, 1998, the Israeli Army stated that "two terrorists were killed near Hebron during a clash with our soldiers."[191] These two terrorists were Imad and Adel Awadallah. Israel claimed the two had been hiding in a small village near Hebron since Imad's escape from prison. When the Israeli Army located the brothers in a small cottage, they encountered resistance and shot them.

To prevent the Palestinians from inciting riots during the brothers' funerals, Israel declined to hand over the bodies to their family. Instead, the Israelis buried the bodies in a secret location. Israel's killing of the two HAMAS military leaders dealt a severe blow to the HAMAS military wing, particularly its ability to prevent Israel from locating and neutralizing its military leaders. [Note: On April 30, 2014, Israel returned the remains of Adel and Imad Awadallah to their family for burial.]

Following the deaths of the Awadallah brothers, HAMAS founder and spiritual leader Sheikh Yassin said HAMAS would not hesitate to retaliate against Israel. During a press conference, Sheikh Yassin said, "Our response is coming soon, God willing. This is the nature of war; one time we gain, one time we lose."[192] Sheikh Yassin said, "Hamas is determined to defend itself, as it is the right of anybody to defend himself. Israel seized our lands, took our freedom, kidnapped our children and girls, killed our sons, and so we will resist by all our power until the holy places are returned and a Palestinian state is established on our land."[193] (See Appendix A-14.)

On October 23, 1998, after he traveled from Milwaukee to Israel, the Israelis arrested Jamil Sarsour for funneling money to Adel Awadallah. An Israeli military court confirmed that Sarsour funneled the money to the mastermind behind the HAMAS bombings. Aware of the importance of this arrest to the VB investigation, the Israelis informed FBIHQ they would like to travel to Chicago to tell me, in

Why Middle East Peace Failed During the 1990s – Part 2

person, of the details regarding the arrest of Sarsour and about the death of Imad Awadallah and his brother Adel.

Jamil Sarsour denied any connection to HAMAS and said, "I only contributed a small [amount of money] to the family [of Awadallah]. That's all I did."[194] Radio reports in Israel reported, "Sarsour gave $40,000 [to Adel Awadallah] over two years."[195] "Awadallah also reportedly asked [Jamil] Sarsour to get him a false passport and any other identification that would allow him to flee the country."[196]

Following the January 1993 arrest of Chicago resident Mohammad Salah, the ITU should have coordinated a logical and thorough investigation of the US-based HAMAS organization. Conducting such an investigation could have prevented many of the HAMAS terrorist attacks previously mentioned. But for the uninterrupted US-financed terrorist attacks by HAMAS against Israel, the Middle East peace process had a good chance of succeeding during the 1990s.

After the killing of the Awadallah brothers and the subsequent arrest of Jamil Sarsour, three DOJ attorneys, FBIHQ SSA Resnick, Milwaukee SSA Ford, Agent Reed, and I traveled to Israel for the second time at the end of April 1999. This time, we met with Sarsour. We intended to talk to him about his material support of international terrorism activities with Adel Awadallah.

I was still concerned about the disruptions caused by the duplicate criminal investigation of Sarsour that the Milwaukee division was still working on. Others and I working the VB case became frustrated daily by the constant interruptions caused by their investigation. Fortunately, we had arranged a meeting with the US Deputy Attorney General in Washington, DC, several hours before our second scheduled flight to Israel. I believed the Deputy Attorney General would recognize and resolve the problem about the Chicago and Milwaukee offices working on duplicate criminal cases and address Attorney Murphy's repeated interferences with the VB investigation.

> "Some terrorism now comes from abroad. Some terrorism is homegrown. But whatever its origin, terrorism is deadly, and the FBI has no higher priority than to combat terrorism; to prevent it where possible; and where prevention fails, to apprehend the terrorists and do everything within the law to work for conviction and the most severe sentences. Our goal is to prevent, detect and deter."[197]
>
> — Louis J. Freeh, Director FBI

CHAPTER 27

THE SECOND TRIP TO ISRAEL

"Do you know what the answer is to peace in the Middle East?"
—Michael Resnick, Supervisory Agent,
FBIHQ International Terrorism Unit,
asked an Israeli official in May 1999

Before traveling to Israel for the second time in four months, Agent Reed and I discussed the trip several times and agreed to sit together on the flights to and from Israel. She called the airline to make our flight and seat reservations.

The US Deputy Attorney General scheduled a meeting in Washington, DC, on the morning we were to leave for Israel. Those required to attend this meeting included Reed, Ford, Gossfeld, the AUSAs from Chicago and Milwaukee, FBIHQ's SSA Resnick, Murphy, and me. The purpose of the meeting was to discuss the problems that occurred during the previous trip and the US government's goals for the pending trip to Israel.

The meeting took place inside a secured chamber on Sunday morning, April 29, 1999. This secured chamber is reserved for a federal judge who "presides over a court established for no other purpose than to decide in secret whether to permit the United States Government (FBI or National Security Agency) to engage in espionage against a foreign government which maintains a presence on United States soil."[198]

The meeting addressed the conduct of the US officials while in Israel during January 1999, as well as the other issues surrounding the FBI investigations. During this meeting, we understood that we could each express our concerns regarding any problems, including issues with Attorney Murphy. Therefore, before the meeting, I prepared a list of topics I wanted to address. I outlined my concerns regarding Murphy's roles in the loss of $200,000 in terrorist funds in 1998, causing Milwaukee to open a duplicate portion of VB, and his refusal to use forfeiture laws against assets of a known US-based HAMAS financier. I then showed my list to Gossfeld. He said, "It would be great if the Deputy AG addresses these issues."

However, once AUSA Flessner began expressing his concerns regarding Murphy's conduct, the Deputy AG cut him off, saying, "We will have none of that here!"

It was clear he would allow no one in the room to discuss their concerns regarding Murphy. Realizing I could not discuss the many problems caused by Murphy during the past eighteen months, I quietly slid my list of issues back into my briefcase.

During the meeting, the Deputy AG clarified that Murphy was in charge during our trip to the Middle East. After the meeting, the FBI agents and supervisors walked to the J. Edgar Hoover FBI Headquarters building.

While Ford, Gossfeld, Resnick, Reed, and I stood in the outdoor plaza at FBIHQ, I stated, "I just want to make one thing clear about this

The Second Trip to Israel

trip. I am the lead investigator of the FBI's National Criminal Investigation of HAMAS. I am going to evaluate potential evidence against Jamil Sarsour." Reed then claimed she was going to investigate the same thing.

Despite feeling frustrated with her comment, I clarified to everyone present that the VB investigation targeted high-ranking HAMAS members, making it absurd for Milwaukee to carry out the same criminal investigation on just one individual. I reasoned Milwaukee had a massive fraud investigation regarding Sarsour and his associates.

I further stated Chicago had four years of experience investigating the overall US-based HAMAS enterprise, of which Sarsour was a primary co-conspirator—Chicago's years of investigation linked him to the primary targets of the HAMAS criminal enterprise, allowing the FBI to pursue RICO criminal charges against many HAMAS leaders, terrorism financiers, and trained terrorists.

Reed shot back by claiming since Sarsour lived in Wisconsin, the Milwaukee office had the right to investigate him over Chicago. Resnick told everyone present, "I am well aware of the problems between Chicago and Milwaukee regarding the duplicate criminal investigation of Sarsour. Following this trip, I will resolve the duplicate investigation in a manner that is in the best interest of the FBI."

At 10:00 p.m. that evening, we left the United States for our second trip to the Middle East to further the FBI's AOT investigation. Reed and I sat together on the flight, talking and laughing, with no signs of hostility between us following our encounter earlier that day.

After arriving in Israel on May 1, 1999, since there were no plans during our first day, we went sightseeing together. We took a taxi to Bethlehem to tour the historic city. Within minutes after arriving at the site, Reed approached me and said, "Bob, I do not feel comfortable here. Will you go back to the hotel with me?" She expressed to me her fear and concern for her safety. I voiced discomfort with our location; however, we would be fine, and she need not worry. Again, she asked me, "Bob, will you please return to the hotel with me." She said she would feel safer at the hotel.

Sensing a problem, the group members asked me what was wrong. I explained how Reed was concerned for her safety and wanted me to return to the hotel with her. Resnick and the others spoke to her and convinced her everything would be fine. As the group walked through Bethlehem, we talked to her to help her stay calm until we returned to the hotel several hours later.

The FBI received permission on May 2 to view the evidence found in Adel and Imad Awadallah's possession at the time of their deaths. With such a large group viewing those items, it would have made the trip far more dangerous. SSA Resnick, and only one FBI agent and one AUSA could travel to the location to view the evidence.

It was Resnick's decision on whether Agent Reed or I would go to view the evidence with him. Resnick, Reed, and I sat at a table in the hotel restaurant to discuss who should view the evidence. Both Reed and I expressed our desire and reasons for believing we should be the one. After the meeting, Resnick said he would call us within an hour to let us know which of us would make the trip.

An hour later, Resnick called me and asked me to meet him on the hotel patio. During our meeting, he said, "Bob, you will travel with Flessner and me in the morning to view the evidence found on the Awadallah brothers."

"Have you told Cybil? She'll be upset," I remarked.

"I do not care. After witnessing her panic attack today in Bethlehem, there is no way I am sending her into a dangerous situation. She will stay behind and conduct some other work," said Resnick.

The Second Trip to Israel

FBIHQ SSA Michael Resnick and me by the Mediterranean Sea, May 1999.

As we sat outside on the hotel patio, Resnick drilled me about VB. He threw a lot of "what if" scenarios at me regarding many avenues of the investigation. He asked me to explain my short- and long-term goals.

After talking for an hour and a half, Resnick stared at me for a few minutes. He then stated, "Bob, you know what you are doing! You get it! You know what needs to be done and how to get it done. You have anticipated future issues and problems that may arise. No one has ever done what you have done. Your efforts, goals and foresight with Vulgar Betrayal can change what happens here between Israel and the Palestinians."

"Do you see how, through Vulgar Betrayal, the FBI can stop future terrorist attacks and allow for a possible peaceful resolution between Israel and Palestine?" I asked.

"Yes, I now understand the full potential of Vulgar Betrayal," said Resnick.

"Why are others unable to see the incredible potential of this investigation? Why is Clinton aiming to kill it?" I asked.

"Bob, Vulgar Betrayal is extremely complex and difficult for many, including some at headquarters, to comprehend fully. There are so many avenues within your investigation. I do not understand how you can keep this so well-organized. In your head, not just on paper," he replied.

"Someone from headquarters now understands Vulgar Betrayal and its significant possibilities," I said.

The following morning, Resnick, Flessner, and I traveled to a US government facility to meet with the driver responsible for taking us to the location where the evidence was located. The driver showed us the vehicle that would take us to the location. The large black SUV was armor-plated and had bulletproof glass throughout. He pointed out that the vehicle was designed to withstand a direct hit from a mortar round and had fire extinguishers integrated into its exterior to counter firebomb attacks. He further shared the driving maneuvers he would take should certain situations arise. We reached the evidence facility without incident.

Upon arrival at the facility, we were guided to a room to observe the belongings of the Awadallah brothers from their time of death. The possessions included weapons, ammunition, and disguises. I found a black bag with something that could aid in advancing the VB investigation. This bag contained items Sarsour had provided Adel Awadallah through a third party. In addition, I came across a receipt in the bag that provided evidence that the items given to Adel were purchased in Chicago, IL by Jamil Sarsour.

I told Resnick and Flessner about the Chicago receipt I found in the black bag. As they reviewed the receipt, I mentioned Reed would not be happy when she learned about its discovery. The receipt was evidence Sarsour had conducted activity within the Chicago jurisdiction.

Resnick offered to break the news to Reed.

The Second Trip to Israel

 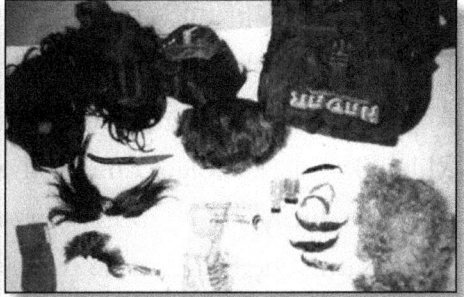

Left: The weapons possessed by the Awadallah brothers. Right: the wigs and other items in their possession to be used to alter their appearances.

Flessner and I thanked him for volunteering.

After viewing the items of interest, a military officer who accompanied us to the facility treated us to lunch in the cafeteria. Resnick and Flessner sat on one side of the table while the military officer and I sat across from them. While discussing security concerns and other issues, Resnick asked the military official, "Do you know what the answer is to peace in the Middle East?"

"No, do you?" asked the military officer.

Resnick pointed at me and said, "He is the answer to peace in the Middle East."

At this moment, I realized Resnick understood what I was trying to do. More importantly, he understood I was not the "out-of-control agent on a fishing expedition" as claimed by Clinton. He realized I had been piecing together a plan that could help bring peace to the Middle East through the dismantling of the entire HAMAS terrorist network and other Middle Eastern terrorist networks.

After returning to our hotel, everyone except Reed gathered in the lobby to take part in a sightseeing tour given by the military official who went with us to view the evidence. Noticing her absence, I asked, "Where is Cybil?"

Someone said she was upset that I had discovered the Chicago receipt.

Resnick and I began discussing the Milwaukee and Chicago criminal investigations during the tour. During our conversation, he pulled me to the back of the group, out of hearing distance from the others. He said, "Bob, you should be the office of origin regarding Sarsour. Milwaukee should receive your leads, not the reverse."

"Mike, I have been saying that since day one. I warned everyone about Attorney Murphy, but no one would listen. He caused these problems. However, no one at headquarters will tell Reed to close the duplicate Milwaukee criminal case. This is so ridiculous, it has caused nothing but problems. Why haven't you or anyone else at headquarters instructed her to close her case these past five months? This is a simple decision. Why will no one tell her to close her case? What am I missing?" I asked.

Photo of Agent Wright and the IDF Officer who FBIHQ SSA Mike Resnick made the statement about Wright being the answer to peace in the Middle East.

"I'll handle this upon our return. Bob, what I need from you is a comprehensive summary of your Vulgar Betrayal investigation. Your summary will help me justify to others at headquarters the Milwaukee case needs to be closed," said Resnick.

"I will work on it when I return to Chicago. The duplicate case has distracted the VB investigation, and things will only worsen if you guys at headquarters do not address this issue soon," I warned.

The Second Trip to Israel

Reed and I sat at a table on the hotel's outdoor patio the following day. Because of the problems we were experiencing with our cases, I tried to explain to her why FBIHQ needed to step in and make a call on which office should be the office of origin regarding the criminal investigation of Sarsour. I did not mention the conversation between Resnick and me the previous evening. I wanted nothing to do with telling her the Milwaukee case would be closed. We expected she would have a negative response to the case closure. FBIHQ would need to instruct her to close her duplicate investigation.

I expressed my disappointment to her regarding FBIHQ's failure to decide before our January trip. I further told her that Murphy caused this mess by convincing Milwaukee AUSA Kern to become involved with the Sarsour matter.

She then began telling me why she believed Milwaukee would remain the office responsible for investigating Sarsour's HAMAS-related criminal activities.

"Cybil, I enjoy working with you, and together we can make this work," I said.

"You are just playing with my head. You are just being nice to me so you can get what you want," she said.

Feeling frustrated by her statement, I suggested we cease discussing it, as it was unresolvable between us.

Frequently during the trip, she told me she and her husband were number one and number two on the FBI Personnel Resource List (PRL) for a transfer from Milwaukee to the Indianapolis division.

"You would be glad to see me go away," she remarked.

I told her that was not true. I enjoyed working with her and only wished that the matter of investigative jurisdiction over Sarsour was resolved by headquarters, ending the friction between us.

On the evening of May 4, the team convened a meeting in one of the hotel rooms to discuss the day's events and prepare for the scheduled interview of Sarsour the following day. After the meeting, Resnick met with Reed and me on the hotel's outdoor patio. He told us he wanted to resolve the problem since he felt Reed would receive her transfer to Indianapolis.

He asked, "Can we resolve this problem between the three of us, or would you rather resolve this matter at a higher level at headquarters?"

"Higher level," said Reed.

"I would rather resolve this between the three of us," I said.

She changed her answer, agreeing we could resolve the matter. Resnick then asked each of us to explain why we believed our office should investigate Sarsour's HAMAS-related criminal activities.

During Reed's presentation, she implied that I intentionally failed to provide Milwaukee with records from the Chicago office associated with Sarsour. This false allegation hurt me, and I could not believe she would imply that I was intentionally withholding documents from her.

I declared. "I would never do that! I have always been open and accommodating to all divisions with regards to individuals, businesses, and organizations identified through the Vulgar Betrayal investigation. I have always told agents throughout the country they are always welcome to visit Chicago to review Vulgar Betrayal records. An FBI Chicago relief supervisor deliberately concealed records from me, something I would never do to any FBI employee."

After briefly allowing her to reply and receiving no response, I continued, "On my own, without being told to do so, I have prepared and distributed detailed summaries of the Vulgar Betrayal investigation over the past three years. In addition, I have provided records

The Second Trip to Israel

to at least a dozen FBI divisions to aid them with their investigative efforts against HAMAS. Until now, no one has opened a duplicate criminal investigation of any subject of the Vulgar Betrayal case. We only have three agents and one support person assigned to the Vulgar Betrayal case. We have issued over 600 subpoenas for records and found hundreds of HAMAS subjects, front organizations, and businesses in the United States. As of last month, the Vulgar Betrayal case file holds over 640 subfiles and is growing daily. The FBI has provided no support personnel to Vulgar Betrayal to help handle the massive volume of records arriving in Chicago daily.

"The point is, Cybil, I am so bombarded by everything else I am working on regarding Vulgar Betrayal that I do not have time to address all the leads coming in from other offices. You are taking it personally, and you believe I have intentionally withheld records from you when I have not. Come to Chicago to review the Vulgar Betrayal records if you need them sooner than our delivery timeline allows. You can copy any records you need and take them back to Milwaukee. Dallas, Kansas City, Detroit, and many other offices have come to Chicago to view and copy Vulgar Betrayal records. You are only forty-five minutes away. You can come down anytime and copy any records you need."

Once I finished, Resnick said his final decision would be based on what he believed was best for the investigation and the FBI. As he continued, it became clear he thought that what was best for the FBI was for Chicago to be named the primary office.

When Reed realized what was about to happen, she became visibly upset and began commenting about this exact thing happening to her in the past with FBIHQ SSA Doug Phillips. I lacked understanding of her comment about Phillips; however, once I realized she was about to cry, I excused myself to allow her and Resnick time alone. I believed he would have an easier time calming her down if I were not present.

Fifteen minutes later, I returned to the table and found her calm and smiling. "I may have a resolution to the problem," said Resnick. As I understood it, the resolution involved the Chicago agents investigating Sarsour and Milwaukee investigating Sarsour's local criminal activities and his associates within the Milwaukee division. Chicago would provide any information it developed regarding him; likewise, Milwaukee would provide Chicago with details regarding its investigation. Reed and I would regularly contact one another to discuss the cases and compare notes. This is precisely what I wanted. I agreed to this solution quickly, and we instantly fixed everything, ensuring there would be no more problems between Reed and me.

Around 10:30 p.m., Resnick returned to his room while Reed and I stayed outside and talked. I inquired why she had such contempt and anger for FBIHQ Supervisor Phillips. She said she had been working a source for over two years before he had caused severe problems, ultimately forcing her to close the source case file. She claimed he made false statements about her conversations with him regarding the source. She further said that because of the false statements made by him, the Office of Professional Responsibility (OPR) conducted a one-year investigation into Phillips's conduct after she filed a complaint against him.

What she said regarding Phillips left me dumbfounded. Unbeknownst to her, I worked with Phillips for over a year after arriving in Chicago in 1993. He was among the most likable and well-respected agents on the Chicago JTTF. He was not a person who would lie or mislead others about anything. He was one of the few JTTF agents who openly shared his investigative results with others on the squad.

The Second Trip to Israel

When he announced he was leaving to take a supervisor position at FBIHQ, the agents on the squad were sorry to see him leave Chicago.

The following morning, I informed Flessner about the agreement reached the previous evening between Resnick, Reed, and myself. I then called Gossfeld in Chicago, left a message on his voicemail regarding the new agreement, and expressed how happy I was the friction between Chicago and Milwaukee was over.

The rest of the trip went well. Reed and I conducted a joint interview and continued socializing without further disagreements. Regarding Sarsour, following our interview, he decided he needed more time to decide if he wanted to cooperate with the FBI.

Hours before our flight's departure to the United States, Resnick, Reed, and I had dinner in a restaurant with five of the host countries' government officials. During dinner, I inquired about obtaining specific HAMAS records, which I knew Israel had in its possession. The highest-ranking government official told me these records would not be available to the FBI. I began joking with one of the other host supervisors about her boss's determination not to release these records to the FBI. "Are these records made of gold? Why is he being so stingy with them?" I asked her, loud enough for her boss to hear. Her boss stared at me as she and I laughed. He was unhappy with my comment.

"Hey, I am just trying to understand why you will not share the records you found buried. I can help you," I said.

"Do you want to know why I will not release these documents to the FBI?" the ranking official asked.

At this moment, everyone seated at the large table stopped talking and listened.

"I would love to know why," I said.

He then said he was concerned with FBIHQ management's lack of understanding of HAMAS and its overwhelming presence within America. His government agency did not trust FBIHQ management, so he would not provide the FBI with the requested documents.

"I agree with your concerns about FBI headquarters. But you know I understand what is happening here and can help. However, I need your help. I need to see those records," I said.

"Bob, do you know what one of your supervisors in Washington, DC, seriously suggested after we apprehended a Palestinian American several years ago?" he asked.

"No, but I can only imagine. During our trip here in January, Attorney Murphy wanted to offer Sheikh Abu Tair immunity and protection in the United States in return for his cooperation in testifying against other HAMAS leaders," I said.

"Seriously?" exclaimed the official.

"Yes. Dealing with that nonsense is a weekly occurrence for me. What did the FBIHQ supervisor suggest to you?" I asked.

"He wanted us to permit a shipment of weapons to be shipped here from abroad, so they could track the destination of the weapons," the official answered.

"Let me guess who suggested this absurd idea. Was it Pat Anderson?" I asked.

"Yes," he replied.

"The guy was clueless about HAMAS and the situation in Israel. I understand your frustrations with FBIHQ. Believe me, I live with it every day. However, you see Mr. Resnick at the end of the table?" I asked as I pointed to Resnick.

I then continued, "We discussed my investigation at length the other night. Despite his recent focus on terrorism, he comprehends

The Second Trip to Israel

the situation. He gets it! If he were your contact at FBIHQ, he would help both of our investigations. We need to work together to identify the HAMAS terrorists in America, Israel, and other countries. We can do this together through him."

"How would these records help you, Bob?" the official asked.

"I have every reason to believe these records came from a fax machine that Abu Saab asked Mohammad Salah to install in a Rahat doctor's office in 1992. The purpose of the fax machine was to communicate with HAMAS leader Abu Abada and other HAMAS leaders in the United States about military activities, transferring reports, and receiving orders for carrying out terrorist attacks against Israel. I believe someone set up the fax machine in Dr. Mahud Rumhi's medical office. If I am right, these documents, combined with the information I have already developed, will help to convict many Palestinian American HAMAS members for the murders that resulted from US-based activities linked to specific terrorist attacks here in your country," I explained.

"Bob, I will think about it," said the official.

"That is all I ask. That's much better than your previous firm 'no,'" I stated.

Everyone laughed, and Resnick assured the official he would discuss this matter further with an Israeli official in Washington, DC.

Before leaving the restaurant for the airport, the official asked to talk to Resnick and me privately regarding two things. Reed walked over as the official was talking to us. The official first told us he and others in the government had read the detailed affidavit I had signed and they understood what I had accomplished regarding the $1.4 million seizure in 1998 and assured us he could provide me with the documents I had requested during lunch. Second, he asked Resnick to tell Murphy to stop calling him.

"I do not care for Attorney Murphy. I find him annoying," said the official.

I laughed and assured him I understood his feelings. I said, "I wish I could have no further contact with Murphy."

He then shared some examples of his contacts with Murphy.

Shortly after our conversation, Resnick asked, "Bob, are these records you requested the same records Director Freeh requested last year, and they declined to turn over to him?"

"Yes. I need these records, Mike. If they are the communications I believe them to be, Vulgar Betrayal will quickly identify HAMAS leaders in America and worldwide. We will know who gave orders to carry out terrorist attacks and who financed the attacks," I said.

"I did not see this coming. This is great!" said Resnick.

"Once I realized who the high-ranking official was, I realized he had the authority to release the documents to us. I had to give it a shot and ask for the documents," I said.

He said, "I didn't know what was happening, but I could tell he was mad about something you said."

"I made a joke with one of his subordinates, and he did not like it when we both started laughing afterward. But it helped start the dialog I was seeking," I said.

"That it did. The opportunity to review those records has made this trip extremely productive for the FBI," he remarked.

Resnick, Reed, and I left the restaurant and traveled to the airport to meet with the attorneys before boarding the plane for the return trip to America. Resnick instructed Reed and me not to mention anything to Murphy or the AUSAs about our discussion regarding the documents I requested with the high-ranking official.

The Second Trip to Israel

"There is no reason to risk Attorney Murphy getting involved in our efforts to get these important documents," he stated.

Shortly after we arrived at the airport, Murphy approached Resnick and me. He informed Resnick he wanted to attend any meetings Resnick held in Washington, DC, with Israeli officials regarding any documents they may turn over to the FBI. Resnick and I looked at one another and wondered why Murphy would make such a statement. Seeming frustrated with his request, Resnick informed Murphy that the high-ranking government official had specified that he no longer wanted to speak with him in the future, and asked that Murphy cease contacting him.

"You clearly misunderstood his words!" Murphy suggested.

"I understood his words clearly. There was no misunderstanding. He does not want to talk to you ever again," said Resnick.

"I do not believe he said such a thing," snapped Murphy.

"Well, he said it to both Bob and me. Bob, did I misunderstand what he said about Mr. Murphy?" asked Resnick.

"No, you did not misunderstand what he said about Mr. Murphy. He told us about specific conversations you had with him. He said you initiated these contacts, and he does not want you calling him anymore," I said.

"I will do whatever I want!" said Murphy.

"You always do! No matter what consequences your actions bring about," I said.

Murphy inquired, "What does that mean?"

I said, "Where do I begin? I know, let us start with the $200,000 in terrorist funds we lost because of you. How about the fact that you made it known that you know nothing about HAMAS? Otherwise, you would not have embarrassed yourself and the rest of us when you suggested whom you wanted to offer immunity to."

"Enough!" Resnick shouted.

"He wants you to know that he no longer wishes to speak with you. As for your request to be present for any meetings between the FBI and another foreign government official in Washington, DC, such meetings are FBI matters, and you do not need to be present during such meetings," said Resnick.

Murphy turned and walked away, saying, "We'll see."

After boarding the plane, Resnick asked Reed and me, "Which of you tipped Murphy off about our dinner meeting conversation?"

Resnick and I learned that as soon as we arrived at the airport, Reed approached Murphy and told him about our dinner conversation with the host country's supervisors and the high-ranking government official.

Since I had misplaced my airline ticket, the airline issued me a replacement ticket with a new seat assignment. With this new seat assignment, I was no longer seated next to Reed. Instead, I was sitting next to another male passenger. After taking my seat, I reclined and closed my eyes for a brief rest. When I opened my eyes a few minutes later, I found Reed sitting in the seat next to me, looking at me.

"Someone is sitting there, he will be back shortly," I said.

"No, he will not be sitting here. I traded seats with him so we can sit together on the way home," she said.

She and I discussed movies and other things during the long flight back to America.

CHAPTER 28

THE EEO COMPLAINT

"The American foot dragging in investigating attacks in which Palestinian terrorists killed American citizens must be politically motivated. It is impossible to explain such indifference to the murder of Americans in any other way."[199]

— David Bar-Illan, Communications Director, Israel Prime Minister's Office

On May 10, 1999, I reviewed the Indianapolis PRL to determine where I would rank in seniority should I place my name back on the list to be considered for transfer to the Indianapolis FBI office. While reviewing the list, I discovered that Agent Reed held the ninth position. I called her and asked, "Cybil, have you seen the PRL for Indianapolis lately?"

"No. Why?" she asked.

I shared I was reviewing the list and found her to be in ninth place instead of first as she had mentioned before.

She said that she had contacted the eight agents on the list ahead of her and learned that each agent would not accept the PRL transfer to Indianapolis if offered to them through 1999. Technically speaking, she was now at the top of the list. She and her husband were offered transfers to the Indianapolis division a few days later. They would transfer from Milwaukee to Indianapolis within the next ninety days, in mid-August. This meant she would leave the Milwaukee criminal terrorism case behind. I also learned I would now be the next agent on the list to be called with the next transfer offer to the Indianapolis office, if I placed my name on the list.

On May 12, 1999, US Magistrate Wayne R. Anderson issued an opinion that the affidavit I swore to support for the June 8, 1998, seizure of HAMAS assets established "a reasonable basis for the government's belief that the [seized $1.4 million] funds are tainted. . . . We also find that the complaint establishes a reasonable basis for the government's belief that the Ford Van and [Salah's] residence is forfeitable because they were traceable to funds that are forfeitable under Section 1956 (a) (2) (a) (Money Laundering)."[200]

Mohammad Salah and the QLI were now required to answer interrogatories, which questioned their participation on behalf of HAMAS. Salah and the QLI were required to prove that the seized funds were not terrorist-related, as claimed in the affidavit.

On May 13, Reed called to discuss our cases. After I congratulated her on receiving her transfer to the Indianapolis office, she stated, "I bet you are happy now. Now, you are finally going to be rid of me."

I expressed my unhappiness about her transfer because we needed her help to investigate Sarsour's role in aiding HAMAS terrorists. I also told her I considered adding my name to the Indianapolis transfer list.

She encouraged me to add my name, assuring me that another agent would be offered a transfer to Indianapolis at the end of September. Upon my inquiry about how she knew about the September

The EEO Complaint

opening, she mentioned that a senior Indianapolis agent would guide new agents through the FBI Academy and retire after their July graduation. She stated, "You would never add your name to the Indianapolis list because you would never be willing to give up Vulgar Betrayal."

I thought, "She is right. I am not walking away from this case now, especially with the arrest of Sarsour and the expected return of HAMAS terrorist Sharif Alwan to Chicago in June."

During the call, she asked me to forward the completed VB analysis to her office. When I asked why she was requesting such information, she said, "I need it for my investigation of Sarsour's criminal activities in Palestine."

Her statement stunned me. I reminded her of the agreement reached in Israel between Resnick, her, and me. She claimed I agreed to analyze Sarsour's records and would provide the finished product to Milwaukee in real time, daily, to assist Milwaukee with its criminal investigation of Sarsour's HAMAS-related activities overseas.

"That's not what we agreed to," I stated.

I then informed her that the agreement was that Chicago would investigate Sarsour's activities abroad, and Milwaukee would investigate all the local criminal activities conducted by Sarsour and his Milwaukee associates. I told her that for Chicago to meet her request, I would have to send most of the VB case files to Milwaukee. I again reminded her that Chicago was working on many HAMAS subjects. We were not working full-time on Sarsour as she assumed. After the call ended, the now predictable phone call came from Milwaukee management to Chicago management, alleging I had again upset her.

A few days later, frustrated with the years of loading data into the databases by hand, I asked the computer section supervisor if she would install a scanner program onto my computer if I purchased the scanner myself. After she agreed to install the program, I purchased a $300 HP scanner from Best Buy with my own money to further the VB investigation. I delivered the scanner and computer to the computer squad the next day.

Two days later, I returned to pick up my computer and scanner. The FBI computer technician who tried to install the program said that she did not know how to load the program onto my computer. She said, "I guess the best thing for you to do is call Hewlett-Packard and ask them how to load the program."

I went to Gossfeld's office and said, "Tim, how pathetic is it that I had to purchase a scanner with my money to help further my investigation. Now I learned the computer section doesn't know how to load a simple program onto my laptop computer."

"Bob, you need to add this to the book you will write about this case in the future," said Tim.

"I have no intention of ever writing a book. Besides, no one would ever believe this story," I said.

On Friday, May 14, 1999, at 4:30 p.m., the Milwaukee office telephoned Gossfeld, seeking permission for Reed to travel to Chicago on Sunday to copy VB records in the Chicago office. Milwaukee said that her purpose for working on Sunday was to allow her to take the following Friday off so she could save a vacation day. After the call, Tim came to me and said, "Bob, Milwaukee called to ask if Reed can come down on Sunday to copy some VB records. Are you interested in working with her on Sunday?"

"There is no way. I have already made plans for the weekend. I will be in Indianapolis visiting friends," I said.

Unable to locate anyone else willing to work on Sunday with such late notice, Tim informed Milwaukee that Chicago had no agents

The EEO Complaint

available to assist Reed on Sunday; therefore, she should not plan on traveling to Chicago on Sunday.

A week later, on May 21, while visiting the Milwaukee office, Chicago SAC McChesney received two communications drafted by Agent Reed. After McChesney returned to Chicago, she forwarded the two communications to Gossfeld. After reading Reed's communications, Tim called me into his office.

"I need you to read these two communications before leaving my office," said Tim.

While I was reading the first communication, it was clear Reed was now breaching into other areas of the VB investigation. The first communication contained a list of demands from her to Chicago seeking the work product of the VB investigators.

The communication stated, "Chicago would conduct the investigation of Sarsour and provide the results to Milwaukee in real time."

She, in writing, told Chicago to conduct her investigation for her and forward the results to her daily.

Her second communication conflicted with the agreement on March 5, when Milwaukee agreed they would not seek or request records outside the State of Wisconsin. The second communication requested VB information and financial records regarding a VB target in New York. After reading the second document, I asked, "What in the hell is she doing, Tim? Why would she write these?"

"Bob, check the date on each communication," Tim stated.

"They are each dated May 16. What is significant about the date?" I asked.

"It was the Sunday she wanted to work in Chicago with you, and you refused because you went to Indianapolis," said Tim.

"So, she worked in Milwaukee on Sunday and created these in response to us because no one wanted to work on Sunday with such short notice?" I asked.

"Bob, that's precisely what she did," said Tim.

After reviewing the two communications, I felt I could no longer trust her and informed Tim I no longer wanted any further contact with her. Realizing she only worked three days a week and would soon transfer to Indianapolis, I said, "Tim, I will no longer answer my phone when I receive any outside calls on Mondays, Wednesdays, and Fridays, until after Reed moves to Indianapolis in August."

"I do not blame you," said Tim.

On May 25, 1999, since FBIHQ had still failed to take action regarding the apparent problems between Chicago and Milwaukee, I drafted the comprehensive summary of the VB investigation, which Resnick had requested when we were in Israel. Although I did not intend to draft this summary for another two months, Reed's actions made it necessary to draft it immediately. Through this summary, I intended to outline the mission and goals of the VB investigation, list identified subjects, summarize the results of VB Conference I and VB Conference II, provide investigative results to date, and list the requirements each division must meet before receiving any records from the VB investigation. Because of other VB matters I needed to address, it would take two weeks to write the summary.

Meanwhile, Chicago SAC Kathleen McChesney split the JTTF squad in half during the first week of June. This split caused half of the agents assisting part-time with the VB investigation to no longer assist VB. They even reassigned Agent Smith, who had been investigating BMI full-time since April 7, to the new squad.

The EEO Complaint

During a squad meeting with McChesney, I said that losing these agents devastated the VB investigation. I asked if the agents could continue working part-time on the VB case. McChesney stated she would look into the matter.

The following day, May 26, 1999, five weeks after Agent Gamal Abdel-Hafiz refused to conduct the covert recording with a Muslim terrorism target, Agent Ron Smith, a criminal agent from the Dallas office, called me seeking permission to travel to Chicago to review financial documents within the VB criminal investigation files for assistance with the Dallas investigations of HAMAS. I told him he was welcome to review anything he wished. However, because I was concerned about Abdel-Hafiz's refusal to secretly record a meeting with BMI president, Solimon Biheiri, and his ongoing contacts with Abu Abu, I explicitly instructed Smith not to share any information he gained from the VB files with Abdel-Hafiz.

Agent Smith inquired why I would make such an unusual request. I shared what had transpired recently, including my conversations with agents in other divisions who claimed to have serious concerns regarding Abdel-Hafiz's unreported contacts with FBI terrorism targets. I also told him about Abdel-Hafiz refusing to conduct a covert recording against another primary Muslim terrorism target in Tampa. I informed him that the financial records he would review were grand jury material, and Abdel-Hafiz was not on the grand jury list.

I told Agent Smith that if Abdel-Hafiz had been on the grand jury list, the AUSAs said that until the matter of his refusing to covertly record a Muslim terror subject was resolved, his name would have been removed from the grand jury list. I further said that although I was not saying he was a member of any terrorist group, the VB criminal investigation had collected evidence that showed at least one member of HAMAS had applied for an FBI Special Agent position.

I also relayed to Agent Smith the story about the Catholic FBI agent, as told by Reed. I told him that she and I found Abdel-Hafiz's statement, "A Muslim does not record another Muslim," to be like the Catholic agent in Milwaukee who did not want to perform his duty at an abortion clinic based upon his religious beliefs.

I told him and others in the FBI that I believed Abdel-Hafiz should execute his sworn duty to protect America, regardless of his religion. I found his religious comment disturbing, particularly under the circumstances. I said the link to the US embassy bombings in Kenya and Tanzania in 1998, the BMI's financial ties to known US-designated terrorists, and the fact the president of the company was reaching out to Abdel-Hafiz through a friend of his made me very suspicious. I informed Agent Smith that Abdel-Hafiz didn't need to review any VB criminal case documents until the matter was resolved.

Following this telephone call, Agent Smith, apparently offended by my comments regarding Abdel-Hafiz, told his supervisor about our conversation. The Dallas supervisor instructed him to write an FBI communication detailing our conversation. Agent Smith's written communication reads, in part:

```
      FEDERAL BUREAU OF INVESTIGATION
Precedence:  ROUTINE              Date: 05/27/1999
To:          Dallas
From:        Dallas IT
Contact:     SA [Ron Smith]
Approved By: [Blacked Out by FBI]
Drafted By:  [SA Ron Smith]
Case ID #:   66F-0
```

Title: CONVERSATION BETWEEN SA [RON SMITH] AND SA ROBERT WRIGHT CHICAGO FBI ON 05/26/1999 RE SA GAMAL ABDEL-HAFIZ

Synopsis: Summary of telcall between SA [Ron Smith] Dallas and [SA Robert Wright], Chicago, 05/26/1999, re SA Gamal Abdel-Hafiz, Dallas.

Details: As directed by SSA [Dallas], the following is a summary of the above-referenced conversation.

On 05/26/1999, SA [Smith] telephonically contacted SA [Wright] re a possible Dallas Division criminal investigation of [a Dallas-based organization which] is the subject of Chicago division [Vulgar Betrayal] case number 265C-CG-101942-Sub H1-J. It was discussed how Dallas could get access to records that were part of Chicago's investigation in order for Dallas to potentially investigate possible violations of US law by individuals within Dallas's territory who are associated with HAMAS.

After this discussion, SA [Wright] asked SA [Smith] if SA [Smith] had heard about what SA Abdel-Hafiz had done. To the best of SA [Smith's] recollection, there was little transition from the previous topic of conversation to this question. SA [Smith] said in the negative to the question.

SA Wright then advised that, recently, SA Abdel-Hafiz had been contacted by an individual who was a subject of [VB] case number 265C-CG101942 and who thought that he was going to be subpoenaed to the grand jury. The subject wanted a meeting with SA Abdel-Hafiz. According to SA [Wright], SA Abdel-Hafiz then contacted Det [Detective Adams] (Dallas, Texas Police Department), North Texas Joint Terrorism Task Force, re Chicago's [VB] investigation.

SA Abdel-Hafiz also requested to review Det. [Adams] file re the [VB] investigation.

SA [Wright] continued stating that he had requested that SA Abdel-Hafiz wear a recording device to the meeting with the subject and that SA Abdel-Hafiz had refused. SA [Smith] responded that perhaps SA Abdel-Hafiz had refused because doing so would jeopardize his standing within the Arab community. SA [Wright] responded that SA Abdel-Hafiz had previously refused to wear a recording device for [the] Washington Field Office in a similar matter.

SA Wright continued, stating that, recently, [FBI blacks full line out]. SA Wright also stated that Muslim agents should not be assigned to international terrorism matters, but to matters such as Bank Robbery and White-Collar Crime. Commenting further on SA Abdel-Hafiz's refusal to wear a recording device, SA [Wright] stated that Catholic agents would lose their gun and badge if they refused to work Abortion Clinic matters. SA [Wright] stated that he did not want SA Abdel-Hafiz to have further access to the files in this [VB] matter, and that SA [Wright] was going to request SA Abdel-Hafiz be removed from the grand jury 6(e) list in this matter.

SA [Wright] responded that he only allows access to grand jury records on a need-to-know basis. The conversation ended with SA [Wright] stating he would forward a copy of an EC, summarizing [VB] case number 265C-CG-101942, to SA [Smith] who agreed to wait until receiving said EC before authoring an EC, recommending the opening of a criminal investigation of [the Dallas HAMAS based organization].[201]

On Monday, May 31, 1999, Gossfeld notified me about a call he had just received from an Equal Employment Opportunity

The EEO Complaint

(EEO) counselor from the Dallas FBI office regarding Agent Gamal Abdel-Hafiz.

"The role of the EEO office is to provide equal opportunity in employment for all persons; to prohibit discrimination in employment because of race, color, religion, sex, national origin, age, or handicap; and to promote the full realization of equal opportunity through a continuing affirmative action program."[202]

Tim said, "Bob, you had better sit down for this one."

"Now, what has happened?" I asked. Tim informed me that Abdel-Hafiz had inquired about filing an EEO complaint against me. "What! What is the basis for his complaint? That I expected him to do his job?" I asked.

Tim told me that, according to the Dallas EEO counselor, Abdel-Hafiz claimed I had harmed his reputation as an FBI agent and questioned his loyalty to the United States. Tim provided me with the counselor's telephone number and asked me to call him. Tim believed that the Dallas EEO counselor wanted to mediate Abdel-Hafiz's concerns to prevent him from filing a formal EEO complaint against me with FBIHQ. I telephoned the counselor to discuss the concerns.

The counselor said that Abdel-Hafiz was claiming I made the following insinuations or statements about him:
1. I telephonically discussed with another Dallas agent that Agent Abdel-Hafiz refused to wear a recording device for agents in the FBI Washington and Tampa field offices, which resulted in damage to his professional reputation, questioned his integrity, credibility, and loyalty to the United States of America.
2. I had insinuated, during the telephone conversation [with Agent Smith], that HAMAS, a terrorist group, had successfully infiltrated the FBI through him.

3. I had stated that Muslims should not be assigned to international terrorism matters but to matters such as bank robbery and white-collar crimes.
4. I was going to request that he be removed from the VB grand jury 6E list.
5. I told Smith that Muslims will always sympathize with each other.
6. I stated to Smith that I hated all Muslims.
7. I did not want Abdel-Hafiz to have access to my case files regarding the Vulgar Betrayal investigation.

I told the EEO counselor I didn't make the second, fifth, and sixth comments alleged by Abdel-Hafiz. I shared the context of the remaining four statements I made to Smith. The counselor asked if I would discuss the matter in a conference call with Abdel-Hafiz. According to the counselor, Abdel-Hafiz wanted me to apologize to him and take Muslim sensitivity training.

"I'm open to a conference call, but those two things he wants me to do will never happen. I have nothing to apologize for. All I did was my job, attempting to stop terrorists from killing innocent people. My only bias is against the terrorists. This work is not what I wanted. I give it my all, and now look at what's happening to me," I exclaimed. The counselor understood my frustration.

At the end of the call, the counselor said, "Bob, keep up the good work you are doing."

Immediately following the call, I returned to my desk. I sat there thinking about the possibility of Abdel-Hafiz filing a formal EEO complaint against me. John, unaware of the EEO matter, sensed something was bothering me.

The EEO Complaint

"Bob, what is going on? Is there a problem?" he asked.

"John, you will not believe what is happening. Abdel-Hafiz is considering filing an EEO complaint against me," I said.

"What! What is wrong with this organization? Bob, do not worry about it. You did nothing wrong," said John.

"I know I didn't, but that's not my concern," I said.

"What are you worried about?" asked John.

"John, hear me out. I am not saying Abdel-Hafiz is a member of HAMAS, but he is good friends with a HAMAS business front accountant. Therefore, he is associated with HAMAS members. Would you agree?" I asked.

"Yes, that makes sense," said John.

"Assume for a moment he is a member of HAMAS. He can now cause serious problems for the FBI agent responsible for seizing 1.4 million dollars of HAMAS's assets. Through a still open criminal investigation that continues to cause harm and financial damage to HAMAS. What would you do if you were a member of HAMAS and were in his position?" I asked.

"HAMAS would encourage him to pursue the EEO complaint against you, no matter what, and file a civil lawsuit against you," said John.

"Exactly. If Abdel-Hafiz files a formal EEO complaint and/or a civil lawsuit against me, the cowards within FBI management will remove me from the Vulgar Betrayal case. At the very least, I will have to focus my attention on an EEO or civil lawsuit instead of the investigation of HAMAS. That's what worries me," I said.

"Bob, I cannot sit here and do nothing about this situation. OPR needs to investigate Abdel-Hafiz for refusing to conduct the covert recording for religious reasons," said John.

"John, they would never investigate him. FBI management would come after me before they did anything to him," I said.

"I have to try. I'll do something without your involvement. I want OPR to get involved with this situation," said John.

Because of the severe nature of the events surrounding the VB terrorism investigation, which included Abdel-Hafiz's refusal to record a meeting with a terrorist target, John was determined to identify the best procedure to request an FBI Office of Professional Responsibility (OPR) inquiry against Abdel-Hafiz. John wanted the OPR unit to investigate Abdel-Hafiz's refusal based on his Muslim religion. John made three attempts, through the Chicago division's security officer, to learn the proper procedure for requesting the opening of an OPR investigation. However, FBIHQ failed, on all three occasions, to respond to John's inquiries.

A few days later, McChesney hosted a meeting in her conference room to discuss the VB investigation. Tim and I briefed the SAC on the VB case and shared the serious issues concerning the FBI's failure to provide VB with adequate resources. Specifically, additional FBI agents, support employees, computers, and other much-needed resources to help us conduct an appropriate and thorough investigation of the Middle Eastern terrorists who were living and operating within the US. She gave me a wink and reassured me that the VB case would finally receive the support and resources it had been lacking.

On June 6, 1999, Abdel-Hafiz filed a formal EEO complaint against me for discrimination based on religion and national origin. Although I was not in the FBI management program, the FBIHQ EEO officer's letter stated, "You were identified as a Responding [FBI] Management Official."

The EEO Complaint

On June 14, 1999, I completed a comprehensive, nineteen-page VB investigation case summary. I forwarded the summary to the FBIHQ National Security Unit and the top fifteen FBI field offices most affected by HAMAS's criminal activities within the US. In addition, I sent a copy to FBIHQ Supervisors Resnick, Clinton, and two other FBIHQ supervisors. The summary details the activities of HAMAS's front organizations and identifies the mission of the VB investigation.

I believed the VB case summary would force FBIHQ to resolve the persistent problems of two divisions, Chicago and Milwaukee, simultaneously conducting the same criminal investigation of Sarsour. The FBI has heavily redacted the nineteen-page VB case summary, which reads, in part:

```
        FEDERAL BUREAU OF INVESTIGATION
Precedence: ROUTINE              Date: 06/14/1999
To:         National Security, Baltimore, Cleveland,
            Dallas, Detroit, Indianapolis, Jacksonville,
            Kansas City, Los Angeles, Memphis, Newark,
            New Orleans, New York, Milwaukee,
            St. Louis, and Washington Field Office.
From:       Chicago CT-1
Contact:    SA Robert G. Wright, Jr.
Approved By: [SSA Gossfeld]
Drafted By: SA Robert G. Wright, Jr: rgw.
Case ID #:  265C-CG-101942 (Pending)
Title:      VULGAR BETRAYAL - AOT-IT HAMAS
            (MATERIAL SUPPORT/EXTORTION/
            INTERNATIONAL MONEY LAUNDERING/
            RICO/CONSPIRACY) OO: CG
```

The FBI's Pre-9/11 Vulgar Betrayal

GRAND JURY MATERIAL—DISSEMINATE PURSUANT TO RULE 6 (e)

[The FBI redacted the initial two paragraphs as "secret."] (End Page 1)

Enclosed for Milwaukee are two FD-302s (FBI document summarizing an interview) [the next two lines are blacked out by FBI]. FD-302 regarding the receipt of records from [name blacked out]. A copy of forthwith subpoena and copies [of records] provided to Milwaukee in the past; FD-302 of [FBI blacked out name], FD-302 regarding the interview of [name blacked out] and a copy of [blacked out] which may aid Milwaukee in its criminal investigation of [name blacked out].

[The FBI blacked out the next full paragraph.]

The following identifies the purpose of Operation Vulgar Betrayal, identifies the creation and extent of the HAMAS criminal enterprise within the United States and covers Vulgar Betrayal's respect for territorial integrity of all FBI field offices.

THE GOALS OF OPERATION VULGAR BETRAYAL

1. a. Identify, prevent, and defeat intelligence operations conducted by any foreign power within the United States, or against certain interests abroad, that constitute a threat to US national security.

   b. Prevent, disrupt, and defeat terrorist operations before they occur.

2. Favor the interest of a national HAMAS strategy by the FBI over any single field office's individual preference for investigative strategy.

3. Have a terrorism nexus to the criminal activity being pursued.

The EEO Complaint

4. Respect the territorial integrity of individual field offices.
5. Protect the lives and welfare of assets and other intelligence sources.

1a. IDENTIFYING THE THREAT TO US NATIONAL SECURITY

[The FBI blacked out the first two full paragraphs]
(End Page 2)

In December 1993, Chicago discovered HAMAS subjects were conducting significant criminal activity. This activity included bank fraud, income tax evasion and welfare fraud. The policy of the Chicago office, as well as many [FBI] offices, was not to interview the subjects of intelligence investigations, and accordingly, this did not allow the pursuit of prevention by criminal prosecution and civil forfeiture.

In 1995, it became clear no FBI field office was conducting a nationwide criminal investigation of the USA HAMAS RICO Enterprise (Enterprise). Each [FBI] division was conducting local intelligence investigations; however, the results of these investigations were not being used in a nationwide effort to fully identify and neutralize the USA-based Enterprise.

The Enterprise consists of individuals/co-conspirators [FBI blacked out names]. The organizations are merely tools used by the Enterprise to aid in terrorism-related activity. [The following two lines blacked out.] Furthermore, any monies given to the organizations by the Enterprise can be criminally seized by the US government, including substitute assets. [The FBI blacked out the following three full paragraphs.]
(End Page 3)

[The FBI blacked out the first full paragraph of page 4.]

In January 1996, [the Chicago JTTF] SSA advised [SA Wright] a criminal case (265A) against the Enterprise or a co-conspirator of the Enterprise could only be opened with sufficient source information linking the Enterprise or co-conspirator to specific criminal activity linked to terrorism activity.

In March 1996, FBIHQ provided a copy [of a document] belonging to Mohammad Salah, a convicted US-based HAMAS terrorist. Agents attempted to interview 60 known associates of Mohammad Salah. During an interview with [one of the 60 associates,] allegations were made that two [Muslim] religious non-profit organizations gave [the interviewee] over $3 million dollars for investment and that they ultimately defrauded [the interviewee] of $750,000. The organizations were the QLI (Quranic Literacy Institute) and the North American Islamic Trust (NAIT) (Indianapolis). The Indianapolis division deferred the investigation of NAIT to Chicago because of the size and scope of the intended criminal investigation of the Enterprise by Chicago.

In July 1996, [Chicago] AUSA Mark Flessner authorized the use of the Federal Grand Jury to investigate the allegation of [the interviewee].

In September 1996, a source familiar with NAIT provided detailed information about the [Enterprise]. The source identified [locations where the FBI could obtain names of members of the HAMAS Enterprise]. The [hundreds of] names [identified by the FBI] were checked in the FBI's Automated Case Support network.

(End Page 4)

50% of the members were identified as intelligence subjects. In addition, one of the members identified had applied for a Special Agent position with the FBI.

The EEO Complaint

[The FBI blacked out the first four lines of this paragraph.] [The FBI blacked out the number] Co-conspirators and organizations were identified. To date, approximately [The FBI blacked out the number] have been subpoenaed.

[The FBI blacked out the next three full paragraphs.]

(End Page 5)

PART A: SOURCE OF FUNDS ESTABLISHED A [HAMAS] BASE IN THE USA

From 1988 through 1994, 17 individuals and nine organizations wire-transferred over $10 million dollars into the bank accounts of four individual college students in the USA. The four [college students] were [FBI blacked all four names out]. These four are directly responsible for the [HAMAS] USA Enterprise and together they laundered the $10 million dollars through various bank accounts throughout the USA. Ultimately, the money was laundered directly to the Middle East either for terrorism or laundered to various locations throughout the US to finance the creation of organizations, which would aid the Enterprise in its [terrorism] mission.

PART B: ORGANIZATIONS ESTABLISHED IN THE USA BY THE ENTERPRISE

In the beginning, the Enterprise used previously established non-profit Muslim student organizations to launder funds of the Enterprise. The Muslim student organizations initially used by the Enterprise to criminally launder funds is the Muslim Student Association (MSA) [The FBI blocked out the remaining information]. There are [currently] hundreds of these organizations located on campuses throughout the US.

The Enterprise used the $10 million dollars in overseas funds to establish the following organizations in the USA, most of which are still in existence today: [The FBI blacked out the entire half-page list of Muslim organizations established by HAMAS within the US].

(End Page 6)

Many of these organizations, such as [The FBI blacked out the name of the organization], have incorporated satellite offices in other states. Additionally, since 1992, many of the above organizations have transferred to other cities and sometimes changed the name of the organization while retaining the same board of directors.

PART C: THE ENTERPRISE'S METHOD OF OPERATION

In order to sustain the rapid growth the Enterprise has enjoyed in the USA for the past decade, the proceeds of illegal activities have been increasingly used not only to finance international terrorism, but also to purchase property, homes, businesses, stocks, and other investments in the USA. In addition, the proceeds have been used to finance the education and living expenses of co-conspirators of the Enterprise while living in the USA.

Enterprise has grown in membership and has amassed a financial fortune at an alarming rate during the past ten years. Enterprise has achieved these successes by using the immigration laws of the USA. Co-conspirators of the Enterprise enter the USA as visitors or students and later apply for citizenship, this, for taking advantage of the greater protection afforded citizens of America.

As a naturalized US citizen, the co-conspirator can better aid the Enterprise in conducting illegal activities, the intent of which is to violate and disrupt US policies and interest,

The EEO Complaint

within the USA and overseas. Should the co-conspirator be investigated or arrested, he will claim his rights as a US citizen and seek to prevent US authorities from investigating him or demand that the US government assist in obtaining his release from custody in another country.

The leaders of the Enterprise appear to understand the weaknesses of the United States Government. For years, the Enterprise has realized that US Government agencies do not share information with one another nor conduct joint investigations.

(End Page 7)

However, in the spring of 1996, a Chicago INS Agent and two FBI agents from the Chicago Joint Terrorism Task Force (JTTF) attempted to interview known associates of [HAMAS Military Commander, Mohammad Salah,] a Chicago-based naturalized US citizen.

Some interviewees boasted they had been in the USA illegally for years, [one for over 18 years] and stated the US Government could not do anything to them. Most of the interviewees, legal and illegal aliens, admitted they had never paid any federal income taxes while in the US. The Chicago leaders of the Enterprise became upset when they learned the INS and FBI were working together to investigate co-conspirators of the Enterprise. They also became extremely upset when they discovered the investigators were inquiring about income taxes and donations to [the Enterprise's] non-profit organizations.

When inquiries of this type or any type are initiated by any [US] Government agency into the Enterprise or one of its co-conspirators, the Enterprise immediately attempts to quash the inquiry by means of intimidation. For example, during the spring of 1996 joint INS and FBI interviews, the Enterprise attempted to protect itself, as it always has, by claiming the joint INS and FBI interviews violated the interviewee's civil rights. The Enterprise further claimed the [INS and FBI] agent's actions were motivated because of the interviewee's religious and political beliefs.

In the summer of 1996, leaders of the Chicago Enterprise traveled to Washington, DC to complain in person to the White House and the FBI Director. When the leaders of the Enterprise realized their trip to Washington, DC failed to stop the joint INS and FBI investigation, the Enterprise leaders threatened to file a civil lawsuit against the three agents [Agent Vincent, Agent Wright & the INS agent] for violating the civil rights of the [Muslim] interviewees. Attorneys of the Enterprise informed the Chicago Enterprise leaders the [INS and FBI] agents were acting within the scope of their employment. There was no violation of the interviewees' civil rights since they were being questioned regarding their known association with a convicted terrorist [Mohammad Salah].

Additionally, the Enterprise uses occasions such as the interviews of community members, arrest of illegal aliens, and the seizure of terrorist funds to gather the support of innocent members of the [Muslim] community who have nothing to do with the Enterprise. The Enterprise issues printed materials, which are intended to scare innocent members of the [Muslim] community into believing they may be the next innocent target of the US Government. The Enterprise also established a new organization to collect monies from the innocent members of the community to fight the US Government.

(End Page 8)

PART D: CRIMINAL ABUSE OF UNITED STATES LAWS

In the very beginning, the Enterprise abused another weakness of the US Government. [The FBI blacked out the remainder of this paragraph.]

THE FOLLOWING PARAGRAPH CONTAINS TAX INFORMATION, WHICH MAY NOT BE DISCLOSED TO ANYONE NOT LISTED ON THE TAX DISCLOSURE LIST IN CHICAGO.

[The FBI blacked out the entire following two paragraphs. Note: The blacked-out information proved, beyond any doubt, that the Enterprise and its co-conspirators were involved in a massive tax fraud scheme.]

On June 9, 1998, over $1 million dollars in terrorist-related funds were seized from the Quranic Literacy Institute (QLI), one of the organizations used by the Enterprise to launder criminal funds. The QLI is located in a two and a half story residential building, which is located in a residential area and occupied by the families of [The FBI blacked the remaining seven lines out].

(End Page 9)

Publicity following the civil seizure prompted [the FBI blacks out the name] to contact the FBI and advise that the QLI had another $1 million [The FBI blacked the remaining eight lines out].

THE FOLLOWING PARAGRAPH CONTAINS TAX INFORMATION, WHICH MAY NOT BE DISCLOSED TO ANYONE NOT LISTED ON THE TAX DISCLOSURE LIST IN CHICAGO.

[The FBI blacked out the following two paragraphs.]

These paragraphs list many of HAMAS's for-profit and not-for-profit organizations.

PART E: USE OF CO-CONSPIRATORS TO DELIVER TERRORIST FUNDS TO THE OCCUPIED TERRITORY

Overseas funds, profits, and donations given to the above US organizations have been transferred to HAMAS leaders in the OT for terrorism [The FBI blacked out the remainder of this paragraph.]

(End Page 10)

[The FBI blacked out the following three entire paragraphs as "secret."]

[The FBI blacked out five words in the first line of this paragraph] confirms that the Enterprise has continued to operate successfully in the USA. More importantly, the material support activities [of the recently arrested US-based HAMAS member] are directly linked to Enterprise activity that occurred in 1992 and 1993, by [Mohammad Salah]. The criminal acts of [the recently arrested US-based HAMAS member, acting] on behalf of the Enterprise established the two criminal acts needed within the past five years to pursue RICO conspiracy charges against the Enterprise. [The FBI blacked out the following two paragraphs.]

(End Page 11)

PART F: CONTACT WITH HAMAS MEMBERS IN THE OCCUPIED TERRITORIES

The Enterprise has been communicating with HAMAS members in the OT [the FBI blacked out the remainder of this paragraph and the next two full paragraphs as "secret."]

The EEO Complaint

PART G: [The FBI blacks out the first four words] CONDUCTED IN THE USA

[The FBI blacked out the entire two paragraphs of PART G.]
(End Page 12)

[The FBI completely blacked out page 13.]
(End Page 13)

PART H: UTILIZATION OF OVERSEAS ACCOUNTS TO LAUNDER FUNDS

The Enterprise has used at least [The FBI blacks out the number] bank accounts to transfer funds to the OT. The financial institution, account holder, and account numbers have been identified and located in [many countries.] [The FBI blacked out the remainder of this paragraph.]

The US Attorney's Office in the Northern District of Illinois has issued letters of rogatory to the countries with which the USA has established treaties. The remaining countries are to be contacted by [FBI] Legats who have received leads from Chicago. The letters of rogatory and leads were forwarded to each country in April and May 1999.

1b: PREVENT AND DISRUPT THE HAMAS RICO ENTERPRISE

[The FBI blacks out the entire first paragraph as "secret."]

On June 9, 1998, the Chicago JTTF, consisting of the INS, Chicago Police Department, US Secret Service, US Customs Service, US State Department, CIA, and the FBI seized approximately $1.5 million in cash and assets from the Enterprise through a civil seizure action. This seizure was the first seizure of terrorist-related funds and assets by the US Government. Since the seizure, the Enterprise has hired a lobbyist, contacted numerous national and local politicians, denounced the seizure on C-SPAN, and met with top-ranking officials of the Department of Justice in an attempt to protect the Enterprise from future criminal and civil actions by the FBI and the United States Attorney's Office.

On 5/12/1999, US Magistrate Wayne R. Anderson issued an opinion that the US Governments affidavit in support of the seizure has "established a reasonable basis for the government's belief that the funds are forfeitable because they were transferred in violation of Section 1956 (a) (2) (A)." The next status hearing is set for July 6, 1999. In order for Mohammad Salah and the QLI to proceed, they must now answer the interrogatories, which question their participation in the Enterprise and ask them to disclose the source of the $1.4 million. By law, the burden of proof now falls upon the [defendants] to prove the funds seized were not terrorist-related funds.

(End Page 14)

During July 1999, Chicago plans to arrest [the FBI blacked out the name of the terrorist] a US-based HAMAS terrorist. He will be taken before the Federal Grand Jury in Chicago. [The FBI blacks out the following six lines.] Following [this terrorist] appearance before the grand jury, several other subjects will be interviewed and subpoenaed before the Federal Grand Jury.

[The FBI blacked out the following three full paragraphs.]

2. FAVOR THE INTEREST OF A NATIONAL HAMAS STRATEGY OVER ANY SINGLE FIELD OFFICE
[The FBI blacked out the first entire paragraph as "secret."]
(End Page 15)

The EEO Complaint

[The FBI blacked out the first three entire paragraphs as "secret."]

On April 26, 1999, Deputy Attorney General Mark Richard advised that the Attorney General ultimately must decide whom, when, and where any prosecutions against the Enterprise would occur. Chicago is confident several co-conspirators will be indicted and convicted in districts outside of Chicago.

3. ESTABLISH A TERRORISM NEXUS

[The FBI blacked out the first full paragraph as "secret."]

(End Page 16)

[The FBI blacked out the first full paragraph on page 17 as "secret."]

Further, the accumulation of all local criminal activities (i.e., tax evasion, tax fraud, food stamp fraud, bank fraud) being committed by Enterprise co-conspirators weakens the nation's economic system, interferes with free competition, seriously burdens interstate and foreign commerce, threatens domestic security, and undermines the general welfare of the USA and its citizens.

[The FBI blacked out the last full paragraph as "secret."]

4. RESPECT THE TERRITORIAL INTEGRITY OF INDIVIDUAL FIELD OFFICES

[The FBI blacked out the following four full paragraphs as "secret."]

(End Page 17)

5. PROTECT LIVES & WELFARE OF ASSETS & OTHER INTELLIGENCE SOURCES

[The FBI blacked out the entire first full paragraph as "secret."]

Chicago considers the Milwaukee leads in the EC dated 5/16/99 covered.

(End Page 18)

LEADS: Set Lead 1: (Admin) ALL RECEIVING OFFICES[203]

[The FBI blacked out the entire paragraph as "secret."]

(End of Page 19)

CHAPTER 29

VULGAR BETRAYAL'S ARREST OF A HAMAS TERRORIST

I took the entire week off on June 28, 1999, fed up with the added problems caused by Agent Reed. I again considered whether I wanted to continue fighting this never-ending battle with Chicago, FBIHQ, and Milwaukee. My sincere goal had always been to prevent HAMAS and its supporters from continuing to operate within the US at the expense of US citizens and to help prevent future acts of terrorism. However, with the repeated failures of FBI management, the case appeared doomed. During my second day off, as a last effort, I called FBIHQ Mike Resnick on Tuesday morning to discuss the nineteen-page case summary I had prepared and sent to him on June 14.

When I asked Resnick if he had read the VB case summary, he informed me he had not seen it; however, he would review it and get back to me.

"Why are you and Clinton refusing to make a final decision regarding the office of origin for Sarsour's criminal acts? You told me during the second trip to Israel how 'Chicago should be the office of origin, and Chicago should send leads to Milwaukee, not the other way around.' This is ridiculous. Something needs to be done. Why will you not fix this problem and tell her to close her case?" I asked.

"We are going to decide soon," said Resnick.

"That is all I keep hearing. You guys know what needs to happen here. Why are you guys not telling her to close her duplicate case? What am I missing here? Why are you reluctant to instruct her to close her duplicate investigation, Mike?" I asked.

"We are going to decide soon," Resnick said again.

I pleaded with him to decide soon since two divisions investigating the same terrorism target had created an atmosphere of competition, which had developed into a lack of trust between Reed and me. He said he would talk to Clinton and call me back by the end of the day.

During a follow-up call, Mike told me he had spoken to Clinton, and they agreed a decision needed to be made soon.

"We are going to make a decision within the next two weeks," he said.

"I simply want what's best for the FBI and the investigation. Mike, I do not care which jurisdiction ultimately indicts Sarsour. Many VB subjects will be indicted and tried in districts outside the Chicago division. The most important thing is that the FBI conducts the best investigation possible to defeat the terrorists and their supporters," I said.

He agreed and again assured me that a decision would be made within two weeks.

Next, I called Gossfeld to inform him about Clinton and Resnick's decision to hold off for another two weeks regarding Reed's duplicate investigation.

"That's not right. It needs to be addressed now," said Tim.

"Tim, Resnick told me, in Israel, Cybil's case needs to be closed, and Vulgar Betrayal is the primary HAMAS criminal investigation of the FBI. What are they scared of? This makes no sense. Why do they refuse to instruct her to close the case?" I asked.

"I have no idea. I will call Resnick tomorrow and explain that this matter needs to be addressed in a few days, not weeks," Tim promised.

On July 2, I traveled to Indianapolis to attend a party with friends from high school and college. During the party, as I was sitting alone, I began thinking about how much I missed Indianapolis and wanted to move back. I thought to myself, "I am miserable in Chicago. I no longer want to be there. This is where I want to be." Moments later, my friend Cheryl introduced me to her friend Brenda.

Within minutes, Brenda said, "You do not seem very happy."

I laughed and said, "Believe it or not, I was just thinking that. I have decided I want to move back to Indianapolis." I said that I missed living in Indianapolis, missed my friends in the area, and would be two hours closer to my family. I told her that the trip had made me realize how unhappy I was in Chicago. Later that evening, I told Brenda and my friends I would be adding my name to the Indianapolis transfer list when I returned to work in Chicago on Monday morning. Brenda and I talked for over two hours, and at the end of the evening, we made plans to meet in Indianapolis two weeks from then.

During the afternoon of July 6, while speaking to Gossfeld about my Indianapolis trip, I said, "Tim, I am sorry, but I cannot do this anymore. No matter what we do to stop the terrorists, we always get screwed over. I am sick of it all. The FBI has no intention of neutralizing any known terrorists. I'm wasting my time here. Tell me something that has gone our way in the past seven months. It hurts to realize I wasted the past six years of my life, but I need to think about myself. No one else cares about this case. Why should I?" I asked.

"You are just vetting your frustrations, I get it," said Tim.

"No, I am not vetting. Before I add my name to the Indianapolis transfer list today, I just wanted to tell you I am now first on the list and should receive my transfer offer to Indianapolis in October," I said.

"Bob, do nothing until I talk to the front office. Give me a few hours before you do anything," pleaded Tim.

"I am sorry, Tim, but I have decided. I've put my life on hold long enough. I met a nice girl this past weekend in Indianapolis and am interested in pursuing a relationship with her. We have made plans to meet in Indianapolis in two weeks," I explained.

"Bob, if you walk away from Vulgar Betrayal, the case will be closed. Only you can manage this case. You have every detail in your head," said Tim.

"I understand what you are saying, but it doesn't matter, Tim. Management is going to shut the case down, anyway. Management does not understand the importance of this case. Headquarters wants Vulgar Betrayal closed down to protect the terrorism subjects of the FBI intelligence files. At some point, management will negligently close Vulgar Betrayal. They do not care," I said.

"Bob, just give me a few hours before you do anything," asked Tim.

"No way, I am done. I am submitting the paperwork to add my name to the Indianapolis transfer list," I said.

As Tim left his office to talk with the SAC about my decision, I returned to my desk, completed the paperwork, and added my name to the Indianapolis transfer list. The front office gave me a printout that showed my name was added to the "Indianapolis transfer list at 3:24 p.m. on July 6, 1999."[204]

Vulgar Betrayal's Arrest of a HAMAS Terrorist

An hour later, Tim informed me about three meetings he had had with front office management concerning my thoughts about transferring from Chicago to Indianapolis. Because I expressed my desire to leave Chicago, Tim said management had scheduled a meeting for July 15 to discuss the duplicate investigations of Chicago and Milwaukee. He said that the supervisors, ASACs, and SACs from both the Chicago and Milwaukee divisions would attend the meeting. The meeting would be at a Cracker Barrel between Chicago and Milwaukee. He said that, during this meeting, FBI management would resolve the problem of both offices working on the same criminal target.

"Bob, if we can resolve the problems to your satisfaction, will you reconsider transferring to Indianapolis?" asked Tim.

"Tim, if the Milwaukee case is closed and I can proceed uninterrupted with Vulgar Betrayal, I will remove my name from the Indianapolis transfer list for one year," I said.

"Just one year?" asked Tim.

"Look, things are coming together. We will have Sharif Alwan locked up shortly, and the AUSAs have agreed to pursue my plan to lock up another dozen HAMAS terrorists by the end of the year. If management can resolve this ridiculous problem with Milwaukee, you will have me for another year. At the end of that time, if things are going as planned and headquarters leaves us alone, I will probably stay longer," I said.

"After listening to the discussions in today's meetings, I am confident that we will resolve the problems during the meeting on July 15," Tim said.

"I hope so. If not, I am leaving," I said.

When Reed called to discuss our cases the following day, I informed her about my decision to add my name to the Indianapolis transfer list. She did not believe me initially; however, when she realized I was serious, she stated, "See, you finally figured out the Vulgar Betrayal case is just not worth it, didn't you?"

"Yes, I realized this case could continue for years with limited success because of Clinton and others at headquarters. The Bureau does not care. I am tired of fighting everyone and no longer want to remain in Chicago," I said.

The problems between Reed and me regarding our cases seemed to disappear once we realized we would no longer work on them soon when we transferred to Indianapolis.

During a subsequent call later in the day, Reed asked, "Bob, what happened? Why did you decide to seek the transfer to Indianapolis?" I told her about my visit with my Indianapolis friends this past weekend.

I said, "During the visit, I realized I wanted to move back to Indianapolis. It does not hurt that I met someone who lives in Indianapolis, and I may date."

"Not that girl you just met! Why would someone date you? No one from Indianapolis would date you!" she yelled.

Although we had joked around with one another in the past, her comments seemed harsh; however, I took her comments as verbal jabs between friends. She said, "Don't move to Indianapolis. I don't want to see your face every day."

I changed the conversation by discussing things we needed to address concerning our cases.

After learning about my decision to add my name to the Indianapolis transfer list, John and another Chicago agent, familiar with the work-related problems between Reed and me, asked why I would even consider transferring to Indianapolis since she would also be there. I told them we would get along well in Indianapolis and that our real problem was not our fault. I said that the fault lay with FBIHQ for refusing to do their job and Murphy's selfish use of Milwaukee to further his personal prosecution goals.

"We'll get along in Indianapolis. Besides, Indianapolis is where I have wanted to move since I joined the FBI. My desire to move back to Indianapolis will not change because I may not get along with someone else who works in the Indianapolis office. Nothing could ever be worse than the agents I have had to deal with on this squad during the years I fought to open the AOT criminal investigation," I said.

After learning Sharif Alwan had a pending application to receive US citizenship with the INS, to entice the HAMAS-trained terrorist to return to America I devised a plan with the two INS agents on the JTTF squad. We were confident Alwan would take the bait and return to Chicago shortly. On July 9, the INS agents advised me that Alwan had contacted them as we had hoped. They placed Alwan's name on a flight watchlist. They said they would notify me when he was aboard a flight returning to the United States from the Middle East.

Alwan had departed the US in 1998 after appearing before the federal grand jury. I had been expecting his return and was planning to prevent him from gaining US citizenship. Now, I needed to make plans to prevent him from leaving the US after serving him with his second grand jury subpoena.

On Monday, July 12, 1999, I received a call from the INS informing me they received a watchlist hit on Alwan. According to the notification, he was aboard a flight from the Middle East and would land in Chicago in less than seven hours. He had taken our bait. The plan was for John and me to serve a grand jury subpoena on him when his plane landed.

However, before I could serve the subpoena, I needed to complete the logistics required to prevent him from fleeing the country after we served him. We could only accomplish this by utilizing an FBI Special Operations Group (SOG) team. Fortunately, on July 9, we wrote an EC in advance, requesting twenty-four hours of surveillance for the unknown date of Alwan's return to the United States. Gossfeld approved the request. The FBI blacked most of the entire "Details" section of the EC, except for, "Twenty-four-hour SOG surveillance is requested from."[205]

The SOG surveillance team's help would be required for a maximum of twenty-four hours and would help prevent Alwan from fleeing the country before his scheduled grand jury appearance in Chicago on the morning of July 13.

Unfortunately, Gossfeld was out of town on July 12, and the acting relief supervisor was Agent Jane Smith. Jane did not believe in the VB investigation. I requested she contact the SOG supervisor to start the twenty-four-hour surveillance as requested in the EC. She questioned me regarding its legitimacy.

After I had explained the flight risk concerns the AUSAs and I had, she said, "The AUSAs are not going to tell us what to do."

"They're not telling us what to do. We are all concerned about the flight risk," I said.

Following this discussion, I believed her concerns were resolved, and there would be no further problems securing the assistance of the surveillance team.

Thirty minutes later, I noticed SSA Pat Garland, the surveillance squad supervisor, entering the JTTF supervisor's office. Five minutes later, Jane called me in. As I entered her office, she began explaining her concerns regarding my request for a surveillance team.

"Bob, I have reread your surveillance request and do not believe it is necessary. Besides, the surveillance team has a more important case to work on tonight," she stated.

"Bob, I have to agree with Jane. We already have another case scheduled to work on; therefore, I cannot fulfill your surveillance request. I am sorry," Garland added.

I thought, "If only the public knew the extent of mismanagement in this organization, they wouldn't feel as secure about the FBI's efforts against Middle Eastern terrorism."

"That is fine. I understand you have a more important case to work tonight," I said.

Walking out of the supervisor's office; I turned to Garland and asked, "Pat, by the way, can you please tell me what the important case is you're working tonight instead of my international terrorism case?"

"Why do you ask?"

"When I relay to the three AUSAs handling the Vulgar Betrayal case that you are choosing to focus on a more important case instead of this international terrorism case, they will probably question me about the case you are working tonight. It must be extremely important if you are refusing to fulfill my request to follow a HAMAS terrorist we have been waiting to return from the Middle East during the past year. We need to prevent him from fleeing the country for the next twenty-four hours," I said.

"I do not understand," said Pat.

"Jane must have informed you about the current situation, correct?" I asked.

"What is going on here?" asked Pat.

"Did Jane tell you the Vulgar Betrayal case is about to be designated as a major FBI case?" I asked.

"No," said Pat.

"I didn't think so. Just to be clear, the person we are targeting is a trained HAMAS terrorist. Trained here in the US and as well as overseas on two occasions with Hezbollah. Two current US-designated terrorists directed and supported his training. He was convicted and served time overseas for terrorism-related activities on behalf of HAMAS. We have waited over a year for his return to the United States. Agent Vincent and I will serve him with a grand jury subpoena tonight when his international flight lands in Chicago, ordering him to appear before the federal grand jury tomorrow morning. When this terrorist realizes he is likely going to be locked up for refusing to cooperate, there is an extremely high risk he might flee the United States. I am not sure why Jane is messing with my request, but Gossfeld approved it on July 9," I explained.

"I did not know about your request until today," he replied.

I continued, "We were unaware of his return date to Chicago. I wrote the request and had Tim approve it in advance in case he arrived in Chicago when Tim was out of the office. I assumed Tim had reached out to you to notify you about this request. Pat, during the past six years I have been in Chicago, I have never seen an FBI agent in this office come this close to locking up an actual Middle Eastern terrorist for anything. The immediate family of this terrorist lives overseas. Again, nothing is keeping him here, and we consider him an extreme flight risk. We want to ensure he does not flee for the next twenty-four hours. Again, I need to know because the United States Attorney's Office is going to ask me why an FBI surveillance team cannot address this international terrorism matter. I'm confident they will find another federal agency who would be more than willing to help us prevent this terrorist from fleeing."

"Bob, there is no problem. We will work on your case tonight. I was unaware of all this information regarding your case," he promised.

"Thanks, Pat." I turned to Jane and said, "Jane, I don't give a damn what you think of Vulgar Betrayal. Never mess with my case again."

Next, I needed to visit Flessner to obtain the grand jury subpoena to serve on Alwan. As I entered his office, Flessner said, "I heard Alwan is aboard a flight from the Middle East and will arrive in Chicago later today."

"Who informed you? I just learned about his flight myself, so I know it didn't come from the FBI. Mark, who told you about it?"

"Bob, I have sources too."

"Will you reveal your source to me?"

"No."

"I was coming here to tell you about his flight so we can get a grand jury subpoena to serve on him when he arrives," I said.

He provided the subpoena for John and me to serve on Alwan when he arrived in Chicago. I was upset that he had learned about Alwan's flight before I could tell him. I knew no one from the FBI or INS had told him.

Note: In the future [2001], because he learned about Alwan's flight from a "source," I would become the subject of an FBI OPR investigation, alleging I provided him with classified intelligence. The alleged classified information was, Sharif Alwan was aboard a flight from the Middle East, arriving in Chicago in seven hours. After being interviewed by the OPR investigators, they were uncertain if I was being honest when I told them Flessner already knew about Alwan's flight.

I told them, "Even if Flessner had not known about the flight, I was going to tell him Alwan was aboard the flight to Chicago because

I had gotten the information through my criminal investigation, and there was nothing classified about Alwan's flight information."

I asked them, "Why is this terrorist's flight information considered classified?" One of them said, "That's the question we were discussing before you arrived. We don't know why this information is considered classified."

Shortly after that, management ordered me to fly to Washington, DC, to take a polygraph exam at FBIHQ because Chicago could not determine whether I was telling the truth or not. When I asked to see the documentation proving the terrorist's flight information was marked classified, no one ever showed me any proof.

After flying to FBIHQ and passing the polygraph exam, I returned to Chicago. The following day, I made a phone call. Through this phone call, I solved the OPR investigation. I learned who told Flessner about Alwan's flight. With Flessner's consent, I called the OPR case agent. I said, "Hi, Ann, I wanted to let you know I solved your OPR case against me this morning after making one phone call."

"You know who told Flessner about the flight?" asked Ann.

"I do. It was a foreign official from Israel."

"How did you find this information?"

"I called Flessner and asked him who told him about it. He told me it was David Cohen."

"This happens a lot. They are not supposed to call one another. They are required to go through certain channels at the Department of Justice. Bob, thanks for letting me know."

A few days later, I received a letter from FBIHQ informing me I had been cleared of the charges.

On the evening of July 12, 1999, John and I "served a subpoena on Sharif Alwan (that) commanded him to appear before the grand jury."[206] On July 13, 1999, Alwan appeared before the federal grand jury.[207] Regarding this appearance, Alwan said, "I was pleading my Fifth Amendment right."[208] Refusing to cooperate with the grand jury, he and his attorney appeared before Judge Aspen, the chief judge.[209] Flessner, John, and I were also in the judge's chambers. "And the government was seeking an immunity order."[210] When asked if Alwan understood what immunizing meant, his attorney said, "He does understand that, Judge. He's asked me to mention to the Court that he appreciates your grant of immunity but that it is not as broad as we think. It will not extend on his trips to Israel or Jordan, and he could suffer some adverse consequences there."[211]

"Well, as you know, that has little legal consequence here," said Judge Aspen.

"I do know that, Judge," said Alwan's attorney.

"Did you explain that to him?" asked Judge Aspen.

"I have," said the attorney.

"All right, is it his intention not to answer the questions before the grand jury in spite of the immunity?" asked Judge Aspen.

Turning toward Alwan, the attorney said, "I think you should answer that so just tell him yes or no. Do not make a speech. Just say yes or no."[212]

"No, sir," said Alwan.

"You are not going to answer the questions, right?" asked Judge Aspen.

"No," said Alwan.

"Even though I have granted you immunity, is that correct?" asked Judge Aspen.

"Yes, because of the reasons my attorney just expressed," said Alwan.[213]

Judge Aspen instructed John and me to take Alwan into custody and deliver him to the federal marshal's office for imprisonment. With the first HAMAS terrorist in custody, the AUSAs, John, and I were ready to pursue the next phase of locking up many more HAMAS members living in the United States.

According to the INS, since many of the Middle Eastern terrorists had not yet become naturalized US citizens, any felony conviction, including a contempt conviction, would prevent them from ever receiving US citizenship in the future. Authorities could hold Alwan in custody for up to eighteen months to force his cooperation. If he did not cooperate, he could be convicted of contempt, a felony, for refusing to cooperate with the grand jury. Once convicted of a felony, he would be prohibited from receiving US citizenship.

Preventing Alwan and many other Middle Eastern terrorists from receiving US citizenship was another primary goal of the VB investigation.

On the evening of July 13, I worked late in the JTTF squad area and identified the HAMAS members that I believed should appear before the federal grand jury soon. Agents Presley and Schiller were also working late in the squad area. They congratulated me on the detainment of Alwan and asked what my future goals were. I shared that I was going to pursue many other Chicago-area HAMAS members and hoped to have them locked up before the end of the year.

I informed them of my intention to pursue and detain or remove all HAMAS members from the United States.

I said that if headquarters would assist in VB's coordinated national effort, the FBI could quickly neutralize HAMAS and eliminate their threat to the economic and national security of both the United States and Israel.

Gossfeld called me into his office the following morning and closed the door. I noticed a serious look on his face.

"Is something wrong?" I asked.

"Yes, Bob, you must be more careful about what you say. You cannot go around saying things about the Vulgar Betrayal case," he stated.

"What are you talking about? What did I say?" I asked.

"Were you working last night?" he asked.

"Yes, I was. Why?"

"Was anyone else working with you?"

"Agents Presley and Schiller were here. I do not remember seeing anyone else. Why?"

"Did you express you wanted to arrest or deport all HAMAS subjects living in the United States?" he asked.

"Yes, I did."

"Bob, you cannot say things like that. Saying such things will upset other agents."

"Tim, I am confused. Are you telling me I upset Presley and Schiller by saying I wanted to lock up all the HAMAS terrorists?"

"No. You upset Agent Ewing. He overheard your conversation while standing on the other side of the squad room wall. He immediately called me on my cell phone last night and started yelling about what you were saying. Bob, he is really upset."

After taking in what Tim said, I stood up from my chair and started looking around his office. I looked in the corners, on the bookshelf, ceiling, and under items on his desk.

"Bob, what are you searching for in my office?"

While continuing to scan the office, I said, "I'm searching for the hidden camera. I hope I find one because this must be a joke. You cannot be telling me, as an FBI agent assigned to the International Terrorism Squad, whose mission is to identify and neutralize international terrorists, that I cannot tell other FBI agents on the JTTF that I want to locate and lock up all the HAMAS terrorists I can find operating in America. Tim, do you realize how ridiculous that sounds?"

Embarrassed, he admitted, "You're right."

"I warned you about Ewing. He is only interested in protecting his unproductive HAMAS intelligence cases. He couldn't care less about actually neutralizing the HAMAS threat to this country. In his eyes, if I lock up the terrorists, he may have to close some of his intelligence files. He is only worried about job security. He wants HAMAS members running around free in this country. I find this type of thinking disturbing, Tim."

"You are right, Bob. I am sorry."

Although I was upset that Ewing had pulled this stunt, I was more concerned that he had convinced Tim to listen to his ridiculous complaint. "That's it. I am going to have a chat with Ewing," I told Tim.

I went to Agent Ewing's office, where he was now the acting supervisor of the squad responsible for HAMAS-related intelligence matters. Calmly and politely, I shared with him how the intelligence squad had failed for years to neutralize HAMAS. I restated how I intended to seek the indictment and criminal convictions of all HAMAS members I could identify through the VB criminal investigation.

I then told him I would listen if he could provide any information to justify my not pursuing a specific HAMAS target. I would cease pursuing the subject if a reasonable reason existed. However, I warned him that a mere request by him for the VB team not to pursue a specific terrorist without actually justifying the request would not suffice.

Tim then walked into his office and asked, "Is everything all right?"

I repeated to him what I had proposed to Ewing. Tim agreed that my proposal was fair.

On July 15, I telephoned Agent Martin of the FBI Milwaukee office to inquire about a set of records he had agreed to forward to Chicago a week earlier. He informed me that Agent Reed had instructed him not to forward the requested documents to Chicago because she was "holding the records hostage" until she received certain records from Chicago.

After the Milwaukee call, I informed Tim and the AUSAs about her intentional withholding of requested documents from Chicago. They asked that I document the communication between Agent Martin and me and forward it to the SAC in Milwaukee. I voiced my disapproval of this idea. I did not want to upset Agent Martin and others in the Milwaukee division since the Chicago agents would work with the Milwaukee agents once Reed transferred to Indianapolis. I recommended Chicago issue a new subpoena for the identical records she was refusing to provide to Chicago. They agreed and issued the new subpoena.

CHAPTER 30
THE CLOSING OF AGENT REED'S CASE

On July 15, 1999, the Chicago and Milwaukee SACs, ASACs, and supervisors met in a restaurant between Chicago and Milwaukee to resolve the problem of the two parallel criminal investigations of Sarsour. Although I had devoted years to establishing and nurturing the VB investigation, I was excluded from attending the meeting. Other than Gossfeld, FBI managers with limited knowledge of the investigation were now going to decide the fate of Vulgar Betrayal.

On the morning of July 16, Gossfeld informed me that the meeting results favored the VB investigation and assured me I would be pleased with the final resolution from the Chicago and Milwaukee managers. According to him, Milwaukee agreed to close Reed's criminal case and merge it into the VB criminal investigation. They would assist Chicago with the VB investigation of Milwaukee HAMAS-related activities. Likewise, the VB agents would aid the Milwaukee agents with their criminal investigation of other ancillary criminal activities related to HAMAS in the Milwaukee area.

In addition, the Chicago and Milwaukee SACs agreed to travel to Washington, DC, and request "Major Case Status" for the VB case, along with an initial $500,000 budget to fund it and necessary office space and equipment.

"Tim, I don't understand why it took so long," I stated.

"It's all over. Focus your efforts on the case. Substantial resources and support are forthcoming," said Tim.

I shared the good news with VB co-case agents Vincent and Tony McDonald.

On July 19, Tim informed me that the only support person assigned to the VB case had requested reassignment from the case. The support employee claimed the case was affecting her emotionally and even disturbed her mentally. He reported she would handle the case for three weeks before she was given a new assignment. No replacement was planned.

Also on July 19, John and I attended a meeting with the three AUSAs. We discussed ways to gain cooperation from some of the many VB subjects we were investigating. After agreeing on an idea, the AUSAs decided the first phase of our plan would begin the following week.

On the morning of July 21, while I was meeting with Tim in his office, Milwaukee SSA Ford called Tim to discuss another concern of Agent Reed. Ford said the VB agents were frustrating Reed. She wanted many boxes of VB records copied immediately and forwarded to the Milwaukee office.

"Brad, listen to yourself! The agreement eliminates the need for record duplication. It is all one case now," said Tim.

Ford agreed with him. Tim then questioned Ford about why he would allow Reed to manipulate him and suggested that he ignore any further complaints from her.

After he hung up, I said, "Tim, I do not understand what is happening. She is transferring to Indianapolis in two and a half weeks.

Why is she doing these things?" I then told him I believed Milwaukee management had not informed her about the closing of her criminal case. "Tim, why is everyone so scared of her?" I asked.

"I don't know, Bob," he said.

Although neither of us understood why others feared her, we were glad she would soon transfer to Indianapolis and we would no longer have to deal with her.

The following day, July 22, at 11:00 a.m., Tim told me about a telephone call he had just received from Ford. Ford had told him Reed was so upset she was "ready to jump off a bridge." He had also mentioned how she had been in and out of his office for the past two hours, complaining and making statements such as, "He won! He won!"

"Bob, I even heard her walk into Brad's office and say, 'He won! He Won!' I think you were right yesterday when you said they had not told her about the closing of her case. I believe they waited until this morning to tell her it was being closed," said Tim.

We agreed that when she said, "He won! He won!" She was referring to me regarding the forced closing and consolidation of her case into the VB case.

"Tim, what exactly have I won? I have to stay and continue working this nightmare while she moves on to Indianapolis," I said.

Again, I expressed my surprise that she was not told about the closing of her criminal case following the management meeting on July 15. Tim suspected Milwaukee was trying to avoid telling her. Instead, they were waiting to close her case after she transferred to Indianapolis to avoid her unpredictable behavior.

Also on July 22, at 1:30 p.m., two and a half hours after learning that Reed was extremely upset about the closing of her criminal case, Chicago A/SAC Walter Stowe entered the JTTF squad area to meet with the agents working VB. He wanted to tell us about the compromise reached between Chicago and Milwaukee management that was finalized within the past hour. The VB agents and Gossfeld gathered around my desk to listen to him as he informed us of the following terms agreed to:

1. Milwaukee would close and merge its criminal case regarding Sarsour into the VB case.
2. The SACs would request "Major Case Status" and funding for the VB investigation.
3. SSA Gossfeld would relinquish his case supervision of VB to an FBIHQ supervisor.
4. The FBI would move the entire Vulgar Betrayal case from Chicago, Illinois, to an off-site in Kenosha, Wisconsin.

I sat at my desk, staring out the window at the Sears Tower, shaking my head in disbelief at what I had just heard from Stowe. The news that Tim would relinquish his case supervision to FBIHQ and the VB case would be physically moved from downtown Chicago to Kenosha left me dumbfounded. Kenosha was over two hours from my home, and located about thirty minutes south of Milwaukee.

"Bob, we realize you will have a long commute since you live in Indiana," Stowe said.

I thought to myself, "Oh my God! I must now drive through three states daily to work on the VB investigation. This is unbelievable!" Depending on traffic, I would have to drive over four to five hours round-trip daily to work the case.

The VB's new plan to detain multiple HAMAS members was ready to be implemented. Everything needed was in downtown

The Closing of Agent Reed's Case

Chicago: the AUSAs, the records, the grand jury, the federal judges, the federal lock-up facility, and most of the subjects. This agreement was absurd! Stowe did not seek any input.

I was deeply upset by these terms. Over the past five years, I had worked diligently to build and nurture the case, often without the support or help of management. Yet, they excluded me from a meeting where critical decisions were made without considering the impact it would have on the VB investigation and my personal life.

After Stowe left the JTTF squad room, Tim informed me this was the first time he had heard about his relinquishing control and the moving of VB to Kenosha. Regarding my commuting to work, he said, "Bob, they cannot make you commute from Indiana to Wisconsin every day. If they try, you should sue the Bureau." We agreed that this would have been avoidable if anyone at FBIHQ had addressed the issue concerning Reed opening a duplicate criminal case over the past seven months. Because of FBIHQ management's failures, Chicago management, under McChesney's leadership, agreed to this ridiculous deal to appease Milwaukee.

Frustrated, I asked, "Tim, what would happen if I drafted a request to be reassigned from the case?"

"Bob, that's what you should do. Without you, there is no case. Maybe they would reconsider the agreement," said Tim.

On July 22, 1999, Tim and I worked together to draft an unofficial one-page request for my transfer or reassignment from the VB case. We wrote the document together on a plain white piece of paper. It was not an official FBI communication. The one-page request reads:

Tim,

Because of our disturbing meeting today with the Associate SAC, I am respectfully requesting to be reassigned from the VB case.

I am responsible for the FBI's criminal HAMAS fundraising case and the first seizure of HAMAS terrorist funds and assets in the US. For more than three years, I have been aggressively pursuing this RICO enterprise with minimal resources and no guidance or support from FBIHQ. Just when things started to become organized this summer after overcoming all the problems with the US Attorney's Office earlier this year, the squad was split in two, and I lost half of the agents who were vital to the success of this investigation.

Because of the numerous obstacles I have faced with this investigation in the past four years, and particularly these past seven months, I added my name to the Indianapolis transfer list on July 6. As I expressed to you prior to your meeting with Milwaukee, I was willing to remove my name from the Indianapolis transfer list and commit myself to remaining in Chicago for at least one more year. I was led to believe the meeting with Milwaukee was to consolidate these two investigations into one, so we would be free from the ridiculous duplication of investigative efforts re: the Milwaukee resident arrested overseas. To date, this investigation has not parceled out any of the other HAMAS subjects or HAMAS front organizations targeted for indictment.

We agreed at two bureau-wide VB conferences last year (1/98 & 10/98) to keep the entire investigation together, and Chicago would be the office of origin of the HAMAS criminal investigation into international terrorism activity. This was not done to benefit Chicago but the entire FBI. Now, I am

The Closing of Agent Reed's Case

told for the first time this case is being moved to Kenosha, Wisconsin, and you are being removed as the supervisor. I am also supposed to make a three-hour commute to work. In addition, the best part is we are relinquishing control to FBIHQ. That is the last thing this case and I need. You know as well as I, no one there truly understands the fabric of what we are delving through here. SSA Resnick is a great guy and was wonderful on my last trip to Israel. He seems to understand and is supportive, but I am not convinced this will move the investigation forward.

I have intentionally prevented any interviews of subjects and potential subjects from taking place for the past year in anticipation Sharif Alwan would be held in 'Contempt.' I did this for the reasons I discussed with you. The plan is coming together. Things are finally working. The AUSAs are working together as a team and keep asking for more information. Things could not be better with the United States Attorney's Office. This is why I told you I would commit myself to this case for at least one more year if things were fixed between Chicago and Milwaukee. You know I have enjoyed an excellent working relationship with many FBI divisions during this case. We both know where the problem lies in Milwaukee.

This investigation has been incredible! I look back now and wonder how we accomplished the things we did with what little support and resources we were provided. The funny thing is that I always believed that if I ever walked away from this case, it would be because of the AUSAs or DOJ. I never thought it would be because of my agency. I have been dedicated to this case above and beyond the call of duty, but no agent should have to endure the difficulties and the lack of support I have endured during this case.

The whole situation has become too difficult to handle, on top of all the pressures from the case itself. Since I have developed a working relationship with a specific foreign country, I would appreciate the opportunity to work on a subject related to that country. In addition, should a briefing of the VB case be needed, I would provide the briefing, which is likely to aid the FBI.

Thank you for your understanding,
Special Agent Bob Wright.[214]

After Tim and I completed the letter, I informed him I was taking the remainder of the week off. Upon returning the following Monday morning, I expected to be reassigned from the VB case. However, when I returned to work on Monday, Tim told me he did not submit my transfer request to management.

He explained, "They won't reassign you. Bob, without you, the case will wither away and die. The SAC is submitting a request to FBIHQ to make Vulgar Betrayal a major case and requesting $500,000 for a new office location, more manpower, analysts, computers, and more. Vulgar Betrayal will proceed according to your wishes. Once Major Case status is approved, you can get everything necessary to identify and bring down these terrorists."

Realizing he was right, I focused on aggressively pursuing the fifteen HAMAS members I wanted to see behind bars before the end of the year.

In July, we started the first stage of the plan to detain over a dozen more. When questioned before the federal grand jury, each member did precisely as John and I believed they would. They all pled to the Fifth Amendment. Everything was now going as planned by the AUSAs and FBI agents.

The Closing of Agent Reed's Case

HAMAS leadership became alarmed over the FBI's legal actions taken against many of its members linked to Mohammad Salah's terrorism training program. HAMAS attempted to interfere with the efforts of the US government by placing Muslim Brotherhood/HAMAS members in the grand jury waiting room to identify the HAMAS members and others who entered the grand jury room. Subpoenaed HAMAS members who entered the grand jury room would see the HAMAS members who could identify them as potentially cooperating with the US government.

Since the Middle Eastern men were the only ones sitting in the grand jury waiting room, the American citizens serving on the grand jury noticed them. They voiced concerns that the Middle Eastern men might attempt to discover their identities and addresses. In order to prevent this continued interference by HAMAS, the court issued a court order that prohibited HAMAS associates from entering the waiting room during grand jury proceedings. When they attempted to enter the grand jury waiting room, FBI agents served them with a copy of the court order and escorted out of the building.

On July 27, 1999, SAC McChesney submitted an official request to FBIHQ seeking "Major Case Status" and funding for the VB investigation. The request was written by Tim Gossfeld and approved by McChesney. The request sought financing for a combined force of a dozen personnel: eight agents, four financial analysts, and an intelligence research specialist. The request sought an initial budget of $275,000 for the first six months to lease building space, purchase rental furniture, computers, scanners, printers, automobiles, financial analysis programs, and many other necessary items. The "PRIORITY" Major Case Status request from SAC McChesney to FBIHQ National Security reads:

FEDERAL BUREAU OF INVESTIGATION
Precedence: PRIORITY   Date: 07/27/1999
To: National Security   Attn: ADIC Neil J. Gallagher,
                              DAD Dale Watson,
              SC Michael E. Rolince, A/UC, SSA
    Deputy Director's Office   Attn: RMA Board
    Finance   Attn: Accounting Section
    Budget Execution Unit & UC
    Milwaukee   Attn: SAC Demery R. Bishop / SSA
From: Chicago Contact: SAC McChesney
Approved By: McChesney, Kathleen L.
Drafted By: [Name blacked out by FBI]
Case ID #: 265C-CG-101942 (Pending) & 265C-MW-
            38118 (Pending)
Title: VULGAR BETRAYAL—AOT-IT (MONEY LAUNDERING) — OO: CG

GRAND JURY MATERIAL—DISSEMINATE
PURSUANT TO RULE 6(e)

Synopsis: Request for Major Case status, funding to support a multi-divisional task force, and designation of a Term-15 Supervisory Special Agent to direct this investigation.

Details: On 7/15/1999, SAC's Milwaukee and Chicago met with respective division management to discuss parallel avenues of investigation being followed by case agents in both divisions concerning the activities of [name blacked out by the FBI].

[The FBI blacked out all but five lines of the next paragraph as "Secret."]

[The FBI blacked out the first two full paragraphs on page three as "Secret."]

The Closing of Agent Reed's Case

There are presently SAs in Milwaukee and in Chicago pursuing their respective investigations. It is believed that a combined force of personnel, including a Term-15 Supervisor, Financial Analysts and/or Intelligence Research Specialists from the CG and MW Divisions, and whom would be TDY, and investigators would be sufficient staffing to move this investigation forward in an expeditious manner.

While neither SSA in Milwaukee or Chicago is asking to be removed from supervisory duties over their respective cases, the Term-15 Supervisor to head the Major Case is being made with the belief that such a supervisor would be able to effectively augment the present supervision, provide daily supervision to the Major Case investigators, and coordinate and prioritize the investigative activities arising from this significant case.

[The FBI blacked out the last two paragraphs of the Details section as "Secret."]

LEAD (s): Set Lead 1: <u>NATIONAL SECURITY— AT WASHINGTON, DC</u>

The National Security division is requested to approve Major Case status for 265C-CG-101942 [VB] / 265C-MW-38118.

Set Lead 2: <u>DIRECTOR'S OFFICE— AT WASHINTON, DC</u>

The Deputy Director's Office is requested to approve a Term-15 Supervisor to supervise a Major Case being worked jointly by the Milwaukee and Chicago Divisions.

Set Lead 3: <u>FINANCE—AT WASHINGTON, DC</u>

The Finance Division is requested to coordinate Major Case funding issues regarding this matter with the National Security Division.[215]

After reading the request sent to FBIHQ, I told Tim, "At least one good thing has come out of this Milwaukee nightmare. Management finally realizes how important this investigation is to the fight against Middle Eastern terrorism. We will finally receive the manpower and equipment which we have been lacking for years."

He agreed. Chicago management was finally going to aid the VB investigation.

The following day, July 28, 1999, I was told to draft a communication requesting a full-time financial analyst to be assigned to the VB investigation. The redacted EC reads:

FEDERAL BUREAU OF INVESTIGATION
Precedence: ROUTINE Date: 07/28/1999
To: Chicago   Attn: SSA (Name blacked out)
From: Chicago
    CT-1
Contact: SA (Name blacked out)
Approved By: (Blacked out)
Drafted By: (Blacked out)
Case ID #: 265C-CG-101942 (Pending)
Title: VULGAR BETRAYAL
    AOT-IT (Money Laundering)

Synopsis: Request for Full-time Financial Analyst.

Details: The Vulgar Betrayal case has proceeded at such a rapid pace that to properly address the financial aspects in a timely manner, a full-time Financial Analyst should be assigned.

The Financial Analyst, at a minimum, would be responsible for the following:

1. Prepare FD-192 and administer/coordinate/liaison with Bulky Evidence.

The Closing of Agent Reed's Case

2. Liaison with (Blacked out) United States Attorney's Office, (full line blacked out).
3. (First line backed out) for presentation to the Federal Grand Jury and trial preparation.
4. (First line blacked out) via subpoena, (following two lines are blacked out).
5. Other duties that have yet to be determined.

For the above reasons, it is requested that (name blacked out) currently assigned on a part-time basis to Vulgar Betrayal, be assigned full-time.[216]

The same day, July 28, the AUSAs informed John and me that they drafted a document regarding Agent Gamal Adel Hafiz's refusal to wear a recording device back in April. One of the AUSAs said he was deeply concerned about the entire situation and feared this matter would be revisited in the future. Therefore, the three AUSAs decided to draft their version of events and concerns regarding the agent's refusal to cooperate with Chicago's request to record a covert meeting with a Muslim terrorism target. Each of the three AUSAs signed the document. The US Attorney's Office in the Northern District of Illinois maintains it for future reference if needed.

On July 30, Gossfeld called me into his office.

"Bob, you will not believe this! I just received a call from Clinton regarding your plans to lock up all those HAMAS-trained terrorists. He requested you slow down the pace of the investigation and avoid imprisoning them," said Tim.

Clinton's request did not surprise me. I realized Agent Ewing had called him at headquarters once he could not prevent me from continuing with my plans.

"Tim, tell Clinton if he can justify a good reason we should not lock up known and suspected terrorists, I will slow the investigation down. I won't slow down our efforts without a valid reason from him. I am going after these terrorists. No valid justification exists for delaying this investigation."

Tim agreed with my position and relayed my response to Clinton.

I understood why Clinton asked me not to jail the trained HAMAS terrorists. However, I wouldn't dare tell why to any FBI manager, including Gossfeld. My exposing the FBI ITU's intentional protection of Middle Eastern terrorists above protecting the American people would've resulted in my removal from the JTTF and retaliation. Particularly if I explained the ITU's justification was to protect the ITU's job security. Job security funded by the US Congress, based upon the open FBI classified intelligence files.

CHAPTER 31

THE RETALIATION OF MORALLY BANKRUPT AGENT REED

On August 4, eight days after Chicago requested Major Case status and funding for Vulgar Betrayal, I ran into Gossfeld in the stairwell.

"Bob, I have been instructed to bring you to the SAC's office," he said.

"You look worried. Is something wrong?"

"Yes, an OPR [internal affairs complaint] has been filed against you."

"What! Are you kidding?"

"No."

"Tim, who filed the complaint, what's the allegation?"

"I know nothing. We'll discover this together," said Tim.

As we entered the office of the SAC, we saw McChesney exit ASAC Stowe's office. McChesney looked at me but did not acknowledge my presence. Stowe asked Tim and me to enter his office. As we entered, we noticed ASAC Van Nuys seated in the office. We sat in front of Stowe, who sat behind his desk.

He informed me that someone had filed a complaint against me with the OPR. He said that, based on the seriousness of the allegation, the OPR had opened an official investigation to address the complaint. He then handed me a copy of the OPR "Notification of Investigation" form.

It read: "On 7/22/99, an OPR inquiry was initiated regarding an allegation that captioned employee (Agent Wright) has engaged in a pattern of sexual harassment against a female SA (Special Agent) assigned to a joint Chicago/Milwaukee Division investigation."[217]

This false allegation dumbfounded me. I asked, "Who is alleging this? I do not know who could have said that!" Stowe refused to identify my accuser. Turning to Tim, I exclaimed, "This is a joke! I have never sexually harassed anyone in my life! I did not do this. This is a mistake!" As I reread the letter, I noticed the section, "An agent assigned to a joint Chicago/Milwaukee Division investigation." I looked up at Tim and said, "It is Cybil Reed. Cybil did this, Tim! She filed this crap shortly before transferring to Indianapolis."

Following this, the most shocking news emerged.

"Bob, there is more. You are no longer the case agent of the Vulgar Betrayal case. You are being reassigned to another squad," Stowe informed me.

I requested that he not transfer me from the VB case since things were coming together, and we would lock up many HAMAS subjects soon. I informed him about my frustrations the past several years, especially the past eight months, because of Milwaukee issues caused by Reed. I also stated that the transfer of VB to Wisconsin and Tim's relinquishment of supervisory control to FBIHQ was simply unacceptable.

"You're finding him guilty without even looking into her allegation!" Tim protested.

The Retaliation of Morally Bankrupt Agent Reed

Stowe mentioned that, considering this OPR complaint and the pending EEO complaint filed by Agent Abdel-Hafiz, "We have decided to remove Bob from Vulgar Betrayal and transfer him to another squad."

"Boss, Bob is Vulgar Betrayal! Without him, there is no case," pleaded Tim.

"I am confident any FBI agent can take over the Vulgar Betrayal case," Stowe remarked.

When I glanced at Tim, I saw him looking down and shaking his head in disbelief at that comment.

After I pleaded not to be removed from the VB case, Stowe said he might reconsider transferring me from the VB case.

I mentioned comments Reed made to me that contradicted someone experiencing sexual harassment. Stowe told me to write anything I could remember that would aid the OPR investigators in proving my innocence. He said I could provide any written information to the investigators assigned to interview me.

The FBI's Disciplinary Process sheet presented to me by Stowe contained the following paragraph:

"You are directed to identify, during your interview or as soon as possible thereafter, any testimony, documents, or other evidence which you believe are exculpatory or favorable, so OPR can conduct an appropriate investigation. Pertinent written documentation or other related material presented by you, or your attorney will be made a part of the OPR file and will be considered before any administrative action is decided."[218]

At the end of our meeting, Stowe informed me he would make the final decision the following morning regarding my reassignment from VB.

After Tim and I left the meeting, a female agent walking past us in the hallway said, "You look nice today, Bob."

As we walked further down the hallway, Tim turned to me and said, "I'll support you as a witness if you choose to file a sexual harassment complaint against her."

We both laughed.

Tim then pulled me into the break room on the ninth floor. "Bob, the ASAC agreed to reconsider reassigning you from Vulgar Betrayal to give me the opportunity to learn if Reed's allegations of sexual harassment are true."

"Tim, they are not true!"

"Could you've said or done something she misinterpreted?"

"Tim, that's the problem; she misconstrued everything. I said nor did anything she could have mistaken for sexual harassment. This is crazy! She and I got along great for two months. She wanted to sit next to me on both plane trips to the Middle East. During the return trip in May, she traded seats with the man seated next to me on the plane so she could sit next to me. She even told me she understood why some people have affairs. Tim, I said nothing sexual or showed any sexual interest in her. Nothing about this makes any sense, Tim. You were at all the meetings. Did you notice anything between us that would lead you to suspect issues of that nature between us?"

"No."

"Did she or her supervisor ever indicate any sexual harassment concerns to you?"

"No, there's nothing. Bob, is there anything on the OPR notice regarding the date she filed the complaint?"

"Why?"

"Something must have happened on the day she filed it."

While looking over the OPR notification letter, it hit me like a ton of bricks. "Oh my God! Tim, she filed the complaint on July 22, the same day she was told her criminal case was being closed and merged into Vulgar Betrayal. It was July 22 when Brad called and told you she was so upset she was ready to jump off a bridge."

Looking at the date on the letter, Tim agreed, "You're right!"

"Do you remember what we did when we heard about the agreement between the SACs? We were so upset that we wrote that one-page note requesting that I be reassigned from the case. What did she do? She intentionally filed a false sexual harassment complaint against me!"

"You're right, Bob."

"Because of decisions made at your Cracker Barrel meeting that I had no involvement with, I will once again bear the consequences of FBI management's failures."

"I will speak to Stowe regarding this. The most important thing is keeping you assigned to the Vulgar Betrayal investigation," said Tim.

"Do you agree that, whatever happens, this was not Stowe's decision. It's McChesney's decision, right?" I asked.

"I agree. She makes the final decision," said Tim.

On the morning of August 5, I visited the AUSAs and informed them about Reed's sexual harassment complaint and the potential for my removal as the VB case agent. I said that Tim was about to meet with Stowe to learn about my fate regarding the investigation. The three AUSAs expressed disbelief over the entire situation. They believed the FBI would resolve the matter in my favor and punish Reed for making false allegations against me.

An AUSA inquired, "Bob, why remain employed by the FBI?"

"I cannot. This is it. I am done. I need to determine my next action. I already know they will punish me for this even though I did nothing wrong."

The AUSA again reassured me that the FBI would clear me and take action against Reed, possibly even firing her for making a false allegation. Tim called and requested that I meet him in Stowe's office in ten minutes.

Ten minutes later, Tim and I met with Stowe to learn if I would remain the case agent. "Bob, I know Tim and you feel you are the only one who can make the Vulgar Betrayal case succeed; however, I believe any FBI agent can assume the responsibilities of the case," Stowe stated.

I glanced at Tim, noticing him again shaking his head while looking down at the floor. We realized Stowe would never have made such a statement if he understood the VB case and the importance of my creation and nurturing of it. He continued, "Bob, we are reassigning you from the Vulgar Betrayal case."

"Will I remain on the terrorism squad?"

"No, we are reassigning you from terrorism to the applicant squad."

This was another devastating blow! My dedication to the FBI and its fight against terrorism meant nothing to FBI management. This is how it ended, with no investigation into Reed's false allegation. They assumed she was telling the truth. I was now assigned to the squad that many agents called the "broken toy" squad. They would assign agents with emotional, medical, or disciplinary problems to the squad. The stigma alone would be embarrassing. I went numb as I sat in my chair and thought about my fate.

"The transfer is effective on August 9. I want to assure you that this transfer has nothing to do with the EEO complaint filed by Abdel-Hafiz and the OPR complaint by Reed. Bob, I have been

The Retaliation of Morally Bankrupt Agent Reed

talking to others who know you, and based on what I have heard, you are a very aggressive agent."

Stowe continued, "Considering your aggressive nature, the applicant squad is not a suitable fit for you. We will discuss reassigning you to a different squad in about three to four months if you maintain a low profile and avoid any trouble."

Following the meeting, Tim and I discussed Stowe's statement about Reed's OPR complaint having nothing to do with my being removed from VB. This was an attempt to hinder me from claiming her allegation had negatively impacted my career in case her false accusation was disproven. We agreed that the two complaint filings, from Reed and Abdel-Hafiz, were the reasons for my removal from both the VB case and the JTTF squad. Instead of these two agents being investigated, the FBIHQ OPR unit and the EEO Unit were investigating me.

On August 9, I began my new assignment on the applicant squad. An agent greeted me with a pointed question regarding my assignment. "So, who did you piss off to get assigned here?" he asked. He was packing his things because he was being transferred to another squad. My new squad had three agents.

I took Stowe's advice and began writing a document that would help prove my innocence of Reed's allegations. This document would chronologically detail most, if not all, contacts and conversations between Reed and me. It would also contain a list of witnesses who could act as character witnesses against her.

During my first week on the applicant squad, I noticed an email from Reed while checking my FBI email account. The email dated July 26, four days after she had filed her false sexual harassment complaint against me. The email contained the following:

"Bob, I have not received your corrections to the [Subject 1] interview. Please send it up ASAP. Next week is my last week here and I would like to have this completed before I leave. If you have completed the [Subject 2] interview from our last trip, please forward it so I can initial it. Thanks, Cybil."[219]

Reading the email, one would not suspect she had filed a sexual harassment complaint against me four days earlier. I thought to myself, "She sent this to me four days after filing the sexual harassment complaint? If she were genuinely concerned about sexual harassment, why would she initiate any contact with me after filing the OPR complaint?" Given the circumstances, it seemed logical that she should have forwarded this or any communication to me through her supervisor or ASAC. I printed the email to give to the OPR investigators during my future interview.

On August 11, I had lunch with agents Vincent and McDonald. Neither of them knew about the sexual harassment complaint. They each believed Stowe had removed me from the VB case because of my expressions of frustration regarding the agreement reached between Chicago and Milwaukee when Stowe communicated the agreement to us on July 22.

During lunch, McDonald expressed frustration over my "abandonment" of the VB case and "lack of consideration" for those I left behind to continue working it.

"You abandoned the case and us. You have placed a heavy burden on John and me. The case will not survive without you. Bob, resolve your issues with ASAC Stowe, and return to the case. It's unfair what you have done to us!" he stated.

I became numb. I understood his frustrations; however, I was too embarrassed to tell anyone about Reed's complaint.

The Retaliation of Morally Bankrupt Agent Reed

On August 16, 1999, McChesney drafted an FBI EC regarding my reassignment from the terrorism squad to the applicant squad and sent it to forty-two people in the Chicago office. The EC reads in part: "Title: Assignment Matters, Details: INTRAOFFICE: Effective 8/9/99: SA ROBERT G. WRIGHT from Squad [Blacked out as "Secret"] to Squad A-3."[220]

Also on August 16, I had lunch with John and two FBI language specialists who had assisted the VB case significantly during the past three years. During lunch, the translators pleaded with me not to give up on the case.

One translator said, "Bob, return to the case. No one will put this case together like you have, especially if it is an agent with no Middle Eastern terrorism experience. Unless you return, Vulgar Betrayal is doomed."

John then informed me he had formally requested a squad transfer from the JTTF squad.

"Bob, if you change your mind and return to the case, I will withdraw my transfer request," said John.

After the translators left, John said, "Bob, I've been an FBI agent a long time, and I believe something is happening here that you are not telling me. I realize if you're not telling me, there's a good reason. I'm sure you will tell me when you are ready."

I thanked John for his understanding; however, I was still too embarrassed to tell even him.

As word of my removal as the VB case agent spread, I received many calls from FBI agents around the country. These agents thanked me for my efforts, support, and commitment to the fight against terrorism. The call I enjoyed most was from retired FBI Agent Barry Carmody of the Tampa division. Barry was now working as a contract employee with the FBI. He said he wanted to thank me for all the support I had provided during the Tampa division's criminal investigation of a terrorist group and my overall efforts to fight terrorism. In particular, he wanted to thank me for providing information seven months earlier regarding the issues discussed at the VB II Conference held in Washington, DC. By providing this information to him and INS Agent Larry Davis, they gained access to FBI intelligence files the Tampa intelligence agents had prevented them from reviewing for years.

Barry expressed frustration over Clinton's failure to provide this information to the Tampa division. I assisted many agents throughout the US by providing them with fresh new ideas, investigative methods and US criminal statutes, which could aid them in the fight to neutralize Middle Eastern terrorists operating within the US.

In late August, I met with Gossfeld to express my concern over Agent Vincent and Agent McDonald not knowing why I had been removed from the VB case, and I wanted them to understand that I had no say in my removal. "Tim, I should tell them why management removed me from the case and squad. What do you think?" I asked.

"You are right, Bob. McDonald was here only this morning complaining about your abandoning the case and co-case agents. He is really upset with you. I believe you are obligated to tell them. They will keep quiet."

"I am not worried about them keeping quiet about it. I am just embarrassed over being accused of sexual harassment."

"They know you, and they know her. They will know you did not sexually harass her."

Later that afternoon, I called John and told him I was ready to explain why I had been removed from the VB case. I visited the JTTF squad room to inform him about the sexual harassment allegation. After I told him, he asked, "Are you allowed to tell me who filed the complaint?"

"John, you will not believe this. It was Cybil Reed."

"She did this! She's responsible for this!"

"John, calm down. Lower your voice, others might notice."

"So, are you telling me the front office believes her? How ridiculous! She has mental issues and needs to be fired!"

"John, I am screwed. I promise you I never sexually harassed her. However, the mere allegation alone is trouble. Headquarters will punish me through her complaint, even though I am innocent."

"Given the aftermath of the 1993 shooting?" asked John.

"Yes, I know it sounds crazy, but trust me, they are going to screw me over, John."

"Bob, if it were anyone else telling me something like this, I would think they were paranoid. Your accuracy on various matters in the past few years has consistently contradicted the opinions of those who believed you were mistaken. I believe you. I hope you are wrong, but I believe you," said John.

"I don't want others to know about the OPR investigation."

"I understand. However, it would be best if you told Tony. He is upset with you, Bob. He deserves to know what happened. He will believe and support you."

"John, I know, but not today. I'd appreciate your presence when I inform him."

"Just tell me the time and location."

"Can we meet tomorrow morning at 9:00 in the squad room? I only want the three of us together when I tell him."

"I will be there," said John.

The following morning, we met with McDonald. I told him about the allegation. He was upset over what Reed had done. He thanked me for telling him. He couldn't believe that Reed had filed such a ridiculous allegation; however, he expressed confidence in my innocence and felt, as everyone else, that she would be the one punished for filing the false sexual harassment complaint.

On August 20, I received the following email from McDonald:

"The [VB] ship is sinking, and I am the only one left on board. Gary wants nothing to do with the case. Vincent put in his memo to get off the squad. [Tracy] is no longer assigned to the case. [SSA] Resnick told [Matt Wilcox] there is a good chance we will get Major Case status. I am here getting documents for Milwaukee and the AUSAs, besides putting out little fires. Things are looking up."[221]

After reading this email, I laughed aloud. I thought to myself, "Poor Tony."

On August 24, 1999, I received my FBI "Earnings and Leave Record." Near the bottom of the document reads: "YOUR AVERAGE AVP [Overtime worked] PERIOD-TO-DATE IS 243 MINUTES PER DAY."[222] This statement showed I had been working an average of four hours and three minutes of overtime a day. This did not include the hours I worked at home each weekend. At the beginning of Vulgar Betrayal, I realized with the time commitment required by the case, no relationship with someone would last. To succeed in this case, I needed to dedicate most of my time to it. When most agents left by 5:00 p.m., I would work till 8:00 or 9:00 p.m. since the squad room was quiet. I would use this time to put the pieces together of the HAMAS information collected to date.

CHAPTER 32

THE FBI'S PUNISHED UNTIL PROVEN INNOCENT POLICY

"We asked that the Bureau adopt an 'innocent until proven guilty' policy for personnel, i.e., that promotions, transfers, etc. be unaffected by an ongoing OPR investigation. FBIHQ has indicated that they want to retain the 'punished until proven innocent' policy."[223]

— FBI Agents Association

For decades, the FBI's OPR unit has adopted and maintained a "punished until proven innocent policy"[224] against FBI employees accused of wrongdoing. Once someone accuses an FBI agent of misconduct, regardless of their innocence or guilt, they awaken to the harsh reality that their commitment and dedication to the FBI mission means nothing.

On August 4, 1999, when I was initially notified that I had been accused of sexual harassment, coupled at the time with a pending EEO complaint filed by Abdel-Hafiz, Chicago FBI management's knee-jerk reaction was to say, "You are no longer the case agent of the Vulgar Betrayal case. You are being reassigned to another squad."

My supervisor responded, "We are finding him guilty before there is even an investigation into this allegation!"

The FBI OPR policy maintains that an accused FBI agent may not receive a promotion or transfer to another FBI division while they are the subject of an ongoing OPR investigation. My situation was a textbook example of how the OPR process can be abused to where an innocent agent, falsely accused of misconduct, suffered undue punishment for the remainder of their career. Any vindictive or mentally unstable person within the FBI wishing to cause problems for an agent, prevent them from receiving a transfer to another office, or prevent them from receiving a promotion need only file a false OPR complaint against them.

Although half of the OPR investigations are ultimately determined to be unfounded, the innocent agent has no recourse and "can be financially punished for the rest of their careers because the delay period of the OPR investigation is never re-compensated."[225] The federal financial regulations do not allow for back pay because of OPR-generated pay/promotion moratoriums.[226]

"Current policy tolerates broad, ambiguous, and unacceptable discretion by both the Administrative Services Division and OPR in delaying personnel actions [such as promotions and transfers] until the resolution of such OPR investigations."[227] Even a superficial investigation that requires three or four interviews can last well beyond one or two years. Therefore, dedicated agents falsely accused of misconduct can face severe punishment. In addition, because of the drawn-out investigation, the agent may suffer mental and emotional distress.

The FBI's Punished Until Proven Innocent Policy

Although "the General Records Schedule, which the FBI adheres to, permits the destruction of disciplinary action files after four years, current FBI policy uniquely requires all disciplinary letters be maintained in the employee's OPF [official personnel file] indefinitely."[228] Such records can brand an agent for their entire FBI career. Unfortunately, this policy provides an excellent opportunity for vindictive managers, such as ASAC Gentry in Kansas City, to harm the remainder of an agent's career long after the supervisor has departed the FBI.

Because of the past comments and actions of Gentry following the 1993 shooting in Jefferson City, Missouri, I expected OPR would attempt to punish me even though the malicious allegation of sexual harassment by Reed was not valid. If the OPR investigation was appropriately done, the investigators would determine that Reed maliciously filed her complaint against me, intending to damage my career, prevent me from receiving a transfer to Indianapolis, and cause me emotional harm. However, I remained confident OPR would find me guilty and impose a harsh punishment against me while allowing her to get away with filing the false sexual harassment complaint.

According to the OPR documentation I received when notified of the complaint and the pending investigation, I was allowed to provide "any written documentation" to aid my defense. When OPR interviewed me later, I would be read my rights and signed a sworn statement saying my answers were truthful and complete. At the time of the OPR interview, I intended to submit a written document outlining my contacts with Reed. The contacts would include meetings, telephone conversations, and our two trips to Israel in 1999. I intended to do everything possible to prevent OPR from finding me guilty of her false allegation. I would also establish her motivation for filing the false complaint against me.

I began drafting a document outlining, in chronological order, the events leading up to her complaint. When finished, the document was forty pages long.

Since the document is long, I compiled a separate thirty-one-page document, breaking down the forty-page document into nineteen sections. I did this to help the investigators access specific information to avoid combing through the forty-page document. The second document included sections such as "Part 14: My Decision to Transfer to Indianapolis" and "Part 16: Events Leading to the Filing Of the Complaint."[229] In addition, the last page of each document contained a list of witnesses. The witness page was titled, "I Request the Following Persons Be Interviewed Regarding This Investigation."[230] The list contained five FBI supervisors, three FBI agents, and three Assistant United States Attorneys as witnesses who could aid in proving my innocence. Each person requested to be added to the witness list to prove my innocence since they each interacted with Reed and had personal knowledge of her irrational behavior.

Once I finished, I had compiled seventy-one pages describing my less than seven-month working relationship with her. I had ensured that FBIHQ OPR officials would feel compelled to conduct a thorough investigation to prove my innocence and to justify their punishment of Reed for maliciously filing the false sexual harassment complaint.

The following four pages, contained in the forty-page document, provide you with some insight into my efforts to prevent the OPR from finding me guilty:

DETAILED SUMMARY OF MY CONTACTS WITH AGENT REED
By Special Agent Robert Wright
September 14, 1999

This document has been prepared by FBI Special Agent Robert G. Wright for providing his attorney with factual events regarding his investigation of the US-based HAMAS Terrorist Enterprise and contacts with FBI Special Agent Cybil Reed during this investigation. This summary will also aid the Office of Professional Responsibility (OPR) investigators in their investigation of Agent Reed's complaint.

Included are facts revealing my many attempts to persuade FBI management to act in a reasonable manner regarding an obvious interference with my Chicago-based Vulgar Betrayal (VB) investigation by Agent Reed. The facts will show supervisors at FBIHQ failed to take necessary and appropriate action because of their fears of retaliation by Agent Reed. The facts will also show that because of the failures of FBI management to take reasonable and necessary action, Agent Reed filed a malicious and baseless complaint of sexual harassment against me.

In October 1993, because of safety concerns, I was transferred from Kansas City to Chicago. I was assigned to the Chicago Joint Terrorism Task Force (JTTF). I began investigating HAMAS terrorists residing in the Chicago area and eventually throughout the US and overseas. The following [40 pages] is a summary of events regarding this investigation, particularly from January 1998 to August 1999.[231]

To the best of my recollection, I have not seen SA Reed in person since May 6, 1999, when we arrived in New York after returning from Israel. In addition, to the best of my knowledge since May 25, 1999, I have initiated no more than one or two contacts with SA Reed. All other contacts were initiated by SA Reed. In fact, on 5/25/99, I informed Supervisory Special Agent (SSA) Gossfeld I would no longer answer incoming calls on Mondays, Wednesdays, and Fridays since SA Reed was a part-time agent and these were the days she worked. I wanted to avoid having any contact with SA Reed because of her continued misinterpretations of our communications and her continued interference with the VB investigation.

At no time during these past eight months (1/99- 8/99) have I knowingly or intentionally harassed or sexually harassed SA Reed. In addition, I also swear that at no time did SA Reed ever confront me and state my behavior was in any way offensive to her. Furthermore, at no time did SSA Ford [SA Reed's Supervisor] ever indicate to my supervisor or me, that SA Reed had informed him I was sexually harassing her, or that my behavior toward her was inappropriate. In fact, on April 8, 1999, I confronted SSA Ford and expressed my concern for having any future contact with SA Reed since she had a habit of misinterpreting our conversations and my messages left on her voice mail system.

It is my contention, once Agent Reed was informed on July 19 or 20, 1999, that her case was to be closed and consolidated into the FBI's Vulgar Betrayal case, of which I was the case agent, she maliciously began drafting this frivolous and baseless complaint. I can understand her anger, since on the same day, I likewise acted in the heat of the moment and drafted an unofficial request to my supervisor requesting I be transferred off the VB case to some other type of investigation on his squad. However, unlike SA Reed, I did not draft a malicious and frivolous complaint against another agent in retaliation because I felt, believed, or suspected that agent was responsible for the closing of my case.

I further contend Agent Reed filed this complaint to achieve one or more of the following goals:
1) Knowing I was seriously considering resigning from the FBI in January, I might do so now.
2) To prevent me from receiving an OP [Office of Preference] transfer to the Indianapolis division.
3) To have me removed from the Vulgar Betrayal case.
4) To harm my reputation and career in the FBI.

Although there were problems between Chicago and Milwaukee, the ultimate reason for this complaint being filed was because of the agreement which was worked out between the Chicago and Milwaukee SACs on July 15, 1999, and finalized on the morning of July 20, 1999. Based upon Agent Reed's two hours of complaining and her statements about my winning on the morning of July 20, I believe SA Reed truly believes I am responsible for her being instructed to close her criminal case. Rather than being rational, she reacted in a reckless and malicious manner by filing this baseless sexual harassment complaint, and has damaged my career as an FBI agent, as evidenced by my removal as the case agent of the FBI's leading HAMAS terrorist criminal investigation, which I started more than five years ago.

In drafting this document, I became concerned SA Reed may have maliciously retaliated against FBIHQ SSA Doug Phillips, after Phillips instructs her to close [another FBI] file. I suspected this since on the evening of 5/4/99, [while in Israel] SA Reed became upset and compared SSA Resnick's beginning suggestion about Chicago being the office of origin, which would ultimately force SA Reed to close her [current] case, to that of another situation in which she was forced to close a file by FBIHQ SSA Phillips.

On August 25, 1999, I contacted SSA Doug Phillips, [now in the] Los Angeles Division regarding his past association with SA Reed. SSA Phillips advised he had serious problems with SA Reed misinterpreting conversations, which eventually led to many problems for him. SSA Phillips informed me that following each phone call with Agent Reed, he would inform his supervisor about the call and provide him with the facts regarding their discussion during the call. He did this since Milwaukee management would constantly call complaining about SSA Phillip's conversations with SA Reed. Eventually, SSA Phillips started recording his telephone discussions with SA Reed.

SSA Phillips said after having serious concerns regarding a source of SA Reed's, he instructed her to close the source [file]. Subsequently, SSA Phillips was the subject of a one-year OPR investigation because of false accusations made by Agent Reed regarding their prior conversations. SSA Phillips believes SA Reed should have been fired in the past and cannot understand why she was not. SSA Phillips highly recommended I contact FBIHQ SSA Don Mercer, regarding his working relationship with SA Reed. SSA Phillips relayed significant information regarding SA Reed's character and demeanor. SSA Phillips advised he would discuss SA Reed's character and demeanor with the OPR investigators.

On August 25, 1999, I contacted [FBIHQ] SSA Don Mercer regarding his past association with SA Reed. SSA Mercer advised he was 'fortunate' in that SA Reed had already been through three FBIHQ supervisors and he was the fourth. SSA Mercer was made aware of SA Reed's past problems with other FBIHQ supervisors, and 'decided to be extra careful with SA Reed,' and was 'professional to the extreme' when dealing with her. SSA Mercer was aware SA Reed 'had some emotional baggage and misconstrued conversations.' SSA Mercer stated he would discuss SA Reed's character and demeanor with the OPR investigators and could provide the names of the other two supervisors from FBIHQ who could provide similar information regarding the character and demeanor of SA Reed.

Following these two conversations, it became crystal clear to me why FBIHQ Supervisors Clinton and Resnick neglected to perform their duty to order SA Reed to close Milwaukee's duplicate investigation of Sarsour. They obviously feared SA Reed's malicious retaliation such as that suffered by FBIHQ Supervisor Doug Phillips after he instructed her to close a file. It is extremely difficult to understand how Milwaukee and/or FBIHQ could allow an agent with SA Reed's character and demeanor to travel abroad for such an important mission. Although FBIHQ had direct first-hand knowledge of Agent Reed's character, demeanor, and emotional problems, unlike SSA Mercer, neither SSA Gossfeld nor I was as fortunate to ever be forewarned of SA Reed's problems.[232]

The following chronological summary of noteworthy events concerning the relationship between Reed and me was placed at the end of the forty-page document:

> On January 28, 1998, at the conclusion of the VB I Conference, [US Department of Justice Attorney] Murphy expressed concern that parts of the VB case not be split away from the investigation by other FBI divisions because a case of this size needed to be coordinated out of one office, and Chicago should be the office.

On September 27, 1998, FBIHQ hosted the VB II Conference in Washington, DC to resolve VB investigators entering the jurisdiction of other FBI field offices throughout the US. At the conclusion of this meeting, it was decided VB was the FBI's National HAMAS Criminal Investigation, and VB investigators could travel to other FBI offices to review files to aid the VB investigation.

Prior to January 4, 1999, I expressed my concerns to SSA Clinton regarding DOJ Attorney Murphy's motivation and problems he may pose in the future between Milwaukee and Chicago.

On March 5, 1999, after learning Agent Reed opened a duplicate investigation already being conducted by Chicago, I specifically said, with the aid of charts, to DOJ Attorney Murphy and Agent Reed the potential problems of duplicate efforts caused by Milwaukee's simultaneous criminal investigation of Sarsour.

On April 8, 1999, I explained to [FBIHQ] SSA Resnick the potential problems for the FBI because of Agent Reed's simultaneous criminal investigation of Sarsour. While on the second trip abroad, SSA Resnick stated to me, "Chicago should be the office of origin regarding Sarsour, and you should be sending leads to Milwaukee."

On May 25, 1999, Chicago received a copy of a communication, which was drafted by Agent Reed on May 16, requesting specific records in violation of Milwaukee's agreement with Chicago on March 5.

On June 14, 1999, because of Agent Reed's blatant attempt to impede further into the VB investigation, I completed a nineteen-page detailed summary of the VB investigation in order to head off any future problems between Chicago and Milwaukee.

The FBI's Punished Until Proven Innocent Policy

On June 29, 1999, I telephoned [FBIHQ] SSA Resnick from my home and requested he make a final decision regarding the office of origin of Sarsour to prevent any further problems between Chicago and Milwaukee. SSA Resnick said he and SSA Clinton realized a decision needed to be made, and they would make one within the next two weeks.

On July 15, 1999, the SACs from Chicago and Milwaukee met and decided to close Agent Reed's criminal investigation and consolidate it into the VB investigation.

On July 19, 1999, [Milwaukee] SSA Ford telephoned SSA Gossfeld and advised Agent Reed was upset and wanted boxes of records copied and forwarded to Milwaukee by Chicago. SSA Gossfeld stated, "Brad, listen to yourself! With the agreement we worked out, there's no longer any reason to copy records. The cases are combined, it's one case."

On the morning of July 22, 1999, SSA Ford telephoned SSA Gossfeld and informed him Agent Reed was upset and had been in his office for two hours complaining and saying, "He won! He won!" She was referring to the closing of her case and consolidation into the VB case, of which I was the case agent.

On or about July 22, 1999, Agent Reed filed a sexual harassment complaint against me.

On August 4, 1999, I was notified I was the subject of a sexual harassment complaint, and I was being removed as the case agent of the VB investigation. The investigation I was solely responsible for creating and nurturing.

On August 25, 1999, SSA Doug Phillips advised he had similar problems with Agent Reed misconstruing conversations. Subsequent to his instructions, Agent Reed closed her informant file. SSA Phillips was the subject of a one-year OPR investigation because of allegations of Agent Reed.

On August 25, 1999, SSA Don Mercer, FBIHQ, advised he was the fourth supervisor at FBIHQ to deal with Agent Reed. SSA Mercer was made well aware of Agent Reed's past problems with other FBIHQ supervisors and was "professional to the extreme" when dealing with her. SSA Mercer was also aware Agent Reed "had some emotional baggage and misconstrued conversations."

Unfortunately, our FBI Headquarters let both of us down and failed to act when they knew it was necessary to do so. Although I respect Agent Reed for her aggressiveness and drive to protect the case interest of the Milwaukee division, I cannot and will not sit idly by and accept her intentional and manipulative disregard for the truth through this malicious and frivolous attack upon my reputation and career.

Since entering the terrorism arena in 1993, I have met with constant resistance from many agents, supervisors and FBIHQ regarding the acceptance of my new ideas and methods in curbing the ever-growing terrorism threats to the US. This situation is just another perfect example of the complete failure of the FBI management to handle and respond to an obvious problem.

The arrangement between Chicago and Milwaukee was a recipe for disaster from the very beginning. All I ever did was try to do the right thing as an FBI agent, conducting the best investigation possible with what little support and resources I had available for the past five years. Because of my loyalty and dedication to this investigation, I have received "Exceptional" ratings on my performance appraisals for the past three years. During this past quarter alone, I have averaged over four hours of overtime a day in pursuit of bringing the HAMAS Enterprise to justice.

I have even purchased office supplies, computer equipment and computer programs out of my pocket to further this investigation, as I could not procure these items from the FBI. Things said between Agent Reed, and I were between "supposed" friends and not intended or received, at the time they were said, in a manner which would amount to sexual harassment. We were two friends who shared the same investigative goal of stopping terrorism.

Again, since May 25, 1999, I have had limited contact with Agent Reed. I am hard pressed to identify any conduct between Agent Reed and myself during the time we worked together from which Agent Reed can claim my actions or words amounted to unwelcome sexual advances, requests for sexual favors, or other verbal or physical sexual conduct, which had the purpose or effect of creating an intimidating, hostile or offensive working environment for her. Neither agent Reed, nor her supervisor, ever indicated to my supervisor nor I, that my conduct toward her was inappropriate at any time during this investigation.

The truth of the matter is the actions of Agent Reed and DOJ Attorney Murphy had the effect of creating a hostile and offensive working environment for Chicago. Their actions caused many problems and a lot of stress for the Vulgar Betrayal investigators, Vulgar Betrayal supervisor, and Assistant United States Attorneys (AUSAs) in the Northern District of Illinois, all of which could and should have been avoided had FBIHQ supervisors performed their duties in a reasonable manner.

Agent Reed filed this complaint in retaliation once she learned her case was to be closed and consolidated into the Vulgar Betrayal case. Her motivation is revenge for the closing of "her" case. Her fear is, I will make a successful criminal case out of the FBI's Vulgar Betrayal investigation and eventually transfer to the Indianapolis division. I believe, in her mind, this would cause her embarrassment. At a minimum, by filing a sexual harassment complaint, she intends to prevent me from transferring to the Indianapolis division in the future.[233]

After completing the forty-page comprehensive summary, I met with the Chicago OPR investigator responsible for conducting the Chicago portion of the investigation. I informed the investigator of the forty-page summary I had prepared, which summarize the events and my contacts with Reed. He understood I was providing this summary to tell a comprehensive story regarding the relationship between Reed and myself and her motivation for filing the complaint. He informed me that my interview would take place shortly.

A few days before the interview, the investigator called to inform me he had talked to the FBIHQ OPR unit regarding my forty-page written statement and the list of eleven witnesses. Witnesses who could aid in proving my innocence. Shockingly, the OPR Unit instructed him not to accept 'my written summary. Their refusal to accept crucial evidence to prove my innocence only reinforced my belief they were going to find me guilty of Reed's false sexual harassment complaint.

"They only want you to answer the specific allegations of Agent Reed," he said.

"OPR requiring me to answer only the specific allegations of Agent Reed is inappropriate and unfair to me. I do not even know what specific allegations are being alleged by Agent Reed," I said.

I further told him that the situation was complicated, and by telling OPR the entire story leading up to her allegation, I would have a fair opportunity to be cleared of her false accusation and justify her termination for filing the complaint. Therefore, submitting my summary and list of witnesses was necessary.

He again called the FBIHQ OPR unit to explain my concerns and share my demand to submit my documents to OPR during my interview. However, the OPR Unit again instructed him not to accept my written summary and witness list. This was the nightmare I had expected for years following the intentional distress I had endured by Gentry following the shooting incident in 1993.

Realizing OPR had no intention of providing me with a fair opportunity to clear myself, I now had to hire an attorney. I needed someone else to witness what I expected the FBI would do to me through the OPR investigation. I needed an attorney who could assist with the sexual harassment matter and was knowledgeable about the FBI disciplinary process.

Knowing the FBI would close the VB investigation and allow the Middle Eastern terrorists to continue operating freely in the US, I also needed an attorney who could assist me with warning members of the United States Congress about the ITU's gross negligence of protecting known Middle Eastern terrorists living and operating within the United States over protecting the American public.

In August 1999, after talking to several trusted friends outside the FBI, I decided I should try to hire Attorney David Schippers. Schippers was the Chief Investigative Council for the US House of Representatives, tasked by US Representative Henry Hyde with gathering evidence against President William Jefferson Clinton during the impeachment process. The US House of Representatives impeached President Clinton on December 19, 1998, for high crimes and misdemeanors. Friends considered Schippers the perfect attorney to assist me with both the OPR matter and my efforts to warn Congress about the FBI's failure.

Ironically, Schippers was the attorney I had met five years earlier. In 1994, I had informed him I was concerned the FBI would continue to retaliate against me in the future. The question then was, should I remind him about our 1994 meeting? Either way, he would think I was nuts when I told him about my current situation. However, I was okay with that because, if someone told me this story, I would believe they were nuts too.

Before meeting with Schippers regarding Reed's allegation, I had chosen not to say anything at that time to him regarding our 1994 meeting. Since I realized that Schippers would suspect I was paranoid or mentally unbalanced after telling him my story, I believed that mentioning the 1994 meeting would negatively affect his decision about whether he would represent me. However, I am confident something will happen in the future that would cause him to realize I was not a nutcase.

During my initial meeting with him, I limited my discussion to Reed. I provided him with a copy of the summary I had prepared for the OPR investigator. I told Schippers how the FBIHQ OPR unit instructed the Chicago OPR investigator not to accept my written summary. He said he would read the summary and call me in a few days to advise if he would represent me.

When Mr. Schippers called me the following morning, he said, "Bob, I want to thank you."

"For preparing the detailed summary?" I asked.

"No. For all the hard work you have done through the years and putting your life on the line to stop terrorists," he said.

His comment dumbfounded me. I had never heard anyone among the FBI management ranks thank me or tell me what a good job I had done, other than through my annual FBI performance appraisals.

The FBI's Punished Until Proven Innocent Policy

He stated, "It would be my honor to represent you, Bob."

We then discussed the upcoming OPR interview.

"Bob, they cannot refuse to accept this detailed summary. This summary is incredible. It covers everything, including her motivation for filing this complaint. I've never had a client present me with such a detailed summary. I know some of these men you listed on your witness list. If they're supporting you, then I believe you are innocent. We must reinstate you immediately to the terrorism investigation. This detailed summary will help get you back on your terrorism case," said Schippers.

We met again on the day of the official OPR interview at the Chicago FBI office. After I was read my rights and I signed a form stating that I understood them, the OPR interview began. During the interview, I shared the history of my relationship and contacts with Reed. While presenting my history with Reed, one of the two OPR investigators cut me off when he said, "Your responses are only limited to the specific allegations. We do not want you to provide any additional information."

Schippers told the OPR investigators I had written a detailed summary covering the allegations and providing significant insight beyond them. He slid a copy of the summary across the table to provide evidence on my behalf. As one of the investigators placed his hand on the detailed summary and slid it back to Schippers, he said, "We are aware of this summary and witness list; however, I was instructed by our headquarters not to accept Bob's detailed summary."

In response to that, Schippers pushed back the detailed summary, demanding its acceptance since it provided the complete story.

He then told the investigators, "This detailed summary will significantly aid you guys in clearing my client of this malicious sexual harassment allegation of Agent Reed."

The two investigators looked at one another, unsure how to respond. Schippers said, "There are eleven witnesses identified by name, address, and telephone number who have expressed to my client that he provide you with their names as witnesses. Witnesses who want to provide you with pertinent information regarding serious issues regarding Agent Reed's demeanor. You will take this document!"

The two exchanged glances again. One reluctantly reached for the detailed summary saying, "We will attach it to Bob's signed sworn statement."

After the interview, in their presence, I told Schippers, "Dave, the OPR unit is going to punish me for Reed's sexual harassment allegation even though I have done nothing wrong."

"Bob, you are going to be cleared. It is obvious you have done nothing wrong," he assured. He then asked the investigators, "This is an open-and-closed matter. Do either of you see any sexual harassment here?"

"Bob, unless you are lying, there should be nothing to worry about regarding the allegations of Agent Reed," the lead OPR investigator replied.

I turned to Schippers and said, "Dave, it does not matter. They are going to punish me. You will understand later; there is more to my situation."

"Bob, I have worked hundreds of these cases, and this is one of the easiest ones I have ever seen. You did nothing wrong, and the OPR investigation is a joke. However, since Reed made the allegation against you, OPR must go through the motions before clearing you. They will probably punish her when they discover why she filed this complaint," he said.

"I wish I could share your confidence. I hope you are still there for me when they return and punish me for this," I said.

The FBI's Punished Until Proven Innocent Policy

He again expressed confidence that I would be cleared and told me I was being paranoid due to the stress of the OPR investigation and being removed from the terrorism investigation.

CHAPTER 33
SAC MCCHESNEY KILLS VULGAR BETRAYAL

"I think there were very serious mistakes made. And I think it perhaps . . . cost people their lives ultimately."[234]
— Mark Flessner, Former Assistant United States Attorney, Regarding the Closing of the Vulgar Betrayal Investigation, *Primetime Live*, 12/19/2002

During the first week of October 1999, my new supervisor on the applicant squad presented me with an "Exceptional Performance" award for my work over the past year on the JTTF. Sitting at my desk looking at the award, I realized my hard work and dedication to the FBI meant nothing.

Also, during the first week of October 1999, a Chicago ASAC asked if I would meet with two Milwaukee FBI agents and Chicago Agent Tim Adams, a senior agent tasked by the Chicago SAC, to review the VB case file. Chicago management selected Adams, who had no terrorism experience, to determine what should happen to the VB case. I agreed to meet with the three agents and answer any of their questions.

I first met with the two Milwaukee agents, Roy and Brian, who had been in Chicago reviewing the Vulgar Betrayal case file for three days before I met with them. After the introductions, Roy said, "Bob, how did you do it? Whenever we look at something you did and decide what needs to be done next, we discover you already did it as we look deeper into your case files. You did an incredible job! Where do we go now? What do we do next?"

"Look, guys, I have to be honest with you. It does not matter what you do. The International Terrorism Unit will not let you go after these terrorists. They will never allow you guys to lock up another Middle Eastern terrorist or have one removed from our country. Vulgar Betrayal is dead. It is over," I said.

"Vulgar Betrayal is still an open case. It will not be closed. It is about to become a major case," said Roy.

"Trust me, it's over. This investigation is the FBI's first and only case that was tracking terrorism funds throughout the world and had identified dozens of Middle Eastern terrorists living and operating in America. One was locked up a few months ago, and we were locking up over a dozen more. I wonder what they are going to do with the $1.4 million we seized from the terrorists in 1998," I said.

"Bob, the FBI cannot justify closing Vulgar Betrayal! Why would they ever consider closing it?" asked Brian.

"I realize this sounds unbelievable, but the intelligence side wants Vulgar Betrayal shut down to protect all the terrorism subjects of their intelligence files. They need them open to justify continued funding from Congress. This is all about job security for the ITU."

"What do you mean?" asked Roy.

"The intelligence side of the house does not want us to lock up the US-based Middle Eastern terrorists nor deport them from America. If we lock them up or deport them, the intelligence agents will have to close their unproductive intelligence files. I know it sounds nuts, but it is the truth. They will never allow Vulgar Betrayal to get Major Case status. Because of its imminent closure, many lives will be lost in terrorist attacks that could be thwarted. This investigation did not focus solely on HAMAS. We located bank accounts linked to other major Middle Eastern terrorists and terrorist groups."

The looks on Brian's and Roy's faces showed they suspected I was paranoid. "I realize what I'm saying to you makes no sense. When the FBI kills Vulgar Betrayal, please remember what I told you today," I said.

Less than a week after meeting with the two Milwaukee agents, a Chicago JTTF agent showed me an FBI communication dated October 12, 1999, regarding the VB case. The FBIHQ National Security document responded to the Major Case status and financial support request by McChesney on July 27, 1999. The document, from the National Security division to Chicago and Milwaukee, states the following:

```
        FEDERAL BUREAU OF INVESTIGATION
Precedence: ROUTINE              Date: 10/12/1999
To:         Chicago              Attn: SAC
            Milwaukee            Attn: SAC
From:       National Security
Case ID #:  256C-CG-101942 (Pending)
            265C-MW-38118 (Pending)
Title:      VULGAR BETRAYAL
            AOT-IT
```

Synopsis: Response to Electronic Communication (EC), dated 7/27/1999, requesting NSD approve Major Case status for 265C-CG-101942.

Details: By above-referenced EC, the Chicago and Milwaukee Field Offices requested the Major Case status, funding to support a multi-divisional task force, and designation of a Term-15 Supervisory Special Agent to direct this investigation.

Based upon the 9/13/99 meeting with Milwaukee SAC Williams, SC and SSA and the 10/05/99 meeting with Chicago ASAC, SC and SSA it is determined that this proposal is no longer supported by the respective Field Offices. As such, [FBIHQ] will take no action to advance this proposal until the Chicago and Milwaukee Field Offices initiate further communication with [FBIHQ] indicating a desire to go forward. [FBIHQ] considers this lead covered.[235]

Another FBI document issued on the same day included the following sentence: "Vulgar Betrayal will remain in a Pending case status until other FBI divisions and FBI Legats have covered the outstanding leads overseas."

The "Pending case status" means the VB criminal investigation was no longer pursuing any further criminal investigation of any known and suspected terrorists, terrorist financiers or the tracking of identified domestic and international terrorism-related bank accounts. Once the investigators completed all outstanding VB leads, McChesney will officially close the VB investigation.

VB was investigating known persons in Saudi Arabia and many other Middle Eastern countries who were financially assisting international terrorism. Likewise, VB had issued similar requests to Israel,

France, the United Kingdom and others. It might be hard for others to understand this but, because of the pending official closing of VB, innocent people throughout the world will needlessly die from future Middle Eastern terrorist attacks that could have been prevented.

Three weeks later, on November 5, 1999, SAC McChesney sent the following letter to US Attorney Scott R. Lassar:

Dear Scott,
  This letter is to inform you of [the FBI has blacked out the remaining four paragraphs of this letter].
  Sincerely,
  Kathleen L. McChesney
  Special Agent in Charge[236]

Since someone placed this letter in the VB case file, I suspect the letter informed Lassar that the Chicago FBI office had discontinued pursuing the VB investigation. This would mean the two active judicial portions of the investigation would be closed. The first was the pending civil seizure of the $1.4 million seized from the terrorists in 1998. The second involved the pending criminal matter regarding Sharif Alwan, the trained HAMAS terrorist. If McChesney decided not to pursue these two matters, the criminal charges against Alwan would be dismissed, allowing Alwan to get US citizenship. The $1.4 million would have to be returned to Yassin Kadi, Mohammad Salah, and the QLI.

In November 1999, while at the FBI firearms range, I ran into Agent Tim Adams, the agent who was then assigned to address the criminal matter regarding Sharif Alwan. I inquired, "Do you get angry every time you review the Vulgar Betrayal records and witness how HAMAS has been harming America for the past thirteen years, while the FBI turns a blind eye to their illegal actions?"

"I'm not there yet. I'm mad that no one knows what this case is about. All the intelligence people are worried about is what this case will do to their program," he replied.

"They are clueless. They could have stopped all the US-based HAMAS terrorism activity years ago. I am serious when I say they will not let you pursue these terrorists. They will do whatever they can to stop you, Tim," I said.

"I understand that. I just don't get it," he said.

"Unfortunately, a lot of innocent people are going to die because of FBI management's negligence," I said.

On January 4, 2000, the FBI Legat assigned to the US embassy in Saudi Arabia sent a reply to a lead I had sent regarding the VB case shortly before my removal from the JTTF. We were seeking Saudi Arabia's help in identifying individuals and organizations in Saudi Arabia who knowingly financed international terrorism. This included financial funds being sent from Saudi Arabia to the United States to support Middle Eastern terrorism activities in America. This January 4 communication contained a copy of a letter from the FBI Legat to the Saudi Arabian government seeking their help in obtaining information about radical fundamentalists living in Saudi Arabia who were transferring money to the US to fund international terrorism. The communication reads:

> DATE: 1/4/2000
> TO: Chicago
> FROM: LEGAT RIYADH
> RE: File number 265C-CG-101942 (Vulgar Betrayal) Serial 871
>
> The Embassy of the United States of America presents its compliments to [FBI blacked out the name.] and has the honor to request your assistance in the following matter:

A network of radical fundamentalists participated in a series of money transfers between banks located in Europe, the Middle East, and the United States. It has been determined that some of these funds were used to further the activities of terrorist groups in violation of US laws.

The continuing investigation of this matter has implicated the following individuals who had, and probably still have active accounts with [The FBI blacked out all the names.]

[The FBI blacked out the name.] is respectfully requested to inform the proper authorities and arrange a meeting between Legat Riyadh and [name blacked out] to discuss a resolution of this matter.

If you have questions about this matter, please do not hesitate to contact Legal Attaché or Assistant Legal Attaché at telephone number [number is blacked out].

The Embassy avails itself of this opportunity to renew to [name blacked out] the assurances of its highest consideration.

Embassy of the United States of America.[237]

Ironically, on the same day, while the FBI Legat in Saudi Arabia was working to gain vital information on Saudi-based terrorism financiers, such as Yassin Kadi, and Saudi terrorism-linked bank accounts, for the Vulgar Betrayal case, McChesney technically killed the case. On January 4, 2000, Chicago drafted an FBI communication, which reads:

FEDERAL BUREAU OF INVESTIGATION
Precedence: ROUTINE   Date: 01/04/2000
To: Chicago   Attn: SSA (Name blacked out)
From: Chicago   FA (Name blacked out)
Case ID #: 256C-CG-101942 (Pending)
            265C-MW-38118 (Pending)

Title: VULGAR BETRAYAL
             AOT-IT

Synopsis: Lead covered.

Details: The RICO criminal conspiracy relating to the above-captioned investigation [VULGAR BETRAYAL] is no longer being pursued. As such, the assistance of the FA [Financial Analyst] is no longer necessary.

FA processed a large volume of evidence, consisting mainly of bank records. FA organized and sorted the records before preparing the FD-192s. FA also prepared communications relating to the evidence. Her assistance to the investigation is appreciated.[238]

Less than five months after my removal from VB, McChesney had started the beginning of the end of VB. In the future, once all the leads I sent to other offices and overseas were completed, Chicago sent an official FBI communication to FBIHQ to announce the official closing of VB. McChesney had killed the investigative efforts of the FBI's only successful international terrorism criminal case. VB identified known and unknown terrorists, tracked international terrorism funding, identified overseas international terrorism financiers, and, most importantly, located domestic and international bank accounts used by known and unknown terrorists and their financiers.

Unfortunately, this meant VB's investigative efforts to learn more about Saudi Arabia's terrorism financiers and Saudi-based terrorism-related bank accounts through the FBI Legat in Riyadh and many other countries would be pursued no longer. VB sought the Saudi Arabian government's help in obtaining information about known terrorist organizations and Saudi citizens linked to terrorist financial transactions within the US.

After learning what McChesney had done, I visited the person in charge of the Chicago evidence room. I asked if she would call me if anyone requested the destruction of any VB evidence at any time in the future. I informed her that many documents and bank records held historical significance and should not be destroyed. She assured me I would receive a call. If she had called me, I would have notified the AUSAs to see if they could prevent the FBI from destroying vital historical HAMAS evidence.

On January 10, 2000, I received a communication from FBIHQ regarding my December 21, 1999, request for permission to participate in outside employment. I made the request since I was no longer spending all my time working on the VB investigation. I needed to fill my free time. I pursued my hobby of making lamps. I planned for this to be my career after retiring from the FBI. The letter from FBIHQ reads in part:

FEDERAL BUREAU OF INVESTIGATION
Precedence: ROUTINE   Date: 01/10/2000
To: Chicago   Attn: SAC Kathleen McChesney
                       SSA [XXXX]
From: Administrative Services, PAS/Employee Benefits Unit
Approved By: [Blacked Out]
Case ID #:   67-HQ-xx
Title: Robert G. Wright, Jr. - Personnel Matter - Special
            Agent Outside Employment
Synopsis: To advise that authorization is given for Special Agent (SA) Robert G. Wright, Jr. to participate in outside employment.
Details: Form FD-331 requested SA Wright to engage in outside employment. SA Wright creates baby lamps and

other baby products as a hobby and would like to sell these items. The items are created on his own time and the craft shows would be on weekends.

FBI approval is being given for SA Wright to create and then sell baby lamps and other items. This activity involves the creation of items which are not contracted for either formally or informally in advance. SA Wright creates his items while off duty and his continued production will not likely affect his availability for any assignments.

Accordingly, although SA Wright will receive some payments for the sale of his crafts, since his receipt of these payments will not adversely affect any discernible operation or administrative interest of the FBI, authorization is being given for him to engage in outside employment.

SA Wright should understand that he will be required to cease selling baby crafts should any conflict arise between his responsibilities as a Special Agent and his hobby. This includes, but is not limited to, his complete availability for the performance of official duties. SA Wright should also be advised that he may not advertise or solicit business during working hours and within FBI space. SA Wright should also ensure that there are no references to his position as a Special Agent with the FBI when selling his crafts.

LEAD(s): CHICAGO at CHICAGO, ILLINOIS

That SA Robert G Wright, Jr., be advised that authorization is given for him to engage in outside employment as it relates to his hobby, the creation of baby lamps and items.[239]

In March 2000, I received another sucker punch when I received a call from the secretary of the ASAC responsible for the JTTF squad.

"Bob, you need to come to the ASAC's office next Tuesday to give a signed sworn statement," said the secretary.

"What is the signed sworn statement for?" I inquired.

"Someone from the EEO section at FBIHQ will arrive in Chicago next week to take your statement regarding an EEO complaint filed against you," said the secretary.

"Oh my God, are you kidding! FBIHQ is pursuing Agent Abdel-Hafiz's claim that I have harmed his FBI career. What a joke!" I said.

Abdel-Hafiz filed his EEO complaint on June 6, 1999. It took nine months for someone at the FBI's EEO unit to contact me regarding the complaint.

When I notified my supervisor of this recent development, he laughed. He believed I was joking. I returned to my desk and thought about everything coming down around me. My supervisor approached me to inquire about my seriousness regarding the EEO complaint.

"Yes. Can you believe this? All I have ever done was act in the best interest of my country by doing the best job possible for this organization, and I am getting screwed over again," I said.

Surprised, he informed me he had encountered nothing like this in his nearly thirty years in the FBI. He was supportive and told me he was available anytime if I needed to talk to someone.

On the day of the EEO interview, I told the investigator the entire story regarding Abdel-Hafiz's refusal to record a conversation between himself and the president of BMI, a front company linked to known designated international terrorists.[240] Upon finishing my story, I inquired, "Throughout your years investigating EEO matters, have you encountered anything like my story?"

"Not until today" was his response.

Before signing the signed sworn statement, I insisted on adding the following statement, "The only bias I have is against terrorists." I then asked how long it would be before EEO made a final decision.

The investigator said, "These investigations take a while. You could be close to retirement before the investigation is concluded."

My FBI career was only nine years old, with over twenty years left until retirement.

The investigator interviewed me on March 21, 2000. The following are some of the pertinent portions of my signed sworn EEO statement:

> I was assigned to the International Terrorism squad at [the] FBI Chicago Field Office during the spring of 1999. I was aware that a member of HAMAS, a terrorist organization, had attempted to secure employment [as a Special Agent] with the FBI. [This was not Abdel-Hafiz].[241]
>
> In April 1999, SA Gamal Abdel-Hafiz had telephoned and advised me that a [long time] friend of his worked as an accountant for a [terrorism-linked] company to which I had served the company President and Vice President with Federal Grand Jury subpoenas. He also advised me that the accountant was concerned about harming his application he had submitted to the FBI to become a [FBI] translator. Through the course of my investigation, it had been determined that this company had received financing from two siblings of Osama bin Laden and United States designated HAMAS terrorist Mousa Abu Marzook. Each of the aforementioned are Muslim.
>
> SA Abdel-Hafiz stated that the accountant had inquired of him if he should quit his employment, as it appeared there was a criminal investigation underway [regarding the company].[242]
>
> A few weeks later I received another telephone call from SA Abdel-Hafiz. He advised he had been telephoned by [his

longtime friend] the accountant, who stated that the President of the company was aware of his relationship with SA Abdel-Hafiz. The President inquired if the accountant could arrange a meeting between SA Abdel-Hafiz and the company President regarding the Chicago [VB] investigation.

The accountant then mentioned his concern to SA Abdel-Hafiz that funds the accountant was transferring overseas on behalf of the company may have been used to finance the [United States] embassy bombings in [Kenya & Tanzania] Africa. [I immediately told SA Abdel-Hafiz the US embassy bombings were one of the things we were looking into regarding the company.]

SA Abdel-Hafiz asked if I desired him to speak with the [company] President. I advised him that I desired him to have the meeting and [told him he would have] to wear a concealed recording device (wire) to record what transpired. I then told my supervisor that SA Abdel-Hafiz may be wearing a wire during a discussion with [the company President]. I then went to the United States Attorney's Office and discussed the matter with them [three AUSAs] and they agreed the wire would be of great interest to our investigation. [However,] when I returned to the [FBI] office, my supervisor summoned me to his office and advised me that SA Abdel-Hafiz was not going to wear the wire and that I should forget about it.

Later, while at the United States Attorney's Office on other matters, the question of SA Abdel-Hafiz wearing the wire was brought up by one of the attorneys. The Assistant United States Attorneys still desired SA Abdel-Hafiz to wear the wire. A conference call was arranged between [three AUSAs & two FBI agents in Chicago and Dallas SA Abdel-Hafiz and his supervisor].

The AUSAs expressed to SA Abdel-Hafiz the importance of this [VB] investigation and the purported wire. SA Abdel-Hafiz stated that he would only record the individual [company president] if he told him he was wearing a wire. One of the AUSAs told SA Abdel-Hafiz they would get a meeting location [in a hotel room] and wire it so that SA Abdel-Hafiz would not have to wear a wire. This was not acceptable to SA Abdel-Hafiz, who then proposed placing a tape recorder on a table [so the company President will know he is being recorded] and speaking with the individual. When this was deemed unacceptable by those present [in Chicago], SA Abdel-Hafiz advised he would meet with the individual and report the meeting on an FD-302 (FBI document summarizing an interview) as he had done before in response to a similar request for FBI Tampa.

The AUSAs present advised this was not what they desired and inquired what the root of SA Abdel-Hafiz's objection was to the wearing of a wire. SA Abdel-Hafiz advised that he feared for his safety. When he was told the FBI could protect him, SA Abdel-Hafiz told them [Chicago AUSAs] he did not trust the FBI to protect him. The AUSAs continued to ask why SA Abdel-Hafiz would not wear the wire. [SA Abdel-Hafiz yelled in anger] 'A Muslim does not record another Muslim.'"[243]

In December 1998, while [I was] pursuing an investigation in Dallas, Texas, SA Abdel-Hafiz assisted me in the review of documents. Following this investigation in Dallas, I expressed to a fellow Chicago SA that I was comfortable with SA Abdel-Hafiz and felt that I could contact him in the future if I had questions regarding Middle Eastern terrorism investigations.

I have not discriminated against SA Abdel-Hafiz based upon his religion (Muslim) or his national origin (Arab/

Middle Eastern), and do not have any knowledge of anyone discriminating against him [SA Abdel-Hafiz] on these bases. My only bias is against terrorists.

I was not the only SA concerned with SA Abdel-Hafiz's refusal to wear the wire. Because of the serious nature of the events surrounding this [VB] terrorism investigation, a senior SA of the Chicago FBI attempted, on three separate occasions, to determine the proper procedure to initiate an inquiry into SA Abdel-Hafiz's refusal [to secretly record the company President]. The attempts made through the FBI Chicago security officer were never responded to by FBI Headquarters.[244]

In April 2000, I received a call from Gossfeld. Tim told me a problem had arisen and McChesney asked him to call me. The issue came about when the Milwaukee agents found a document I had written, and it appeared to FBI management the document was part of a more extensive diary. According to Tim, both Milwaukee and Chicago SACs wanted to know if I had kept a diary of the VB investigation while working on the case.

I burst out in laughter.

"What is so funny?" asked Tim.

I informed him that the document in question contained my notes, in chronological order, regarding the many problems caused by Murphy during 1998 and 1999. I reminded him that this was the document I had shown him before the meeting with the deputy attorney general in April 1999 before my flight to the Middle East. I had intended to mention the listed items to the deputy attorney general before he had said he did not want to hear such things after someone else started complaining about Murphy.

"I thought this looked familiar. So, there is no diary?" asked Tim.

"Tim, you can tell McChesney there is no physical diary," I said.

"What exactly does that mean, Bob?" he queried.

"Although there is no physical diary, there is a diary in my head. We both know how good my memory is regarding everything that has to do with Vulgar Betrayal. I remember everything that happened, including conversations. Ask McChesney what she plans to do about that," I said.

"Yeah, I am going to leave that out of my conversation with her," he said, laughing.

On April 18, 2000, I received my annual performance appraisal and it was another overall rating of "Exceptional." My supervisor wrote:

FBI PERFORMANCE APPRAISAL
04/18/2000

CONDUCT INVESTIGATIONS - Exceptional: Since Agent Wright was assigned to the squad (August 9, 1999), he has conducted his investigations in an exceptional manner, displaying great initiative and a sincere desire to get the job done correctly. Agent Wright is very methodical in his work, knowing the required investigative steps and quickly determining how extensively each case should be worked. He is meticulous in his investigative work, which speaks to his years of experience in successfully conducting major investigations.

Agent Wright has continuously demonstrated his exceptional work ethic, which is reflected in both his attitude and organization. This attention to his work has resulted in his being able to work on many cases simultaneously with outstanding results. Most of his cases have been presidential Appointments, which are sensitive in nature.

Agent Wright's greatest attribute is his unfailing professionalism and dedication. He personifies the best attributes of the "ideal Agent" by his always positive attitude, his sincere determination to "get the job done" and his genuine desire to turn in the best possible work product.

In summary, Agent Wright performs his work in this element in an exceptional manner. His high level of performance is routine and continuous, not periodic or intermittent. Agent Wright merits an exceptional rating in this element, as he has sincerely earned it.

REPORT INFORMATION - Exceptional: Agent Wright's reporting is done in a detailed and meticulous fashion, which gives his documents a thoroughness that distinguishes them. His work ethic and pride are clearly displayed in his paper output and its content.

Besides producing well-written communications, Agent Wright provides outstanding oral reports on the status of his cases. He articulates the details and gives his perspective as to the events that have occurred, which enables the supervisor to better access the direction of the investigation and what action needs to be taken. Agent Wright always makes sure he knows the facts of the case and any developments before he provides his oral reports, which eliminates any confusion or future misunderstandings. His oral reporting and insight are almost as equally important as his written documents. Agent Wright is rated exceptional for his work in this element.

DEVELOPMENT OF AN INTELLIGENCE BASE - Exceptional: Agent Wright has performed exceptionally in maintaining the squad's current contacts, but also striving to develop new ones when the opportunity presents itself. His contacts have enabled Agent Wright to quickly obtain reports and general information regarding the presidential appointment (PA) investigations. These liaison contacts respect Agent Wright's professional demeanor and his adherence to the developed protocol to obtain information. Agent Wright meticulously follows the procedures and does not attempt to "take shortcuts" in order to obtain the needed information. His reputation has enhanced his liaison capabilities.

Agent Wright has displayed an exceptional ability to obtain information from outside sources. He has consistently performed in this respect, demonstrating outstanding oral communicative skills and the personality to "win people over." This blend has enabled him to successfully work in PA investigations.

In order to work these cases successfully, one must be a skilled investigator, can work well with others, possess the determination to obtain results and the judgment to assess details, separating important information from hype. Agent Wright possesses all these qualities plus the motivation and drive to perform at the highest level. Agent Wright is rated exceptional for his work in this element.[245]

On June 15, 2000, I learned I was transferred from the applicant squad to the FBI Chicago South Resident Agency office (SRA) in Tinley Park, Illinois. When I had arrived in Chicago in 1993, I had asked to be transferred to the SRA office. Gossfeld told my current supervisor that the Chicago OPR investigators resolved the sexual harassment allegations. According to him, the Chicago OPR investigators concluded I did not sexually harass Agent Reed. Therefore, to make up for the wrongs that management had done to me following her false sexual harassment allegations, they transferred me to the SRA office.

However, no one in Chicago management could officially confirm the OPR investigation found me innocent until the FBIHQ OPR unit reviewed the investigative report and concluded I did not sexually harass Reed. After reviewing the investigation, FBIHQ OPR will issue their written final ruling and forward their decision to Chicago. Although the Chicago investigation cleared me of wrongdoing, I remained confident the FBIHQ OPR unit would ignore Chicago's findings and punish me over Reed's false complaint. It had been ten-and-a-half months since I was first notified of her complaint, and the OPR investigation was still pending. I transferred to the SRA office on July 5, 2000.

Agent Tim Adams, the agent tasked with reviewing the VB file after my removal from the VB case, also worked in the SRA office. He approached me one evening to talk about the frustrations he had endured since taking over the criminal matter regarding Sharif Alwan.

"I have almost twenty-five years in the bureau and will retire in three years. I wish I had never worked on this case. I wish I could have left the FBI without knowing what I learned this past year. I am looking for a way out of the case," he vented.

"Do not take this the wrong way, but I am glad you took over a portion of the case and endured the same frustration I have endured for years. At least now someone else knows what I had to put up with for all of those years." I continued, "Have you figured out why headquarters and the intelligence squad have continually hampered your efforts to stop the HAMAS terrorists?"

"Yes," he said.

"Why?" I asked.

"Job security," he replied.

"Bingo!" I said.

"I have a list of everything they did to hinder my efforts. I actually kept a list," Adams shared.

"Good, hold on to that list. You may need it in the future. I am not done fighting yet. I intend to expose everything I have been through and FBI management's efforts to hinder my fight against the terrorists," I said.

"Be careful, Bob. They will come after you and fire you," said Adams.

"I know. That is why I hired Attorney Schippers last year. I am doing everything by the book because I know how vindictive they can become against a street agent. Eventually, they will try to fire me, but I will be ready for them. I will not let them get away with closing the only FBI case that could help prevent future terrorist attacks by Middle Eastern terrorists living and operating within the United States," I said.

During my first week in the SRA office, I had to interview two police officers from a local police department. The two officers had approached the Illinois State Police about corruption of the assistant police chief of their department. Another Illinois State Police officer and I interviewed the two officers. They shared how the assistant police chief accepted $150 from someone to have his car released from the city impound lot. They then added how he had retired several months earlier.

After the two officers left the interview room, the other officer said, "I noticed a look on your face during the interview. Was this something you already knew about?"

"No. I was just thinking how sad it is there are terrorists throughout this country who need to be investigated by the FBI. I am here wasting my time listening to a story about a retired officer who possibly took $150 to help someone get his car out of an impound lot. This is a long way from the terrorism work I was working on less than a year ago," I said.

Another SRA case I was working on involved a former bank supervisor who had embezzled $100,000 from the bank days before she resigned and moved out of state. After reviewing the evidence, I called her and told her I had evidence that she had embezzled the $100,000. I asked her to return to Chicago the following week to return the money and provide a full confession regarding her embezzlement. In addition, I promised I would not place her under arrest when she arrived at the SRA office. Other agents thought I was nuts for believing she would arrive at the SRA with the money and provide a confession.

As promised, the former bank supervisor arrived at the SRA office, returned all the money, and provided a full confession. Although the case was simple and the file contained only four to six documents, I warned her it might be a year or longer before she heard anything from the US Attorney's office regarding a court date. Over a year later, she was convicted and imprisoned. I spoke to the AUSA assigned to the case regarding her five-year prison sentence. I believed she should have received probation or a lighter prison sentence. The AUSA said that she received a five-year prison sentence because of the federal sentencing guidelines.

A year had passed since Agent Reed filed the sexual harassment complaint with OPR. I was still awaiting the final decision. I continued to warn my fellow agents, Schippers, the AUSAs, and my supervisor that the OPR unit would punish me by finding me guilty and recommend that I receive thirty days off without pay or fire me from the FBI. Everyone believed I was paranoid and continued to assure me that OPR would rule in my favor and punish Reed.

In early September 2000, the FBI offices and Legats had completed all outstanding Vulgar Betrayal leads. McChesney could now officially announce the case's closure.

On September 11, 2000, thirteen months after my removal from VB, and one year to the day of the future 9/11 terrorist attacks, under the leadership of Chicago SAC Kathleen McChesney, Chicago officially closed the Vulgar Betrayal investigation. An EC from Chicago to FBIHQ National Security is read below:

> FEDERAL BUREAU OF INVESTIGATION
> Precedence: ROUTINE   Date: 09/11/2000
> To: National Security   Attn: [XXXX]/SSA [XXXX]
>   Criminal Investigative   Attn: IRS, IRU-1
>   Paris   Attn: [XXXX]
> From: Chicago
>   CT-1
> Contact: SSA [XXXX]
> Approved By: [Blacked Out]
> Drafted By: [XXXX] rml.
> Case ID #:   265-CG-101942 (Closed) - 896
> Title: VULGAR BETRAYAL
>   AOT-IT (MONEY LAUNDERING)
>
> GRAND JURY MATERIAL—DISSEMINATE
> PURSUANT TO RULE 6 (e)
>
> [The FBI blacked out the first two pages, except for the last sentence.]
>
> No further investigation is being conducted in this matter.
> Lead(s): ALL RECEIVING OFFICES—Read and clear.[246]

SAC McChesney Kills Vulgar Betrayal

It was official. As of September 11, 2000, SAC McChesney officially closed Vulgar Betrayal, the FBI's only AOT criminal investigation identifying Middle Eastern terrorists and tracking their domestic and international money trails. This included VB's investigation of the money trails in Middle Eastern countries, such as Saudi Arabia, and efforts to identify others in the Middle East who were financing international terrorism. No one in FBI management would give the closing of VB a second thought.

The ITU helped to convince McChesney to kill the VB investigation. They could now resume protecting all their Middle Eastern terrorism targets. They had no intention of ever neutralizing the actual threats the targets of their intelligence files posed to the American public.

However, Agent John Vincent, the AUSAs, and I understood what closing VB meant. It meant that FBI management negligently failed the American people and their law enforcement partners worldwide by refusing to investigate and neutralize Middle East international terrorism activities and terrorism funding from within the United States and overseas. The FBI now had little to no chance of preventing future terrorist attacks and saving innocent lives in America and around the world.

Adding insult to injury, my supervisor broke the news in September 2000 that I had to be in McChesney's office the following week to receive my tenth FBI anniversary pin and certificate.

"You cannot be serious. There is no way in hell I am ever going to shake her hand and have a picture taken with her after what she has done to me and Vulgar Betrayal," I told him.

"Bob, you must go. She expects every agent to participate in this ceremony," he said.

"I can assure you I will not attend her ceremony. You are nuts if you think I will take a friendly photo with the person responsible for killing my Vulgar Betrayal investigation," I restated.

"Bob, please do it for me. She will not be happy if you do not show up," he said.

"I don't care how she feels about it," I said.

"Bob, I know how you feel, but she will be mad at me if you do not attend. Since I am your supervisor, she will hold your failure to attend against me," he pleaded.

"I will think about it. Give me a few days," I said.

A few days later, I told him I would attend the ceremony only because he was fair and supportive of my situation. I reluctantly went to her office the following day to receive my ten-year pin and certificate. It was unpleasant taking a photograph with her, but I sucked it up and took the photo with a smile, as my supervisor had asked me to do.

I accept my 10-year gold pin and certificate from SAC McChesney, September 2000.

CHAPTER 34

THE DOUBLE STANDARD OF FBI MANAGEMENT

"It's unbelievable. This was perhaps the bureau's most important case ever, with tons of evidence plus a confessed killer—and they screw it up! They have become the gang that can't shoot straight. And, worse yet, the McVeigh case isn't their only bungle. It's just the latest."[247]

— Bill Press, CNN's *Crossfire*, and *The Spin Room*

In May 2001, as I was nearing the completion of this manuscript, I was concerned others would not believe my story. Specifically, I was concerned others would not believe my allegations regarding FBI management's lack of support for the Vulgar Betrayal international terrorism investigation and their double standard of discipline for street agents.

I expressed my concerns to Agent Vincent during the FBI Chicago All Agents Conference. After thinking about my problem, John said, "I have an idea. I know how you can address your concerns about others not believing how screwed up FBI management is now. But you will not like it."

"John, please tell me it has nothing to do with writing another chapter in the manuscript," I said.

"Bob, you can bring the FBI's most embarrassing mistakes to light in your book by exposing only the past eighteen months of FBI management's serious mistakes. Tell the readers about these embarrassing mistakes and the criminal conduct of FBI management. This will give your readers an insight into the genuine problem of the FBI overall, not only within international terrorism investigations. Bob, you can do this with one more chapter," said John.

I was thinking about his suggestion when he added, "Bob, all the material you need is already in the public domain. You can write another chapter in no time."

"John, the thought of writing another chapter just makes me sick. However, you have always given me great advice, and as much as I do not want to do it, I know you are right. I will write another chapter regarding FBI management's recent unforgivable and deadly screwups. For readers to understand how messed up the management of the FBI is at this time, I will only cover issues that have occurred during the past eighteen months," I said.

After publicly researching FBI management's embarrassing and negligent conduct, I found many examples I could use in a new chapter. I called John and thanked him for the idea. Although I knew a little about some of the issues, I learned much more about FBI management's efforts to protect one another, even if it meant throwing hard-working FBI street agents under the bus to cover their own wrongful and sometimes criminal actions.

The Double Standard of FBI Management

"John, some of these FBI issues will help reinforce issues I have already written about. Such as the lack of a modern computer system and FBI managers getting away with serious misconduct while throwing street-level agents under the bus," I stated.

This chapter addresses, through public source documents, seven critical incidents that caused the FBI great embarrassment over the twenty months from January 2000 through August 2001. The essential mistakes of many high-profile cases caused the US Congress to recommend conducting several investigations and overhauling the FBI.

This chapter will provide insight into how FBI management is above the law. How can they be above the law? It is easy when you are in the higher ranks of the "premier law enforcement agency in the world." Many FBI managers, such as ASACs, SACs, Deputy Assistant Directors (DADs), and Assistant Directors (ADs), believe they do not need to answer anyone outside the FBI. They can get away with anything they want, including fraud, lying, destroying evidence, obstruction of justice, and other criminal violations.

In theory, FBI managers are accountable to the US Congress. However, most of the time, they ignore Congress's requests for information by claiming the subject inquired about is under an active FBI investigation. They claim to be prohibited from discussing ongoing investigations, especially when the subject has anything to do with their disciplinary process, which favors managers over support employees and street agents.

In addition, there is no one outside the FBI to investigate the abuse of the OPR process by management. They use the OPR to retaliate against hard-working street agents and whistleblowers. They also protect their managers from facing any punishments for their wrongful conduct and illegal activities, which usually result in the termination of a street agent.

Seven embarrassing incidents occurred within the FBI during 2000 and 2001, which, when taken individually, would be troubling for the FBI. However, the accumulation of so many serious incidents was so tumultuous for the FBI that they caught the eye of Congress and the rest of America.

The seven FBI critical mistakes include:

1. The Wen Ho Lee "embarrassment."
2. The act of treason against the United States by twenty-seven-year-veteran FBIHQ Supervisor Robert P. Hanssen.
3. The FBI failed to provide over 3,000 documents to the Oklahoma City Bomber defense team of Timothy McVeigh. The FBI's gross incompetence led to the delay of McVeigh's scheduled execution in 2001.
4. The Ruby Ridge matter revealed how FBI management cleared FBI managers of wrongdoing while throwing street-level agents under the bus.
5. FBI executive managers used a sham FBI management conference to finance FBI managers throughout the US to attend the retirement dinner of an FBI executive in Washington, DC, at taxpayer expense. Many of these FBI managers lied during the OPR investigation. Lying during an OPR interview would cause a street agent's firing. Not one of these lying managers was fired.
6. News about the missing 459 FBI weapons and 184 FBI laptop computers, some with highly classified information.
7. Last, news concerning the FBI's ancient and neglected computer system.

The Double Standard of FBI Management

As these embarrassing FBI incidents arose, friends, coworkers, and family members questioned why I was not coming forward with my story. I said I would not allow myself to be rushed into exposing my situation because the American people were now being exposed to the many "embarrassments" of the FBI. My priority remained unchanged: legally warn members of the US Congress, with Schippers' help, about the FBI's gross protection of Middle Eastern terrorism organizations and terrorists living in America over protecting the American public.

The following are summaries of the seven FBI embarrassments listed above.

1. The Wen Ho Lee Case

Wen Ho Lee was a sixty-year-old naturalized US citizen who immigrated to the US from Taiwan. Lee worked at the Los Alamos National Laboratory in Santa Fe, New Mexico, "where he worked in the top secret X Division designing the nation's nuclear arsenal."[248]

In 1993, Wen Ho Lee wrote letters to "eight nations, apparently seeking employment [with] Australia, France, Germany, Hong Kong, Singapore, Switzerland, Taiwan and China."[249] According to papers filed by the US government, he sent the letters around the same time "when Lee had begun to download nuclear secrets from the Los Alamos computers."[250]

Seven years later, on December 10, 1999, the FBI arrested him and placed him in solitary confinement in a detention center near Santa Fe. The FBI charged him with "59 counts of downloading volumes of nuclear weapons design and testing simulation data from secure computers to a non-secure computer and tapes."[251] The FBI could not locate seven computer tapes on which he had downloaded the classified information. "Lee was arrested when Congress expressed fear of the Chinese spies in US nuclear labs."[252] US officials (FBI & DOJ) claimed he was a severe national security threat. He was facing life in prison if convicted on all fifty-nine counts.

US District Judge James Parker denied Lee's bond twice since the government insisted he was a national security threat. In August 2000, after Lee was held for nine months in solitary confinement, Judge Parker released him on a $1 million bond with stringent terms, including house arrest. Parker's "reversal came after a senior FBI agent admitted he had given inaccurate or misleading testimony about Lee's alleged deceptions. Under Judge Parker's bond proposal, Lee would have remained under house arrest until his November 6 trial date, wear an electronic monitor, have his mail and phone calls monitored, and [leave] his home only to go to court or the Los Alamos lab with his attorney."[253] Anticipating his imminent release, "about 30 FBI agents and support personnel searched for more than 12 hours at Lee's home, looking for any sensitive scientific materials."[254]

Simultaneously, the government appealed Judge Parker's bail-release order to the Tenth US Circuit Court of Appeals. "The appeals court agreed not to release Lee until it reviews whether the Asian American scientist should be allowed to go home until his trial in November."[255] In affidavits unsealed (the day before), "two former government counterintelligence chiefs said they believe Lee was targeted because he is an Asian American. The same day, leaders of three prestigious scientific organizations objected to the government's treatment of Lee."[256]

A few days later, as their case fell apart, the US government dropped fifty-eight of the fifty-nine counts and asked Lee to plead guilty to a single count of mishandling classified information. As

The Double Standard of FBI Management

part of the plea deal, he agreed to help the FBI account for seven computer tapes on which he had admitted to downloading sensitive materials. Although he claimed to have destroyed the tapes, prosecutors said they could not prove that he destroyed the tapes. The plea deal brought an abrupt end to what was initially touted by the FBI as a significant case of Chinese nuclear espionage.

On September 13, 2000, to the surprise of many, "US District Court Judge James Parker accepted a plea bargain that called for Lee to be sentenced to the nine months he had already served while awaiting trial. The judge told Lee that he 'deserved to be punished' but that he had [already] been 'punished harshly.' Parker went on to criticize federal prosecutors and investigators for holding Lee in solitary confinement, saying their actions had 'caused embarrassment.'"[257] The government never charged Lee with espionage. "In fact, Lee was not only set free but also received an apology from a federal judge [Parker] for having spent nine months in custody."[258]

President Clinton found the Department of Justice's turnaround in the case troubling and expressed concern that Lee "was kept in a county jail with no bail for nine months because federal prosecutors claimed he was a threat to national security."[259] He stated, "The whole thing was quite troubling to me, and I think it is very difficult to reconcile the two positions that one day he is a terrible risk to the national security, and the next day they're making a plea agreement for an offense far more modest than what had been alleged."[260] In addition, "Clinton said he 'always had reservations' about the claims mounted by federal prosecutors to deny Lee bail. 'We ought not to keep people in jail without bail unless there's some real profound reason,' It means he spent a lot of time in prison that any ordinary American wouldn't have, and that bothers me."[261]

The following day, White House officials announced they would launch a review of the government's action regarding the Lee case. Administration officials "made clear the initial White House view is that most of the blame rests with the FBI."[262]

Likewise, the Justice Department announced it would investigate the matter. Attorney General Janet Reno said in a written statement, "Dedicated lawyers and investigators worked very hard on this case. I want to be as open as possible about the work they did, as well as about the decisions I made."[263]

Senators Arlen Specter, R-Pennsylvania; Charles Grassley, R-Iowa; and Robert Torricelli, D-New Jersey, requested the General Accounting Office (GAO), the investigative arm of Congress, investigate the Lee case. On June 28, 2001, "GAO officially unveiled its finding that Assistant FBI Director Neil Gallagher gave 'inaccurate and misleading' information to a Senate committee probing the government's handling of allegations against nuclear physicist Wen Ho Lee."[264]

2. Espionage Activity of FBIHQ Supervisor Robert Hanssen

In December 1996, authorities arrested FBI Agent Earl Pitts for spying for Moscow. Pitts had received "over $200,000 from Moscow between 1987 and 1992 while assigned to the FBI's Quantico, Virginia, training facility. He later agreed to a plea bargain."[265] As part of a plea agreement, the FBI debriefed Pitts for seventy hours to learn what information he had supplied to Moscow and if anyone else within the FBI was involved.

When asked if he suspected anyone else within the FBI of committing espionage, Earl Pitts "told FBI interrogators that (Robert) Hanssen may have been involved in suspicious activity."[266] Specifically, "Pitts recalled an incident involving an agent who was angry because Hanssen had broken into her computer. Pitts thought the incident was odd because 'ordinarily that kind of incident would have been investigated.'"[267] Nina Ginsberg, Pitts's attorney, was present during the interrogation. Ginsberg said Pitts "told the FBI in 1997 he thought there was another mole within the FBI because he felt his Russian handlers knew too much inside information about the bureau. 'He didn't feel that they [Pitts's Russian handlers] were taking full advantage of what he might have been able to do,' Ginsberg said."[268] Regarding the seventy hours of Pitts's debriefing, Ginsberg said, "Hanssen was the only person Pitts named as suspicious."[269] Hanssen "held the highest security clearance and was fully aware of US intelligence operations."[270] Pitts only received a twenty-seven-year sentence for committing espionage against the United States thanks to his cooperation.

On February 18, 2001, almost four years after Pitts named Robert Hanssen by name, the FBI arrested Agent Robert Hanssen, a twenty-seven-year FBI veteran, for providing classified information to Russia. The arrest of Hanssen happened "as he tried to leave a package of classified documents at a secret drop-off location in a park near his Vienna, VA, home."[271] Following his arrest, "The FBI said it had been watching Hanssen, in his mid-50s and a father of six, for four months after obtaining documents from the Russian KGB indicating he was spying."[272]

Earl Pitts had identified Hanssen as another possible FBI spy "more than three years before the FBI said it began to focus on Hanssen as a spy in late 2000."[273] About Pitts mentioning of Hanssen's name in 1997, "FBI (spokesperson) John Collingwood said in a statement, 'Pitts described as unusual' a computer hacking incident involving Hanssen. Pitts did not identify Hanssen as a spy."[274]

Adding to the gravity of the matter, Hanssen's brother-in-law, a Chicago FBI agent, alerted the FBI twice that he had reason to believe Hanssen was operating as a Russian spy. The FBI ignored his suspicions. They would have promptly investigated any FBI street agent if someone had made similar allegations against him/her. However, since Hanssen was a high-ranking FBI manager, FBIHQ management ignored Earl Pitts's and Hanssen's brother-in-law's two reported suspicions.

Common sense dictates that the "premier law enforcement agency of the world" would at least investigate the possibility that Hanssen was a spy. They should have given him a polygraph test to clear questions regarding the computer hacking incident. Yet, they did nothing with the information.

Why did they not look into Hanssen as a spy? Everyone within the FBI knows you are untouchable once you become a high-ranking FBI manager. Managers cover for one another and protect each other from internal investigations. Rarely do they face disciplinary action if an OPR investigation finds them guilty of wrongdoing. High-ranking managers can do whatever they want and get away with it since they are not accountable to anyone outside the FBI.

Hanssen identified Russian spies to Russia. He had "spent the past twenty-five years [working] in counter-terrorism operations intended to catch spies, most recently at the US State Department where his job was to help ferret out Russian spies."[275] Hanssen was the most highly placed agent of the three FBI agents who have faced spy charges. Ron Kessler, the author of *A History of the FBI,* stated, "The other two previous FBI agents who've been charged with espionage just don't compare in terms of the access that this person [Hanssen] had."[276] "Hanssen's high-security clearance and sensitive job assignments gave

The Double Standard of FBI Management

him access to details of US security operations, including methods the United States used to conduct electronic surveillance."[277]

An FBI 110-page affidavit filed with a federal court accused "Hanssen of dropping off intelligence information for the Russians on more than 20 occasions. The material included more than two dozen computer diskettes and thousands of pages of US documents."[278] Hanssen "was indicted by a federal grand jury on May 16 [2001] on charges of selling US intelligence secrets to the Soviet Union and Russia beginning in October 1985. Fourteen of the 21 counts carry the death penalty. The indictment said Mr. Hanssen betrayed his country for over 15 years and knowingly caused grave injury to the security of the United States."[279]

The indictment said Hanssen "conspired with agents from the Soviet KGB and its successor intelligence agency, the SVR, to deliver to Moscow 'information relating to the national defense of the United States.'"[280] Hanssen "is accused of giving his Russian handlers classified information concerning satellites, early warning systems, means of defense or retaliation against large-scale attacks, communications intelligence, and major elements of defense strategy."[281]

Director Freeh said, "Hanssen never identified himself to his Russian handlers and showed no outward signs that he was receiving large amounts of money. His conversations with them were done purely by an anonymous channel, so if there was a compromise on their side, no one could identify him by name, by where he worked or by what he looked like. In exchange for US secrets, Hanssen is accused of receiving about $600,000 in cash and valuables such as diamonds, and another $800,000 was placed in escrow in another country for him."[282]

Director Freeh said Hanssen was trusted with some of this country's most sensitive information, but he betrayed that trust by passing volumes of highly classified information to Moscow. When asked if Hanssen's betrayal was one of the worst cases of espionage encountered by the FBI, Freeh said, "I would clearly characterize it in that fashion."[283] "Freeh said the losses that Hanssen inflicted were 'exceptionally grave.'"[284]

Specifically, some of the damage caused by Hanssen's espionage included his providing Russia with "upgraded versions of software to his Russian handlers, who then sold it for $2 million to [Osama] bin Laden."[285] The software allows Osama bin Laden "to monitor US efforts to track him down. The sophisticated software gives bin Laden access to databases on specific targets of his choosing and the ability to monitor electronic banking transactions, easing money laundering operations for him or others."[286]

"Bin Laden, now believed to be in Afghanistan, is a self-proclaimed international terrorist being sought in the bombing of two US embassies in Africa that killed 224, including 12 Americans. A federal grand jury in New York indicted the 41-year-old fugitive millionaire in November [2000] in the simultaneous explosions on August 7 [1998] at the US Embassies in Nairobi, Kenya, and Dar es Salaam, Tanzania. US authorities believe he directed the attacks as part of a campaign aimed at changing US foreign policy by killing US civilians and military personnel worldwide."[287]

Hanssen also provided his Russian handlers with "a technical manual on the US intelligence community's secure network for online access to intelligence databases."[288]

On October 1, 1985, he gave the names of three active KGB agents who were working for the United States as double agents to his Russian handlers. Moscow then executed two of these three KGB agents after they returned to Russia.

US officials believe he revealed the existence of a tunnel built under the Russian embassy. The tunnel "was built by American intelligence services and packed with millions of dollars' worth of sophisticated equipment."[289] Within days of Hanssen's arrest, the Russian Foreign Ministry "summoned the US Embassy in Moscow for an official explanation on the tunnel, said to have been jointly operated by the FBI and the National Security Agency."[290]

Following Hanssen's arrest, Attorney General John Ashcroft said his arrest was "a difficult day for the FBI. It is extremely difficult because the person who was investigated was one of our own. Individuals who commit treasonous acts against the United States will be held fully accountable. I will devote whatever resources are necessary within the department to ensure that justice is done in this case and any other case like it."[291]

President George W. Bush called Hanssen's betrayals extremely serious and deeply disturbing. He said, "It was a difficult day for those who love our country. To anyone who would betray its trust, I warn you, we'll find you and we'll bring you to justice."[292]

On February 19, 2001, speaking before the Senate Judiciary Committee, Director Freeh said, "As an agency responsible for protecting our national security, this is a difficult day for the FBI. It is especially difficult because the person who was investigated, arrested, and charged is one of our own. The FBI has done an exemplary job of investigating this sensitive matter and ending this breach of our national security."[293]

A committee member asked Freeh, "In all due respect, how can you call this a counterintelligence success when you had a spy working inside the FBI for over 15 years without being detected? Why wasn't he detected earlier? And how did he manage to pass, presumably, numerous polygraph examinations for a person in those positions?"[294]

Freeh said, "The reason I call it a success is that, as an operation and as an investigation, it is an immense success. To conduct this investigation securely, clandestinely, without any leaks, and to do it to where we could catch, red-handed, an experienced intelligence officer laying down classified documents for his handlers, in the business of counterintelligence I think by any expert, would be judged a huge success."[295]

Another senator asked, "Can you confirm that he did in fact take polygraph tests?"

Freeh said, "I don't want to comment on that."[296]

Months after Hanssen's arrest, Plato Cacheris, Hanssen's attorney, worked to secure a plea agreement that would prevent his client from receiving the death penalty. Although the FBI claimed Hanssen began spying in 1985, Cacheris said Hanssen's "activities commenced in '79 to '81 and that period the government knew nothing about it, and they will learn about that."[297]

The July 2001 plea agreement terms called for Hanssen to plead guilty to espionage and conspiracy and cooperate with the FBI and CIA. His wife would receive partial benefits provided she cooperated with the investigation. The death penalty would be taken off the table, and he would serve a life sentence with no chance of parole. After reaching the plea agreement, Cacheris said, "The death penalty is no longer an option in this case, and the government receives, as a result, the full debriefings from Mr. Hanssen as to the breadth of his activities with the Soviet Union."[298]

"Deputy US Attorney General Larry Thompson said that accepting a plea deal was difficult, given the gravity of Hanssen's betrayal. We determined that the interest of the United States would be best served by an agreement requiring Hanssen to tell what he knows about his activities."[299]

The Double Standard of FBI Management

On July 7, 2001, Hanssen appeared in US District Court in Alexandria, Virginia, dressed in a green prison jumpsuit with "prisoner" stamped on the back. He pleaded guilty to fifteen counts of espionage and conspiracy as called for in the plea agreement. During his court appearance, "he held his hands behind his back, fidgeting as he answered questions from US District Judge Claude Hilton. At one point during the proceedings, Hanssen turned around and looked FBI agents squarely in the eye and smiled."[300]

Congressional leaders became concerned about the many "mounting problems at the FBI and what they call a growing lack of public confidence in the bureau. They have issued a bipartisan call for renewed scrutiny of the federal law enforcement agency. Both Republicans and Democrats are suggesting outside commissioners and new internal watchdogs to oversee the beleaguered agency."[301]

Senator Patrick J. Leahy from Vermont, the chairperson of the Senate Judiciary Committee, was concerned about internal security secrets being turned over to US enemies. "In the wake of reports that classified software made its way to terrorist Osama bin Laden, [Leahy] said the FBI internal security safeguards will be a major focus of pending committee hearings."[302] Leahy stated, "'We have spent millions of dollars on computer security for federal agencies, and much of it goes to the FBI. Keeping secrets from outside enemies of this country is only as good as our internal security. If the FBI is doing a poor job on internal security, all the money in the world will not effectively keep outsiders from breaching our most critical and secure systems,' he said, adding that the committee would hold as yet unscheduled oversight hearings on the FBI internal security safeguards."[303] He also stated, "Unfortunately, the image of the FBI in the minds of too many Americans is that this agency has become unmanageable, unaccountable and unreliable."[304]

US Representative James Sensenbrenner from Wisconsin, the chairperson of the House Judiciary Committee, announced he "wants a deputy Inspector General named to oversee only the FBI. He said he is worried the bureau has lost its way. Like a slugger who has lost his swing, I think it is time for this new administration to focus on fundamentals. If the department can't get the basics right, the American people will inevitably lose confidence in it—one of our most trusted institutions."[305]

3. The Missing 3,000+ Oklahoma City Bombing Documents

On April 19, 1995, Timothy McVeigh, a decorated Gulf War Army veteran, bombed the Alfred P. Murrah Federal Building in Oklahoma City, Oklahoma, killing 168, which included nineteen children. Before his trial in 1997, the US government was bound to provide his defense attorneys with copies of all FBI documents and a list of all evidence the FBI had compiled against him. This information was to be reviewed by the defense attorneys to decide if there was any evidence that may help prove his innocence.

In 1997, the court found McVeigh guilty of the bombing and murders and imposed a death sentence by lethal injection. He would become the first person to be executed by the federal government since 1963. He later dropped his right to appeal the verdict and death sentence, opting to die rather than remain in prison for the rest of his life.

Almost four years later, in January 2001, five months before his scheduled execution, "At least one FBI field office suspected as early as January that some [FBI] documents in the Timothy McVeigh case had not been entered into the agency's database system."[306] The

The Double Standard of FBI Management

mistake was discovered when "[an FBI] archivist began compiling information about the convicted mass murderer during December (2000). As early as March (2001), a cross-check of paper documents with the (FBI) central database confirmed the field office's January suspicions and showed that some documents had never been entered into the database."[307] The FBI realized they had never turned over many of the FBI documents to the US attorneys or McVeigh's defense team of attorneys.

During early May 2001, the FBI admitted, "It failed to turn over more than 3,000 documents to McVeigh's attorneys, saying they were not discovered until officials found hard copies of the records to be delivered to [an] archivist."[308] The 3,000 pages of investigatory documents included interview reports, photographs, letters, and tapes. This also included form FD-302 "documents that give the essence of interviews the FBI agents conducted following the Oklahoma City bombing."[309] "Agents in the FBI Oklahoma City field office did not realize the magnitude of the oversight and waited until all the information had been gathered before alerting superiors at FBI headquarters."[310] According to FBI reports, Director Freeh was not told about the potential problem until early May.

On May 9, 2001, Sean Connelly, Special Attorney to the US Attorney General, sent the following letter to McVeigh's attorneys and the federal judge who presided over the 1997 trial:

Dear Counsel,

As I told each of you in separate telephone conversations yesterday, the FBI has discovered additional materials generated by its field divisions outside Oklahoma City in connection with the OKBOMB investigation. I first learned of the existence of these materials yesterday and received them today after they were flown from Oklahoma City to Denver on an FBI plane. FBI Special Agent in Charge (SAC) Danny Defenbaugh, who headed the OKBOMB investigation and currently heads the FBI's Dallas field division, brought the documents to my attention. FBI Director Louis Freeh and Agent Defenbaugh had requested on numerous occasions prior to trial that each field division and legal attaché forward all OKBOMB-related materials to the Oklahoma City division and had received assurance that all such materials had been forwarded. The belated discovery of additional such materials came after an FBI archivist requested that all OKBOMB-related materials be sent to the Oklahoma City field office for archiving.

The materials consist of FBI reports of investigation ("302s" and "inserts") and physical evidence, such as photographs, written correspondence, and tapes (1As, 1Bs and 1Cs). All reports, and all physical evidence capable of being photocopied, are being delivered to you. The physical evidence not capable of being photocopied is identified in the photocopied materials. For control, we have Bates-stamped all the materials being produced from each field division. For example, the documents from the Albany field division are Bates-stamped numbered 1-153; the documents from the Albuquerque field division are Bates-stamped numbered 1-102, etc.

We do not believe anything being produced is Brady material bearing on the federal convictions or sentences of Timothy McVeigh or Terry Nicholls. Similarly, we do not believe anything in the materials makes even prima facie showing of either man's actual innocence. Many of the materials are similar to the previously litigated leads sheets, in that they involve interviews and information regarding persons whom at one time were thought to resemble the UNSUB sketches. Nonetheless, many of the materials—in particular, the FBI 302s and inserts—should have been produced under the reciprocal discovery agreement. We are producing the materials now so you can make your own determinations. Please contact me if you have questions."[311]

Within days of the FBI's announcement of the error, the Senate Judiciary Committee called SAC Danny Defenbaugh to explain what happened. Defenbaugh was "the lead investigator of the Oklahoma City bombing case, was in charge of collecting investigative documents, [and] said the FBI had an inkling that something was amiss as early as January (2001)."[312] Congress wanted to know why the FBI waited until just a week before McVeigh's execution to admit it had failed to turn over the 3,000 pages.

During further questioning by the committee, "Defenbaugh told lawmakers that archivists discovered a single document that had not been turned over to McVeigh's attorneys as required. By early February, more items that had not been turned over began to arrive. Over the next several weeks, many other items were discovered."[313] When committee members asked Defenbaugh why he waited until May to notify FBI headquarters, "[SAC] Defenbaugh said he wanted to be completely sure what the problem was and how bad it was. [SAC] Defenbaugh took offense at the question, according to a source familiar with the conversation. He was affronted."[314]

"Danny Defenbaugh, now in charge of the bureau's Dallas office, released a statement outlining how the undisclosed documents were uncovered."[315] "Defenbaugh failed to explain why the documents were missing from the databases. [Attorney General] Ashcroft has ordered the Justice Department's Inspector General to look into why the material was not disclosed [to the defense team ahead of McVeigh's 1997 trial]."[316]

Bill Press on CNN's *Crossfire* said, "It's unbelievable, this was perhaps the bureau's most important case ever, with tons of evidence plus a confessed killer and they screw it up! They have become the gang that can't shoot straight. And, worse yet, the McVeigh case is not their only bungle. It is just the latest."[317]

On May 16, 2001, Director Freeh testified before the House appropriations committee. He said the FBI committed a serious error on the agency's failure to release the over 3,000 pages.

Freeh stated, "Regardless of how extraneous these documents are, if they were covered by the discovery agreement, they should have been located and released during discovery. As director, I have taken full responsibility. The buck does stop with me. The FBI committed a serious error by not ensuring that every piece of information was properly accounted for and, where appropriate, provided to the prosecutors so they could fulfill their discovery obligations. The underlying case and his [McVeigh's] guilt remain unchallenged. Most offices of the FBI failed to locate the documents and items in question, misinterpreted their instructions and likely produced only those that would be disclosed under normal discovery, or sent the documents only to have them unaccounted for at the other end. Any of these cases is unacceptable."[318]

Regarding the cause of the serious error by the FBI, Freeh stated, "We will have to wait for the Inspector General [Glenn Fine] to complete his investigation before we can know what actually happened. Nothing in the documents raises any doubt about the guilt of McVeigh or Mr. [Terry] Nichols."[319] When the committee inquired about the old and troublesome FBI computer system as a cause for the "serious

The Double Standard of FBI Management

error," Freeh told the committee, "The mishandling of the Oklahoma case documents was a management problem and not a problem with the FBI computer system."[320]

Following the news of the FBI's serious errors on the 3,000 pages and the delay of McVeigh's execution, many involved in the Oklahoma City bombing [case] issued statements regarding the FBI's latest blunder and appeal by McVeigh. The McVeigh case prosecutor, Patrick Ryan, "called failing to turn over the documents 'embarrassing' and 'totally unacceptable.' 'I think the government ought to go along with it,' he said, referring to the granting of more time for the defense to review the documents. He said he thought the government should be the one to ask for a stay [of McVeigh's execution]."[321]

A Justice Department spokeswoman said, "While the department is confident the documents do not in any way create any reasonable doubt about McVeigh's guilt and do not contradict his repeated confessions of guilt, the department is concerned that McVeigh's attorneys could not review them at the appropriate time."[322]

She then said, "Once the government was made aware of the documents, they were turned over to the defense. If the defense disagrees, they will contact us."[323]

Nathan Chambers, McVeigh's lead attorney, said, "This is the FBI's most important investigation, ever, and they hold themselves out as being the premier law enforcement agency in the world. If they are incapable of handling their most important investigation in a matter that instills confidence, we all need to be concerned."[324] He further stated, "The Department of Justice faced a public relations nightmare, and it's through their own doing that they are in this circumstance. They are trying to spin it in a way that makes them look like the good guys."[325]

Oklahoma Governor Frank Keating, a former FBI agent and US Attorney, blasted the FBI's failure when he "called failing to disclose documents an 'unforgivable screw up.'"[326]

"If there is information that the agents knew [was] supposed to be present at trial in Denver, [and was] not presented in trial at Denver in violation of the discovery order, severe disciplinary action needs to be taken against those people,"[327] said Governor Keating.

On May 11, 2001, US Attorney General John Ashcroft "ordered a one-month postponement of the execution of Oklahoma City bomber Timothy McVeigh that was scheduled by lethal injection for Wednesday, May 16, at the US Penitentiary in Terre Haute, Indiana. Ashcroft set the new execution date as June 11, [2001]."[328]

"There's not much [McVeigh] can accomplish, because unfortunately, against his lawyer's advice, he went public and said, 'I did it.' Once he says that, then it's kind of hard for him to come back and say, 'Well, these documents may exonerate me,' because he's pulled the rug out from under that argument. Jones has long contended McVeigh is part of a larger conspiracy and stated his guilt to protect others. 'Not everybody is locked up,' he told CNN. 'There are still others out there,' Jones said. The document glitch elated McVeigh. 'There is egg on the face of the FBI this morning,' said Jones."[329]

Kristi McCarthy, the daughter of a bombing victim, said, "Having this man die is not going to bring back my father. My mother is a widow, and you can't replace that. You can't fill that kind of void in your life and extending this more is, it just adds to the pain, it adds to fury."[330]

Congressional leaders again called for an investigation of the FBI. Wisconsin Representative Sensenbrenner threatened "To hold public hearings to probe what he describes as serious questions on the bureau's ability to store and retrieve sensitive information."[331]

"I am troubled by the revelation that documents pertinent to the discovery agreement between the government and Timothy McVeigh's attorneys were not produced prior to trial. This raises serious questions about the ability of the FBI to comply with other discovery procedures."[332]

New York Senator Charles Schumer, "the ranking Democrat on the Senate Judiciary subcommittee with oversight of the FBI, said he would ask Mr. Bush for a special commission to examine the FBI from top to bottom. He cited a number of problems at the FBI, including the arrest of Agent Robert P. Hanssen, who is charged with selling national secrets to Moscow, and a botched investigation last year [2000] of former nuclear scientist Wen Ho Lee."[333] "We've had mistake after mistake and mistake,"[334] he said.

Iowa Senator Charles E. Grassley criticized the FBI and Director Freeh. Grassley said, "I think there is a management culture here that is at fault. I call it the cowboy culture. It is a culture that puts image—public relations and headlines—ahead of the fundamentals. I don't think he [Freeh] has been willing to challenge the management culture."[335]

Glenn A. Fine, the DOJ Inspector General (IG) responsible for investigating the FBI's failures, which led to the one-month delay in McVeigh's execution, recommended disciplinary action against four FBI managers for what he called a "significant neglect of their duties." He also recommended disciplinary action against Danny Defenbaugh for withholding FBI documents during McVeigh's trial.

Two weeks after the IG report was issued, FBI Director Robert Mueller ordered Defenbaugh to his FBIHQ office to discuss his future with the FBI. "The FBI Director said, during a ten-minute meeting, that he wanted Agent Defenbaugh to leave his Dallas post for an administrative job in the bureau's Washington training division."³³⁶ Rather than take the demotion, Defenbaugh said he told Mueller that he would retire rather than lose the Dallas post and move across the country."³³⁷ "He [Director Mueller] agreed to take no disciplinary action if I chose to retire, said Agent Defenbaugh."³³⁸ Defenbaugh retired on April 30, 2002.

Defenbaugh was the person who permitted Gamal Abdel-Hafiz to decline the secret recordings of the two terrorism targets of the Tampa division (1998) and Vulgar Betrayal (1999). These terrorism targets reached out to Abdel-Hafiz to discuss the Tampa and Chicago FBI investigations. The VB investigators suspected that the terrorism target of VB had possible financial links to Osama bin Laden's bombing of the two US embassies in Africa in 1998.

Rather than instructing Abdel-Hafiz to conduct the secret recording of the VB target, Defenbaugh instructed Abdel-Hafiz to file an EEO complaint against me in 1999. In the future, my attorneys receive documentation proving Defenbaugh told Abdel-Hafiz that he (Defenbaugh) would file the EEO complaint against me if Abdel-Hafiz did not.

4. Ruby Ridge

On August 21, 1992, US marshals attempted to arrest white separatist Randy Weaver at his log cabin in Ruby Ridge, Idaho, for failing to make an ordered court appearance on gun-related charges. During the arrest attempt, a gunfight ensued, killing Deputy US Marshal William Degan and Weaver's fourteen-year-old son, Sammy.

The FBI was called in to take charge of the matter. The FBI "activated its Hostage Rescue Team (HRT), a tactical unit of agents trained in handling high-risk situations."³³⁹ In August 1992, the

The Double Standard of FBI Management

FBI's "Use of Deadly Force Policy," (Rules of Engagement) stated, "Agents are not to use deadly force against any person, except as necessary in self-defense or the defense of another, when they have reason to believe that they or another are in danger of death or grievous bodily harm."

"The FBI Assistant Director (AD) for the Criminal Investigative Division, Larry Potts, and his deputy Danny Coulson discussed the need for an operations plan containing [new] rules of engagement that would provide guidance for the HRT's actions. The (new) rules of engagement were drafted, which provided that if any adult male is observed with a weapon, deadly force 'can and should be deployed' if the shot could be taken without endangering any children."[340]

Potts and Coulson's operations plan violated the existing FBI policy. Authorizing an FBI agent to shoot and kill any adult male who was simply holding a weapon is unconscionable and grossly negligent.

"On August 16, 1992, the HRT (FBI Hostage Rescue Team) was deployed to the site and surrounded Weaver's cabin. When an HRT helicopter took off and flew near the cabin, Weaver, his sixteen-year-old daughter Saraha, and Kevin Harris came out of the cabin, all armed with rifles. HRT sharpshooter Lon Horiuchi fired one shot, wounding Weaver. Weaver, his daughter, and Harris began running back to the cabin." Under the FBI's policy, since all three were retreating to the cabin, there was no reason to believe the agents, or anyone else, were in any danger of death or grievous bodily harm.

However, the new rules of engagement set up by Potts and his deputy Coulson were relied upon by FBI sniper Horiuchi, who "fired a second shot that penetrated the open door of the cabin. This second shot killed Weaver's wife, Vickie [Vicki] Weaver, who was behind the door (holding their 10-month-old daughter) and seriously wounded

Harris."³⁴¹ Weaver and Harris surrendered 10 days later. Weaver served 16 months in prison on weapons charges.³⁴²

FBIHQ tasked Michael Kahoe, Chief of the Violent Crimes and Major Offenders Section, to lead an investigation and prepare an internal "after-action critique" of the FBI's actions at Ruby Ridge. Kahoe organized a Ruby Ridge conference at FBIHQ in November 1992, during which he ordered a report be prepared regarding the FBI's conduct at Ruby Ridge.

The FBI's initial internal investigation in 1992 resulted in disciplinary action against some street-level agents. Potts, Coulson, and other FBI managers sloppily conducted this internal investigation to protect themselves and other senior FBI managers. An inquiry revealed that the investigators had not conducted "significant interviews" and had never investigated misconduct accusations by senior FBI managers. In addition, "'critical interviews' of agents assigned to a command post during the standoff were never conducted."³⁴³ "Two FBI agents believe that the bureau's disciplinary process [conducted by the OPR unit] has shielded top-level supervisors from sanctions for wrongdoing in the deadly 1992 shootout at Ruby Ridge, Idaho."³⁴⁴

Michael Kahoe and other high-ranking FBI managers did not believe anyone outside the FBI would ever see the FBI's internal report. To protect themselves, management ignored any allegations of wrongdoing while simultaneously throwing street agents under the bus to take the blame for management's wrongdoing.

There were rumors that high-ranking managers had created their deadly force policy for the Ruby Ridge situation. Following Agent Horiuchi's shooting, they tried to destroy any documents regarding their newly created deadly force policy. This led to distrust between FBI management and the street agents. Agents were upset because management was trying to cover up their unconstitutional new "use of deadly force policy" and throw Horiuchi under the bus to protect themselves.

On August 22, 1997, Horiuchi faced charges for using a firearm recklessly or negligently, resulting in the involuntary manslaughter of Vicki Weaver. On January 8, 1998, a judge ruled Horiuchi would stand trial for the death. In June 2001, almost nine years after the shooting, Prosecutor Brett Benton of Boundary County, Idaho, released a statement declaring that Horiuchi would not face trial in Idaho. He would retire from the FBI in October 2006 with the title of FBI Program Manager.

Fortunately, while federal prosecutors were preparing for Horiuchi's trial, they asked the FBI "for FBI materials pertaining to the [Ruby Ridge] incident. Kahoe and certain unnamed superiors at FBI headquarters resisted the request."[345] When the FBI forwarded all related documents to the federal prosecutors in Idaho, "Kahoe withheld the [internal] critique from the documents to be delivered to prosecutors . . . and ordered a subordinate FBI headquarters official to destroy all copies of the [internal] critique and to make it appear as if the critique never existed."[346] Kahoe "concealed and destroyed an FBI headquarters document that was sought by prosecutors in preparation for the murder trial pertaining to the Ruby Ridge incident."[347]

Kahoe and others concealed the destruction of the "critique document" from others. In 1995, when the first indications of Kahoe's cover-up surfaced, Freeh ordered the OPR unit to investigate the matter. This investigation led Freeh to suspend six top FBI officials, including Kahoe, who was placed on administrative leave with full pay. In addition, Freeh also suspended Potts, who had been "promoted to No. 2 at the FBI, even as he was destroying evidence in the case."[348]

Angry congressional hearings on Ruby Ridge as well as the 1993 siege at Waco, Texas, followed these suspensions.

In October 1996, the US Justice Department charged Kahoe with obstruction of justice for concealing the internal critique of the siege and then destroying the document. AUSA Robert Goldman, referencing an interview with Kahoe, said, "He [Kahoe] made a mockery of that interview. This was a joke to Mr. Kahoe."[349] Goldman noted, "Kahoe continued to lie about it [destroying the internal critique], in the face of a renewed inquiry in 1995 until under intense questioning and a polygraph test, 'he grudgingly half-admitted he did it.'"[350] "Besides destroying his own copies of the report, according to the factual proffer in the case, Kahoe went to his FBI Violent Crimes Unit Chief, Gale Evans, and told Evans to get rid of his [copy of the report]. Knowing that Evans often kept documents on floppy computer disks, Kahoe told Evans to get rid of the disk containing the critique as well."[351]

On October 10, 1997, before sentencing, "Kahoe told the court that no matter what the punishment, he had already suffered a greater one. 'I will always be known as the FBI agent who pleaded guilty to obstructing justice in the Ruby Ridge matter. I cannot undo that. And that is the worst punishment of all.'"[352] James Richmond, the defense lawyer for Kahoe, "argued that Kahoe's crime was not as serious as government prosecutors portrayed it, that no other evidence had been destroyed, and that Kahoe had simply been trying to protect what he wrongly perceived as the institutional best interest of the bureau."[353]

US District Judge Ricardo M. Urbina sentenced Kahoe to eighteen months in federal prison for destroying the internal critique of the deadly siege at Ruby Ridge, ordering Evans to wipe out all traces of the report, and then lying about it to two sets of investigators.

The Double Standard of FBI Management

The FBI management's handling of Ruby Ridge surfaced again in 2001 during a judiciary committee hearing. Current and former FBI agents pointed out the incident at Ruby Ridge and its aftermath was the perfect example of an FBI management culture that disciplined street agents while protecting FBI management from disciplinary action.

I realized many diligent, loyal, and dedicated street-level agents had to endure the same fate I have suffered because of FBI management retaliation. Unfortunately, they had no recourse to fight against this retaliation. FBI higher-ups could do anything since they did not answer to anyone outside the FBI. Someday, Congress will work to solve the FBI's management problems before things become worse. Fortunately, because I was aware of what FBI management would likely do to me, I hired Schippers in August 1999 to fight them in the future.

While the Senate Judiciary Committee was looking into the Ruby Ridge matter, they learned that, in 1999, "Justice Department officials who reviewed the FBI's flawed investigations of the 1992 siege at Ruby Ridge called for disciplinary action against FBI Director Freeh and three other FBI veterans, but the recommendations were secretly rejected in the closing days (January 3, 2001) of the Clinton administration. Stephen Colgate, an Assistant Attorney General who had the authority to issue final sanctions in the Ruby Ridge case, denied a recommendation to censure Freeh for condoning the shortcomings of the FBI investigations. Colgate, now in private practice, said he stood by his January 3 decision. He said a prominent FBI ethics official also favored no action."[354] In addition, "officials at Justice had urged that disciplinary actions Freeh took in January 1995 against three other unnamed agents involved in Ruby Ridge be rescinded, because the punishments were unwarranted. Nothing was done about the recommendations until Jan. 3, (2001) when Colgate decided no new discipline would be imposed."³⁵⁵

The FBI agents responsible for the 1999 investigation, which turned up the "flaws in the FBI's initial inquiries into the events at Ruby Ridge, denounced Assistant Attorney General Colgate's refusal to impose sanctions on top bureau officials as 'outrageous' and 'a whitewash.' The agents told the Senate Judiciary Committee, which learned last month (June 2001) of Colgate's decision, that they were especially dismayed because senior FBI officials had subjected them to threats and retaliation for conducting a thorough investigation."³⁵⁶ According to John Roberts, unit chief of the FBI's internal affairs investigations, one agent assigned to conduct the reinvestigation of Ruby Ridge "testified that he was threatened and faced retaliation for pursuing wrongdoing within the FBI."³⁵⁷

Roberts was the lead agent assigned to the 1999 investigation. He testified before the committee that his investigation "uncovered the fact that several senior FBI supervisors were involved in 'serious misconduct' during the incident, but nobody was ever charged or disciplined because of FBI cronyism."³⁵⁸ He "described the senior FBI supervisors involved in the standoff as 'popular individuals' within the bureau and suggested that some FBI managers sought to favor their friends and associates at the highest levels of the agency."³⁵⁹ He told the committee that he and former FBI Agent John Werner, a co-case agent of the 1999 investigation, "were told by senior FBI managers 'that we worked for the FBI, that our assignment to the Ruby Ridge investigation could have an impact on our careers and that being assigned to the investigation would not be good for us in the end.'"³⁶⁰

Roberts testified that because of his efforts to do the right thing, "his wife, an FBI support employee, was hounded from her job in

The Double Standard of FBI Management

the Boston division and his attempts to win a promotion have been rejected 14 times."[361]

During John Werner's testimony, he "spoke of a cadre of senior FBI managers, 'often referred to as The Club by street agents, who are motivated by self-preservation and self-interest at any cost.'"[362] Werner further testified he "was told senior FBI supervisors sought to protect 'certain peers' from discipline in the Idaho standoff by 'conducting a sloppy and incomplete investigation,' but noted that the same supervisors were 'most willing to hang lower tier FBI employees [street agents] out to dry.'"[363] "'Hiding behind a wall of arrogance, senior FBI managers are intolerant of any suggestion that their way is wrong,' he said. 'They use intimidation and retaliation against anyone who would be so impertinent as to challenge their interest.'"[364] He said "that some FBI supervisors are motivated by 'self-preservation and self-interest at any cost,' adding that Mr. Roberts's career at the FBI—which continues—had been 'seriously impaired' because of his pursuit of high-profile cases involving senior FBI personnel. 'These retaliatory practices send a chilling message to any other agent who might be charged with similar investigations.'"[365]

After reading what Roberts and Werner said above, I thought to myself, "If FBI management will do all this to these two honest agents to protect known negligent FBI managers, what are they going to do to prevent me from telling Congress and the American public about the negligent closing of Vulgar Betrayal in the future?" But, knowing what I knew, I would be derelict in my duty as an FBI agent not to do everything I could to protect innocent people from future terrorist attacks. Try as they might, they would not silence me. People had died because the ITU had negligently failed to fulfill its duty to prevent Middle Eastern terrorists from operating on US soil.

Unfortunately, because the FBI failed to neutralize known terrorists who were operating and financing terrorism from within the US, more innocent people in Israel and other countries will die.

Both Roberts and Werner "believe that the bureau's [OPR] disciplinary process has shielded top-level supervisors from sanctions for wrongdoing in the deadly 1992 shootout at Ruby Ridge, Idaho."[366] During the hearing, Roberts stated, "I believe the ability to conduct complete, objective, and competent investigations of the leadership of the FBI has been questioned. Of concern to me is the apparent deference paid to [senior] personnel who are found to have violated FBI policy, rules and regulation."[367]

Vermont Senator Patrick Leahy, the Senate Judiciary Committee Chairperson, said, "Ruby Ridge has been a textbook example of [FBI] abuses. It appears from this that the 'good old boy' network had been allowed to persist at the FBI."[368] "The aftermath of events at Ruby Ridge, Idaho, where an FBI sniper killed the wife of separatist Randy Weaver, is an example of what even Justice Department officials acknowledge is the FBI's unwillingness to police itself, especially when top officials are involved."[369] Leahy complained decisions regarding Ruby Ridge were "shrouded in secrecy." He slammed "the Justice Department [for] rejecting recommendations to censure former FBI Director Louis J. Freeh [Mr. Freeh left the FBI on June 22, 2001]."[370] He stated, "This double standard is unfair and demoralizing, but with strong new leadership at the FBI and some hands-on congressional oversight for a while, I expect this part of the culture to change."[371]

Because of the FBI's unconstitutional conduct during the Ruby Ridge incident, the US government paid "$3.1 million to Weaver and his three surviving daughters and revamped regulations on FBI rules of engagement. 'Bureau performance during Ruby Ridge and after was

The Double Standard of FBI Management

terribly flawed,' [FBI Director] Freeh tells a Senate panel."[372] In 2001, "A federal appeals court ruled the (FBI) agents (at Ruby Ridge) were acting under rules of engagement that 'are patently unconstitutional for a police action."[373] The unconstitutional rules of engagement were established by FBI management and relayed to the street agents on the SWAT team. Afterward, to protect themselves, FBI management denied giving the SWAT team the unconstitutional rules of engagement and did not take responsibility, and thereby threw the FBI street agents under the bus.

In the wake of the FBI's unwillingness to appropriately investigate its managers and its history of continued retaliation against street-level agents, on August 5, 2001, the Justice Department said, "Attorney General John Ashcroft considers this issue and any double standard at the FBI, very serious."[374]

5. FBIHQ Management's Sham Conference

In March 1997, FBI Director Freeh set up new disciplinary procedures for the FBI's rank-and-file agents and directed the disciplinary measures involving the senior managers to conform "as closely as feasible to rank-and-file disciplinary measures."

The following will show how arrogant top-level FBI managers continued to abuse and violate FBI rules and regulations, which apply to all FBI employees, support employees, street agents, and all FBI managers.

Remember Larry Potts? He was the assistant FBI director who helped create the new unconstitutional FBI "Use of Deadly Force Policy" at Ruby Ridge. Afterward, he was promoted to the number two position of the FBI as evidence was being destroyed in the Ruby Ridge case. He and five of the FBI's top officials were suspended for their roles in the Ruby Ridge cover-up.

He planned to retire from the FBI in 1997, and his retirement party would become the focus of much attention. "Two months before the [retirement] party, Mr. Potts—a onetime FBI deputy director—was still under criminal investigation over his questionable handling of Ruby Ridge, where three people had died."[375]

His fellow FBI executives scheduled a sham training conference at the FBI's training academy in Quantico, Virginia. This sham training conference would allow his FBI management colleagues to attend the retirement party at taxpayers' expense. The conference, "Integrity in Law Enforcement," was scheduled for October 10, 1997.

Over 140 people, including many FBI executives and SACs from bureau field offices, including the Chicago SAC, attended the party, which lasted an hour and a half in Arlington, VA.

Only five FBI managers attended the "Integrity in Law Enforcement" conference at the FBI Academy. The conference, which included lunch, lasted only ninety minutes.

On October 22, 1997, the OPR started an inquiry into the "accusations that the conference 'was a sham, intended to be used as justification to allow financial reimbursement to [FBI] SACs to travel to a peer's [Potts] retirement party.'"[376] The OPR investigation "focused on whether the Quantico conference was illegally used to justify travel reimbursements to senior [FBI] managers, who otherwise would have been on personal business."[377]

OPR later found the conference to have been a cover for senior FBI managers to get improper reimbursements for personal travel to Washington, DC, for Potts's retirement party.

In September 1999, the FBI's Law Enforcement Ethics Unit (LEEU) prepared a separate report regarding OPR's investigation of the party at the FBI Academy. "The 24-page LEEU report was part of a study commissioned by FBI Director Louis J. Freeh to monitor the integrity of the bureau's organizational components."[378] In July 2001, Senate investigators received this report as they looked into recent FBI mismanagement issues.

The LEEU "Potts Retirement Party," report was critical to the OPR investigation and its conclusions, particularly the punishments against the senior FBI managers. The report stated, "Although this paper only summarizes a complicated case, there can be little question that OPR was correct in its initial suspicions, the LEEU report said, adding that a 'fair and reasonable reading' of the OPR report 'clearly shows both voucher fraud and lack of candor [lying] by several' senior FBI executives who attended the party."[379]

"The report said a board of FBI executives who oversaw punishment for senior managers in the Potts case ignored warnings by Mr. Freeh in a 1994 'Bright Line' memo that said voucher fraud and lack of candor—lying or making false statements—would result in dismissal [being fired from the FBI]. The board [of FBI executives] recommended only letters of censure. In addition, the report said, the board [of FBI executives] never addressed accusations that senior FBI managers lied concerning travel vouchers they submitted to attend the Potts party."[380]

The report summarized significant conduct that the FBI executive board chose to ignore. Some of these included the following.

"One SAC, in a sworn deposition, said his trip to Washington was to attend a 'career board' meeting, although no such meeting was scheduled."[381] Rather than being fired for lying, as any FBI street agent would be, the board of FBI executives recommended this SAC for a letter of censure for "inappropriate travel."

"Another [FBI manager] said his trip to Washington was to assist an employee seeking a hardship transfer. Arriving in Washington at

1:30 p.m. on October 9, 1997—the day of the Potts party—he left the city at 10 a.m. on October 10, 1997. The employee with whom he said he met about the transfer was actually out of the country [at the time of the alleged meeting]."[382] Rather than being fired for lying, the board of FBI executives recommended this FBI manager also receive a letter of censure for "inappropriate travel."

"A third [FBI manager] who filed travel documents to 'attend meetings' in Washington had been censured, suspended, demoted, and placed on probation 15 years earlier for using government travel for personal business."[383] Instead of being fired, as a street agent would for even the first offense, this FBI manager, who committed his second offense, received a letter of censure for "inattention to detail."

The report also said, "an FBI section chief told OPR the Quantico conference was set up after Potts party had been planned, and he realized senior managers could use it to pay for their travel to attend the Potts party."[384] "The report said the section chief admitted to OPR he did not believe 'an objective observer would conclude this was a legitimate conference, as opposed to a cover for SAC travel' [to attend the Potts party]."[385]

The report concluded, "the section chief failed to exercise proper oversight. The executive board [of FBI executives] recommended a 15-day suspension. The recommendation later was determined by top FBI officials to be 'unnecessarily harsh' and was downgraded to a letter of censure."[386]

The "OPR investigators believed senior FBI managers filed false vouchers, misused government property, lacked candor, or lied under oath. They cited 15 prior [FBI street agent and support employee] cases involving similar accusations resulting in dismissals [firings from the FBI]."[387]

The LEEU report concluded, "Because of the Potts dinner cases, one could argue that the director's 'Bright Line' [disciplinary policy] promulgated in 1994 has been relegated to a faded chalk mark in the history of FBI discipline."[388]

The LEEU report outraged members of the Senate Judiciary Committee. Senator Charles Grassley had already been focusing on "what he called a 'double standard' of discipline between the FBI's senior managers and rank-and-file agents, saying the bureau's management system is 'broken.'"[389] He said, "This story shows the clash of cultures between the culture of arrogance that pervades FBI management and the culture of ethics that is taught to new FBI recruits. We need FBI leadership that gets back to practicing what it preaches at the FBI training facility in Quantico."[390]

6. The Missing FBI Guns and Computers

On July 18, 2001, the FBI received another bipartisan flogging from yet another Senate committee for their "serious management problems at the bureau, including the unsaid loss of hundreds of weapons and laptop computers."[391] The 459 missing weapons included rifles, pistols, and submachine guns. The 184 missing laptop computers included several which contained classified information.

News of the missing weapons and computers happened one day after Ashcroft "told a congressional hearing that a string of publicized troubles over the past decade have damaged public trust in the bureau."[392] He asked Inspector General Glenn A. Fine "to inventory the Justice Department's stock of firearms, laptops, and other items with the potential of compromising public safety, national security, or current investigations. 'In order for law enforcement organizations to be effective, they must have the public's confidence in their ability to perform not only the most complex duties but also the most basic responsibilities,' Mr. Ashcroft said in a statement."[393]

A long-scheduled [Senate] hearing to scrutinize FBI's management practices "turned into a free-for-all as senators and witnesses, including current and former FBI agents, depicted the lost items as symptomatic of an insular, self-protective management culture that seeks to hide problems rather than solve them."[394] The lawmakers "emphasized that the vast majority of [FBI] agents are competent and dedicated; [however], they attacked the bureau's management."[395] Utah Senator Orrin Hatch "called the loss of the guns and laptops simply inexcusable."[396]

Illinois Senator Dick Durbin said, "It is hard to believe the situation has deteriorated and disintegrated to where it has. There is a wall that has been built between the FBI and the Justice Department. And the agencies that are supposed to look over that wall failed. They have failed miserably."[397]

New York Senator Charles Schumer said, "If it were just this last revelation, I would say, 'OK, they made a mistake.' There has been incident after incident after incident and you have to say to yourself, 'What's going on at the FBI?' Schumer then proposed an 'outside comprehensive review of the FBI' by a blue-ribbon committee."[398] "'It is an issue of public trust and the FBI is taking a beating,' he said. 'Polls show Americans have more confidence in local law enforcement than in the FBI.'"[399]

Vermont Senator Patrick J. Leahy said, "What bothers me greatly as (chairperson) of this committee is that some computers were supposed to be containing classified information and you would think after the total fiasco of the FBI's handling of the Hanssen matter, they would learn from this matter."[400]

Iowa Senator Charles E. Grassley said, "To have laptops missing that could have national security information on them would be atrocious. For the FBI to have lost firearms and failed to account for them is inexcusable. We need to know if proper procedures for sensitive inventory have been enforced by the FBI."[401]

7. The FBI's Ancient and Neglected Computer System

During 1998, the FBI began promoting its new modernized computer system and program to be launched in 1999 or 2000. The FBI claimed this new system would store documents and make it easier to find them. A year before the new system was to be launched, agents had to learn about the new system through a series of videos and written material available for review on the existing computer system. When I inquired who was creating the new FBI system, I was told it was an FBI technician employee. Not someone from IBM or another well-known computer company.

I am not sure how other FBI offices selected their computer technicians, but in Chicago, they chose computer technicians from among the current support employees of the FBI. The support employees included secretaries and others who had no previous computer training. Once selected, the FBI transferred the employee to the computer team and assigned them the role of a computer technician. I am not exaggerating. Therefore, when the FBI announced it was creating a modernized computer program named Trilogy, I chose not to waste my time taking the mandatory training sessions for the new system.

In June 1999, Tim called me into his office and asked me why I was the only agent on the JTTF squad not to have conducted any required training for Trilogy.

I said, "Tim, I have no intention of conducting even one minute of training for a computer system, which I know will never work. I do not care how much they exaggerate this thing. I assure you it will never work." I also shared how the new computer system and program were being created by an FBI employee, not an actual computer expert.

He replied, "You are right! I did not know. I am going to hold off on the mandatory training myself. We can always catch up on the training after they launch the program."

Of course, due to too many problems, they never launched the costly Trilogy computer system that had been under construction for almost two years.

The system was inferior to even my home computer. "When the typical agent turns on a computer, it displays not the multicolored screen familiar to many — with its landscape of toolbars, boxes, browsers, and icons — but a green-and-black screen that was obsolete a decade ago."[402]

One afternoon, while my supervisor and I were discussing how pathetic the computer system was, the supervisor asked, "Bob, with all that is going on right now with the bureau, why doesn't someone come forward and talk about our computer problems?" Coincidently, news stories about the FBI's serious computer problems surfaced a few days later.

Throughout the FBI's "700 offices, investigations are routinely slowed, and crucial information missed, while data is downloaded on the (FBI's) ancient systems. Processes that many teenagers could perform at home in minutes take the nation's top investigators hours."[403] Nancy Savage, president of the FBI Agents Association, said, "Some of our smaller offices don't even have Internet access. We don't always have the ability to transfer photographs. Those kinds of things are basic to law enforcement now."[404]

The Double Standard of FBI Management

"'The average person in America would think the FBI, as the premier law enforcement agency, would have top-of-the-shelf automation, but they are far from it,' said William Esposito, the bureau's deputy director in the late 1990s. 'The system definitely needed upgrading, and it was a frustration by a lot of people, at both the management and agent level, as to why this could not happen sooner and faster.'"[405]

The FBI hired a former IBM executive, Bob Dies, as an FBI assistant director in 2000. His job was to evaluate and upgrade the computer system. In 2001, he told a Senate committee that, while the bureau had tried to correct problems, "no meaningful improvements have been made to the system in six years."[406] He said he was "appalled at the state of the bureau's technology. 'The [agents] are better than I thought,' Dies said. 'The technology, on the other hand, is worse than I thought. And I had a very low expectation level.'"[407] He further stated, "Agents and support personnel are forced to use outdated and ineffective equipment, asked to 'do their jobs without the tools other companies use or that you may use at home on your system.' He said agents cannot electronically store investigative information in primary investigative databases, including photos, graphical and tabular data."[408]

The above comments of Mr. Dies confirm why I say I had no choice but to load data manually, such as checks, travel dates, terror training camp dates, and all other information collected through the VB investigation, in chronological order on a single-spaced Word document. I was thankful there was a search feature in the Word program so I could quickly find dates and other information. My only other choice was to write the information chronologically into a notebook.

Dies further said that Congress had given $300 million during the fall of 2000 to upgrade the FBI's computer network. "While that should bring the bureau to a basic functioning level, the FBI will still lag far behind the rest of the world. They have been starved for support for so long, they do not know what to ask for," Dies said.[409]

In 1999, the FBI hired Kenneth H. Senser, a former CIA executive, as an acting FBI assistant director to assess security programs and countermeasures. Senser "testified that 'most if not all' federal agency computer systems are ahead of the FBI, and that he was 'bringing in people to oversee security measures and changes,' many of them from the CIA. He said that during an assessment of the FBI computer system, he found that security initiatives were 'often poorly coordinated, inefficient and not as effective as possible.'"[410]

Senator Leahy said, "There is absolutely no reason for this. The FBI has had an extraordinary increase in its budget. It is a lack of management. It is an attitude of some that 'We are the FBI, and we have done it in this way for a long time, and this is how we are going to do it.'"[411]

In 1995, as I was planning for the future of my criminal terrorism investigation, specifically the entry, storage, and retrieval of vital records, i.e., checks, photographs, INS information, tax information, travel records, and more, I realized the FBI computer system was incapable of storing this data and worse yet, could not link any dates and individual events with other relevant dates and events.

For example, when HAMAS held its training camps in the US, Mousa Abu Marzook drafted personal checks for each HAMAS trainee. These trainees were attending US colleges and universities throughout the US. Simply entering the date of the training camp and the date of each check into the FBI's database, one would expect the FBI database would automatically conduct a link analysis and notify an FBI agent of the link. However, this was not the case. In fact, during 1995, the FBI's computer system was grossly outdated.

In 1995, to remedy this problem for my investigation, I visited a computer store one block from the Chicago FBI office. I shared my needs without saying who I worked for and inquired how much such a system would cost. After analyzing the current description of the computer system I was working with, the salesperson advised me to discard the outdated system and develop a separate, more advanced system for my project. The system would comprise a separate mainframe, four complete IBM state-of-the-art computers, and other necessary cables and items. The total cost was $17,000. I believed that international terrorism was important enough to justify the expense of $17,000, considering that each case had a budget of up to $20,000 for essential case support items to further the investigation.

After receiving the written estimate, I drafted a request summarizing my need for modern IBM computer equipment and asking for $17,000 in case funds to pay for the computer system. My supervisor and others laughed at my "ridiculous request" and told me it would never get approved. In addition, I was told all computer purchases needed to go through the computer section.

I visited the computer section supervisor to learn how to purchase the equipment. The supervisor told me that the US government's purchase list did not include the equipment on the computer store estimate. She said that the government was required to accept computer bids on its list. She further said the bid process would take over a year to complete. Under the existing computer purchase list, I could purchase comparable computers one to two years older for $30,000.

Wondering why, I asked, "Why would anyone in their right mind pay $30,000 for a two-year-old computer system when you can buy a current state-of-the-art system for only $17,000 right now?"

Ultimately, FBI management would not approve the computer system, forcing me to continue entering my information into a Word document.

To make matters worse, only one of the three computers available for the entire JTTF squad had Microsoft Word installed from 1995 to 1997. Thirty JTTF squad members shared three computers. Other squad members constantly complained about me "hogging" the squad's only movable stand-alone computer.

Very little had changed concerning the FBI's computer system between 1995 and 2001. In fact, "The congressional committee with oversight over the FBI sent a letter last month [April 2001] to Director Freeh saying it is 'concerned that the FBI had information technology systems that are slow, unreliable, and obsolete systems that cannot address the bureau's critical needs.'"[412] The letter encouraged Freeh to use the expertise of the GAO, a congressional agency, as it decides how to upgrade its computer system. "The GAO (General Accounting Office) is prepared to assist the bureau throughout the process to ensure that this technology upgrade becomes a model program instead of another government IT failure like those which GAO found at other agencies, the letter said."[413]

Wisconsin Representative F. James Sensenbrenner Jr. announced in May 2001 "that a lengthy investigation of the FBI's information technology systems by the Justice Department's Office of Inspector General (IG), which concluded in 1999, found that there were problems in the way information was entered or searched in the FBI databases. He said the IG's office found that the way search results were handled within the FBI resulted in 'incomplete data being provided.'" [414]

"A report by the IG said the FBI's practices and policy handicapped the usefulness of the FBI's databases and that many of the document's investigators discovered regarding key task force subjects . . . [they] could not be found using the FBI system."[415]

"The FBI's procedures for culling information from its teletypes and electronic communications and inputting it into its databases essentially makes it impossible for the FBI to state with confidence that a database search has yielded all information in the FBI's files about a particular subject,"[416] the (Inspector General) report said. The report also said, "Many of the FBI personnel were not well versed in using the bureau's database system. Mr. Sensenbrenner said the American people 'need to be confident' that its federal law enforcement agencies adhere to the highest standards of integrity, professionalism, and competence."[417]

On May 12, 2001, FBI spokesperson John Collingwood said, "There is complete agreement within the bureau, the Department of Justice, the administration, and Congress that the FBI's automated record system is antiquated and based on obsolete technology. Regarding the system, there is a total lack of internal confidence and a lack of ability to do basic data searches. This is an issue on which all parties agree."[418]

The above FBI statement is precisely why I had to create my VB database system to help put the pieces of the HAMAS puzzle together. At some point, my Word document contained well over 1,000 pages. This was the only way I could link events, money, individuals, terrorist attacks, travel, vehicles, terrorist training camps, and everything else together. The FBI did not possess any financial link analysis programs, accounting programs, or other resources that street agents could use to conduct complicated investigations successfully. The FBI refused, even after the $1.4 million seizure of terrorism funds, to let me buy a commercial accounting program to aid the investigation. It's amazing that VB was as successful as it was with no reliable computer system.

Suggested Solutions from Congress Regarding the FBI Include Having the DOJ Inspector General Investigate All FBI Employee Misconduct

On June 24, 2001, Illinois Senator Richard Durbin and Pennsylvania Senator Arlen Specter, both members of the Senate Judiciary Committee, introduced bipartisan legislation to create a separate, independent Inspector General to oversee the FBI. They said this would increase accountability for the nation's top federal law enforcement agency.

The senators said that while the DOJ had the Office of Inspector General (OIG), which investigates allegations of misconduct of employees within the DOJ family, the OIG "lacks authority without permission from the Attorney General to investigate accusations of FBI employee misconduct."[419] Instead, the FBI had used its own supervisors to investigate misconduct allegations through the OPR Unit. The senators said their proposed legislation called for "an independent Inspector General for the FBI who would report directly to the Attorney General."[420]

Senator Durbin said, "The lack of accountability at the FBI has reached a level of national concern. It is time for the nation's top law enforcement agency to be held to the same level of professionalism as every other agency of the government."[421] In addition, he said, "There is no reason the FBI should be protected from the same level of professional scrutiny the Central Intelligence Agency (CIA) and virtually every other agency faces."[422]

On July 18, 2001, Ashcroft announced he was transferring the FBI's OPR authority to investigate all misconduct allegations by FBI employees to the Justice Department's Inspector General. In a brief statement, the DOJ said, "The expansion of the Inspector General's authority was designated to provide 'consistency' throughout the department. Misconduct allegations in other Justice agencies, such as the Immigration and Naturalization Service (INS) and the US Marshals Service, are already under the control of the Inspector General. This action now gives the Office of Inspector General the same authority to investigate misconduct allegations against employees of the FBI and DEA that the Office of Inspector General has regarding all other components of the Department of Justice, thereby promoting consistency in the disposition of such allegations. The change takes effect immediately."[423]

When news of Ashcroft's delegating the authority of reviewing all OPR complaints and making decisions on investigations to the OIG, agents familiar with my situation called. They asked if the Inspector General would now review my pending OPR situation.

"Maybe the Inspector General will review your case regarding Reed's false allegations," said one agent. I was relieved when I learned about Ashcroft's decision. The possibility that the OPR would have to answer for their sloppy and incomplete investigations of hard-working street agents would finally end.

Unfortunately, my confidence in the IG was short-lived. Following the 9/11 attacks, two incidents occurred regarding the new IG who oversaw the alleged misconduct of all FBI employees. These incidents caused my attorneys and me to lack confidence in the IG's investigations of any alleged wrongdoing.

The first incident happened on November 4, 2001, seven weeks after the 9/11 attacks, after my attorneys filed an official thirty-eight-page complaint with both the OPR unit and the IG's office. Enclosed with this complaint, to prove the complaint did not contain any grand jury or classified information, were copies of all the public sources and redacted documents from the FBI. The complaint had the title: "DERELICTION OF DUTY BY THE FEDERAL BUREAU OF INVESTIGATION IN FAILING TO INVESTIGATE AND PROSECUTE TERRORISM AND OBSTRUCTION OF JUSTICE IN RETALIATING AGAINST SPECIAL AGENT ROBERT WRIGHT, JR."

Rather than address the serious allegations in the thirty-eight-page complaint regarding FBI management's dereliction of duty to protect American citizens from Middle Eastern terrorism, the IG forwarded the complaint to the FBIHQ OPR unit. The IG included a recommendation letter requesting the OPR unit open an OPR investigation against me for possibly releasing classified and grand jury information to my attorneys, who drafted the complaint.

The FBI immediately opened a 'secret OPR investigation' I was never supposed to know about. However, I learned about it when a Chicago supervisor, who became the acting ASAC for a week, called me to his office. Upon my entering, he handed me a copy of the outcome of this 'secret OPR investigation.' The document concluded that my complaint to the IG contained no classified or grand jury information. At a later date, the FBI will falsely claim to a US District Court Judge this document contains classified and grand jury information.

The second matter involved the FBI assistant director and FBI deputy director of the OPR Unit. These two men jointly decided they were going to terminate me, conducting no investigation into a fabricated accusation against me. The issue resulted from my efforts

The Double Standard of FBI Management

to expose, legally, the FBI's negligent terrorism efforts to the US Congress and the American public to prevent more deaths. However, there was one obstacle standing in the FBI's way. As required by the Attorney General, the IG had to review all OPR matters to determine whether the DOJ or the FBI should investigate the matter.

To circumvent the IG, FBI Assistant Director Robert Jordan and FBI Deputy Director Jody Weis directed the OPR Unit Chief, John Roberts, to draft the necessary paperwork 'in such a way as to deceive the IG.' Once the DOJ returned my case to the FBI OPR Unit, Jordan and Weis could illegally fire me, without cause, and get away with it because my only recourse would be to file an appeal with the FBI OPR Unit.

Fortunately for me, the honest OPR Unit Chief, John Roberts, who had direct knowledge of Jordan and Weis's conniving plan, sought to protect the integrity of the FBI. After discovering Jordan and Weis's illegal conduct, he wrote a sixty-page letter. With the help of an attorney, he delivered the letter to the Senate Judiciary Committee. The letter informed the senators that Robert Jordan and Jody Weis were repeatedly told that the worst punishment for my alleged misconduct was a letter of censure. After reading the letter, US Senators Charles Grassley (R) and Patrick Leahy (D) became involved with my situation.

Had it not been for Roberts's bravery, courage, and integrity in coming forward and notifying the US Senate Judiciary Committee, Jordan and Weis would have wrongfully fired me and escaped punishment. If they had fired me, I could not legally challenge my FBI termination.

To this day, I wonder how many FBI employees have been wrongfully fired throughout the past decades by corrupt FBI managers.

Avoiding accountability each time, FBI management got away with it because they knew they did not have to answer to anyone. Again, fortunately in my case, Roberts, a person of courage and integrity, reported the illegal conduct of the top two OPR unit managers. Unfortunately, he and his wife, who was Robert Jordan's secretary, each paid a high price for their dedication to protecting the integrity of the FBI.

In the next book, *The FBI's Post-9/11 Vulgar Betrayal*, I extensively describe the above two matters, as well as many other acts of retaliation that the FBI directed toward me after the 9/11 attacks.

> "The FBI also has an institutional arrogance in how it deals with its own employees. In order to regain the trust and confidence of the American people, the FBI must be open and fully responsive to differing points of view within its ranks. Retaliation against FBI Whistleblowers who "break the code of silence" within the Bureau is oftentimes subtle and inconspicuous, but no less devastating to an Agent's career."[424]
> —US Senator Charles E. Grassley, Senate Judiciary Committee, 07/29/2001.

CHAPTER 35

THE FBIHQ OPR DECISION

"OPR brings greater rights and transparency to the important process of increasing objectivity and fairness for all employees, which are essential in any government dedicated to the rule of law. My goal is for the American people to have total confidence that the disciplinary system (OPR) is fair and promptly identifies and punishes misconduct, without fear or favor. I am proud of the men and women of the FBI who carry out their work with total honesty and integrity. By erecting rigorous safeguards, we can reduce impropriety to the absolute minimum."[425]

—Louis J. Freeh, FBI Director (1999)

On September 20, 2000, my supervisor in the SRA office called me into his office and informed me he had received a phone call from ASAC Walter Stowe. I was told that the OPR unit had reached a final decision regarding Agent Reed's sexual harassment allegations, and Stowe requested I meet with him in his office at 9:00 a.m. on September 21 where he would present me with the ruling. Although all indicators pointed to me being found innocent of Reed's sexual harassment claim, I remained confident the FBIHQ OPR unit was going to punish me unjustly.

On September 21, 2000, at 9:00 a.m., I arrived at Mr. Stowe's office. He was polite and professional when he informed me the final ruling had been made. Before he could say anything else, I asked, "Sir, can I say something to you before you tell me their decision?"

"Sure, go ahead, Bob," he said.

"I just want to tell you what I think the decision is before you tell me. First, I told my supervisors, the AUSAs, Agent Vincent, and my attorney that although I did absolutely nothing wrong, the OPR Unit would punish me. If the SAC's recommendation was zero to seven days off without pay, they will give me a minimum of thirty days off without pay. If the SAC recommended over seven days off without pay, I will be fired. I just wanted to say this before you tell me their decision because there is a reason this is happening, and I do not want you to think I am mentally unbalanced when I tell you the reason."

"Bob, you are right. They recommended thirty days off without pay," he confirmed.

I looked out the window and let out a loud "Whew!"

As I turned back to Mr. Stowe, I noticed a look of confusion on his face.

"Sir, although I did nothing wrong, this outcome was my best-case scenario under the circumstances. If you do not mind my asking, what was the Chicago office recommendation after you completed the OPR investigation?"

"We recommended no time off. Bob, you are innocent!" he replied.

"At least you guys came to the right conclusion. I am thankful for that," I said.

The FBIHQ OPR Decision

"Bob, if you had sexually harassed her, I would have recommended you be fired," he said.

"I agree with you. If I had sexually harassed her, you should have fired me. But I never sexually harassed her or anyone else in my life," I said.

"Bob, why do you believe OPR recommended giving you thirty days off without pay?" he asked.

"I know the reason. The problem is, no one cares to investigate why this is happening, and I continue to get screwed over," I said.

"What is the reason? Their decision does not make any sense," he questioned.

I said what the Kansas City ASAC, William Gentry, had done to me following the shooting incident in 1993. I explained how Gentry told me he held a grudge against me and, after that, retaliated against me repeatedly. I then shared that besides Gentry prejudicing the Chicago office against me before I arrived in Chicago, I was confident he had contacted a friend at FBIHQ to prejudice me should I ever be involved in any OPR matter in the future.

"Such a thing could not happen. They could not do such a thing. It is just not possible," said Stowe.

"I understand where you are coming from, but can you explain why this is happening and how since day one of Reed's allegation, I knew, even though I was innocent, I would get screwed over when this day arrived?" I asked.

He reasoned the recommended thirty days off was because of the "political climate" of the times regarding sexual harassment.

"Did you see my OPR file in Washington, DC, to find out if someone had not included what I suggested in my file?" I asked.

"No, I have not looked at the file," he replied.

He and I agreed to disagree about why the OPR Unit recommended thirty days off without pay. But we both agreed I was innocent and the decision was a severe miscarriage of justice. He said there were many problems with the OPR decision and he wanted to go through the OPR letter, sentence by sentence.

"Bob, there are some serious problems with OPR's conclusions. The most disturbing thing to me is the accuser's lack of credibility," he stated. He continued, "Bob, I would like to point out where the credibility problems lie in her statements. This is just between you and me."

"Sir, then do not tell me because I will repeat whatever you tell me," I said.

"Okay, then let me tell you where you need to look to find the credibility issues you need to bring up when you appeal this OPR decision," he suggested.

"Sir, I have no intentions of appealing this decision," I said.

"Bob, I believe in this OPR process, and I strongly recommend you appeal this decision," he urged.

"Look, I am sure you believe in the OPR process; however, I do not. I already know they will deny any appeal I make and never change their decision," I said.

Remembering my graduation day at the FBI Academy, I laughed.

"What is so funny?" he asked.

I explained, "I was just thinking about how an assistant director welcomed us into the 'FBI family' during my graduation ceremony at the FBI Academy. He mentioned members of the FBI family looked out for and cared for one another. You were even on the stage since you oversaw the FBI Academy during my training and graduation. What a family! All I have ever done was to perform the best job possible, and my so-called family has continued to screw me over every time it gets the chance. This is no family. If the management of this organization had done its job, we would not be having this discussion right now. I would still be working Vulgar Betrayal and would have locked up a lot of Middle Eastern terrorists."

After taking in what I said, he asked, "What do you mean by 'if management had done its job'?"

I explained, "In early 1999, I warned Clinton that the Milwaukee office was unaware of the scope of the Vulgar Betrayal case and that they would interfere with the investigation by opening a duplicate criminal investigation on Sarsour. Clinton told me he was not aware of what the Vulgar Betrayal case was about. Yet, behind my back, he is ruining my reputation and harming the case by telling other supervisors and agents around the country I have no idea what I am doing. During our second trip to Israel, Mr. Resnick told me Agent Reed should not have been allowed to open the duplicate criminal case of Sarsour, and Chicago should run the entire HAMAS criminal investigation. I asked why Resnick and others at headquarters refused to do the right thing and instruct her to close her duplicate criminal investigation. I later discovered why none of them ever instructed her to close her case."

"Why did they not tell her to close her case?" asked Stowe.

"They were all scared of her. They feared she would file a retaliation OPR complaint against them. Because of their intentional failure to do their jobs, you had to decide to close her case during your meeting with Milwaukee in July of '99. On the day she learned her case was to be closed, instead of coming after you guys for closing her case, she took it out on me by filing this false sexual harassment complaint that same day. I am being punished for your guy's decision to close her case. I lost my Vulgar Betrayal case in which I had invested years of my life. And now, although you all know I am innocent of this vindictive sexual harassment allegation of hers, I am being punished by being labeled a sexual harasser and being hit with thirty days off without pay for something everyone knows I did not do," I said.

"Bob, you need to appeal this decision and list any witnesses you believe need to be interviewed," said Stowe.

"Sir, during my OPR interview, I provided a forty-one-page document, which included a list of eleven witnesses. These witnesses wanted to be interviewed by OPR; they specifically wanted to provide information regarding Reed's mental status during their interactions with her. Several witnesses are supervisors from FBIHQ who asked me to list them as witnesses. OPR contacted none of these eleven witnesses."

Looking through the investigation file, Mr. Stowe said, "Bob, there is no copy of the summary you're referring to in the OPR file I have here."

"You must be kidding! I drafted a complete summary of my relationship with Agent Reed, and they did not even read it, let alone place it in the file. The Chicago supervisors who conducted my OPR interview must have thrown it away. Are you certain it isn't in the file?" I asked.

"No, I do not see it here," he confirmed.

"Sir, this is just wrong! My attorney repeatedly insisted on attaching the summary to my signed sworn statement. The OPR interviewers said FBIHQ instructed them not to accept it. They reluctantly took it and told us they would submit it along with my sworn statement." I continued, "Sir, I am not lying. Ask those two Chicago supervisors who conducted my OPR interview what they did with my summary and witness list. They threw it away because headquarters instructed them not to accept it from me. Do you see how unfair this OPR

The FBIHQ OPR Decision

investigation has been toward me? Why would the OPR unit tell the OPR interviewers not to accept a document from me, a document which helped prove my innocence?" I asked.

Unable to answer my question, Mr. Stowe said, "Bob, add your document to your appeal paperwork. I want to point out a few things I believe are wrong with OPR's conclusions. You need to stress these points in your appeal."

"Sir, you do not understand what I am saying about the appeal. The appeal is a waste of time. They have already made up their minds and will not reverse this thirty-day off decision," I said.

"Here is one problem which stands out in their final ruling. They have concluded you requested a transfer to Indianapolis to follow Reed. They concluded that there was nothing to suggest that you were ever interested in transferring to the Indianapolis division until she received her transfer. You live in Indiana now, right?" he asked.

"Yes, but at the time of the shooting in 1993, management asked me about my preferred transfer location. I said Indianapolis. I was told the closest I could get to Indianapolis was Chicago, which is why I am here now. I lived in Indianapolis for three years. I worked for the Indianapolis Mayor's Office in 1988, the Indiana Attorney General's Office in 1989 and 1990, and attended law school in Indianapolis through 1990. I entered the FBI through the Indianapolis division in 1990. Before entering, I spent my entire life in Indiana from age three, except for the year I attended law school in Michigan. How can they conclude there is nothing to suggest I was never interested in transferring to the Indianapolis division?" I asked.

"That is the problem, Bob! These conclusions are disturbing, as well as the credibility of Agent Reed. You must appeal this decision," he remarked.

"Sir, honestly, my days in this organization are numbered. I appreciate your support in filing an appeal, but again, I do not share your confidence that they are going to do the right thing regarding this matter. I do not wish to appeal the decision. If I believed it would do any good, I would appeal; however, I know they will never reverse their decision," I said.

"Bob, think about this carefully. You must send in a request to review the OPR file within ten days from today. Do this, and once you read her statements, you will understand why her credibility is an issue. Bob, she is mentally unbalanced. Once you read her statements to the OPR agents, you will understand why I can say that. You must appeal this decision!" said Stowe.

"Sir, I am just glad you guys came to the right conclusion. Again, I appreciate your time," I said.

I then shook hands with him and left his office.

Following our meeting, I visited one of the AUSAs assigned to the VB case. I informed him about the decision to punish me, although the Chicago OPR investigation concluded I was innocent and determined Reed was mentally unbalanced. During the meeting, the AUSA also encouraged me to appeal the decision. He told me to deliver a copy of the OPR letter to Schippers immediately.

I took his advice and delivered a copy of the letter to Schippers. Since Schippers was in a meeting, I left a copy along with a note explaining that the Chicago office concluded I was innocent. I then returned to the SRA office.

After arriving at the SRA office, I found the following voicemail from Schippers, "Bob, it's Dave. I just read this piece of garbage! My philosophy is that I thoroughly agree with the front office, and I thoroughly agree that you should not take one minute off for that garbage! Call me when you get this message."

The FBIHQ OPR Decision

When I called Schippers, he said, "We are going to take this thing to The Wall! This is wrong! How can they think they will get away with this injustice?"

Schippers said he would start the appeal paperwork immediately.

"Dave, do you remember what I told you in front of the interviewers after the OPR interview?" I asked.

"I remember. I thought you were being paranoid," he said.

"Dave, you can file the appeal, but OPR will never reverse their decision," I said.

"They have no choice, Bob. They must reverse this garbage," he stated.

During the weekend, I reflected on all I had been through during the past fourteen months because of Reed's malicious allegation. It genuinely pleased me that the FBI Chicago leadership understood her intentional motive was to harm my reputation and career and prevent my transfer to the Indianapolis office.

The other frustrating fact about her malicious complaint was that the cowards in the OPR Unit had no intention of punishing Reed for filing a false complaint against an innocent agent. Aware she would subject another unsuspecting agent to the same treatment in the future, I decided I must pursue a civil lawsuit against her for the intentional infliction of emotional distress and damage to my FBI career. By filing the civil lawsuit, I would publicly disclose her real name in the court filing, enabling other FBI agents to realize her malicious conduct toward another agent.

The following Monday morning, September 25, 2000, I discovered a voice message from Mr. Stowe, requesting I call him to discuss the OPR letter he had presented to me on Friday. When I called, he stated, "Bob, I have done something I have never done in my entire FBI career."

"What is that?" I asked.

"I called the Assistant Director (AD) responsible for the OPR Unit. I told the AD they got this one wrong, and I believed this was an unfair punishment against you. I also told the AD I questioned the credibility of the agent who filed the complaint against you. We spoke for about twenty minutes, and he said there was nothing they could do unless you file an appeal of their recommendation," said Mr. Stowe.

"Thank you for making the call," I said.

"Bob, I just want to reiterate my strong recommendation that you appeal this decision. I strongly believe this is a miscarriage of justice. You must request to review the file and request an extension to respond to their decision," he restated.

"Mr. Stowe, I provided a copy of the letter you gave me to my attorney, and he is extremely upset with OPR's ruling. We will appeal the decision. Thank you for your genuine concern in this matter."

"I just could not stand by and allow this injustice to happen," Mr. Stowe replied.

"Sir, there is one thing I would like to request," I said.

"What is it?" he asked.

"I want my Vulgar Betrayal case back. I just want my terrorism case back. I've dedicated years to that case, and I'm the only one who knows it inside and out. Assigning Vulgar Betrayal to another agent is unfair. I know things they will never know, no matter how often they read the files," I said.

"Bob, both the civil and criminal Vulgar Betrayal cases have been officially closed," said Stowe.

"How can the FBI justify closing it?" I asked.

"The statute of limitations had run on the criminal activities of the Vulgar Betrayal subjects," he explained.

The FBIHQ OPR Decision

"What are you talking about? With the arrest of Sarsour, the FBI could link his HAMAS activities with Adel Awadallah back through 1989 and beyond, including the activities of Salah and Marzook. Because of Sarsour's activities, the FBI can pursue a RICO investigation, which carries a ten-year statute of limitations for all criminal activity linked to the US-based HAMAS members. How can you justify closing the case? These terrorists are still committing criminal activities today to support international terrorism. There is no way the US Attorney's Office agreed to the closing of Vulgar Betrayal because they knew the statute of limitations had not expired because of the RICO activities of Sarsour. We can still shut these terrorists down," I said.

"Bob, the case has been closed. I think it is better to let sleeping dogs lie," he said.

When he said both the criminal and civil cases had been closed, it was hard to realize the consequences. As for the closing of the criminal case, there were no longer any further investigations of the criminal activities of the US-based HAMAS terrorist organizations. This also included VB efforts in Saudi Arabia, France, Great Britain, and many other countries. As for the closing of the civil case, this case covered the $1.4 million in terrorism funds we had seized from Mohammad Salah, the QLI, and Yassin Kadi in June 1998. If this was true, returning the $1.4 million to the HAMAS terrorists would be necessary. If McChesney allowed that to happen, the return of the terrorism funds would amount to nothing less than gross negligence on her part.

Chicago FBI management refused to reopen VB and allow me to pursue the only large scale FBI criminal terrorism case. It was hard to accept the FBI was intentionally ignoring the criminal activities of known Middle Eastern terrorists, their non-profit and for-profit organizations, and the financing of international terrorism from within America. I had done all I could do. There is nothing left to do but to keep drafting this manuscript to warn politicians in Washington, DC, about the ITU's gross negligence before more innocent people died from future Middle Eastern terrorist attacks.

Something disturbing happened days before Sharif Alwan would learn his fate from the VB criminal trial in Chicago. Gossfeld, still the supervisor of the Chicago JTTF, told a fellow agent he hoped Alwan would win the criminal case by being found not guilty. I could not believe the answer when I asked the agent why Gossfeld would say such a thing. The agent explained that Gossfeld, McChesney, and others in the ITU at FBIHQ expressed their frustration with the US Attorney's Office for continuing the criminal pursuit of Sharif Alwan after McChesney closed the VB investigation. Fortunately, the United States Attorney's Office ignored the FBI's request and continued to pursue Alwan's criminal conviction.

On October 20, 2000, the federal court found Sharif Alwan guilty of contempt. Subsequently, Alwan was sentenced to two years in prison "for his refusal to testify before the grand jury investigating US fundraising efforts by the Islamic militant group, HAMAS."[426]

During the trial, Alwan said in part, "I have two kids and I have my wife, my parents there, and I can't give up on going back there [Palestine] because it is my homeland. I consider my second homeland here [USA]."[427]

The US Attorney asked him, "And would you tell us, please, again why it is that you don't have a fear now, [about testifying], but you did three months ago?"

"I do still have a fear, and three months ago, the stand was different. And today the consequences I might face after not testifying will be harder on me. I won't be able to get my citizenship as a US citizen of this country. I might lose my green card. I am subject to deportation," said Alwan.

"You understand, Mr. Alwan, that as a citizen of this country, you have an obligation to obey the lawful court orders that are entered?" asked the US Attorney.

"Yes, I do," said Alwan.

"And you did not do that, did you, Mr. Alwan?"

"I did not obey that, that's correct," said Alwan.

"And you knew that you were required to obey the order of the court to testify?"

"Yes," answered Alwan." [428]

"Mr. Alwan, your testimony is that if there is something about you that you care about, then you will obey a court order or not obey a court order." asked the US Attorney.

"Would you repeat the question, please?" asked Alwan.

"Today, you have it in your mind that you want something for yourself. You do not want to go back to your homeland. Do I understand you correctly?" asked the US Attorney.

"That's correct," answered Alwan."[429]

During the redirect examination of Alwan by his attorney, the attorney asked, "Mr. Alwan, do you believe that becoming an American citizen requires that you jeopardize the safety of your wife, your family and your father?"

"I believe becoming an American citizen would give me more rights, more rights to protect myself here and in my country too, when I go back,"[430] said Alwan.

With Alwan's felony conviction, he would never become a US citizen in the future. This was one of my ultimate goals regarding him and all the other Middle Eastern terrorists we had identified through VB. Unfortunately, VB's closing prevented John and me from continuing our efforts to locate hundreds of other Middle Eastern terrorists living in the US who were seeking to gain US citizenship to help them travel in and out of the US whenever they wished.

During Alwan's sentencing proceeding, the Honorable Ruben Castillo stated the following in part:

> I have been involved in the criminal justice system for over 20 years. I know that the criminal justice system only operates on the basis of information, information that is given when required and that people that come to this country to create a new life for themselves. As everyone by definition who is American has somewhere in their generational history has come to create a new life, has to accept that this country is one of the rules of law. That means that if you are on the street, be it the South Side or the West Side of Chicago, and you witness criminal activity, it is your obligation as a citizen to give that information, even if it means that your life then is at risk; because, that is the nature of this country.
>
> And you had information, Mr. Alwan. You could certainly have given that information whenever you decided in a confidential setting, which is the nature of the federal grand jury, and you decided not to give that information, not once, not twice, three times in a very conscious and contemptuous proceeding.
>
> And that is why the jury, after a fair and impartial trial, where you were well represented by your attorneys . . . Mr. Hill and Ms. Jarad represented you to the best of their ability, but they could not challenge the fact of what had already occurred in the transcripts of the repeated proceedings before the chief judges of this court.

And you decided for whatever reason, because you are a stand-up person, you are a person who does not want to be seen by your community as an informer or a snitch, in your own words. I do not believe, and I tell you this straight to your face, that this is out of fear of the Shin Bet [Israeli Intelligence Agency]. I just cannot conclude that based on my life experience because, if you did have fear of the Shin Bet, you would not have testified in the manner in which you did which fully disclosed the manner in which you had been tortured and made to give a statement to the Israelis.

I do not believe that that would have occurred if you had this fear for your family or otherwise. I believe, as I've already indicated here, that the fear is that you'll be labeled an informant by your community and the repercussions that would come from that. That's what I believe has driven your decision not to testify.

And that is a decision that the criminal justice system just cannot take because if everyone can have it within their own power, when they are going to decide when to give information and when they are going to decide not to give information, then the criminal justice system in this country would just collapse, and that is something that I cannot allow as a representative of this criminal justice system.

And so, in looking at your situation and looking at the sentencing range of 24 to 30 months, I conclude, on the basis of everything that's before me, that it is appropriate to sentence you to the custody of the Attorney General for a period of 24 months, and I will do that.[431]

Agent Tim Adams, the agent tasked to address the Alwan part of the VB case following my removal as the case agent, was the FBI agent who testified on behalf of the US government during Alwan's criminal trial. Following Alwan's conviction, the FBI presented Adams with a "Cash Incentive Award" for his work and testimony during the trial. Someone later informed me that he was uncomfortable receiving the cash award. I congratulated him and told him he deserved the award and much more.

> "Clear procedures have been created to process complaints and FBI management officials will promptly investigate such incidents. Disciplinary action will be taken against such misconduct, and the discipline can range from an oral reprimand to dismissal. FBI employees are assured they can seek redress without fear of reprisal from anyone."[432]
> — Louis J. Freeh, FBI Director (1999)

CHAPTER 36

THE OPR APPEAL AND MY MEETING WITH SAC MCCHESNEY

Before my OPR oral appeal, Mr. Schippers and I could review the Chicago OPR investigative file, which comprised my interview and two interviews with Reed. In January 2001, Schippers arranged, through A/SAC Walter Stowe, a date and time to view the OPR file.

On the OPR file review day, Schippers and I met with Stowe in his office.

As Mr. Stowe reached out to shake Schippers's hand, he said, "Bob's innocent!"

"You're damn right he's innocent! However, what bothers me is how Bob knew from the day he learned of this OPR complaint that OPR would punish him even though he was innocent. Even today, Bob is confident OPR will not reverse this miscarriage of justice," said Schippers.

"Trust me, I'm serious. I am happy you guys realize I am innocent and that what she did was wrong. For the record, OPR will not reverse its pathetic finding. I will end up taking thirty days off, without pay, for something I did not do. There is nothing anyone here can do about that. OPR can do whatever it wants to do because they do not have to answer anyone," I said.

The two men agreed that OPR had no choice but to reverse its decision.

Stowe then told Schippers what to focus on while reviewing the OPR file. Stowe clarified that Reed was interviewed first, and the second interview was mine. According to him, the Chicago OPR investigators compared our two statements, and all agreed that something was wrong. The investigators concluded they needed to re-interview Reed. Stowe emphasized to Schippers that he needed to focus on Reed's second interview statements.

"Something in her second interview will jump out at you. There is something that would cause someone to question her mental stability," said Stowe.

He told us we could not copy any documents within the OPR file but could take notes.

He then took us to a room where we could review the OPR file privately. While reading Reed's second statement, Schippers blurted out, "What is this crap!? Bob, you must read this garbage! I understand why Mr. Stowe questions her mental stability."

As I read Reed's second interview, I was surprised to learn that she told OPR investigators that four FBIHQ supervisors had harassed her over the past few years.

I turned to Schippers and said, "I guess in her mind, every guy who talks to her is sexually harassing her. Dave, what is happening here?"

After reading the entire OPR file, Shippers said, "How can OPR think they are going to get away with this crap? Everything in here proves you are innocent, and she needs to be fired for filing a false sexual harassment complaint against you!"

The OPR Appeal and My Meeting with SAC McChesney

"Because they can, and they will get away with punishing me because FBI management does not have to answer to anyone, Dave. I know you still do not believe me, but they will not reverse the thirty days off finding no matter how innocent I am," I said.

"They have to reverse the ruling. Their outcome is a complete joke!" he said.

"Again, I am happy you and Chicago management know I am innocent. I know you're an incredible attorney, Dave, but not even you can convince them to reverse their decision," I said.

January 11, 2001, was the scheduled date of my OPR oral appeal of the proposed thirty days off without pay. Knowing that OPR would not reverse its decision and that they would record the appeal, I drafted a three-page statement that was critical of them, which I intended to read to the appeal board.[433] After reading my prepared statement, Schippers said, "Bob, if you read this statement, you will seal your fate."

"Dave, you still do not get it. They will not change their minds. I will tell you what, if you can point out one thing in that statement that is not true, I will not read the statement," I said.

Schippers agreed that everything in the statement was correct and that I should read my statement to the appeal board.

The appeal took place by phone. Schippers and I were in his Chicago law office while the appeal committee members were at FBIHQ in Washington, DC. At the onset of the oral presentation, Schippers complained OPR did not receive my forty-one-page statement with the list of eleven witnesses to be interviewed, even though he had insisted the interviewers accept it. He then expressed dismay when he learned OPR had contacted none of the eleven witnesses. He also informed the OPR appeal board that the eleven witnesses could provide critical information regarding the accusing agent's questionable character, reputation, and perpetuity for misinterpreting conversations. In addition, he said there were many mitigating factors in my favor, which OPR chose not to follow up on and, sometimes, outright ignored.

The OPR Assistant Director (AD) revealed that the appeal committee had discovered a problem with the OPR investigation. Sitting behind his desk, Schippers gave a thumbs-up sign, showing that OPR realized they had made a mistake. The AD stated, "Our procedures do very much contemplate that an employee's version of facts and any information they consider exculpatory or leading to exculpatory information should be in the file, but it was not particularly focused on or brought to our attention at the decisional level. Therefore, we are now going to have to go back and examine it in-depth."

Leaning back in his leather executive chair, Schippers gave me two thumbs-ups.

The AD continued, "One of the things which I think would help would be if you, at your earliest convenience, could either have Special Agent Wright do it, or you do it on his behalf, identify for us what kind of information those eleven witnesses would be anticipated to present. For example, just looking at the description of the names, it does not look like all of them necessarily have personal knowledge of the particular events in question that occurred or, subsequently, that they might have general knowledge about what may have been a bureaucratic battle between two offices."

"That is part of it, but the witnesses would cast grave doubt on the complaining witness's credibility," said Schippers.

"Well, that is why it would be very helpful for us if we could have a description of the evidence which you think could be elicited from those various witnesses," said the AD.

The OPR Appeal and My Meeting with SAC McChesney

Leaning back in his leather executive chair, Schippers gives me a big smile and two thumbs-up again.

Near the conclusion of the appeal conference call, the AD asked me to resubmit the list of my witnesses with an explanation of what each could contribute to the investigation. The appeal board assured us they would read the summary. Schippers believed they would do the right thing and clear me of Reed's false allegations. Because of the positive tone of the appeal, I decided not to read my three-page prepared statement. It seemed the appeal board intended to fix their wrongful finding against me.

However, following the appeal call, I said, "Dave, if OPR doesn't interview any of the eleven witnesses on my list, they will not change their ruling."

"Bob, it is a done deal. They got it wrong, and they know it. You are going to be cleared. Just get your summary and witness list together so we can send it to the FBI," said Schippers.

On January 18, 2001, I completed the witness list and faxed it to Mr. Schippers.[434] I then called him and said, "Dave, I know it sounded as though they are going to do the right thing here, but I am telling you, if they do not interview these witnesses before April, we will need to file a civil lawsuit against Agent Reed before July."

"What are you thinking?" asked Dave.

I explained that if OPR did not begin the interviews by April, they would not conduct them at all. They would then continue with their initial thirty-day off ruling and get away with it because they would not have to answer to anyone. "Dave, that's how FBI management works," I said.

"Bob, I think you are being paranoid; however, you have warned me since day one that the FBI was going to find you guilty, even though you were innocent. Considering what has already happened, I understand your concerns. Therefore, if they do not interview any of these eleven witnesses within three to four months, we will file a civil lawsuit against Agent Reed," he said. He sent my witness list to FBIHQ on January 19, 2001.

In late March 2001, I informed Schippers that the OPR unit had interviewed none of my eleven witnesses. We again discussed the filing of a civil lawsuit against Reed for causing "intentional infliction of mental distress and intentional interference with prospective advantage."

In addition, we discussed filing a second lawsuit against the FBI concerning my manuscript in the future. I knew that once the FBI discovered the contents of this manuscript, they would go to any lengths to stop it from ever being shown to any member of the US Congress. The last thing the FBI wants is for the American public to learn about their intentional failure to protect them from Middle Eastern terrorist attacks in favor of protecting the terrorists. Schippers agreed that if OPR had conducted no interviews before May 1, he would prepare and file a civil lawsuit against Reed.

Although we knew the FBI would have the civil lawsuit against Reed dismissed, knowing the FBI was punishing me for Reed's false allegations, I wanted to create a legal public record regarding her malicious conduct. In addition, filing the civil lawsuit would legally identify the actual name of Reed, allowing other FBI agents to learn about her malicious filing of the sexual harassment complaint against another agent. Unlike myself, other agents would have prior knowledge of her demeanor.

My supervisor in the SRA had supported me since my arrival in July 2000, and I did not want him to learn about any lawsuits filed

The OPR Appeal and My Meeting with SAC McChesney

on my behalf from any source other than me. Therefore, I gave my supervisor a heads up about the potential lawsuits that may be filed against Reed within the next two months and another against the FBI, on my behalf, at a later date, concerning a manuscript I had been writing and was nearing completion.

The supervisor said he was now bound to notify the front office of the possible pending lawsuits to be filed on my behalf. Within fifteen minutes of receiving an email from my supervisor about the pending lawsuits, SAC McChesney called him. He told me that she wanted to see me in her office at 9:00 a.m. the next day. March 8, 2001, would be the first time she had spoken to me since 1999 when she removed me from the VB investigation and the JTTF. During our photo taken in September 2000, she and I did not speak other than to say "hi" and congratulate me on my ten years with the FBI.

The following morning, I met with her in her office. We sat at a small round table. She asked, "Bob, how are you doing?"

"Fine," I said.

"How do you like the SRA?" she asked.

"It's all right."

"What type of investigations are you working?" she continued.

"Low-level bank fraud cases. Several of which include low-level Middle Eastern subjects linked to major terrorism subjects from my Vulgar Betrayal case you took me off of in 1999 and then killed shortly after that," I said.

"Bob, sometimes the best way to attack these groups is to go after the smaller players," she remarked.

That last comment left me speechless. After taking a minute to digest what she had said, I stated, "Ma'am, I identified the creation of the entire US-based HAMAS network, including the financiers and those who established the HAMAS network in America. HAMAS is going strong today because the FBI is doing absolutely nothing about their terrorism activities. The International Terrorism Unit (ITU) is a complete joke. It is so screwed up."

"The Terrorism Unit has many problems which need to be addressed," she said.

I continued, "Hundreds of people have died, including five American citizens, because the FBI did not do its job. A lot more people are going to die from Middle Eastern terrorist attacks in the future because the FBI is not doing its job. I cannot believe you allowed the Vulgar Betrayal case to be closed. Could you please explain your justification for closing it?"

"The United States Attorney's Office would not identify the criminal violations which would be used to prosecute the subjects," McChesney said.

"If you had asked me the same question, I would have given you the same answer. We were in the middle of a major international terrorism investigation, which was nowhere near completion," I said.

"There was a statute of limitations problem," she claimed.

"That is not true. With the recent arrest of Sarsour in Israel, I could link his 1999 material support in the aiding of HAMAS terrorism activities to the activities of other US-based HAMAS members dating back to 1989. Using the RICO statute, we could have gone back ten years and have gotten all of them for their HAMAS-related activities," I informed her.

"Bob, why didn't you pursue a RICO violation?" she asked.

"What? That is exactly what I was doing. I wrote it in my case summaries, which I sent to other divisions and FBIHQ, telling them we were conducting a RICO investigation. On October 23, 1998,

The OPR Appeal and My Meeting with SAC McChesney

in a priority teletype from the FBI director to Chicago regarding the Vulgar Betrayal investigation, the subject title was Vulgar Betrayal; Act of Terrorism—Racketeer Influenced and Corrupt (RICO).[435] On June 14, 1999, just six weeks before you removed me from my case, I sent a nineteen-page summary titled AOT-IT HAMAS, listing violations under investigation as material support, international money laundering, conspiracy, extortion, and RICO.[436] The summary detailed the RICO activities we were investigating. On July 27, 1999, you requested that National Security designate Vulgar Betrayal as a major case. Two weeks later, you took my case away and shut it down. A lot of innocent people are going to die because of your closing of Vulgar Betrayal. How will you ever explain your closing of Vulgar Betrayal in the future?" I asked her.

While she was staring at me and failing to reply to my question, I said, "Ma'am, there was no credible or justifiable reason to ever close this successful international terrorism case."

She remained silent as she continued staring at me.

As I sat in the chair shaking my head in disbelief, I thought about how SSA Ewing and FBIHQ SSA Clinton had continually obstructed the VB investigation throughout the case. I now realized McChesney clearly had no clue how dangerous the US-based Middle Eastern terrorists were to the national security of the US. I broke the silence by saying, "The problem is, the people you relied upon to determine the fate of Vulgar Betrayal misled you and lied to you. People like Clinton and Ewing, whom you promoted as the new supervisor of the HAMAS squad."

Again, McChesney did not respond as she stared at me. As I continued shaking my head in disbelief, I again broke the silence: "Let me ask you another question. If I said I wanted to lock up and deport all HAMAS terrorists from the US, would you find anything wrong with my making this statement?"

"No," said McChesney.

I then told her what occurred after Ewing overheard me make this comment. I explained how Ewing purposely concealed evidence and provided false information with the intent to obstruct the VB investigation. I also informed her about Clinton's comments to others nationwide to discredit and obstruct VB.

Not wanting to discuss international terrorism further, she changed the subject by asking, "I understand you intend to file some lawsuits. Can you tell me why?"

"I will talk to you about the first lawsuit, but I will not discuss the second lawsuit we expect we will be forced to file in the future against the bureau. I have no confidence in the OPR unit, and I realize they will not rescind the thirty-days-off recommendation and, worse yet, that Reed, who should be fired, is going to get away with filing the false sexual harassment complaint against me. Therefore, my attorney and I agree that a civil lawsuit needs to be filed against her."

To my surprise, she said, "I agree. You need to pursue legal action against her. However, we expect OPR will reverse its ruling shortly."

"Thank you for understanding why I need to sue her. This whole situation was wrong, and I continue to be punished for something I did not do. Stowe called this matter 'a serious miscarriage of justice.' The first time he met my attorney, the first words out of his mouth were, 'Bob's innocent.' It is inexcusable how others can stand by and allow this to happen to me," I said.

"We will have to wait for their appeal decision. Bob, would you provide me with advanced notice of any lawsuits that you may file in the future?" she asked.

The OPR Appeal and My Meeting with SAC McChesney

"Sure, that will not be a problem. I do not intend to blindside anyone. I have nothing to hide. I only want the truth to come out about what happened here regarding the OPR matter and the wrongful closing of the Vulgar Betrayal investigation," I said.

"I understand you are authoring a book. Is it about the FBI?" she asked.

"Yes, I am almost finished with it. I wish you could read it," I responded confidently, knowing what it contained.

"Can you tell me what it covers?" she asked.

"Absolutely not," I said.

"You realize that as an FBI employee, you must submit the book to the FBI for review before publishing it," she said.

"I know the rules inside and out. I know exactly what the requirements are of the pre-publication unit before I can publish any of the information," I said.

"Are you unhappy in the SRA? Would you like a transfer to some other squad or one of the other RAs?" she asked.

"I am not unhappy in the SRA. Before arriving there, I had lost faith in the FBI and its investigation ability while working on the International Terrorism squad. However, since arriving, it is the first time in a while that I have seen so many agents working hard on their cases. This has restored my faith in the FBI and the dedication of the street agents. Unfortunately, I rarely saw that type of dedication while assigned to the International Terrorism squad," I said.

"Historically, the RAs are the bread and butter of the FBI. There is much challenging work conducted," she said.

"I worked in a three-man RA in Kansas City before transferring here. You are right, there is much more challenging work in the RAs," I agreed.

"Bob, if you want to transfer to another RA or a squad downtown, do not hesitate to let me know," she stated.

"I will. Thank you," I said.

The meeting ended.

When I arrived at the SRA following our meeting, I told the other agents about the meeting. Senior agents exchanged glances after being informed of my conversation with McChesney. They then warned me that she would retaliate against me for threatening to file lawsuits and speaking my mind to her regarding her closing VB. Being naive, I was confident she would not retaliate against me.

I told Schippers about my meeting with McChesney the following day. We discussed the manuscript I had been writing and submitted the paperwork to the FBI to allow me to meet with publishers. Schippers published *Sell Out*, number three on *The New York Times* bestsellers list. He said he wanted me to meet with the publisher of his book in the future. However, we both agreed that the number one priority was to provide a copy of the manuscript to members of Congress to warn them about the FBI's intentional failure to pursue known Middle Eastern terrorists living and operating in the United States.

The FBI pre-publication review approval process had two parts. First, I needed approval to engage in outside employment before agreeing with a publisher to publish my manuscript. Second, I was required to submit my manuscript to the FBI for pre-publication review to approve the public release of the manuscript. Since I was an FBI employee, I needed to submit the manuscript to my SAC, who would read it and forward it to FBIHQ with their recommendation. The FBIHQ pre-publication review unit would review the manuscript and respond to my request for permission to publish it within thirty business days from the date I submitted the manuscript to the SAC.

The OPR Appeal and My Meeting with SAC McChesney

Many believed the FBI would never permit me to publish this manuscript because the subject of the manuscript concerned an international terrorism investigation that was negligently closed by FBI management. However, according to the FBI pre-publication review rules, the FBI review was to decide whether the manuscript contained any classified or sensitive information within FBI files. In addition, the FBI rules state, "No objection to disclosure or publication by a current employee will be interposed solely because a work is critical or disparaging of the FBI, the government, or its officers and employees. The FBI will not object to the disclosure or publication of such material, but the author may be warned that disclosure is not without potential consequences."[437] Although I was almost finished with the book, I still needed another three to four months to complete it.

On March 31, 2001, as many FBI agents had done in the past, I sent the FBI's request for an "Outside Employment" form to the Chicago front office requesting permission to meet with a list of six book publishers. Chicago was required to forward my request to headquarters. However, the next day, I found the "Outside Employment" paperwork in my mail folder with a note requesting a written summary of my manuscript. I refused to share the manuscript's subject matter and argued that I was not required to submit such a summary. The Chicago front office declined to forward my "Outside Employment" request form to FBIHQ to prevent me from talking to any publisher. However, other active FBI agents could and had done so before. McChesney wanted to know what I wrote in this book. She had every right to be worried about contents of the book, which detailed how she killed the VB case.

The front office then claimed that as long as the civil suit regarding the $1.4 million was still pending in court, I would not receive permission to publish my manuscript. The rationale was that I would have to testify at trial regarding the 1998 seizure; therefore, I could compromise my testimony to sell more books. Specifically, the FBI said it was concerned that during my testimony at the civil trial, I could say something that would cause more sales of my book and profit from it. I concurred with the conclusion of the Chicago front office and confirmed that I would hold off on submitting my manuscript for FBI pre-publication review until the civil case ended. It was confusing to read that the $1.4 million civil case was still pending, despite Stowe and FBI documents stating that the Chicago FBI office had closed the VB criminal and civil investigations. However, I was relieved to learn efforts were continuing to prevent the HAMAS terrorism funds from being returned to Mohammad Salah, the QLI, and Yassin Kadi.

CHAPTER 37

MR. SCHIPPERS'S CONFESSION

"Due to the repeated failures of FBI Management, the FBI has taken one of this country's greatest weapons in the fight against terrorism and turned that weapon on itself."

— David Schippers, Schippers and Bailey Law Firm, Chicago, IL

During the first week of June 2001, Mr. Schippers called me at work and asked me to meet him in his office at noon. In the past, he never made this kind of request. When I asked if something was wrong, he said, "I want you to meet someone and listen to her story. Bob, whatever you do, do not tell her your name. Listen to her without reacting or revealing your identity. I want you to tell me if the information she has is correct. You will understand what is happening when she tells you her story."

I agreed to be in his office at noon.

When I arrived, Schippers was excited and reiterated that I should not react to anything the woman said and to not tell her my name.

I agreed not to say anything. As we entered his office, an attractive, young, dark-haired woman sat on the sofa.

Schippers said, "Jayna, this is a friend of mine, and I would like him to hear what you have told me."

Mrs. Jayna Davis said she had worked for *NBC News* in Oklahoma City during the bombing of the Alfred P. Murrah Federal Building by Timothy McVeigh on April 19, 1995. She shared how she was working to identify the unknown terrorist whom the FBI linked to the bombing. She detailed her efforts to identify the unknown person and said the FBI and other federal agencies met her with much resistance. She told me she was authoring a book titled *The Third Terrorist* about evidence the FBI ignored following the bombing.

About fifteen minutes into her story, Jayna surprised me when she said, "I have a high-level government official in Washington, DC, who recently told me about a Chicago FBI agent named Robert Wright. Back in 1998 and 1999, Agent Wright was involved with finding specific information linking international terrorists to international terrorism activities, some based here in America."

Jayna Davis, Author, The Third Terrorist.

She continued, "My source told me about Agent Wright and how the FBI intentionally shot him down and killed his very productive Middle Eastern terrorism investigation. They messed with him because of his successful efforts in identifying and arresting Middle Eastern terrorists operating in the United States."

As she looked through a folder for a document, I looked over at Schippers, who motioned for me to remain quiet by putting his finger up to his mouth.

Mr. Schippers's Confession

Mrs. Davis continued to tell us about the VB investigation, which included specific things that no one outside the FBI could have known. She again implied that the FBI intentionally did things to force its closing. She shared why certain people in the government wanted it closed.

She then said, "The things they did to this poor FBI agent."

Schippers said, "Jayna, I want to introduce you to my friend. This is FBI Agent Robert Wright."

Jayna instantly jumped to her feet and hugged me. What she had just told us completely overwhelmed me.

After she left the office, I verified the information she mentioned regarding the VB investigation was accurate with Schippers. As I sat in a chair in front of his desk, looking through the file folder he asked me to review, he said, "Bob, I have to confess something to you. Before Jayna informed me about the FBI's actions toward you, I genuinely believed you were nuts!"

"I know, Dave," I said as I continued looking through the file folder.

"No, Bob, I thought you were nuts!" he reiterated.

"I know. It's all right, Dave," I said, still looking through the folder.

"Bob, look at me!" he said.

I looked up and asked, "What is it?"

"I am being serious when I tell you I thought you were nuts!" he restated.

I remarked, "Dave, it is all right. I have always known you thought I was nuts. Hell, if someone told me the story I told you, I would think they were nuts too. If you do not believe me, I can prove to you right now that I knew you thought I was nuts."

Perplexed, he asked, "How can you prove you knew I thought you were nuts?"

"Do you have a copy of my manuscript here in your office?" I asked.

"Yes, it's locked in my credenza. Why?" he asked.

"Pull the manuscript out and hand it to me," I said.

I located the page I wanted him to read.

Handing the manuscript back to Mr. Schippers after marking the paragraphs, I said, "Here, read these three full paragraphs on this page."

Mr. Schippers read the following three paragraphs from Chapter 32:

"In August 1999, after talking to several trusted friends outside the FBI, I decided I should try to hire Attorney David Schippers. Schippers was the Chief Investigative Council for the US House of Representatives, tasked by US Representative Henry Hyde with gathering evidence against US President William Jefferson Clinton during the impeachment process. The US House of Representatives impeached President Clinton on December 19, 1998, for high crimes and misdemeanors. Friends considered Schippers the perfect attorney to assist me with both the OPR matter and my efforts to warn Congress about the FBI's failure.

Ironically, Schippers was the attorney I had met five years earlier. In 1994, I had informed him I was concerned the FBI would continue to retaliate against me in the future. The question then was, should I remind Schippers about our 1994 meeting? Either way, he would think I was nuts when I told him about my current situation. However, I was okay with that because, if someone told me this story, I would believe they were nuts too.

Before meeting with Schippers regarding Reed's allegation, I had chosen not to say anything at that time to him regarding our 1994 meeting. Since I realized that Schippers would suspect I was paranoid or mentally unbalanced after telling him my story, I believed that

Mr. Schippers's Confession

mentioning the 1994 meeting would negatively affect his decision about whether he would represent me. However, I am confident something will happen in the future that would cause him to realize I was not a nutcase."

After Schippers finished reading the three paragraphs, he leaned back in his chair and stared at me as he ran his hands down the sides of his face. "Oh my God! You knew all this time I thought you were nuts!"

"Yes, but now you know I am not, right?" I asked.

"No, you are not nuts, Bob," he confirmed.

"In 1994, I sat in this chair as you sat behind that desk, and we had over an hour-long conversation over my concerns about the FBI's retaliation against me in the future. At the conclusion of our meeting, we both agreed there was nothing you could do. You told me if the FBI retaliated against me in the future, I should come back and see you. I warned you then I would be back in the future," I said.

Unsure of what to say, he stared at me.

"Hey, Dave, I am back!" I said, laughing.

"Bob, I do not remember meeting you," he said.

"I remember the meeting as if it were yesterday," I said.

Mr. Schippers stood up and said he would be back shortly. Ten minutes later, he returned and sat at his desk. As I looked up, he was staring at me.

"What's wrong?" I asked.

"You were really in my office in 1994, telling me this day would come in the future," he stated.

"Scary, isn't it?" I remarked.

"Bob, I did not remember you being here, so I just checked the law firm records, and you were with me for over an hour in 1994," he confirmed.

"Dave, all kidding aside, I want you to consider everything I have told you during the past two years regarding what the FBI has done to my VB investigation and me as the absolute truth. Do you now realize how bad my situation will become once they read my manuscript? The manuscript details how they intentionally and negligently killed the VB case to protect the terrorists over protecting the American public."

"I was just thinking the same thing," he remarked.

"Dave, although everyone knows I am innocent regarding Reed's sexual harassment complaint, FBIHQ OPR ignored all the evidence proving my absolute innocence. No one, not you, Walter Stowe, Agent Vincent, or others, can explain why this is happening to me. This is happening to me because FBIHQ intends to use their pathetic ruling against me in the future when this manuscript goes public. After the things I said to SAC McChesney in March, I am certain she wants to see OPR continue with their 30-day off recommendation." I said.

"Bob, the FBI must now clear you of their finding that you sexually harassed that mentally unbalanced woman," he said.

"Dave, we heard everything Jayna just said about what the FBI has been doing to me. Please trust me when I say headquarters will not change their guilty ruling against me. They will punish me by making me take thirty days off without pay for something we all know I did not do. Even though they know I am innocent. They know about the manuscript, and I promise you, they are going to tell the media, members of Congress, and the American people not to believe me because they found me guilty of sexually harassing another agent. Not to mention the new OPR investigation McChesney hit me with following my meeting with her in March. Unfortunately, I expect they will begin hitting me with more false OPR investigations in the future," I further said.

Mr. Schippers's Confession

"Bob, how can they justify opening more OPRs against you?" asked Schippers.

"Dave, after everything Jayna told us, you must now realize they are going to come after me, with everything they have, to prevent me from telling Congress and the American people the truth," I said.

Looking concerned, he said, "Bob, this is much bigger than I ever suspected. What is about to happen is beyond the capacity of my small law firm. Would you mind if I bring in another law firm from Washington, DC, to help assist with your case?"

"Dave, we need all the help you can provide. When FBI management reads the manuscript in the future, they are going to come after me with OPRs and anything else they can to fire me. Once they fire me, they will claim I am a former disgruntled employee making things up about them in retaliation for being fired. They will get away with it unless we stay a step or two ahead of them. I do not have a problem with you bringing in another law firm," I said.

"I have a law firm in mind. I will call the head of the firm after you leave," he said.

He then informed me someone who wanted to help with my book had contacted him.

"Bob, to protect you, I will not tell you why or who contacted me."

"Okay," I said.

"I have a question for you. Are there any documents you need that will help you tell your story regarding the FBI's terrorism failures?" he asked.

"Dave, I am confused by your question," I said.

"I remember you saying something about needing confessions of some terrorists arrested overseas. Do you still need those confessions?" he clarified.

"Yes, there are confessions of two terrorists arrested in Israel I could use. But I can't get them since the FBI classified them as secret documents," I said.

Schippers asked for the names of the two men.

"Sheik Abu Tair, from Palestine, and Jamil Sarsour, from Milwaukee," I said.

"What about Mohammad Salah? Do you need his confessions?" he asked.

"No, I have already legally gotten all of Salah's confessions and interviews," I answered.

"Please print the names of the two you need on this paper. We will have no further discussions about this," he requested.

On Friday, June 8, 2001, following a meeting with another AUSA in the United States Attorney's Office regarding one of my cases, I ran into AUSA James Robertson. Robertson asked if I had time to talk with him in his office. After entering his office, he closed the door and asked, "Bob, can you tell me why you are doing the things you are doing to expose the problems with the FBI's terrorism efforts?"

"My main reason is to save lives," I said.

"What do you mean?" he asked.

"We could have shut down the entire HAMAS criminal enterprise, but they intentionally killed the case. Because of that, they have allowed HAMAS to continue growing, and HAMAS is continuing to kill innocent civilians, with funds gained from the criminal activities that the FBI has ignored. It is only a matter of time before a Middle Eastern terrorist attack happens here. I hired Mr. Schippers in August 1999 to help with Agent Reed's false allegation and to help me reach members of Congress to warn them about the FBI's terrorism failures before it's too late. Vulgar Betrayal needs to be reopened to pursue HAMAS and the other terrorist organizations we discovered," I explained.

With a look of relief on his face, he said, "That is good."

Confused by his look, I asked, "Why did you think I was doing what I am doing to expose the FBI's incompetence?"

"We were not sure. We were concerned it might be because you were bitter, disgruntled, or wanted to get even with the FBI after what they did to you," he explained.

"How can I live with myself if I do not do everything I can to expose the FBI's incompetence? Eventually, it will happen here, and I must do anything I can to prevent it from happening. The truth will be embarrassing for the FBI, but that is not my problem. Saving lives is my top priority. The terrorism responsibilities must be removed from the FBI and given to a new agency whose sole mission identify and neutralize the terrorists," I said.

"Bob, we have a problem with the $1.4 million we seized in 1998," he added.

"What is the problem?" I asked.

"Vulgar Betrayal has been closed, and the FBI refuses to assist our office with our pending civil action concerning the $1.4 million we seized. This is a copy of one of two letters we sent to SAC McChesney, asking her to reopen the FBI Vulgar Betrayal case and to bring you back on the case," he shared.

After reading the letter sent to McChesney, I asked, "What did she say?"

"Nothing. She has not responded to the two requests," he stated.

"So, what happens to the $1.4 million?" I asked.

"Since the FBI will not assist us with the case, we will have to return the money to the individuals from whom it was seized," he informed me.

"You cannot let that happen!" I exclaimed.

"Remember when I once asked you if Yassin Kadi might be Osama bin Laden?" he asked.

"Yes, I answered it was not likely, but Kadi may be an associate of bin Laden's," I said.

"Did you discover anything about Kadi?" he inquired.

"I sent a lead to FBI legats in several Middle Eastern countries to ask our counterparts about bank accounts and individuals we had identified through Vulgar Betrayal within each country. There were many questions for authorities in Saudi Arabia regarding the bank accounts of Yassin Kadi and others living there. Shortly after I sent these leads, McChesney removed me from Vulgar Betrayal. Oh my God! You cannot give the $1.4 million back to the terrorists!" I restated.

"Can you stay here longer?" he inquired.

"Yes, I am not in any hurry," I said.

"I will be right back," he promised.

To my surprise, a few minutes later, he returned with one of the highest-ranking officials from the United States Attorney's Office. The supervisor sat beside me and said, "Hi, Bob."

"Hello ma'am, it has been a long time," I said.

"Yes, it has. I understand you have been brought up to speed about our situation regarding the $1.4 million," she mentioned.

"I have. McChesney will never reopen the Vulgar Betrayal case or let me work on any FBI terrorism matter ever again," I said.

"We have figured that out. That leads us to why we're here with you now. We have a question for you," the supervisor informed.

Mr. Schippers's Confession

"What is your question?" I asked.

"Bob, this will be a highly unusual request. If you say no, we will understand. Would you be willing to come to our office after your workdays end at the FBI and on weekends to help us with the civil seizure case?" asked the supervisor.

"To prevent the $1.4 million from going back to the terrorists, I have no problem with helping you. When do you want me to start?" I asked.

The supervisor said, "You two can decide that."

"However, there is one thing I must do first. I must run this by my attorney, Dave Schippers," I said.

"That is fine," said the supervisor.

After leaving the United States Attorney's Office, I went to Schippers's office to inform him about the request. I told him I wanted to assist them in preventing the return of the $1.4 million to Middle Eastern terrorists. Dave was unhappy about my offer to help them.

"No way! Bob, I understand why you want to do this, but once the FBI finds out what you are doing, and they will find out, they will fire you!" he protested.

"Dave, no one else can help them with this case. I am the only one who knows what needs to be done," I said.

"Bob, now that I realize you are not nuts, I have initiated several things to help you get your message out to Congress before there is an actual terrorist attack in the United States. I have called several congressional representatives. I am working on identifying well-known media reporters to assist us in the future and contacting a law firm in Washington, DC. I appreciate that you want to help, but if you get fired, and you will get fired, this will all be a waste of time," he stated.

"Fine, I will not help them. I just cannot believe headquarters and McChesney wants the $1.4 million returned to the HAMAS terrorists. How pathetic is all this, Dave?" I asked.

"Bob, I understand, but we need to protect you. I am here to protect you," he said.

"I understand. Thanks, Dave," I said.

"Bob, do you know of any effort by the FBI to blame you for closing the Vulgar Betrayal investigation?" he asked.

"No, why? What are you thinking?" I asked.

"If something bad happens, such as a terrorist attack in the future, and it comes out the Vulgar Betrayal investigation should never have been closed, McChesney and others at FBIHQ will need a scapegoat. And you, my friend, will become their scapegoat," said Dave.

"There is no way in hell they could ever blame me for the closing of Vulgar Betrayal, Dave," I said.

"After all they have done to you, I would not put it past them to make some false claim, such as you did something illegal, which forced them to close Vulgar Betrayal," he remarked.

I assured him, "I understand where you are going with this, Dave, but others could come to my defense and say the FBI is lying. The US Attorney's Office has asked me to help them prevent the $1.4 million from being returned to the terrorists without the FBI's knowledge. All because McChesney refuses to allow the FBI to help them. They even sent her two letters requesting she reopen the case and bring me back to help prevent the $1.4 million from being returned to the terrorists. They let me read one of these letters, and she refused to reply to the letters. How pathetic is that?"

Mr. Schippers's Confession

"Yeah, the US Attorney's Office is really desperate to keep that money from being returned to HAMAS and Kadi. Bob, I was a federal prosecutor with the Department of Justice, and until today, I have never heard of a US Attorney's Office making such a request to an active FBI agent. I understand and do not blame them for asking for your help to prevent the money from being returned to the terrorists. But I must protect you. You are right, if the FBI ever tries to use you as their scapegoat, I am confident the US Attorney's Office would come to your defense," said Dave.

"Dave, the person responsible for closing Vulgar Betrayal and allowing the $1.4 million to be returned to the terrorists, is SAC McChesney. Unfortunately, she will never be held accountable for her negligence unless my manuscript becomes public," I said

"I agree. But if something really bad happens in the future, and it comes out she closed VB, she will pay a heavy price for what she has done, Bob," said Schippers.

Following our meeting, I called the US Attorney's Office. I shared why I could not assist their office in preventing the $1.4 million from being returned. The US Attorney's Office understood Schippers's concerns and warned me to listen to his advice in the future when the FBI came after me.

The following day, Saturday, June 9, 2001, because AUSA Robertson had questioned my motive for exposing the FBI's dereliction of duty in the terrorism arena, and aware many others would ask Schippers the same questions, I drafted a mission statement. On Monday, June 11, I provided a copy of my mission statement to Schippers. My mission statement reads the following:

MISSION STATEMENT
OF SPECIAL AGENT ROBERT WRIGHT, JR.
June 9, 2001

The FBI is America's top law enforcement agency, and as such, its mission is to protect America and its citizens at home and abroad. The strength of the FBI has always been the public trust in the integrity and quality of FBI investigations. However, in light of the many FBI mistakes which have surfaced during the past decade, and additional mistakes which will be exposed in future legal actions and a book I am writing titled, Fatal Betrayals of the Intelligence Mission [aka: VULGAR BETRAYAL], America's confidence level in the FBI will further erode. However, as a nation we must work together in seeking to regain the confidence level we once had in the FBI to achieve its vital mission of protecting the safety and welfare of America and its citizens throughout the world.

The FBI is going through a difficult time; however, I am confident the FBI and the American people can overcome these difficulties. Together, we can and must resolve the difficult issues surrounding the problems within the FBI. America cannot afford to have its top law enforcement agency continue to be lax in areas fundamental to the national security of this country. I love America and likewise I love the FBI, particularly its purpose and mission; however, the mission has been seriously jeopardized to the point American lives have been needlessly lost. Accordingly, I am seeking a thorough review and complete "house cleaning" to identify and fix the FBI's problems, whether they be managers, agents, procedures, policies, and/or inadequate laws.

There [is] a combination of reasons the FBI has failed to maintain public trust. These reasons include:

1. The lack of quality managers.
2. The lack of program goals & objectives.
3. The lack of modern computer technology.
4. Failing to modernize investigative objectives.
5. The agency is overwhelmed with too many investigative violations.
6. A lack of independent oversight of the agency (incompetent managers are not held accountable for their mistakes).
7. The FBI's internal affairs unit (OPR) is biased and unfair.
8. Serious Intelligence vs. Criminal investigative conflicts have contributed to the preventable deaths of American citizens.
9. The FBI's duplication of the investigative jurisdictions of other federal law enforcement agencies, such as the DEA and ATF.

As an eleven-year veteran of the FBI, it is my opinion the management of the FBI is incapable of resolving these issues on its own. Any cosmetic attempt by the FBI to fix itself is not realistic. Little would change, because of the mentality of the poor FBI leadership. Therefore, in the interest of America's National and Economic Security, I believe President Bush and Congress should work together to implement a task force made up of experts from outside the FBI. To conduct a top to bottom review of the FBI's hiring procedures, investigative procedures, outdated or unnecessary investigative violations, information technology, records management, overall organizational structure, and the FBI mission.

The task force should include experts from state and local law enforcement offices, computer technology experts, management information specialists, and state and federal prosecutors. Anyone affected by or [who] relies upon the FBI should be involved in this critical and necessary restructuring of the FBI. Programs and administration of each FBI office should be effective. The information collected by the FBI should be used to effectively protect American citizens and the national and economic security of America.

A significant percentage of the criminal activity investigated by the FBI is directly linked to the sale or use of illegal drugs. The FBI has even established drug squads to investigate drug related matters. However, a separate federal agency, the Drug Enforcement Agency (DEA) already exists. Therefore, I believe the task force should seriously consider consolidating the DEA into the FBI.

More importantly, the task force must seriously consider removing the terrorism investigative matters from the hands of the FBI. For reasons of consistency, reliability, and national security, these responsibilities should be assigned to a new federal anti-terrorism agency. The assets of the DEA could be used to fund the new anti-terrorism agency. Switch the terrorism responsibilities of the FBI with the nation's illegal drug responsibilities.

Knowing what I know, I can confidently say that until the investigative responsibilities for terrorism are transferred from the FBI, I will not feel safe. The FBI has proven for the past decade it cannot identify and prevent acts of terrorism against the United States and its citizens at home and abroad. Even worse, there is no effort by the FBI's International Terrorism Unit (ITU) to neutralize known and suspected international terrorists residing within the United States. Unfortunately, more terrorist attacks against American interests coupled with the loss of American lives will have to occur before those in power give this matter the urgent attention it deserves.

Realizing more American lives are going to be needlessly lost; no one should expect me to consciously sit idly by and pretend to forget the things I know. By sharing what I know, the terrorism problems plaguing America may be corrected. Knowing what I know, I truly believe I would be derelict in my duty as an American if I did not do my best to bring the FBI's dereliction of duty to the attention of others. Therefore, to prevent more deadly terrorist attacks against American interests at home and abroad, I have made it my mission, with the legal assistance of Attorney David Schippers, to legally expose the problems of the FBI to the President of the United States, US Congress, and the American people.[438]

Six days later, on June 15, 2001, FBIHQ issued a national press release to announce that FBI Director Freeh had promoted Chicago SAC McChesney to one of the FBI Assistant Director positions.

"McChesney will become the assistant director in charge of training, based at the FBI Academy at Quantico, Virginia."

Freeh said McChesney has distinguished herself in a variety of assignments.

He said, "As an investigator, supervisor, program manager and as twice head of a field office, Kathleen had demonstrated success at every level. She is an innovator with a vision for the future, which makes her extremely well-suited to lead one of the most important divisions of the FBI."[439]

"The FBI has 14 Assistant Directors—eleven who head divisions at FBI Headquarters and three who head field offices in New York, Los Angeles, and Washington, DC. The assistant director position is the third highest in the FBI after the Director and the Deputy Director."[440]

After learning about McChesney's promotion to assistant director, I thought about my meeting with her on March 8. Specifically, when I asked her, "How are you going to explain your closing of Vulgar Betrayal in the future?" To which she never replied as she stared at me.

Unfortunately, now, with her promotion, she will never have to justify her gross negligent closing of VB. Even worse, she may become the first female FBI director in the future.

Also on June 15, Schippers discovered that the OPR unit had interviewed none of my eleven witnesses. He asked, "Bob, what are they doing? It has been six months. Why are they taking so long to interview them?"

I admitted that I would sound paranoid by expressing my belief that I knew what they were up to.

Perplexed, he said, "Tell me because this makes no sense."

"I am still on the transfer list for Indianapolis, and as long as they keep this OPR investigation open, I cannot transfer to Indianapolis. They usually issue the transfers near the end of the fiscal year, during August and September. If the OPR unit upholds the decision of thirty days off without pay before August or September, I will be placed on probation for one year. During this probation period, I cannot receive a transfer to Indianapolis or any other FBI division. In effect, the FBI will have prevented me from receiving my transfer to Indianapolis from 1999 through 2002. That's over three years after Agent Reed filed her complaint. This is what they're waiting for, Dave. If this occurs because of her complaint, I will have lost the VB case, not be able to transfer to Indianapolis for over three years, and face a thirty-day unpaid leave for her false accusation," I clarified.

He asked, "Do you truly believe this is what they'll do to you?"

"Yes, I do. Dave, the forty-one-page document we provided was more than enough to find me innocent. If OPR had relied only on the document, they would have cleared me of her allegations by now. They should have already conducted at least one interview with the eleven witnesses to confirm what's in the document. You do not understand the retaliation of FBI management. I do. I warned you from the beginning that the FBI would wrongly punish me. Dave, they have no intention of reversing the punishment, no matter that the investigators and Stowe determined I was innocent and Reed is mentally unstable," I said.

"Do they think they'll get away with giving you a thirty-day unpaid leave for this crap?" he asked.

"It is easy, Dave. They do not have to answer anyone. I will have no recourse against them. I have no choice but to appeal to the same people who punished me unjustly. Dave, please believe me, I am going to get hit with the thirty days off," I said.

"Bob, I believe you. We need to sue Agent Reed before OPR announces their final decision," he said.

"I agree. I want to stay one step ahead of them by getting this lawsuit filed against her as soon as possible," I said.

Since federal law prohibits anyone from suing an agent of the US government in federal court, Schippers filed a civil suit against Reed as an individual, not as an FBI agent, in an Illinois state court. He said how the DOJ might rule she was acting within the scope of her employment when she filed the false complaint. If so, the DOJ would request to transfer the matter from state court to federal court. Once the case moved to federal court, the DOJ would file to dismiss the case since federal law prohibits such lawsuits against an agent.

After Schippers said the DOJ would dismiss the lawsuit, I said, "Dave, I do not care what they do. It's not about money. This lawsuit will serve as a warning shot to let Reed and the FBI know we are coming after them for what they have done. By suing, we will warn other agents about Reed's vindictiveness by publicly recording her name and actions toward me."

"I cannot believe what they've done to you, Bob. Due to the repeated failures of FBI management, the FBI has taken one of this country's greatest weapons in the fight against terrorism and turned that weapon on itself," remarked Schippers.

I thought about what he said and realized he was right. I had taken all of my focus and energy used to pursue the Middle Eastern terrorists through VB and redirected it in exposing the FBI's gross negligence to Congress and the American public.

"Dave, I have done everything possible to prevent this. They have left me with no choice," I said.

"I agree," said Schippers.

"Dave, I need you to do me a favor before you file the lawsuit. Please call McChesney and tell her we are suing Reed. I promised her I would give her advance notice before filing any lawsuits. She will not have a problem with our suing Reed because, in March, she agreed I needed to sue her," I said.

"No problem, I will call her after you leave," he said.

On June 18, 2001, Schippers filed a nine-page complaint containing two counts in the Circuit Court of Cook County against Cybil Reed, seeking $150,000 in damages per each count. The complaint reads, in part, the following:

FACTS GIVING RISE TO THE CAUSE OF ACTION
COUNT ONE
Intentional Infliction of Mental Distress

10. In or about 1995, Wright developed and implemented an investigative plan to identify and neutralize foreign Middle Eastern terrorist organizations operating throughout the United States.

11. During his investigation, Wright identified a resident of the United States who was directly involved in the terrorist activities in the United States and elsewhere. Wright opened a case and began an intense in-depth investigation of that individual's financial and other activities.

12. In or about 1999, Wright became aware that [Reed] had also opened a criminal case in Milwaukee concerning the same individual and his activities.

13. Reed demanded that her case be given precedence and that she be assigned to be the lead agent, with the Chicago investigation as secondary.

14. In order to avoid confusion and duplication of effort, the FBI decided that the investigation must be coordinated out of one office.

15. As a result, in July 1999, a meeting was arranged, and an agreement was reached between Milwaukee and Chicago Special Agents in Charge.

16. On the morning of July 20, 1999, [Reed] was instructed to close her case and Wright was told to proceed with his investigation.

17. [Reed] became extremely angry. She complained for two hours and bemoaned that Wright "had won."

She held Wright responsible for her being instructed to close out her case.

23. On July 22, 1999, two days after she was ordered to close her case and defer to the Chicago investigation being conducted by Wright, [Reed] filed with the FBI Office of Professional Responsibility a false and malicious charge against Wright in which she alleged that he had engaged in a "pattern of sexual harassment."

26. The conduct of the Defendant as stated above was extreme and went beyond all bounds of decency. The conduct was, accordingly, outrageous within the purview of the laws of the State of Illinois.

27. As a direct and proximate result of the Defendant's intentional and outrageous conduct as alleged, he suffered irremediable injury to his personal and professional reputation, was subject to a full investigation and disciplinary proceedings by the FBI and was relieved of his cases in international terrorism.

28. As a direct and proximate result of the Defendant's intentional and outrageous conduct, Plaintiff has in fact suffered severe and permanent mental and emotional distress as was specifically intended by the Defendant when she engaged in that outrageous conduct.

WHEREFORE, Plaintiff, Robert G. Wright, Jr. prays judgment against the Defendant, Cybil [Reed], for damages in the amount of One Hundred Fifty Thousand dollars ($150,000) and such other relief as this Court deems just in the premises.[441]

COUNT TWO
Intentional Interference with Prospective Advantage

35. With full knowledge of the results and with the specific intent to interfere with and harm Plaintiff's reasonable expectation of future advantage, on July 22, 1999, Defendant filed a charge of sexual harassment with the FBI/OPR.

36. The actions by the Defendant as alleged in paragraph 35, were done with malice in that:

a) The Defendant knew her charges to be false.

b) The Defendant knew that her charges would result in a disciplinary investigation.

c) The Defendant acted with the specific intent to destroy the Plaintiff's career; and

d) The Defendant filed the false charges two days after the Plaintiff prevailed in a work-related jurisdictional dispute over the Defendant.

37. As a direct and proximate result of the actions of the Defendant, as alleged, and as the Defendant specifically intended, the Plaintiff was publicly humiliated, and embarrassed. He suffered irremediable injury to his personal and professional reputation, was subject to a full investigation resulting in a recommendation of disciplinary action against him and was relieved of his duties in international terrorism.

38. As a direct and proximate result of the false and malicious statement and actions by the Defendant and the actions of the FBI caused by such statements and actions, Plaintiff's career as a Special Agent of the FBI had been destroyed. He will never attain the prospective advantage that he enjoyed prior to the Defendant's false and malicious statements and actions in that he will no longer advance financially

and professionally within the FBI as he had previously anticipated.

WHEREFORE, Plaintiff, Robert G. Wright, Jr. prays judgment be entered against the Defendant, Cybil [Reed], for damages in the amount of One Hundred Fifty Thousand dollars ($150,000) and such other relief as this Court deems just in the premises.[442]

The following morning, the *Chicago Tribune* and *Chicago Sun-Times* ran stories about the filing of the suit. The *Chicago Sun-Times* article reads below:

> *FBI agents take fight over duties to court.*
> A spy vs. spy conflict in the Chicago and Milwaukee offices of the FBI spilled into the courthouse Monday as one FBI agent sued another. Robert G. Wright, an agent on the FBI's International Terrorist Squad in Chicago, was investigating a suspected terrorist in 1999 when he learned that a Milwaukee-based FBI agent, [Cybil Reed], was investigating the same person, Wright said in a suit filed Monday in Cook County Circuit Court.
>
> FBI agents from Milwaukee and Chicago held a meeting and decided to make Wright the lead agent on the case, the suit states. "[Reed] became extremely angry," and two days after she was ordered to close her case, she filed a charge of sexual harassment against Wright with the FBI's Office of Professional Responsibility.
>
> The office investigated the complaint and recommended disciplinary action against Wright, the suit states. He was relieved of his duties in international terrorism. Wright is still an agent, but his career has been "destroyed," the suit states.

Mr. Schippers's Confession

Wright's attorney is David P. Schippers, who gained fame as investigative counsel for the House Judiciary Committee during the impeachment proceedings against former President Bill Clinton.

[Reed] could not be reached for comment. Wright demands $150,000 from her for intentional infliction of mental distress, among other claims. The suit does not name the individual the FBI was focusing on in July 1999, when the actions in question took place.[443]

Although the above news article, and a similar one published on the same day by the *Chicago Tribune*, are public source documents that contain the actual name of Agent Reed, the FBI insisted I change her actual name in this manuscript. Therefore, I would be required to change her name in the above *Chicago Sun-Times* article. Her name change was the last remaining issue that allowed the publishing of this manuscript.

Although I wanted to continue pursuing legal means to use her actual name, my attorney convinced me to agree to the FBI's request to change her real name in the book. He convinced me after he pointed out a way around the agreement. He pointed out that the FBI could not delete the public source news stories published by the two Chicago newspapers.

Therefore, a Google search for the *Chicago Tribune* article, "FBI agents, wind up fighting selves" (https://www.chicagotribune.com/2001/06/19/fbi-agents-wind-up-fighting-selves) or the *Chicago Sun-Times* article "FBI agents take the fight over duties to the court" may show the actual name.

The same applies to the lawsuit filed against Reed on June 18, 2001, In the Circuit Court of Cook County, County Department, Law Division—Robert G. Wright, Jr., Plaintiff.

Also, on the same day these two news articles were published, there were newspaper articles published regarding FBI Director Freeh's promotion of Chicago SAC McChesney to FBI assistant director. McChesney would be transferring from Chicago to her new assignment on the last day of September 2001.

CHAPTER 38

THE FBIHQ OPR APPEAL BOARD'S DECISION

On June 21, 2001, three days after filing the civil lawsuit against Agent Reed, my supervisor informed me that ASAC Pat Daly wanted to see me in his office on the morning of June 22. After I arrived in his office, Daly said, "Bob, before we begin, we need to wait for SAC McChesney. She said she wanted to be present for this meeting."

"Is this good news or bad news?" I asked.

"Bad, I guess," said Daly.

Minutes later, wearing a red dress, McChesney entered the office and sat across from me on the north side of the room. Daly sat behind his desk at the east end of the room.

McChesney said, "Bob, I need to inform you that after learning about the filing of your lawsuit, Agent Reed informed the Indianapolis SAC that she now fears for her life. She believes you are going to come after her and harm her."

"What is her justification for making such an absurd claim?" I asked.

"I am obligated to notify you of this development. In addition, you are not allowed to visit the Indianapolis office, enter Agent Reed's residential neighborhood in Indianapolis, or attempt to make any contact with her. A communication from the Indianapolis office to Chicago is being sent saying the same."

"This is so pathetic. I am being wrongly punished for her malicious act in the first place because the OPR cannot conduct a competent and thorough investigation, and now this. What a joke!" I said.

"Bob, I do not understand why you had to file this lawsuit against her. I wish you could have just worked past it and moved on," said McChesney.

I could not believe the words that came out of her mouth. I thought, "That's it, the gloves are off. I'm no longer going to hold back." I spoke out, "Are you serious? You think I should have worked past it? That is all I have done for the past seven years! Now, I am going to fight back. This is just the beginning of my fight to expose what has happened here. Most of which occurred under your leadership, Ma'am. You even told me I needed to file a civil lawsuit against Reed. When Mr. Schippers called to inform you we were suing her, you did not discourage it."

"Bob, there were two positive stories about the FBI the day your story ran. They were both overshadowed by your lawsuit against Reed," she said. Looking at ASAC Daly, she remarked, "I do not recall any FBI agent ever suing another FBI agent."

Of course, one of these positive news stories concerned her promotion to assistant director. She was upset with the lawsuit because it "overshadowed" a story about her promotion. However, the coincidence of these two stories occurring simultaneously gave me a bit of satisfaction since I believed she would never have to answer for her

The FBIHQ OPR Appeal Board's Decision

negligent closing of VB. I couldn't let her criticize me for working to expose those in FBI management who closed VB.

"If those of you in FBI management had done your job, none of this would be happening. I do not know what you are upset about. Besides, this lawsuit is nothing compared to the next lawsuit coming down the road concerning my manuscript."

"As for the book, you cannot publish it without prior FBI approval," she said.

"Again, I know the pre-publication rules inside and out. Believe me, I know exactly what I am doing. I truly wish you could read it. My true story would disturb you. Unfortunately, the manuscript is the work product for the second lawsuit we will be forced to file against the FBI in the future. Therefore, I cannot allow you to read it now," I said.

"You are just filing lawsuits to cause problems for the FBI!" she claimed.

"Do you believe Mr. Schippers would put his reputation on the line if he did not believe we had a winnable case? He has admitted that the second lawsuit we will file against the FBI is too big for his firm to handle. Right now, he is working to bring in a major law firm from Washington, DC, to assist with the second lawsuit. Without belief in our winnable case, he wouldn't do this. We are not playing games. As I told you in March, many people have died, including American citizens, because the FBI failed to do its job, and a lot more people are going to die in the future. I am going to do whatever I can to prevent others from dying," I said.

"What do you want to achieve in the second lawsuit?" asked McChesney.

"I want to save lives. I want Congress to investigate the FBI's failure to investigate the Middle Eastern terrorists who are living and operating in America. I also want to see five agents fired for obstructing the Vulgar Betrayal investigation, including Agent Reed," I said.

"Bob, based upon what you just said, you are indicating you have information you should have turned over to FBI management to address," she pointed out.

"I told management. Nobody cared! They did nothing. I tried, but the FBI management did not care. I told you in March, and you did nothing about it," I said.

"Bob, it is your responsibility to go to the next management level to report any violations," she stated.

"Don't you dare try to put this off on me! I reported an ASAC for gross negligence in 1993, which is another reason we are here today. If I had reported your negligent closing of the Vulgar Betrayal investigation to OPR, they would clear you. Then you and many other FBI managers would retaliate against me for years," I said.

To calm things down, Daly changed the subject. "Bob, there is more. I have to notify you that you are the subject of another OPR investigation."

I asked, "What is this about, and who started it?"

"The SAC attended a meeting with members of the United States Attorney's Office a few weeks ago. During the meeting, the SAC learned you showed a classified 'Secret' document to one of the AUSAs in early 1998. The SAC then reported this matter to OPR to start this investigation."

I looked at McChesney and said, "You did this to me!"

The revelation that she had started this investigation against me dumbfounded me. I thought, "The senior agents were right. Management is going to mess with me and hit me with multiple OPR investigations." After a few moments of thinking about her retaliation effort against me, I began laughing.

The FBIHQ OPR Appeal Board's Decision

"Bob, this is not a laughing matter. This is very serious," said McChesney.

"No, this is pathetic. This is an absolute joke! I cannot believe you did this to me. Ma'am, you can hit me with all the OPRs you want. You will not silence me," I said.

Her face turned red. I remember thinking, "Her face is almost as red as her dress." No one would dare be so direct with her, let alone a street agent. At that moment, I had lost all respect for her and her leadership ability.

The OPR notification letter states, "On 6/4/01, an OPR inquiry was initiated regarding an allegation that captioned employee made an unauthorized disclosure of classified information to an Assistant United States Attorney, Northern District of Illinois in violation of a July 19, 1995, Attorney Generals Order."[444]

To again restore calm, Daly asked, "Bob, do you recall this incident?"

"Sir, I remember AUSA Robertson asking to review the classified file in question; however, I do not recall physically sitting down with him and showing him the file. Robertson needed to review this file to clear up the statute of limitations issue before the $1.4 million seizure could happen in 1998. The money was being moved. $200,000 had already been withdrawn, and we needed to move quickly to seize the remaining funds. I do not recall showing him the file. I have a tremendous amount of respect for Robertson, and if he said it happened, then it happened. That was almost three and a half years ago, and a lot was happening. However, I know one thing, there is no way in hell I would have shown him the classified file without my supervisor instructing me to do so, and my supervisor was present himself when I showed Robertson the file. I will tell you this, there is no way in hell I would have signed off on the $1.4 million seizure as an AUSA without having reviewed that classified file myself."

"Why not?" asked McChesney.

"It was the first ever civil seizure of terrorist funds by the US government. As the AUSA, I would have confirmed that no statute of limitations problems existed. The issue was when the FBI first knew about the transfers of specific terrorism funds. This information was contained inside Salah's classified intelligence file. What an embarrassment it would have been for the United States Attorney's Office and the FBI if the AUSA had not verified the issue in advance. Are we finished, or is there more?" I asked.

"Bob, you may return to the South RA," said Daly.

While leaving the office, I turned around and said, "Oh, by the way, Ma'am, congratulations on your promotion to Assistant Director of the FBI."

Clearly flustered by my comment, she turned around and said, "Thanks."

On Monday, June 25, 2001, Schippers presented me with the confessions of HAMAS terrorist Sheik Mahamad Abu-Tair and US-based HAMAS financier Jamil Sarsour. When I asked him how he got these confessions, he gave me a letter dated June 22, 2001, from Michael C. Kotzin, vice president of the Jewish Federation of Metropolitan Chicago. Mr. Schippers said, "Bob, you can use these in your book. The letter reads in part:

> Dear Mr. Schippers:
>
> Per your request, I am enclosing non-classified materials involving two cases brought before the military prosecutor

The FBIHQ OPR Appeal Board's Decision

in the State of Israel. One involves the case of Mahamad Mahmud Hassan [Abu-Tair]. The other involves the case of Jamil Salam Saliman Sarsour.

It is my understanding that these materials are intended to be used by your client, Robert Wright, in a personal capacity, as research documents for a book which he intends to have published in the future regarding terrorism in the Middle East, with emphasis on the terrorist group Hamas.

I am enclosing both the Hebrew originals of the documents and the English language translations.

I hope this is helpful,
Sincerely,
Michael C. Kotzin
Executive Vice President.[445]

Two weeks later, on July 10, 2001, Schippers asked if I would be available to meet with a reporter from *60 Minutes* on July 11 for a get-acquainted meeting. He wanted the reporter and me to become acquainted before a future terrorist attack occurred in the US. I informed him I first needed to find out if such a meeting would be a problem for me at work.

After consulting with my supervisor and the FBI Chicago Associate Division Counsel, I sent the following email to ASAC Daly:

Subject: Lunch meeting with a member of the media.

Sir, my attorney, David Schippers, has invited me to have lunch with him and Carol Marin (from) *60 Minutes*. Marin has expressed interest in the recent civil action filed on my behalf by Schippers. Marin has been told, and she agrees, that anything discussed during this lunch meeting is off the record. The lunch will allow us to become acquainted with one another. There will not be *any* news stories or news articles written because of this lunch meeting.

I am aware of the bureau constraints regarding the discussion of bureau matters with the media. I have no intentions to discuss pending cases, policies &/or classified information. However, should HAMAS &/or Mohammad Salah arise, my statements will be limited to available public source information, such as the affidavit from June 1998, which was filed in support of the seizure of HAMAS assets.

On 7/10/01, I discussed this matter with the Chicago Associate Division Counsel. He saw no problem with this lunch meeting provided I was aware of the bureau constraints. I also informed my supervisor about this matter.[446]

On July 11, 2001, Schippers introduced me to *60 Minutes* correspondent Mrs. Carol Marin. She said that she had been friends with Schippers for many years and was interested in my story. She said she had learned about me from Schippers and requested to meet with me in person. Although she realized I could not discuss my situation, she said she wanted to meet with me because she realized my story would interest the public in the future. I said I was not ready to go public and would not submit to an interview. She understood my concerns and gave me her business card and cell phone number.

I told her how frustrating it was to know that many Middle Eastern terrorists were living in the US and that one day, they would strike America with American-earned funds. I also showed her the nearly completed manuscript with thirty detailed colored charts. Per my employment agreement, I said she could not read the manuscript since the FBI must first approve its release to the public. Following lunch, I returned to the SRA.

The FBIHQ OPR Appeal Board's Decision

Two days later, on July 13, 2001, at 7:19 a.m., McChesney sent the following email to my SRA supervisor regarding my meeting with Mrs. Marin on July 11:

> As I told [A/SAC] Pat Daly, our policy precludes this type of meeting and furthermore, even if there is publicly available information on the case it is in litigation and should NOT be discussed. Advise SA Wright he is not to have contact with the media regarding Bureau related matters, to 'get to know' a reporter, etc. Though he is involved in a private lawsuit it centers on FBI operations and he cannot discuss that either. I suggest you document your advice to Bob regarding this. – KM.[447]

My supervisor responded to her email at 8:41 a.m. with the following message:

> Kathleen—It is my understanding that SA Wright has met with the reporter and did so after consulting [Chicago Associate Division Counsel] as to Bu policy. I will ensure that SA Wright is aware of your instructions, and I will document the same.[448]

At 9:38 a.m., the Chicago Associate Division Counsel sent the following email to McChesney with the subject listed as "Bob Wright luncheon with a reporter."

> I just spoke with [Agent Wright's supervisor] regarding this and saw your email response to his message to you and thought it would be prudent (for me) to give you my end of it. Wright did call me the other day to ask for my input on a proposed meeting over lunch he was having with his attorney and a reporter. He told me this meeting was simply

to introduce him to this individual. He also told me that his attorney had advised him the bureau could not prevent him from having lunch with someone, but that he did not want to run afoul of anything and so sought [his supervisor] advice and mine.

"My first question to him was, whether any ground rules regarding his lawsuit had been proposed or established by his supervisor or the front office, and he emphatically told me 'No.'" I did tell him that while I did not think I could prevent him from having lunch with someone on his own time, that he absolutely could not discuss anything regarding FBI cases or files. He assured me that he would not, and indicated his attorney had set this up and that he did not know much more about it other than it was just to be an introduction.

If there is the possibility that he will be seeking advice from a number of parties during this litigation, we should have a POC [point of contact] for him regarding questions like this, so there is a single voice. If there was a POC, I was not aware of it or I would have referred him to that person. If we need to talk about this, let me know.[449]

McChesney sent the last email at 11:35 a.m. regarding my lunch meeting to the Chicago Associate Division Counsel. The message says,

"This may be the result of bad timing, but I told Pat Daly on Wed. that Bob was not to do this, despite what [name blacked out by FBI] said. I will talk to Pat about it. Thanks –KM."[450]

On July 31, 2001, Schippers informed me I needed to be in his office the following morning, August 1, to meet with a group of legal representatives from Judicial Watch, a DC-based legal foundation.

The purpose of the meeting was to explain my story to their legal team. According to him, depending on my presentation, they would decide whether they would assist him in representing me in my efforts to warn Congress and others about the FBI terrorism negligence.

Having never heard of Judicial Watch, I did some research. Judicial Watch is a non-partisan educational foundation promoting transparency, accountability, and integrity in the US government, politics, and law. They advocate exceptional standards of ethics and morality in our nation's public life. They seek to ensure that political and judicial officials do not abuse the powers entrusted to them by the American people. They fulfill their mission through litigation, investigations, and public outreach. Their motto is "Because no one is above the law." They use open records or freedom of information laws and other tools to investigate and uncover misconduct by government officials and litigate to hold to account politicians and public officials who engage in corrupt activities.

The best part about Judicial Watch, at least for me, is that they are a 501(c)(3) non-profit organization. Contributions from individuals, foundations, and corporations finance the legal operations and are tax deductible to the extent allowed by law.

"If Judicial Watch agrees to take you on as a client, you may not have to pay any legal fees," said Schippers.

According to him, if Judicial Watch filed any lawsuits against the FBI on my behalf, they would recover all legal fees from the FBI when they win the lawsuit against the FBI.

I asked him how long it would take them to decide if they would represent me.

He answered, "It depends on how many representatives they send to the meeting. If there are only a few representatives, they must go back to Washington and consult with the full legal team before deciding. It may take one to three days before they let us know."

The following morning, August 1, 2001, when I arrived at Schipper's office, he introduced me to five Judicial Watch representatives. He then took me into his office and said, "Bob, those five guys are the top five legal representatives of Judicial Watch. They are taking your situation seriously. You tell them your story, answer any of their questions you can to the best of your ability, and we should have an answer from them by the end of the day."

Dave and I met with the Judicial Watch representatives in the law firm conference room. For the next hour, I gave my presentation and answered their questions. The last thing I said before leaving the room was, "I realize my story sounds unbelievable, but I promise you, everything I have told you is true. Because the FBI refuses to do anything to stop the Middle Eastern terrorists who are living and operating here in America, it is only a matter of time before one of these terrorist groups carries out a terrorist attack on American soil. I need your help to warn Congress and the President before such an attack happens. Thank you."

Schippers and I then walked out of the conference room. "Dave, I hope they do not think I am nuts. How did I do?" I asked.

"Bob, you nailed it! They do not think you are nuts," said Dave.

"I am heading back to work and will wait for your call with their decision," I said.

He grabbed my arm and said, "Bob, after what you told them, I know they will offer to take you on as a client. Go to my office and wait for me. It will not take long."

Ten minutes later, Dave entered his office with Larry Klayman, Chairperson and Chief Counsel of Judicial Watch. Klayman approached

The FBIHQ OPR Appeal Board's Decision

me, shook my hand, and said, "Agent Wright, we would be honored to work with you and Mr. Schippers to warn Congress about the FBI's investigative failures regarding Middle Eastern terrorists."

I was so relieved that I began to tear up.

"I want you to know two things. First, we don't think you're crazy. Second, you will not pay one dime for our legal services. The FBI will pay your attorney's fees in the future. We need to sign a legal representation agreement to get started representing you," said Mr. Klayman.

Larry Klayman and Thomas Fitton, President of the Judicial Watch, signed the Legal Representation Agreement on August 1, 2001. I signed it too. Paragraph two of the agreement states, in part, "JW (Judicial Watch) shall not invoice the Client for any attorney's fees or expenses in prosecuting the Lawsuit or any other legal action taken on behalf of the Client. Rather, only in the event the Client receives an award of attorney's fees at the conclusion of any lawsuit or other mutually agreed-upon legal action, JW shall be entitled to receive any such court-awarded attorneys' fees as a donation for its public interest legal services."[451]

On August 17, 2001, upon our arrival at the Chicago FBI office, Schippers and I met with the two Chicago OPR investigators to discuss the investigation McChesney had initiated against me. Before giving my signed sworn statement, I was called into ASAC Daly's office.

Mr. Daly informed me that the OPR appeal board had rendered a final decision regarding the sexual harassment complaint Reed had filed against me over two years prior. Fully aware they had conducted no further investigation following my appeal, including interviewing any of my eleven witnesses and my recent comments to McChesney, I expected the news would not be favorable for me.

"Bob, I am sorry to inform you of this, but OPR has affirmed its thirty days off without pay recommendation and one-year probation," said Daly.

"Sir, this is pathetic. Do you mean to tell me McChesney is doing nothing about this injustice? I am innocent, and she knows it. How can she allow this to happen?" I asked.

"Bob, once the report is sent from Chicago to the OPR office in Washington, it is completely out of our hands," he stated.

"I knew they would not reverse this injustice. The retaliation continues and nobody cares," I said.

After I signed the notification document, Daly said, "Bob, normally, when we tell the employee about the OPR decision, the employee is suspended on the same day. However, in light of the circumstances concerning your OPR case, we (the Chicago ASACs) all agree you should be allowed to decide when you would like to begin the thirty days off. Would you like to start today or at a later date?"

"I do not want to start today. I want to wait until September 1st and take the entire month of September off. I guess I will finish my manuscript and play a lot of golf," I said.

Laughing, Daly said, "That will be fine with me. Considering the circumstances, I am glad to see you have a sense of humor about this."

"Sir, I must keep a sense of humor about all of this, or it would drive me nuts. What keeps me sane is knowing the truth about all that has happened will be exposed in the future," I said.

Schippers said to Daly, "My client is innocent! I will send a letter to the new FBI director, Robert Mueller, requesting the suspension of this OPR punishment until the final appeal process is completed."

The FBIHQ OPR Appeal Board's Decision

"Dave, I appreciate you wanting to send a letter to the director, but it will be a waste of time. He will not be made aware of your letter. This ends now; I will take the thirty days off," I said.

"How can you remain so calm?" inquired Schippers.

"Since day one, I knew this would happen. You always disregarded my warnings about this outcome, thinking I was stressed and paranoid. I know the entire truth will come out in the future. Dave, we now need to focus on all the things you have put in motion to warn others who can help us before more terrorist attacks kill more innocent people," I said.

After we left Daly's office, Dave asked, "Bob, didn't McChesney get promoted to assistant director?"

"Yes, why?" I asked.

"She must have it in for you. She could have stepped in at any time and called the assistant director in charge of the OPR to insist they reverse this injustice!"

"I agree. I even asked Mr. Daly why she was not fixing this mess. Mr. Daly said it is out of Chicago's hands after it sends their report to Washington," I said.

"McChesney's failure to fix this injustice tells me she wanted you to be punished, even though she and everyone else knew you are innocent. What is going on here, Bob?" asked Dave.

"Welcome to the FBI, Dave. I suspect her refusal to correct this injustice concerns my meeting with her in March. I told her that her closing of Vulgar Betrayal amounted to negligence, and she could not justify closing it in the future. Plus, she knows about the manuscript, which covers what she did to the FBI's only criminal investigation of Middle Eastern terrorists and organizations that could have prevented future terrorist attacks," I said.

"What's the connection between that and her correcting this injustice?" asked Dave.

"I told you why they were doing this the day Jayna Davis was in your office. In the future, when the manuscript is published, McChesney and others at FBIHQ will inform others in the media and Congress that I am not a credible person because the OPR found me guilty of committing sexual harassment of a coworker. In addition, they have already hit me with three additional OPR investigations since I met with McChesney in March. She initiated the first, and the same day I was informed of my being cleared of any misconduct related to her first investigation, I was informed about a second OPR investigation against me. This investigation originated from the first OPR initiated by McChesney as it involved disclosing classified information to another AUSA. I am certain there will be many more OPRs in my future," I said.

"Why do you believe they will open more against you?" asked Dave.

"Because when the manuscript is published, they'll be able to tell the media and Congress I am not credible because the FBI has conducted so many OPR investigations on me," I said.

"You believe McChesney intentionally wanted you to be found guilty of the sexual harassment, and she initiated at least one of the OPRs against you, which also has now led to another OPR against you, so the FBI could use these things to discredit you in the media and with Congress in the future?" asked Dave.

"Absolutely," I said.

After thinking about it, Dave said, "I'll be damned. Bob, when you explain it that way, it makes sense. It sounds like a logical explanation for everything they have done to you during these past six months."

The FBIHQ OPR Appeal Board's Decision

"Unfortunately, I fear the three OPR matters will be nothing compared to what they will do to me once they learn what the manuscript contains," I said.

"I agree," said Dave.

On August 30, 2001, while conducting research, I found an article dated August 29, 1997, titled "Islamic Terrorist Groups Operating in the United States," by Steve Mack. While reading the article, I discovered I was not the only FBI agent who held the belief that Middle Eastern terrorists would strike inside the United States. The article reads, in part,

> Very few people realize it, but at this very moment, militant Islamic groups that have been officially described as international terrorist organizations—such as Hezbollah, HAMAS, Palestine Islamic Jihad, and others—are operating very quietly within the borders of the United States, from New York City to San Diego. What these terrorist groups do is acquire money in the US to send back to their parent organizations overseas. They also use their US addresses to purchase US equipment, use US internet sites to communicate, and use US universities to bring Middle Eastern students into the US, get teaching positions, and bring terrorist leaders from the Middle East as guest speakers to influence American college students.
>
> John O'Neill, the man who formally headed the FBI's counterterrorism unit until 1996 and who now heads those efforts in New York City, said, "Almost every one of these [terrorist] groups have a presence in the United States today. A lot of these groups now have the capability and the support infrastructure in the United States to attack us here if they choose to do so."

The group of men involved in the 1993 World Trade Center bombing that killed six people and injured more than 1,000 included even US citizens converted to the radical Islamic fundamentalism craziness.

It is known that US-based HAMAS militants have been involved in surveillance operations against prominent Jewish people in the Chicago area. What could their intentions only be?

World renown terrorism expert Brian Jenkins of Kroll Associates said, "The fact they are using the United States as a launching pad, a depot and a bank is not new. What is different is the fact it is done so with an open hostility toward the US government and US society."[452]

What could be the reason for Middle Eastern terrorist groups to be openly hostile toward the US government and US society? It is because the only US government agency responsible for investigating and neutralizing international terrorism organizations operating in the US, the FBI, has failed miserably to do its job of neutralizing the terrorists to protect the American people. Instead, the FBI's fundamental goal has been to protect all terrorists who are the subjects of FBI intelligence files. Why? They need these files to remain open indefinitely because they need justification for continued funding from the US Congress. Job security! Protecting the terrorists from being neutralized is more important to the FBI's ITU than protecting the American public.

When the ITU prevents FBI agents from interviewing both suspected and known international terrorists and likewise prevents the leadership of known US-based terrorist organizations, who are openly raising money to fund global terrorism, from being interviewed, the terrorist groups can get away with whatever they want in America.

The FBIHQ OPR Appeal Board's Decision

After Mohammad Salah's arrest in 1993 and his subsequent confession, which detailed the US-based HAMAS leadership and organizations in America, the FBI only opened a few terrorism cases. However, there was no effort by the FBI to coordinate any national investigation to address HAMAS's widespread US-based criminal enterprise. Even after receiving Salah's address book, FBIHQ told me I could not use it to conduct interviews to identify other HAMAS members associated with Salah. The ITU prevented the interview of Salah and his trained terrorists.

The most disturbing thing that should have awakened those in the ITU occurred after John and I attempted to interview people in Chicago who were listed in the HAMAS Military Commander's address book.

The Chicago HAMAS delegation visited the White House and top leadership at FBIHQ to complain about the few interviews John and I had attempted. HAMAS leaders were furious. How dare FBI agents investigate HAMAS within the United States? I could not blame them. Ten years after establishing their US-based criminal enterprise, without any FBI interference, they have to deal with two FBI street agents who are trying to interview associates of a convicted terrorist, Mohammad Salah, the HAMAS Military Commander. No one in the FBI had ever done such a thing.

Regarding FBI Agent John O'Neill, I was pleased to learn someone else in the FBI also believed it inevitable that a Middle East terrorist group would attack the United States at home. I searched for additional information online to learn more about him.

I learned the FBI hired him as a fingerprint clerk in 1972 and made him an agent in 1976. During his first fifteen years, he worked in organized and white-collar crimes. In 1991, he was reassigned to the Chicago FBI office as an ASAC. He established a Fugitive Task Force that included federal agents and local police departments.

In February 1993, after the World Trade Center bombing, where six were killed and hundreds were injured, the FBI took action by arresting some suspects and identifying Ramzi Yousef as the mastermind of the bombing. The FBI also declared Ramzi Yousef as a wanted individual. O'Neill was still working in Chicago and was not involved with the investigation.

In 1995, he was promoted to FBIHQ Chief of the Counterterrorism Section. On his first day on the job, he learned that Ramzi Yousef had been located in Pakistan. He spent the next several days working day and night, trying to capture Ramzi Yousef. His FBI agents, working with the DEA and State Department, located and arrested Yousef. Following this arrest, he learned everything he could about Islamic terrorists.

John O'Neill got it! He understood that, to work against international terrorism successfully, you must learn as much as you can about the terrorist groups. In order to combat international terrorism, it is crucial that you gain extensive knowledge about the terrorist groups, such as the reasons for their formation, the identities of their leaders, their objectives, their sources of funding, and various other details. But, once you learn these things, you will realize how much these terrorist groups hate America and what they are willing to do to harm America.

On June 25, 1996, a bomb attack targeted the Khobar Towers in Dharan, Saudi Arabia, killing nineteen American soldiers and injuring five hundred. Both O'Neill and FBI Director Louis Freeh were leading the investigation. O'Neill believed the Saudi government was not fully cooperating with the FBI's investigation. When

The FBIHQ OPR Appeal Board's Decision

Director Freeh disagreed, O'Neill allegedly told him that the Saudis were, "blowing smoke up your ass." "O'Neill's friend and *ABC News* producer, Chris Isham, confirms that O'Neill was frustrated with the investigation. 'He felt the Saudis were definitely playing games and that the senior officials in the US government, including Louis Freeh, just didn't get it.'"[453]

In November 1996, in a speech at a technology conference in New Jersey, O'Neill told attendees that "'interesting times lie ahead' and that the main terrorist threat now came from transnational groups not backed by national governments. He also warned, 'We see the intent is for a large number of casualties.'"[454]

On January 1, 1997, he was promoted to ASAC of Counterterrorism & National Security in the New York Office. He was in charge of 350 agents. In May 1997, the Associated Press quoted him as saying, "A lot of these groups now have the capacity and the support infrastructure in the United States to attack us here if they chose to." Weeks later, during a National Strategy Forum in Chicago, he told the attendees that the Afghanistan insurgency against the Soviets was "a major watershed event." He said that Afghan war veterans were now a significant security threat.

He stated, "They were trained in terrorist activity, and now they are back in their various countries and around the world with the training and having the network capabilities to know other Jihad players around the world who have the same like mind, the same fundamentalist thinking and the same type of training."

In March 1997, when *CNN*'s reporter Peter Arnett asked Osama bin Laden about any future terrorism plans, bin Laden said, "You'll see them and hear about them in the media, God willing."[455] According to bin Laden, "The US will drive them [Muslim terrorists] to transfer the battle into the United States." As promised, he orchestrated the next attack on August 7, 1998, bombing the US embassies in Kenya and Tanzania. The attack killed 230 people and injured over 4,800 in nearby neighborhoods. He again attacked the US on October 20, 2000, when the USS *Cole* suffered a suicide attack, killing seventeen American sailors serving onboard. But the concern needed to be bin Laden committing a terrorist attack on US soil. O'Neill recognized this and committed to doing everything in his power to prevent bin Laden and terrorist organizations from carrying out any attacks on US soil.

In 1998, FBI Deputy Director Robert Bryant "consulted with O'Neill and others to draft a report calling for the FBI to change the way it fights terrorism. The report advocated a centralized information system to collect data and help predict future terrorist attacks. Bryant also endorses assigning some agents to spend their entire career working counterterrorism cases. 'It was never funded. It was put on the back burner somewhere,' Bryant told *Frontline*."[456]

On June 10, 1998, the day after the Chicago division's seizure of the $1.4 million in Middle Eastern terrorist funds, John Miller of *ABC News* interviewed Osama bin Laden. "O'Neill's friend, *ABC* producer Chris Isham, arranges the interview [with bin Laden]. Some of O'Neill's information helps Isham and Miller draw up their questions for bin Laden. Isham tells *Frontline* that O'Neill was desperate to watch the footage of the entire interview, even though *ABC* had a policy against releasing outtakes. 'He wasn't taking no for an answer,' he said."[457] *ABC* compromised by putting the entire interview online.

O'Neill had learned a great deal about Middle Eastern terrorism organizations. He had narrowed in on Osama bin Laden and his Al-Qaida network because he considered them the biggest threat to the United States. Because of his extensive knowledge of Osama bin

The FBIHQ OPR Appeal Board's Decision

Laden, he could better understand things bin Laden said during the *ABC News* interview than those who did not understand the motives and mindset of bin Laden and other terrorists.

On August 7, 1998, trucks loaded with explosives bombed the US embassies in Kenya and Tanzania., killing 224 and thousands injured. O'Neill told Assistant Director Lewis Schiliro that only Al-Qaida had the means to carry out these attacks. He requested to be named the on-scene commander and for the New York FBI office, not the Washington Field Office, to be designated to oversee the investigation. An FBI turf war erupted between the New York and Washington offices. Although FBIHQ allowed New York to oversee the investigation, it refused to send O'Neill.

In July 2000, O'Neill attended a retirement conference in Orlando, Florida. He left a briefcase containing highly classified FBI documents concerning national security matters in a room with other FBI agents. After returning to the room following a phone call, the briefcase was missing. He called the local police. They found the briefcase, and it seemed unopened.

He returned to New York and reported the incident to the FBI. A fingerprint dusting of the documents showed no documents were touched. The matter was so serious that the Justice Department opened a criminal investigation. "O'Neill's friend Jerry Hauer tells *Frontline*, 'I think he felt that some people were going to use it as a wedge, as a way of painting him in a bad light.'"[458]

O'Neill faced disciplinary measures in 2000 for the briefcase security breach. "While still in New York, O'Neill's rise in the FBI bureaucracy begins to stall as he is passed over three times for promotions. [Assistant Director] Bryant tells *Frontline* he recommended O'Neill. 'I think that if you are being investigated by OPR, Office of

Professional Responsibility, and there's a question, they don't want to promote somebody that's got a cloud over them, even a minor thing, like [misuse of] a vehicle.'"459

Seventeen American sailors lost their lives when the USS *Cole* was bombed while docked in Yemen on October 12, 2000. O'Neill advocated for the New York office to handle the investigation and was appointed as the on-scene commander. Again, these were investigations that the DC field office always handled. Many in Washington, DC, were not pleased with O'Neill's encroachment of their turf.

However, Assistant Director Barry Mawn and Director Freeh agreed with O'Neill. After arriving in Yemen, O'Neill confronted issues concerning the safety of the FBI agents. He also wanted the resources needed to investigate the attack thoroughly. He clashed with Barbara Bodine, the United States ambassador to Yemen. He wanted a heavy security presence to protect his investigators. The US ambassador wanted the FBI agents to be unarmed. O'Neill intended to have direct access to interview Yemen officials, but the ambassador wanted to supervise the FBI encounters with Yemen officials.

The friction between the two was so bad that the ambassador sent cables to the State Department critical of O'Neill. It became so bad that FBI Director Freeh and Attorney General Reno became involved in the dispute between O'Neill and Bodine.

In November 2000, O'Neill returned to the US to take a break from the Yemen investigation. he worked tirelessly to solve terrorist attacks against the US while simultaneously working to prevent future Middle Eastern terrorist attacks within the United States. After working four weeks nonstop in Yemen, he had lost over twenty pounds. Unfortunately, unlike him, very few within FBIHQ management knew how easy it would be for a Middle Eastern terrorist group

The FBIHQ OPR Appeal Board's Decision

to commit a terrorist attack inside the US. At this time, Osama bin Laden was the major threat to US interests around the world.

In January 2001, O'Neill had plans to return to Yemen to continue overseeing the USS *Cole* investigation. However, Bodine denied him clearance to enter Yemen. "'I had to act as a cultural interpreter. They have endured first British colonialism and then the Soviets. These people have only had foreigners telling them what to do. Now Mr. O'Neill and his men were coming in, doing the same thing,' Bodine told Britain's *The Sunday Times*."[460] FBIHQ decided the situation between O'Neill and Bodine was so irreconcilable that they chose not to fight for O'Neill's return to Yemen.

On May 2, 2001, FBI Director Freeh, a supporter of O'Neill, announced he would be retiring in June. It was well known that others at the FBIHQ, who might be the next acting FBI director until the new FBI director was announced, did not support O'Neill's hardline terrorism efforts. They couldn't care less that he had been working tirelessly for years to prevent future terrorist attacks against the United States, attacks he knew were coming.

In June 2001, O'Neill and Assistant Director Barry Mawn agreed that FBI agents in Yemen could not be protected. Because of severe security threats, the FBI pulled out of Yemen. O'Neill promised family members of those killed on the USS *Cole* that the FBI would not abandon the investigation and promised they would return to Yemen to complete it.

"We were operating with three SWAT personnel as support as far as security goes, and an open hotel just was not going to work. We could not provide protection, said former FBI agent Clint Guenther."[461]

On June 21, 2001, Freeh retired from the FBI. Tom Pickard became the acting FBI director until a new director was sworn in. There were allegations that Pickard was not a fan of O'Neill. With

Freeh's retirement, O'Neill had lost one of his best allies in the FBI. Freeh understood his drive to pursue Osama bin Laden to prevent future terrorist attacks against America.

By July 2001, O'Neill "is more marginalized than ever at the FBI because of his relationship with [others at FBI] headquarters. O'Neill discusses the [terrorism] threats with his friend Chris Isham, who tells *Frontline*, 'He knew there was a lot of noise out there and that there were a lot of warnings, a lot of red flags, and that it was a similar level that they heard before the millennium [threats], which was an indication that something was going on. Yet, he felt that he was frozen out, that he was not in a capacity to really do anything about it anymore because of his relationship with the FBI [leadership]. So, it was a source of real anguish for him.'"[462]

I understand the anguish O'Neill felt. After my removal from VB in August 1999, I felt so helpless. Knowing people would die because FBI management closed the case, I knew I had to do something. Knowing what I knew, there was no way I could ever move on with my life and pretend to forget what I knew. When you know innocent people are going to die, you must do something, anything, to prevent those deaths. I hired Schippers in August 1999 to help me warn Congress.

Also, in July 2001, the DOJ decided not to file any criminal charges regarding O'Neill's short loss of the briefcase in July 2000. However, the FBIHQ opened an OPR investigation regarding his removing of the classified documents from FBI space. Although the OPR was unnecessary, some high-ranking managers at the FBIHQ sought to embarrass O'Neill and cause him additional stress.

During July 2001, O'Neill learned about a "job opening as the head of security at the World Trade Center. It would mean a significant salary increase, but also it would mean leaving the FBI. By this point, however, O'Neill realizes his chances for a promotion were severely hurt by the briefcase incident."[463]

On August 19, 2001, less than two weeks before O'Neill's official retirement from the FBI, *The New York Times* published a news story about him. The article's title is "FBI is Investigating a Senior Counterterrorism Agent." The article covers the negative matters regarding O'Neill's FBI career. This article was a hit piece and smear campaign by some FBIHQ higher-up cowards. FBIHQ called a newspaper, in this case, *The New York Times*, and asked for a favor.

The favor was for an unfavorable article to be written and published about O'Neill. Their goal was to cause O'Neill embarrassment and harm his reputation to protect FBI management and the image of the FBI. FBIHQ did this to keep him from making any public comments to the media in the future regarding FBI terrorism matters and to harm his employment opportunity at the World Trade Center.

NOTE: In my next book, *THE FBI's POST 9/11 VULGAR BETRAYAL*, I detail how top FBI officials attempted to commit two similar media smear campaigns against me. The first media smear occurred on May 10, 2002, after FBIHQ read this book. They called *Washington Post* reporter James Grimaldi to request he write and publish a news article about me regarding my sexual harassment of Agent Reed and my racial bias against a Muslim FBI agent, Gamal Abdel-Hafiz. Their smear campaign backfired. After I talked to the reporter, he wrote and published in *The Washington Post* on May 11, 2002, an article titled, "Agent Alleges FBI Ignored HAMAS Activities—Chicagoan Sues, Saying Bureau Refused to File Charges, Disrupt Pre-Sept. 11 Crimes."

The FBI's second confirmed attempted media smear campaign occurred in June 2003, following a press conference I gave at the

Washington Press Club. A few days after the press conference, a Chicago ASAC requested permission from the FBI assistant director and the deputy assistant director of the FBI OPR Unit to allow several Chicago FBI agents to conduct a media smear against me. This media smear was to be done by a reporter at the *Chicago Tribune* newspaper. Although I am confident that there were additional FBI attempts to conduct media smear campaigns against me, these two attempts were confirmed.

Fortunately, at the end of the *New York Times* article, some defended O'Neill. Barry Mawn said, "Mr. O'Neill was a tireless worker and had his 'complete confidence.' John is recognized worldwide as probably one of the best in conducting both counterterrorism and counterintelligence operations."[464]

"James K. Kallstrom, the head of the New York office in the mid-1990s, said that Mr. O'Neill 'has been a major force for the public safety of the United States and the security of the United States for over two decades.' Like many of O'Neill's friends and supporters, Mr. Kallstrom made clear that he thought Mr. O'Neill had been the victim of a smear campaign by people [FBI leadership] seeking to damage his reputation, perhaps because he was being mentioned for a national security job at the White House, a job he never sought.

"Mary Jo White, the United States Attorney for the Southern District of New York, praised Mr. O'Neill in a statement Friday as 'one of the unsung heroes in our nation's effort to combat terrorism in the United States and around the world.'"[465]

The New York Times cited the cowardly unnamed sources for the article as "government officials," "law enforcement officials," "several officials," and "State Department officials."

The FBIHQ OPR Appeal Board's Decision

O'Neill believed Pickard was the source of the *New York Times* article. "Mr. O'Neill confronts Pickard, who denies that he was the source of the leak."[466]

On August 22, 2001, three days after *The New York Times* published the O'Neill hit piece article for the FBI, O'Neill retired from the FBI. O'Neill wanted to keep his promise to the families of those killed in the USS *Cole* that the FBI would not abandon the investigation and they would return to Yemen to complete the investigation. Keeping his promise, "in his final hours on the job, O'Neill signs an authorization for the FBI to return to Yemen. O'Neill explains, 'I was not leaving here until I did it because I promised that we would send them [FBI agents] back. When I pulled them out, I had to. But I was determined to be the one who signed the piece of paper to send them back.' O'Neill also emails Lou Gunn, whose son had died in the Cole attack, to tell him that he was retiring but that the FBI was returning to Yemen."[467]

After O'Neill retired, the FBI higher-ups rescinded his effort to send the FBI back to Yemen to investigate the USS *Cole* terrorist attack.

The day after O'Neill retired, August 23, 2001, he began his new job as head of security at the World Trade Center in New York. According to Chris Isham. O'Neill recognized the threat still posed to the World Trade Center. When he first had gotten the job at the World Trade Center, he told me, "I have this great job. I am head of security at the World Trade Center."

And I said, "Well, that will be an easy job. They are not going to bomb that place again."

"Well actually," he immediately came back and said, "Actually, they have always wanted to finish that job. I think they are going to try again."[468]

From the summer of 1999 through August 2001, Glenn Meade, a fiction writer, authored a novel, *Resurrection Day*, about a terrorist attack based around an Al-Qaeda attack on Washington, DC. "Meade is helped by numerous US counterterrorism experts. One of these is John O'Neill, the FBI's counterterrorism chief and top expert on Osama bin Laden. Meade says the feeling he got from O'Neill was that the threat posed by Islamic extremists 'is a bigger danger than a lot of people in the FBI are prepared to admit; some are sticking their heads in the sand.'"[469]

Los Angeles FBI Agent Pat Patterson was in Yemen in 2000 to assist in the USS *Cole* bombing investigation. While there, he spent time with John O'Neill.

Patterson said, "I thought it was unlikely they would hit a target [the World Trade Center] a second time, but John was convinced of it. He said, 'No, they definitely want to bring that building down.' He just had that sense and was insistent about it."[470]

Following the publication of the *New York Times* article on August 19, two Chicago supervisors told me about the article. One supervisor handed me a copy of the article. They recommended I mention this negative story regarding O'Neill's loss of his briefcase in Orlando in my manuscript. The supervisors did not like O'Neill. I assumed it had something to do with O'Neill's time in Chicago from 1991 to 1994.

I clarified to each supervisor that I did not know this man and that he had no connection to what happened to me or the closing of Vulgar Betrayal. I said to each, "I cannot add this information to my manuscript." At the time, I did not read the news article or know anything about Agent O'Neill.

However, while conducting researching for this manuscript on August 30, 2001, I printed a news article titled "Islamic Terrorist

The FBIHQ OPR Appeal Board's Decision

Groups Operating in the United States," by Steve Macko, dated August 29, 1997. The second paragraph reads, "John O'Neill, the man who formerly headed the FBI's counterterrorism unit until 1996 and who now heads those efforts in New York City, said, 'Every one of these groups has a presence in the United States today. A lot of these groups now have the capability and the support infrastructure in the United States to attack us here if they choose to do so.'"[471]

After reading O'Neill's statement, I placed his quote at the top of the next chapter. I then spent a few days learning more about Mr. O'Neill. I realized this man shared my passion to help stop future Middle Eastern terrorist attacks against America. I then realized I must include the above summary, a positive summary, regarding O'Neill's tireless efforts to prevent more terrorist attacks by Osama bin Laden against America.

I wish our paths had crossed while I was working on VB. It would have been nice to talk to a high-level FBI manager who also understood an attack was coming in the future.

CHAPTER 39

SEPTEMBER 2001

"Almost every one of these [terrorist] groups has a presence in the United States today. A lot of these groups now have the capability and the support infrastructure in the United States to attack us here if they choose to do so."[472]

— John P. O'Neill, Unit Chief,
FBI Counter Terrorism, 05/22/1997

On September 1, 2001, I began serving my thirty-day suspension, without pay, for something I never did. During my first week off, I put a new roof on my home and worked on several projects around the house. During the evenings, I worked on completing this manuscript.

On September 7, Director of Security John O'Neill at the World Trade Center in New York, "has engrossed himself in discovering what security systems are in place there, and what will be needed in the future. On this day, he runs into Rodney Leibowitz, a friend. Mr. Leibowitz is the president and CEO (Chief Executive Officer) of a company called First Responder Inc., which provides bioterrorism preparedness training to healthcare professionals. First Responder Inc. is in fact scheduled to send in a team to conduct a threat assessment of the World Trade Center for O'Neill on September 15."[473]

On September 10, O'Neill called Howard Rubinstein, "a famous public relations man for powerful New Yorkers, [which included] Larry Silverstein, the World Trade Center leaseholder."

According to Silverstein, O'Neill said, "Why don't you come down on September 11, come to a breakfast meeting at 8:00, where we'll talk about what we're doing to prevent terror attacks."

Silverstein said, "Okay."

O'Neill added, "Bring your staff, two people."

Silverstein said, "That's fine."

O'Neill said, "Come at 9:00 instead of 8:00."[474]

Because of a scheduling conflict, Rubinstein canceled the 9/11 meeting with O'Neill.

Also, on September 10, O'Neill "meets up with his old friend Raymond Powers, the former New York City Police Department Chief of Operations, to discuss security procedures. Their conversation turns to Osama bin Laden. According to journalist and author Murry Weiss, 'Just as he had reiterated since 1995 to any official in Washington who would listen, O'Neill said he was sure bin Laden would attack on American soil and expected him to target the Twin Towers again.'"[475]

He told Powers, "It's going to happen, and it looks like something big is brewing."[476]

"Later on, O'Neill goes out in the evening (09/10/2001) with his friends Robert Tucker and Jerome Hauer. Again, he started discussing bin Laden. He told his friends, 'We are due. And we are due for something big.' He said, 'Some things have happened in Afghanistan. I do not like the way things are lining up in Afghanistan.' He added, 'I sense a shift, and I think things are going to happen.' Asked when he said, 'I don't know, but soon.'"[477]

I did the same thing O'Neill did. I told whoever would listen about the future Middle Eastern terrorist attack inside the US. There were times I even told myself to stop talking about it because I knew others could not possibly understand. It was difficult to keep what you knew to yourself when you knew innocent people were going to die. This was why O'Neill and I talked about what we knew: a US-based Middle Eastern terrorist attack was coming in the future. Knowing the things you know eats away at you. Even more so when you know that the FBI division's SACs and FBIHQ management were doing nothing to prevent the genuine threats to America.

Instead of the FBI helping us pursue the known Middle Eastern terrorists we were seeking, they marginalized us and forced us out of the international terrorism program. FBIHQ requested *The New York Times* write and publish a hit piece on O'Neill, forcing him to retire three days later. Regarding myself, I lost my VB case, and McChesney wanted the $1.4 million to be returned to the Middle Eastern terrorists.

After two years and one month since I began drafting this manuscript, on the evening of September 10, 2001, I worked late into the night to complete it. At 2:30 a.m. on September 11, I finished it. I wanted to submit the manuscript to the Chicago FBI office in the morning. However, with McChesney in Chicago until September 30, I would never give her access to this manuscript. I was sure that if she discovered what the manuscript contained, she would hit me with additional OPR investigations to aid in protecting herself in the future. Therefore, I would wait until October 1, the day I return to work following my thirty-day suspension. After completing this manuscript, I went to bed at 3:00 a.m.

On September 11, at 8:46 a.m., O'Neill was in his office on the thirty-fourth floor of the South Tower when the first plane struck the North Tower. He exited the South Tower and called his girlfriend. He informed her about scattered body parts and inquired if she knew the cause of the building's damage. He told her he was okay and would call her back later.

Rubinstein, who canceled his 9/11 meeting with O'Neill at the World Trade Center, said, "I am sitting in my staff meeting, and my secretary runs in and said the World Trade Center got hit, and you were supposed to be there. Everyone at that breakfast meeting died, including John O'Neill."[478]

"Wesley Wong, an FBI agent who had known Mr. O'Neill for more than twenty-five years and was in the command center, with O'Neill, that had been set up following the North Tower crash. [Agent Wong] last saw O'Neill walking toward a tunnel leading to the South Tower, likely to assist in that building's evacuation and gather surveillance footage from the security offices located there."[479]

When I woke up on the morning of September 11, I noticed a voice message I had received after going to bed. The message was from my friend Gretchen Yordy, an Indiana State Trooper whom I attended college with at Indiana State University. "Bob, Oh my God! As soon as you get this message, turn on your TV," was her message. By the time I had turned on my television, the second plane had already struck the South Tower. The moment I learned two planes had crashed into the Twin Towers, I knew it was an attack by Osama bin Laden.

September 2001

The next call I received was from my brother, Kevin. While we were speaking on the phone, we witnessed the first collapse of the World Trade Center tower.

"Oh my God! Did that building collapse?" I asked.

"Bob, that building is gone!" said Kevin.

For the next several minutes, neither of us said a word. I broke the silence by saying, "Kevin, I have to go. I cannot even talk right now."

Like all Americans, I watched the news unfold on television. Then, there was news of the Pentagon attack and plane crash in Pennsylvania. Throughout the day, I received many calls from friends and family members. Everyone said, "Bob, you were right! You warned about this for years."

One of my many calls was from Judy Miller, a reporter from *The New York Times*. She was in downtown New York City when the terrorists struck the World Trade Center towers. She was emotional when she said, "Bob, I lost some of my friends today. You need to go public with what you know. You can help save lives! You need to go public."

She asked, "Are you willing to go public with your story now?"

Judy Miller, Reporter, The New York Times.

I told her how I had completed my manuscript about five to six hours before the attacks. I informed her I could say nothing publicly until I submitted the manuscript to the FBI for a pre-publication review.

"Judy, if I go public before they review the manuscript, they will fire me. They will then claim I am simply a former disgruntled employee who is not telling the truth," I said.

The FBI's Pre-9/11 Vulgar Betrayal

After further pleas for me to go public, I said, "Judy, the holy war is now in America. We both know this is only the beginning. I will submit my manuscript to the FBI for a pre-publication review on October 1, 2001. Once they approve the manuscript, I promise you will be the first to receive a portion of its contents."

She said she understood but doubted the FBI would allow the manuscript to be released to the public. I informed her I had read the pre-publication review rules and saw no reason for them to deny its release. The following day, I saw Judy being interviewed by Katie Couric on the *NBC Today Show* about Middle East terrorism.

At 9:45 a.m., I received a call from Jayna Davis, who was in Oklahoma. She said, "Bob, I received a call from a friend telling me Carol Marin was supposed to be at the World Trade Center this morning at the time of the attacks."

Carol Marin was the *60 Minutes* correspondent who Schippers and I met on July 11. At 10:40 a.m., I saw Carol seated at the *CBS News* desk with Dan Rather as I changed news channels. Her body was covered in soot from the collapse of the World Trade Center towers. She was explaining how a New York firefighter and police officer saved her life after one tower collapsed and a ball of fire was coming toward the three of them.

Carol Marin, Reporter, CBS News and 60 Minutes.

It was surreal! The only news reporter I had met with regarding my story was actually at the World Trade Center on the morning of the attacks. We met only two months ago, on July 11. We were sitting in Schippers's conference room when I warned her that Middle Eastern terrorists were going to attack the US in the future and kill a lot of innocent people. Carol was almost one of those killed during the 9/11 attack. Moments after her live conversation with Dan Rather, she called Mr. Schippers. She inquired if she could interview me and review my manuscript. He informed her that I could not make any public comments at that time or show the manuscript to anyone until the FBI approved the release of it.

The next call was from Larry Klayman. He said, "Bob, in a millisecond after learning about the attacks, I thought of you and what you told us during our meeting in Chicago five weeks ago."

He said that one of his partners, Tom Fitton, was on board a flight to Los Angeles, and the plane was now sitting on the tarmac at Reagan National Airport. He said Fitton could see the smoke rising from the Pentagon.

He informed me that my case with Judicial Watch was now priority number one.

"Larry, had the FBI supported my efforts, we might have been able to prevent these attacks from happening. Maybe not, but we will never know because the management of the FBI did not understand Vulgar Betrayal. You need to find someone in Congress who can help transfer terrorism responsibilities from the FBI. The FBI is incapable of doing what needs to be done to prevent Middle Eastern terrorists from operating in America," I said.

"Bob, I have been calling several members of Congress. We will get you to Washington as soon as possible so you can tell them your story," he assured.

It was inconceivable to believe the FBI would ignore the criminal activities of known Middle Eastern terrorists living in the US for decades. Likewise, they refused to pursue the $1.4 million civil action to prevent the terrorism monies seized in 1998 from ever being returned to the terrorists. Even more disturbing is the fact that the US Attorney's Office sent two written requests to McChesney requesting she reopen the VB case to prevent these funds being returned to the terrorists. McChesney's arrogance prevented her from acknowledging the importance of these two letters.

The following day, I learned the flight that struck the Pentagon was carrying a passenger named Barbara Olson, a conservative commentator and wife of US Solicitor General Theodore Olson. According to Klayman, she was also traveling to Los Angeles. Both Fitton and Olson were traveling to California to appear on the television program *Politically Incorrect* with Bill Maher.

"It is my understanding they should have been on the same flight. There must have been a scheduling error," said Mr. Klayman.

SSA Ewing, SSA Clinton, the ITU, and many others got what they wanted. My removal from the FBI's terrorism program, over two years before the 9/11 attacks, the Vulgar Betrayal criminal investigation closed, their HAMAS intelligence subjects and HAMAS terrorism activities protected from any FBI criminal investigations.

Because of the combination of their poor management skills, ignorance of enforceable criminal laws, job security concerns, and protecting their terrorist subjects from ever being interviewed, arrested, and removed from the US, a Middle Eastern terrorist attack on US soil, such as these 9/11 attacks, was inevitable. They did it all to the terrorists of their unproductive intelligence cases.

Congratulations to those of you in the FBI's international terrorism arena who failed to prevent the attacks on 9/11. I have a question for you, "Was it worth it? Were the very lives of so many innocent American citizens, the very lives you swore to protect, worth your sabotaging of the FBI's Vulgar Betrayal criminal investigation?

September 2001

This was the FBI's first and only criminal investigation, which was employing new, previously untested weapons in the battle against Middle Eastern terrorists living and operating within the United States. The leading criminal investigation, which, if allowed to continue through September 2001, could have helped prevent the events of 9/11. But we will never know for certain because you helped kill Vulgar Betrayal over two years before the 9/11 attacks. All those lives were lost because you continued playing your worthless and unproductive spy games, with no intent ever to neutralize the Middle Eastern terrorists living and operating in America over protecting the American public. Again, was it worth it?"

I hoped that someday, someone in the US Congress will review the FBI's so-called intelligence files to discover for themselves how unproductive they were leading up to the 9/11 attacks.

To members of the US Congress, you must do whatever it takes to review the FBI intelligence files of Mohammad Salah and all other intelligence files of HAMAS and all other Middle Eastern terrorists throughout the FBI. The lack of work products, the lack of any interviews with terrorism targets, family members, their associates, employers or anyone, will disgust you. You will not find any efforts to neutralize the terrorism subjects via criminal charges or any efforts to have visitor overstays and illegal immigrants removed from the US via the Immigration and Naturalization Service. Even worse, you will discover the FBI allowed many terrorism subjects to become naturalized US citizens while under active FBI classified intelligence investigations. Worst of all, you will find there was absolutely no effort by the FBI intelligence unit to use any collected intelligence to identify and link any of the subjects together. The FBI's only case making such an effort was Vulgar Betrayal, which was negligently killed under the leadership of Chicago SAC Kathleen McChesney, who will become on October 1, 2001, FBI Assistant Director McChesney.

On September 12, I spoke to Judicial Watch President Tom Fitton. He shared how his plane was stuck on the tarmac when the passengers aboard noticed smoke coming from the direction of the Pentagon. He said, "While still on the plane, we heard there had been a terrorist attack. I immediately began thinking about what you told us in Chicago last month. It was surreal."

I had previously scheduled to play eighteen rounds of golf with three others at a local golf course on 9/12. The others called and told me I needed to stop watching the news and come to play golf with them. I had hoped someone from the FBI would have called and requested I come back into the office to help do something, anything, to help with the investigation of the 9/11 attacks. Since no such call came, I played golf. It was the most depressing game of golf I have ever played. I felt guilty for even playing following such a national tragedy.

Later that evening, news stations reported that retired FBI Agent John O'Neill was likely killed when the Twin Towers collapsed. On September 21, the recovery teams discovered his body in the debris of the South Tower.

On September 13, 2001, I called AUSA Robertson about the terrorist funds we seized in 1998.

"James, please tell me you did not give the money back to the terrorists," I said.

"Bob, because the FBI refused to pursue the civil case, we have been negotiating to return the money. The negotiations call for the funds ($1.4 million) to be returned next month (October 2001). However, considering what has happened, I promise you, we will not give them back their money," he stated.

Next, to prevent known international terrorists from harming any more Americans, I called Judicial Watch and again informed Klayman that I needed to share my knowledge regarding the FBI's severe problems with Congress. Problems which led to the successful terrorist attacks on September 11. He wasted no time scheduling congressional appointments for me and purchasing my round-trip airline ticket for "September 20, American Airlines 6:20 a.m., flight #1002, from Chicago O'Hare to Washington, DC."[480]

However, on the evening of September 18, a DOJ official in Washington, DC, learned of my plans to meet with members of Congress. They called my attorneys and leveled a threat against me through them to prevent me from meeting with any members of Congress.

After the call, my attorneys called to inform me about what occurred during the call.

"Bob, this is a game changer! Bob, the highest levels of the DOJ and FBI view you as a serious threat. You are now on their radar," said Mr. Klayman.

I was told that, based on the DOJ official's demeanor, they believed the FBI might arrive at my home within a few hours with a search warrant to retrieve my manuscript and all associated documents.

My attorneys asked me to gather all of my documentation, computer disks, memory sticks, laptop computers, and anything related to my manuscript and hide them somewhere away from home.

With the worry of a potential search of my home and seizure of my manuscript and supporting documents weighing on me, I did what my attorneys asked. I gathered all my records, files, computers, and memory sticks and took them to a friend's home. The work product resulted from two years of research, and I couldn't risk the FBI taking the legally gathered documents from me. The FBI taking these items would likely mean I would never see them again.

Fortunately, there was no search. However, I am confident there were discussions between Washington, DC, and FBI Chicago about searching my home to seize my manuscript and supporting documents. The DOJ officials notified Assistant Director McChesney of my plans to travel to Washington, DC, to meet with members of Congress. When this happened, I was serving my thirty-day suspension from the FBI without pay.

On the morning of September 19, I received a call at home from my FBI supervisor.

"Bob, this is a little far-fetched, but I have been instructed to call you and ask you a question," said my supervisor.

"Who instructed you to call me?" I asked.

"McChesney," said the supervisor.

"Go ahead. What does she want to know?" I asked.

"Is it true you are planning to travel to Washington, DC, to meet with members of Congress?" asked the supervisor.

"Yes, it is true. My attorneys have scheduled the interviews and purchased my airline ticket," I said.

"I have been instructed to inform you that you may not leave the Chicago division without permission from the FBI," said the supervisor.

"You are kidding. I am currently suspended without pay for something I didn't do. Do you seriously believe the FBI can tell me I cannot travel anywhere I want to go right now? Go back and tell McChesney I will travel wherever the hell I want to go," I said.

"Bob, I cannot go back and tell McChesney that," he said.

"Sure, you can. It's easy. The only problem is she will hit you with an OPR investigation," I said.

"That's not funny, Bob," he responded.

"What is not funny is that the FBI's failure to do its job has led to the deaths of thousands of innocent Americans. All I want to do is warn those in power about what is really going on within the FBI's international terrorism program before more innocent people die," I told him.

"Bob, please help me out. Give me something I can go back and tell her without making her mad," he pleaded.

"I am sorry she brought you into this mess. She should have called me herself. However, I may have a solution," I said.

"What is it?" he asked.

"Tell her I will fly to Washington, DC, as scheduled, per my attorney's recommendation. However, if she wants to call Mr. Schippers and talk to him about this, I do not have a problem with her making the call. Tell her I will do whatever Mr. Schippers tells me to do," I said.

"That is much better! I will relay the message. Thank you, Bob," he said.

Following McChesney's call to Schippers, she sent the following email to FBIHQ Assistant Director John Collingwood and Chicago ASAC Patrick Daly:

From:	KATHLEEN MCCHESNEY
To:	[FBI ASSISTANT DIRECTOR] COLLINGWOOD, JOHN E. [CHICAGO A/SAC] DALY, PATRICK
Date:	Wed. Sep 19, 11:48 a.m.
Subject:	Wright & Congress

Bob Wright's attorney just told me that although Bob had intended to fly to WDC this AM to meet with attorney Larry Claman [Clayman] from Judicial Watch and meet with Bill Barr and/or Chris Cannon, he is NOT doing any such thing.

Bob's Chicago attorney, Dave Schippers said he has directed Bob to not speak to anyone in Congress absent a subpoena. KM[481]

A few days later, a Chicago supervisor told me, "FBI Assistant Director McChesney has given instructions that when you return to work following your thirty-day suspension, you are not allowed to perform any work related to the 9/11 attacks." According to the supervisor, she also wanted me to stay seated at my desk and not answer any incoming calls from the public. She instructed Daly to draft an email confirming her decision to ban me from taking any part in the FBI's 9/11 criminal investigation and forward the email to my supervisor for delivery to me when I returned to work on Monday, October 1. This was so far-fetched, the supervisor had to be joking.

On September 23, 2001, President Bush issued Executive Order 13224, authorizing the blocking of property and prohibited transactions with persons who commit, threaten to commit, or support terrorism. Executive Order 13224 states in part:

> By the authority vested in me as President by the Constitution and the laws of the United States of America, I, GEORGE W. BUSH, President of the United States of America, find that grave acts of terrorism and threats of terrorism committed by foreign terrorists, including the terrorist attacks in New York, Pennsylvania, and the Pentagon committed on September 11, 2001, acts recognized and condemned and the continuing and immediate threats of further attacks on United States nationals

or the United States constitutes an unusual and extraordinary threat to the national security, foreign policy, and economy of the United States, and in furtherance of my proclamation of September 14, 2001, Declaration of National Emergency by Certain Terrorist Attacks, hereby declare a national emergency to deal with that threat. I also find that because of the pervasiveness and expansiveness of the financial foundation of foreign terrorists, financial sanctions may be appropriate for those foreign persons that support or otherwise associate with, and sharing of information by, the United States and foreign financial institutions as an additional tool to enable the United States to combat the financing of terrorism.

I hereby order: all property and interest in property of the following persons that are in the United States or that hereafter comes within the United States, or that hereafter come within the possession or control or United States persons are blocked: (a) foreign persons listed in the Annex to this order.[482]

The first "List of Terrorists and Groups Identified Under Executive Order 13224, [was published on] September 23, 2001."[483] The list contained twenty-seven names of terrorists and terrorist organizations. Number twelve on this list was "Osama bin Ladin (Most Wanted Terrorist)." US authorities announced they would release another list of Middle Eastern terrorists shortly.

On Sunday, September 30, 2001, the image of Muslims covered the front page of the Sunday *Sun-Times*, burning an American flag. Under the burning US flag was the caption, "TERRORISTS GET MILLIONS FROM AMERICA – Some Give Money and Cheer the Carnage. Others Are Only Unwitting Backers. And Illinois Is a Major Hub; Pages 8-9A."[484]

On page 8A of the *Sun-Times*, there is an article titled "Chicago may be a key hub for charities funneling cash," which reads in part:

> The Chicago area has been on the government's radar screen for some time, mostly because of a highly publicized case [Vulgar Betrayal] in which federal authorities say a man raised hundreds of thousands of dollars for Hamas.
>
> [Mohammad] Salah of suburban Chicago was arrested in Israel in 1993 and confessed to working as a Hamas military operative. From 1991 to 1992 alone, he funneled more than $100,000 to Hamas military activities in the Middle East, the FBI says.
>
> Before his arrest, Salah told authorities he worked as a computer analyst for the Quranic Literacy Institute [QLI] in Oak Lawn, according to a court affidavit by FBI Special Agent Robert Wright. The affidavit was submitted as part of a pending civil assets seizure case against Salah and the institute, which authorities alleged was involved in a Hamas fundraising scheme. The FBI has frozen $1.4 million in assets.
>
> Salah admitted to Israeli interrogators that he knew of 31 [Muslim] institutions collecting funds for the Islamic world and that Chicago was one of the hubs, according to court transcripts from an extradition hearing of another Hamas member [Mousa Abu Marzook].
>
> Since there is a large Islamic community in Chicago, they collected an enormous amount of money, Salah is quoted as saying in the transcripts.[485]

On Sunday evening, the night before I returned to work from my thirty-day suspension, I packed a box with my manuscript and binders containing hundreds of documents I used to write it. I aimed

September 2001

to present the manuscript and supporting documents to my supervisor, who would then present them to the new FBI Chicago SAC, Thomas Kneir who would be starting his first day in Chicago on October 1st.

CHAPTER 40
AFTERWORD

On October 1, 2001, after completing my thirty-day suspension, I returned to work in the Chicago FBI SRA office. I brought the finished 500-plus page manuscript and binders with my supporting documents in a large box. I placed the twenty-four-pound box on my desk.

The documents in several large binders contained all public source documents from the US and the Middle East, federal court records and transcripts, Israeli HAMAS confessions, and FBI documents I legally got through the Freedom of Information Act (FOIA). I relied upon these documents, listed in over nine hundred endnotes, to accurately and legally share my story. Neither the manuscript nor the supporting documents contain any classified or grand jury information that is not legally in the public domain.

Moments later, when other agents were at my desk welcoming me back to work, my supervisor came to my desk to deliver a message from the FBI management. Although most agents in the SRA office were working on the 9/11 investigation, my supervisor informed me, in front of other agents, that the front office had banished me from working on anything regarding the 9/11 terrorism investigation. In addition, I was told I could not answer incoming complaint calls regarding terrorism-related matters from the public. The supervisor then handed me a document he had drafted, following ASAC Daly's call to relay McChesney's decision to ban me. The document drafted by the supervisor, dated September 25, 2001, reads:

> PFH: pfh
> A/SAC Patrick J. Daly advised that when SA Robert G. Wright, Jr. arrives back at work from his 30-day suspension, he is not to work 265A-NY-208350 [the 9/11 investigation]. A/SAC Daly also said he would discuss this with SA Wright upon Wright's return.
> 1 - SA Wright
> 2 - SRA 2 Personnel Folder SA Wright.[486]

My supervisor said, "Bob, I need you to sign a copy of this notification that tells you that you are not to work on anything related to the FBI's 9/11 criminal investigation."

I signed the document, and as I handed it to him, I said, "They can do whatever they want to me, but I promise they will never silence me."

While standing at my desk, with three other agents present, my supervisor said, "Bob, do not rock the boat. The FBI has changed since the 9/11 attacks."

After being told 'not to rock the boat,' I said, "Don't rock the boat? The FBI's negligence led to the collapse of the towers and loss of thousands of lives!"

"What do you want me to do about it?" yelled my supervisor.

"I don't want you to do anything. I'm going to do something. I finished my manuscript, and I am going to submit it for pre-publication review. I want the truth to come out regarding the gross negligence of the ITU and McChesney's negligent closing of my Vulgar Betrayal case," I exclaimed.

I then turned around and picked up the twenty-four-pound box from my desk. I turned to my supervisor and said, "Here, I need to present this to you."

"What is it?" asked the supervisor.

"This is my rock, and I am going to throw it through the bottom of the boat and sink it. This is my manuscript. It will help others learn why 9/11 happened. According to the FBI's pre-publication rules, I must present it to you, and you must present it to the SAC. The SAC must then forward it to FBIHQ," I said.

"I am not taking that box from you! I will not deliver your manuscript to our new SAC!" he yelled.

He then turned around, rushed into his office, and slammed the door shut.

Thirty minutes later, I entered the supervisor's office with the twenty-four-pound box. I restated that the FBI rules required me to submit the manuscript to my supervisor, who must then present it to the SAC. He again refused to accept the manuscript and suggested I deliver it to the Chicago SAC myself.

"I thought about doing that, but knowing how vindictive FBI management can be, I would likely get hit with another OPR investigation for misuse of my bureau car to transport the manuscript to the SAC," I said.

I didn't enjoy having to put my supervisor on the spot. He supported me since the first day of my arrival on the SRA squad in July 2000. Near the end of the day, he told me that Mr. Daly had permitted me to deliver my manuscript to him the following morning in his office.

On the morning of October 2, I delivered the manuscript and supporting documents to Mr. Daly. He was pleasant and asked me to sit with him and discuss the manuscript's contents. He liked the full-color charts I had prepared and asked for the program's name. He believed the Chicago office should purchase the program and make it available to all Chicago agents.

I inquired about my being banned from working on any aspect of the FBI's investigation of the 9/11 attacks. He informed me that McChesney had banished me from investigating the attacks because of concerns over my relationship with one supervisor, Jack Ewing, who was now overseeing Chicago's portion of the 9/11 investigation. "Of course he is," I said laughing.

I knew the real reason had to do with the many things I had said to McChesney during our March 2001 meeting. On the morning of 9/11, I wondered what she was thinking, in the wake of the terrorist attacks, about all the things I said to her only six months earlier. For a little while, I thought she would call me back to help reopen the Vulgar Betrayal case. But then reality hit me. There was no way she would ever admit her closing of Vulgar Betrayal was a mistake.

During our March 2001 meeting, I warned her about the Middle Eastern terrorist threats. As a reminder, some of the many things I said to her were:

1. "Hundreds of people have died, including five American citizens, because the FBI did not do its job. A lot more people are going to die from Middle Eastern terrorist attacks in the future because the FBI is not doing its job. I cannot believe you allowed the Vulgar Betrayal case to be closed. Could you please explain your justification for closing it?"

Afterword

---

2. "On July 27, 1999, you requested that National Security designate Vulgar Betrayal as a major case. Two weeks later, you took my case away and shut it down. A lot of innocent people are going to die because of your closing of Vulgar Betrayal. How will you ever explain your closing of Vulgar Betrayal in the future?"
3. "Ma'am, there was no credible or justifiable reason to ever close this successful international terrorism case."
4. The problem is, the people you relied upon to determine the fate of Vulgar Betrayal, misled you and lied to you. People like Clinton and Ewing, whom you promoted as the new supervisor of the HAMAS squad.

Remember, in 1994, when I asked my terrorism squad supervisor, "What are we doing? Waiting for the bombs to go off so we can look good because we will know who to arrest after the attacks?"

Between 1996 and September 11, 2001, I expressed my belief to fellow agents, the AUSAs, and my attorneys that the Middle Eastern terrorists were going to attack the US at home.

One afternoon in July 1999, Agent McDonald and I were in one AUSA's office. While looking down at the street, I told him how easy it would be for a Middle Eastern terrorist to blow up the Chicago federal building, which housed the FBI.

McDonald asked, "Bob, do you think they would do that?"

"In a heartbeat. They do not care. They will commit suicide against those they perceive as their enemy," I said.

"Why don't we tell the SAC? Maybe she could talk to the mayor of Chicago and have the streets around the federal building closed down?" he asked.

"They would laugh at us. They do not understand. I do know one thing though," I said.

"What is that?" asked McDonald.

"It is coming. There will be an attack here in America. It is only a matter of time. When it happens, many people are going to die. That is what it will take before the terrorism unit at headquarters takes this matter seriously," I said.

For seven years, I pleaded with FBI management to abandon the unproductive intelligence methods in favor of criminal methods in pursuing the financial trial of Middle Eastern terrorist groups operating within the US and abroad. My overall goal was to prevent future acts of terrorism within the US and abroad. Unfortunately, the attacks of September 11 and loss of almost 3,000 innocent lives exposed the FBI's fatal intelligence flaws to the world.

Following the 9/11 attacks, fearing Congress was considering removing the responsibility for investigating international terrorism from the FBI, FBI management began pursuing the criminal methods I pursued against the Middle Eastern terrorist organizations operating in the United States. They realized the investigative techniques I had been preaching and pursuing, against the wishes of the ITU since 1995, were the correct methods of pursuing, identifying, and capturing the international terrorists and their financiers.

Three weeks after the 9/11 attacks, on October 3, 2001, Dennis M. Lormel, Chief Financial Crimes section, FBIHQ, appeared before the House Committee on Financial Services to address cutting off the financial lifeline of the terrorists.

He stated, "As you well know, the FBI, in conjunction with law enforcement and intelligence agencies throughout the US and the world since the 9/11 attacks, is in the midst of the largest, most

Afterword

complex, and the most critical criminal and terrorism investigation in our history. The FBI has dedicated all available resources to this investigation, including over 4,000 special agents and 3,000 support personnel. Nothing has a higher priority than determining the full scope of these terrorist acts, identifying all those involved in planning, executing, and/or assisting in any manner the commission of these acts, and bringing those responsible to justice. Foremost, our priority is doing everything in our power to prevent the occurrence of any additional terrorist acts.

"So, while I wish none of us needed to be here today, circumstances sadly have made this hearing all too necessary. Therefore, I welcome the opportunity to work with this Committee and all members of Congress in our efforts to cut off the financial lifeblood of the individuals and organizations responsible for these terrorist attacks. Identifying, tracking, and dismantling the financial structure supporting terrorist groups is critical to successfully dismantling the organizations and preventing future terrorist attacks. I thank this Committee for realizing the importance of the financial structure of terrorist organizations to their activities and for calling this hearing to focus attention on cutting off the financial lifeblood to these organizations."[487]

He added, "The FBI's strategy in the investigation of terrorist organizations emphasizes identifying and tracing funds used to finance and fund these organizations. As is the case in so many types of criminal investigations, identifying and following the money plays a key role in identifying those involved in criminal activity, establishing links among them, and developing evidence of their involvement in the activity. Locating, seizing and/or freezing assets tied to terrorist organizations plays a key role in cutting off the financial lifeblood of these organizations and in not only dismantling the organization, but in preventing future terrorist acts. Because of the international nature of terrorist organizations, these investigations require considerable coordination with foreign authorities and the CIA and the intelligence community to ensure that the criminal investigation does not jeopardize or adversely impact sensitive national security matters. This requires careful adherence to restrictions [aka The Wall] separating criminal investigations from those involving national security and classified intelligence matters."[488]

Note: Lormel is talking about the same "Wall" that FBIHQ National Security attorneys agreed with my legal theory that FBI criminal agents had the right to review previously collected intelligence contained within the FBI's intelligence files. After Vulgar Betrayal was shut down, the FBI International Terrorism Unit told agents that the "Wall" remained.

Regarding the necessity for all government agencies to work together, Lormel told the committee, "The acts of terrorism on September 11 highlighted the need for a comprehensive law enforcement response to international terrorism. In the initial stages of this investigation, it was financial evidence that established direct links among the hijackers of the four flights and helped to identify a web of co-conspirators. To provide a comprehensive analysis of the financial evidence, the FBI has established a Financial Review Group to conduct this analysis and determine the source and movement of funds both within and outside the United States that supported these acts of terrorism.

"The Financial Working Group will strive to coordinate the financial investigative efforts; organize, catalog and review personal and business records; develop linkage and time lines concerning the cells and groups responsible; facilitate Mutual Legal Assistance Treaty (MLATs) requests and Letters Rogatory; develop financial and investigative leads in support of this investigation and future terrorism investigations; and identify criminally related fundraising activities by terrorist organizations. Contributions from other law enforcement agencies are critical to the success of such a group. The FBI considers this Financial Review Group to be an integral part not only of the response to the acts of terrorism of September 11 but of future terrorism investigations as well."[489]

Everything, and I mean everything, Lormel described that was now being done by the FBI after the 9/11 attacks, was being pursued by only three FBI agents working the VB investigation before McChesney closed it over two full years before the 9/11 attacks. Chicago sent the official closing letter of the VB case to the FBIHQ National Security Unit on 9/11/2000, one year to the day before the 9/11/2001 terrorist attacks happened. It took over a year, 8/99 – 9/00, for all VB outstanding leads to be completed before Chicago could officially close VB on paper on 9/11/2000.

It makes me sick to my stomach, knowing it took the lives of nearly 3,000 innocent people, not to mention the future loss of life of many members of the US military following the 9/11 attacks, before the FBI finally pursued the investigative techniques and goals which were being achieved, with only three FBI agents, through the Vulgar Betrayal investigation. To prevent the US Congress from removing their national terrorism responsibilities, the FBI decided, after the needless loss of almost 3,000 lives, now was a good time to assign 7,000 agents and support personnel to investigate international terrorism groups.

However, knowing how the FBI works, I'm confident that over time, the FBI will revert to its pre-9/11 rules regarding intelligence investigations. This would include preventing any known or suspected terrorists, their associates, and family members from being interviewed; ignoring the criminal activities of the terrorists; allowing terrorists to get US citizenship; and not allowing agents to open AOT criminal investigations.

On October 10, 2001, while President Bush was visiting FBIHQ, he said, "Eventually, no corner of the world will be dark enough to hide in. I want to thank the American people for understanding that we are engaged in a new war that will require a new way of thinking. Our war is against networks and groups, people who coddle them, people who try to hide them, people who fund them. This is our calling. This is the calling of the United States of America, the [freest] nation in the world. A nation built on fundamental values that rejects hate, rejects violence, rejects murder, and rejects evil. And we will not tire. We will not relent. It is not only important for the homeland security of America that we succeed; it is equally as important for generations of Americans who have yet to be born."[490]

On Saturday morning, October 13, 2001, John Vincent called and asked, "Bob, have you seen the front page of the *Chicago Tribune* this morning?"

"No, why?" I asked.

"You need to find a copy now and read it. After you read it, call me back," he said.

"What should I read?" I asked.

"Trust me, you will know when you see it," he remarked.

I drove to a nearby gas station, purchased the paper, and returned to my Jeep. Once in the Jeep, I opened the paper, and there on the front page was an article titled, "Chicago link emerges as the US freezes more assets." The front-page story told how Yassin Kadi and the Muwafaq Foundation became the targets of an FBI Chicago investigation (Vulgar Betrayal) in 1998.

The article states, in part, the following:

> The government on Friday (Oct 12th) expanded its efforts to disrupt Osama bin Laden's financial network, freezing the assets of dozens of his supporters, including a Saudi business executive who allegedly financed a real estate deal in Chicago's western suburbs to raise money for terrorist activity in Israel.
>
> Yassin Kadi is among the 39 people, businesses and charities whose assets were frozen by the Treasury Department. They joined 27 other individuals [including Osama bin Laden] and groups named in a similar order by President Bush last month.
>
> Kadi's extensive business activities span three continents and include dealings with relatives of the bin Laden family. His money surfaced in the Chicago area in 1991, when Kadi sent $820,000 for a land deal in Woodridge to fund the militant Islamic group Hamas, according to an FBI affidavit.
>
> According to a US government source, Kadi provided $3 million to Osama bin Laden and his Al-Qaida organization.
>
> The government has made a priority of identifying and seizing the financial assets of bin Laden and his supporters. The president's order blocks those named from doing business with anyone in the US and freezes their bank accounts.
>
> Kadi first drew attention in the US in 1998, when he emerged as a key player in an alleged plot to funnel money to Hamas. The scheme was detailed in an FBI affidavit filed in a federal civil case to confiscate the assets of an Islamic charity and a southwest suburban man named Mohammad Salah, described as a "high-level Hamas military operative."

Kadi also is an executive with a Saudi company, M.M. Badkook. The institutional food caterer who supplied 15,000 meals a day to the Kuwaiti and US Army during the Persian Gulf war, according to reports in Saudi Arabian business journals.[491]

After reading this article, frustrated by what the FBI had done to both VB and me, I began pounding my fist into the ceiling of my Jeep five or six times. I just sat in the Jeep thinking about how VB had been on the right track all along and how much we could have discovered two full two years before the 9/11 attacks.

Following Kadi's money trail, we worked to identify Kadi through Saudi Arabia and other countries that were financially linked to Kadi. Not only Kadi but also other known and unknown terrorism financiers. It was only a matter of time before we would have confirmed his connection with Osama bin Laden.

I wondered how the FBI was going to explain VB's negligent closure. How would they explain that I had sent still-pending leads, weeks before VB was closed, overseas to learn more about Kadi, such as identifying his associates and tracking his financial activities, which would have led us to other financiers and associates of Osama bin Laden. Unfortunately, we will never know what we could have achieved prior to 9/11 since VB was closed down by now Assistant Director McChesney.

As of October 13, 2001, since the closing of the Vulgar Betrayal investigation, the following is true:

1. Yassin Kadi financed HAMAS terrorism activities that included terrorist attacks in Israel, leading to the deaths of Israeli and American citizens.

Afterword

2. US-Designated Terrorist Mohammad Salah sent Kadi an email thanking him for his support.
3. Kadi was financially involved with BMI. The president of BMI was the terrorism target FBI Agent Abdel-Hafiz refused to record. According to Abdel-Hafiz, he refused to conduct the covert recording because "A Muslim does not record a Muslim."
4. FBI Assistant Director McChesney refused to acknowledge two letters from the United States Attorney's Office in Chicago regarding the VB investigation. These letters requested she reopen the Vulgar Betrayal case and bring me back to aid in preventing the return of the $1.4 million in terrorist funds, seized in June 1998, back to the Middle Eastern terrorists. Of the $1.4 million seized, $1 million belonged to Yassin Kadi to whom McChesney wanted the money returned. Kadi was now identified, four weeks after the 9/11 attacks, by the US government as a chief financier of Osama bin Laden and officially named as a "Specially Designated Global Terrorist."

After learning that about Yassin Kadi, I contacted a friend on the JTTF squad. I inquired about the identity of the FBI agent assigned to search through the VB files to learn all they could about Yassin Kadi. Since the VB case contained over 600 files, I could help save the agent much time, probably weeks, by directing the agent to all files associated with Kadi and the other files of targets linked to Kadi.

My friend told me since VB was a closed case, FBI management wanted nothing further to do with it, even after the 9/11 attacks. Again, I was dumbfounded.

He said, "Bob, no FBI agents are reviewing any of the Vulgar Betrayal materials. Management has no desire to revisit it, not even to prevent the $1.4 million from being returned to the terrorists. They are going to act as if VB never existed."

"I will not let that happen. I will make it my mission to expose them to force the reopening of Vulgar Betrayal," I said.

In the wake of the 9/11 attacks, why, after the above story and the Chicago *Sun-Times* story published on September 30, would the Chicago FBI office not reopen and pursue the VB terrorism investigation? Because it would amount to FBI management having to admit they made a grave mistake. Rather than admit they were wrong, they would rather pretend the VB case never existed.

The FBI's primary missions following the 9/11 attacks were to protect FBI management, protect the image of the FBI, and protect the FBI's counterintelligence jurisdiction from being transferred to another, more competent federal agency, which is what some members of Congress were threatening following 9/11.

I believe McChesney ignored it to prevent the exposure of her negligent closing of the case over two full years before 9/11.

As of October 2001, my three goals were:

1. Warn the US Congress about the FBI's terrorism failures leading up to the 9/11 attacks.
2. Do whatever I must do to force the FBI to reopen Vulgar Betrayal.
3. Seek the removal of the jurisdiction over the nation's counterintelligence and terrorism responsibilities from the FBI to a new federal agency whose sole mission would be to identify and neutralize terrorism threats against American citizens at home and abroad.

I realized that in the future, the FBI might force me to tell my story to the public against their wishes. I met with Mr. Schippers in his office

Afterword

to discuss my concerns. After I explained my concerns about speaking publicly in the future to him, he informed me he was not aware of any FBI agent ever making public comments regarding the negligent conduct of the FBI without being fired or forced out of the FBI.

"Dave, I agree with you. I hired you over two years ago to help prevent them from firing me in the future."

"Bob, I do not know how to keep them from firing you should you hold a press conference in the future without their approval."

"Dave, we can make it happen. I can give a press conference in the future, and they cannot fire me."

"How?" he asked.

"I know the FBI's rules inside and out, and there is no way anyone within the FBI has reviewed the FBI's rules and regulations regarding an FBI employee legally speaking publicly about serious issues within the FBI. I have discovered a way to speak publicly without being legally fired. I have a plan."

"Tell me how this is possible," Schippers demanded.

"First, I need you and Judicial Watch to file separate complaints with the DOJ Inspector General's office."

"Why should we file two separate complaints with the IG's office?"

"I will get to that shortly. But we also need to send both of the complaints simultaneously to the FBI OPR Unit."

"Bob, why would we file the complaints with both OPR and the Inspector General?"

"Dave, what are the odds the FBI will investigate the complaints, let alone acknowledge receipt of the complaints?"

"Since you are filing them, they would likely ignore both complaints."

"Exactly! What about the DOJ?"

"I have no idea. Why?"

"According to the FBI's rules and regulations, if I file a complaint with OPR or the DOJ Inspector General, they must acknowledge receipt of my complaint and notify me they are actively investigating the allegations within the complaint. According to the FBI's rules and regulations, should they fail to notify me they have received my complaint and are investigating my allegations, I then have the legal right to speak publicly regarding the issues within the complaints. However, before I can speak out publicly, I must give a seven-day written notice of my intention to speak publicly about the issues the FBI and DOJ have failed to investigate."

"Do you have this in writing?"

"I do. Here is a copy. I recommend we file the complaints two months apart."

After reading the FBI rules, Dave said, "I'll be damned. How did you find this?"

"I read most of the FBI's rules and regulations. It's likely no one in management even knows about this seven-day written notice. I doubt if any FBI employee has ever used it."

"Bob, I will file the first complaint during the first week of November. I will talk to Klayman about Judicial Watch filing the second complaint in January 2002," said Schippers.

On March 14, 2002, *USA Today* published a news article titled, "FBI zeroes in on Hamas fundraising in the US." The article quoted retired FBI ASAC Stowe as saying, "If Bob Wright said that had he been able to conduct an unfettered (Vulgar Betrayal) investigation, he somehow could have predicted Sept. 11, that is absolutely ludicrous."[492] Judicial Watch lawyer Larry Klayman said, "His (Wright's) position is he was obstructed from doing his investigation, and if he had been allowed to do that, Sept. 11 may have been averted."[493]

Afterword

Because of Stowe's honesty and high integrity, I have admired and respected him since the day I first met him while attending the FBI Academy in 1990. He was the agent in charge of the FBI Academy. In 1999, he became the Associate SAC of the Chicago FBI office. He did his best to reverse OPR's wrongful conclusion of the Agent Reed matter.

I concur with Mr. Stowe's statement to *USA Today*, that if I said I "somehow could have predicted Sept. 11, is absolutely ludicrous." I never said that I could have predicted the 9/11 attacks.

However, I have said that had VB not been closed, the FBI's probability of thwarting the 9/11 attacks would have proven far greater than the 0 percent chance the FBI had on the morning of 9/11. VB might have even prevented the 9/11 tragedy altogether.

To justify my comments above, I will recount a negligent order made by the International Terrorism Unit (ITU) three weeks prior to the 9/11 attacks. The order prohibited a NY FBI terrorism criminal agent from locating two Saudi terrorists. Before I share the NY FBI agents' story, I need to explain some things.

Achieving the ultimate aim of preventing future terrorist attacks before 9/11 might have been possible. VB was the FBI's first of its kind, national and international criminal terrorism investigation. It had many investigative tentacles being pursued simultaneously. The investigative tentacles included identifying unknown Middle Eastern terrorists; identifying for-profit and non-profit terrorist organizations; identifying US and international bank accounts used to finance international terrorism; identifying and pursuing the arrest of over a dozen known terrorists residing in the US; identifying and interviewing those knowledgeable about Middle Eastern terrorism activities; identifying and seizing terrorist funds and property; working with other countries to further identify known financiers of international terrorism; and identifying the names of account holders of known international terrorist-related bank transactions and accounts.

This was all accomplished through the VB chronological database. It played a crucial role in linking terrorists to each other.

All the above was being done by one FBI support employee and three FBI agents, Agent Vincent, Agent McDonald, and me. VB received little to no support and funding from the ITU. Rather than help VB protect the American people, the ITU was busy seeking ways to obstruct and kill VB to protect the terrorists.

In 1996, an ITU supervisor admitted to the Chicago JTTF that the ITU did not read the communications received daily from FBI intelligence agents. When I asked what they did with the intelligence information, the ITU supervisor said they "filed it away" to be retrieved and reviewed once a future terrorist incident occurred.

I have seen terrorism intelligence files dating back to the 1960s. There are decades of FBI-collected intelligence records, many with vital information to the national security of America. They filed this information away without reviewing it. Not even the intelligence agents could review other offices' classified intelligence files to find links to their terrorism targets.

To prevent any criminal agents from ever accessing the intelligence files, some unnamed person fabricated an imaginary "Wall." It prevented any FBI criminal agent from reviewing any FBI classified intelligence files to further a criminal investigation. After discovering there was no written rule about the made-up Wall, I reviewed the legal statue regarding the FBI's classified information gathering authority passed by the US Congress.

Afterword

The law states that criminal agents may not use any intelligence collection tools established by the law to further any criminal investigation. The law Congress passed does not prohibit FBI criminal agents from reviewing intelligence files to aid in their investigations. They are not allowed to use intelligence methods to gain evidence for their criminal case(s).

Therefore, I reasoned that, since the classified information collected by the intelligence agents already existed within the intelligence files, there was no risk the criminal agents had used intelligence gathering tools to collect this existing information.

VB's most strategic achievement in the fight against international terrorism was the tearing down of the imaginary Wall. This happened during the FBIHQ VB II Conference in October 1998. After presenting my legal opinion about the imaginary wall, the National Security Unit (NSU) attorney agreed with me. Removing The Wall allowed all criminal agents to review the classified intelligence files to further their terrorism investigations.

The NSU attorney told all conference attendees that Chicago VB criminal agents can visit other FBI divisions to review collected classified intelligence to further the VB criminal case. The attorney declared that because the classified information was "previously collected," there was no possibility the FBI criminal agents used intelligence collection tools to obtain the information.

It's crucial to comprehend there were no circumstances under which any FBI criminal agent would ever need or want to use any intelligence gathering tools to gather evidence for a criminal case. The FBI's intelligence collecting methods are laughable because of their required procedures and long processing times.

For example, when an intelligence agent needs financial or telecommunication records of a terrorist, the agent must request a National Security Letter (NSL). The intelligence agent then drafts a communication which is approved by the agent's supervisor. This communication is then forward to FBIHQ for review. FBIHQ then forwards the communication to the DOJ in Washington, DC.

I once submitted a request for an NSL to obtain the financial records of a terrorist. The NSL process took over ten months before I received it. It took over two months more to get the bank records. Through the NSL intelligence collecting tool, it took over one year to obtain the financial records of the terrorist. That was the last time I would ever make an NSL request for financial records.

To get the same financial records as a criminal terrorism agent, I consulted with the assistant US Attorney. I would express my justification for needing the financial records of the terrorists. Within ten to fifteen minutes, I would depart the office with a federal grand jury subpoena for the financial records.

Six weeks after the VB II Conference, five Chicago FBI agents visited the Dallas office in December 1998 to review all HAMAS-related classified intelligence files. We discovered much information vital to the VB criminal investigation. We tagged the pages we needed. The Dallas office copied the pages and forwarded them to Chicago. VB had to create a separate classified subfile to place those documents in.

Weeks after the Dallas trip, FBI Tampa Agent Barry Carmody called me. The Tampa intelligence agents' refusal to allow Barry access to Sami Al-Arian's classified intelligence files frustrated him. He was the case agent of the Tampa criminal terrorism case of Al-Arian. He claimed, four months after the VB II Conference, Supervisor Clinton

Afterword

told the Tampa intelligence agents the Wall prevented any criminal agents from accessing any FBI classified intelligence files.

I told Barry that Chicago VB agents had examined all the classified intelligence files in the FBI Dallas office. I informed him that Clinton was lying because he was continuing to protect the terrorists from terrorism criminal investigations. I assured Barry that he now had the right to review all of Al-Arian's classified files in Tampa or any in other FBI offices where records may exist.

I gave him the National Security Legal Unit (NSLU) attorney's contact information. The NSLU attorney helped Barry and his Tampa colleagues access the Tampa division's classified intelligence files to help further their terrorism criminal investigation. A few days later, Carmody called and expressed his gratitude for helping him gain access to Tampa's classified files.

FBIHQ Supervisor Clinton refused to inform all FBI agents that FBI criminal agents could review previously collected classified information contained within the intelligence files. Instead, Clinton continued telling FBI intelligence agents the imaginary Wall remained intact. The only rule of the Wall was that FBI criminal agents could not review any classified intelligence files to further a criminal investigation.

In August 1999, McChesney killed the VB investigation and moved me off of the JTTF. There was nothing I could do to warn criminal agents they could review the classified intelligence files to further their criminal cases.

Just imagine if the FBI criminal agents could review the classified terrorism intelligence files for three full years before the 9/11 attacks. The possibilities of preventing the 9/11 attacks would have been significant. The criminal agents could have been connecting the terrorism funding, non-profit organizations, bank accounts, and trained terrorists of all Middle Eastern terrorist groups active in America.

Meanwhile, many within the ITU considered VB the greatest threat to their job security. They needed to find a new way to protect their Middle Eastern intelligence subjects from another VB-type criminal investigation. To achieve this goal, someone made up a new second rule for the imaginary Wall.

The FBI's new made-up restriction prohibited Act of Terrorism criminal agents from conducting any criminal investigation of any terrorist who is the subject of an FBI classified intelligence file.

This new made-up rule prevented AOT criminal agents from investigating and even trying to locate any terrorist(s) who were the subject of a classified FBI intelligence file. Even if the criminal investigation began before the classified intelligence file was opened.

The ITU's made-up rule gave the ITU the authority to stop any criminal investigation opened against any terrorist(s) who was the subject of a classified intelligence investigation. Even more disturbing, if a criminal investigation had already begun, the ITU could open a classified case and then instruct criminal investigators to cease their criminal terrorism investigation, without providing any justification, other than saying a classified case was opened. This made-up rule even prevented the criminal agents from attempting to locate the residential addresses of the terrorists, even through the use of criminal tools.

Personally, I would have told the ITU to go to hell and continued working on my criminal investigation. I can say this because I know how worthless the FBI's terrorism intelligence cases are. Again, I also know the real reason the ITU made up this second rule. It was to protect their job security. They needed to protect the terrorists of

Afterword

classified intelligence files from being criminally pursued, arrested, convicted and deported from the US.

Unfortunately, the ITU could now protect the terrorists, by prevent criminal agents, who were working to protect the American people, from neutralizing (i.e., arrest, charge, convict, and/or deport) the terrorists.

The ITU never had any intention of ever neutralizing any Middle Eastern terrorists who were the subjects of their classified intelligence files. Again, the ITU needed their intelligence files to remain open for statistical analysis, to justify their continued congressional funding. Job security was the primary motivation of the ITU.

The following is the story of a New York FBI agent with seven years of terrorism experience. His story illustrates how the new made-up Wall rule proved deadly.

On September 20, 2002, an FBI Special Agent from New York presented a prepared three-page statement to a Joint Intelligence Committee. The statement reads below, in part:

> I am a Special Agent of the Federal Bureau of Investigation (FBI) assigned to the New York Field Office. I appreciate your invitation to appear before your committee today in connection with your Joint Inquiry into the tragic events of September 11, 2001.
>
> I am before you today to address practices that frustrate us all. Much has been written about how the FBI does not share information with local law enforcement agencies, but the American people must realize that the FBI does not always have access to the information itself, nor is all [the intelligence] information the FBI possesses available to all of its [criminal] agents. It is my belief that the former problem is due to fear

that the bureau may 'run ahead' or 'mess up' a current or future operation of one of our sister agencies and later primarily because of decisions that have snowballed out of the Foreign Intelligence Surveillance Act (FISA) Court. A concept known as "The Wall" has been created within the Law Enforcement and Intelligence Communities. From my perspective, and in its broadest sense—"The Wall" is an information barrier placed between elements of an intelligence investigation and those of a criminal investigation. In theory—again, same perspective—it is there to ensure that we, the FBI, play by the rules in our attempts to gather evidence in a criminal case and federal prosecution.

I joined the FBI in December 1995, and was assigned to the New York Field Office's Joint Terrorism Task Force in July 1996. In October 1997, I was assigned to the squad that had responsibilities for Taliban and Pakistan matters. [After] the East Africa Embassy bombings in August 1998, I was part of a team on the ground, spending a cumulative total of over 30 weeks abroad investigating the bombings.

In early 1999, I joined the New York Field Office's Usama Bin Laden (UBL) case squad, which is responsible for the overall investigation of UBL and Al-Qaeda. Immediately after the attack on the USS *Cole* in Aden, Yemen on October 12, 2000, I was assigned as one of the case agents and worked on that case—Adenbom—until the attacks of September 11, 2001.

Briefly, "The Wall," and implied, interpreted, created or assumed restrictions regarding it, prevented myself and other FBI agents working a criminal case out of the New York Field Office from obtaining information from the intelligence community regarding Khalid Al-Mihdhar and Nawaf Al-Hamzi in a meeting on June 11, 2001. At the time there

Afterword

was reason to believe that Al-Mihdhar and Al-Hamzi had met with a suspect connected to the attack on the USS *Cole*.

The situation came to a head during the fourth week of August 2001, when, after it was learned that Al-Mihdhar was in the country [USA], FBIHQ (intelligence) representatives said that FBI New York was compelled to open an 'intelligence case' and that I nor any of the other 'criminal case' investigators assigned to track Al-Qaeda could attempt to locate him. This resulted in a series of emails between me and the FBIHQ analyst working on the matter.

In my emails, I asked where this, 'The New Wall,' was defined. I wrote on August 29, 2001: "Whatever has happened to this—someday someone will die—and wall or not, the public will not understand why we were not more effective and throwing every resource we had at certain 'problems.' Let's hope the National Security Law Unit (NSLU) will stand behind their decision then, especially since the biggest threat to us now, UBL [Osama bin Laden] is getting the most 'protection.'" I was told in response that "we [at FBI Headquarters] are all frustrated with this issue," but "These are the rules. NSLU does not make them up."[494]

Let's assume after the VB II Conference in 1998, Clinton had issued a bureau-wide communication to all offices and agents announcing the dismantling of the imaginary wall. Three years later, the New York agent would have been able to review the intelligence case files of the terrorists he was seeking to find. If the intelligence files contained the address information to find the terrorists, the NY criminal agent could have secured a search and/or arrest warrant, through the US Attorney's Office, based on the NY agent's personal knowledge of the two terrorists' links to terrorism.

I have no doubt the NY agent would have found these two terrorists through criminal investigative tools. Unfortunately, the new made-up rule prevented him from even searching for the terrorists through criminal methods.

If the arrest and/or search had taken place, the NY agent might have discovered information during the search of the terrorists' residences that might have aided the FBI in preventing the 9/11 attacks.

I can say this because the two terrorists, Khalid Al-Mihdhar and Nawaf Al-Azmi, were two of the five Saudi hijackers who crashed American Airlines Flight 77 into the Pentagon on September 11, 2001, at 9:37 a.m.

Nineteen hijackers took part in the 9/11 terrorist attacks. Had FBIHQ informed all FBI agents in 1998 the imaginary Wall no longer existed, it is conceivable that the FBI could have found more of the nineteen hijackers before the 9/11 attacks.

Eighteen years after the 9/11 attacks, I learned something so disturbing I could not believe it. The most important evidence relied upon to justify opening the VB investigation were the financial records of the terrorists, their businesses and non-profit organizations. Following the money is essential for the success of any investigation worldwide. In the world of international terrorism, if you cannot follow the money of your terrorism subject, your case is worthless.

In 2019, I discussed with an FBI intelligence agent how simple it was, since the 9/11 attacks, for intelligence agents to get the financial records of the terrorists they were investigating. The agent told me the intelligence agents are not allowed to request, get, or review any bank records of their terrorism intelligence subjects and their businesses. This is beyond disturbing on so many levels.

Afterword

With the FBI keeping the responsibility of protecting the American people from terrorism after the 9/11 attacks, I fear for the future loss of innocent lives in both the US and overseas.

The US Congress must create a new counterterrorism agency and relieve the FBI of all its terrorism-related responsibilities. The mission of the new counterterrorism agency must focus on neutralizing the terrorists and their organizations, such as HAMAS and all other Middle Eastern organizations operating in the United States against US interests around the world.

The only FBI AOT criminal case to identify and seize terrorism funds linked to international terrorist attacks was Vulgar Betrayal. Six weeks after 9/11, the US government labeled Yassin Kadi, a central figure in the VB case and Osama bin Laden's alleged chief financier, a "Specially Designated Global Terrorist." Yassin Kadi owned $1 million of the $1.4 million seized.

Kadi's $820,000 contribution to the Woodridge land development project, channeled through QLI, aimed at generating tax-free income to fund HAMAS's international terrorism that included attacks that killed innocent people. In 1998, for the first time, the FBI, through VB, seized funds linked to a previously unknown scheme or method used by a Middle Eastern terrorist group operating within the United States.

In the 1980s and 1990s, BMI, also known as The House of Money, backed by Yassin Kadi and HAMAS leader Mousa Abu Marzook, spearheaded many similar land development projects across America. Through VB, our investigation into BMI's projects aimed at uncovering other Middle Eastern terrorist groups receiving terrorism financing via similar American tax-free land development schemes. QLI sent a bank document to a Chicago bank, which identified BMI as a participant in the Woodridge land deal. This was one of the many terrorism financing issues we investigated. Unfortunately, with VB closed, none of these FBI terrorism financial investigations took place.

On October 15, 2001, *CNN* anchor Paula Zahn and correspondent Allan Dodds Frank explored Yassin Kadi's alleged role in financing international terrorism.

"Let's get an update now on the investigation into the funding for the suspected terrorist. Allan, there have been some news reports about the role of Saudi Arabia in this investigation. How critical is the kingdom to the investigation of the money trail? And are they going to cooperate?" asked Zahn.

"Paula, good questions. The kingdom is all important. It is of course, the source of Osama bin Laden's money originally," answered Allan.

"Well, let's, for starters, talk about some of those names that we saw surface on that government list that came out Friday night. How vivid an example is that of any Saudi role in all of this?" asked Zahn.

"Well, one of the names on the list is a man named Yassin al-Qadi [Kadi]. Now, my sources in the government tell me that the foundation he ran funneled at least $3 million to bin Laden as contributions from wealthy Saudi business [executives]. One of the main ways bin Laden has been raising money, according to my sources, is essentially a protection racket, and so these wealthy business [executives], and sometimes even governments, my sources believe, have been paying off Al-Qaeda through these [non-profit] relief organizations that purport to be helping Afghan refugees in order to have the trouble erupt elsewhere rather than right at home,"[495] said Frank.

Concerning donations to Osama bin Laden, Yassin Kadi's response was a definitive, "Absolutely not. I have never been associated to this

Afterword

guy in any way and never sent any money to him."[496] When asked why his name ended up on the Treasury Department's list, "Al-Qadi [Kadi] said a London-based newsletter 'African Confidential,' had accused the foundation [Muwafaq] of involvement in an assassination attempt on Egyptian President Hosni Mubarak."[497] He said, "The Bush administration needs to realize, you need to make friends at a time like this, not make enemies by pointing fingers at innocent people. We should all be together against international terrorism. We are all in the same boat."[498]

Kadi's reaction to reports of his terrorism financing was typical of one who finances Middle East terrorism. The financier tried to insulate himself as much as possible and later denied any knowledge of or association with the terrorists when his involvement in financing terrorism in the Middle East is discovered. In keeping with this mentality, Kadi's attorney said he "will be demonstrating that at no time has he had any link with terrorism, nor has he supported Hamas, Osama bin Laden or al-Qaida or any other terrorist individual, group or organization."[499]

The fact is, Kadi financed the terrorist activities to include actual terrorist attacks of Mohammad Salah. He also had a business interest in the same company, BMI, as Mousa Abu Marzook. The problem was many people, US officials included, thought of terrorists as uneducated and anti-social and expected them to fit a specific stereotype. People did not suspect clean-cut, well-educated medical doctors, engineers, and businessmen to be linked to the financing and directing of international terrorism activities.

On October 30, 2001, I was called into ASAC Daly's office regarding the June 2001 OPR investigation filed against me by McChesney. Mr. Daly informed me that OPR investigation resulted in a "no action" recommendation in my favor. This meant OPR could not prove McChesney's allegation that I showed classified documents from a classified FBI file to an Assistant US Attorney in Chicago.

However, I was not ready for what came next. Mr. Daly handed me another piece of paper, telling me I was now the subject of a new OPR investigation. This was the third OPR investigation opened against me since my March 2001 meeting with McChesney.

Daly said that the new OPR investigation was initiated based on new information the OPR agents discovered during the second OPR investigation. This third OPR notification letter reads the following:

> TO: SAC, CHICAGO DIVISION   10/11/2001
> FROM: OFFICE OF PROFESSIONAL RESPONSIBILITY
> TITLE: SA ROBERT G. WRIGHT JR.
>
> On 5/16/01, an OPR inquiry [OPR #2] was initiated regarding an allegation that unknown subject(s) were involved in the unauthorized disclosure of classified information to the United States Attorney's Office, Northern District of Illinois. On 10/11/01, this OPR inquiry was expanded to include an allegation that the captioned employee engaged in investigative dereliction resulting in violation of the Intelligence Oversight Board (IOB-2001-37) requirements and was involved in the unauthorized disclosure of classified information.[500]

OPR alleged I provided classified information to another Chicago AUSA, Mark Flessner, also working on the VB investigation. The classified information I allegedly disclosed to Flessner was that a known terrorist and target of the investigation was aboard a flight from the Middle East and would land at O'Hare International Airport within seven hours.

Afterword

There was nothing classified regarding the terrorist being aboard the flight to Chicago. The fact is, two INS agents and I had devised a plan, through the VB case, to lure Sharif Alwan from the Middle East back to Chicago. The agents and I knew the terrorist would return to the US within two weeks. Unfortunately, we were unaware of his return date. Upon my request, the INS agents placed this terrorist name on a flight watchlist used by the INS for notification when a foreign national was aboard a flight destined to arrive in the United States. The FBI could not show me any written proof Alwan's flight information was classified as secret.

On July 12, 1999, when the INS agents received notification via the watchlist, they discovered that Sharif Alwan was on a flight and scheduled to arrive in Chicago that evening. After they notified me, I went to Flessner's office to obtain a grand jury subpoena to serve on Alwan when his flight arrived in Chicago. As I entered Flessner's office, he stated, "I heard Alwan is aboard a flight from the Middle East and will arrive in Chicago later today." When I inquired how he learned about Alwan's flight information, he refused to reveal the source of his knowledge. I got the subpoena from Flessner and left. Later that evening, John and I located the terrorist and served him with the grand jury subpoena.

After reading the third notification letter, I laughed and told Daly, "Tell OPR they can bring these OPR investigations against me all they want. I have done nothing wrong. The only thing I am guilty of is trying to stop terrorists. No one is going to silence me from exposing the truth about the FBI's failure to stop Middle Eastern terrorists."

I then realized that the FBI would continue retaliating against me because of my efforts to expose its dereliction of duty. After discussing it with my attorneys, they drafted the first complaint to be filed with the DOJ Inspector General's office and the OPR.

On November 4, 2001, my attorneys filed a thirty-seven-page complaint with the DOJ Inspector General's office, titled:

> COMPLAINT TO THE FEDERAL
> BUREAU OF INVESTIGATION
> OFFICE OF PROFESSIONAL RESPONSIBILITY
> AND
> UNITED STATES DEPARTMENT OF JUSTICE
> OFFICE OF INSPECTOR GENERAL
> FOR
> DERELICTION OF DUTY BY THE FEDERAL
> BUREAU OF INVESTIGATION
> IN FAILING TO INVESTIGATE AND
> PROSECUTE TERRORISM
> AND
> OBSTRUCTION OF JUSTICE IN
> RETALIATING AGAINST
> SPECIAL AGENT ROBERT WRIGHT, JR.[501]

On November 23, 2001, to prevent future terrorist attacks against Israel and its citizens, the Israeli government sent a military helicopter into the West Bank to locate and kill Mahmoud Abu Hunud. Abu Hunud was a HAMAS terrorist leader "involved in terrorist activities dating back to 1997, including deadly attacks on a Tel Aviv discotheque in June [2001] and a Jerusalem pizzeria in August [2001]."[502] The Israeli gunship located Hunud in a taxi, along with another HAMAS member, and opened fire, killing both.

On December 1, 2001, in retaliation for the November 23 attack by the Israeli gunship on the two HAMAS members, HAMAS conducted a series of three terror attacks in a popular, crowded Jerusalem pedestrian mall. At least two HAMAS "suicide bombers detonated explosives near Zion Square just before midnight. A third explosion, about ten minutes later, came from a car bomb, which was timed to explode as rescue workers arrived to tend to casualties."[503] HAMAS caused at least twelve deaths, all ages fourteen to twenty, and injured over 180 people, nineteen of them critically, in a series of three terror attacks at the mall.

Twelve hours later, another HAMAS suicide bomber calmly boarded a bus in downtown Haifa, paid his fare, and, within sixty seconds, ignited an explosion that caused the bus to explode into a massive fireball. The force of the explosion launched the bus into another bus. As a result, the explosion claimed sixteen lives and injured thirty-five innocent people.

On December 2, 2001, "President Bush said he was 'horrified and saddened' by the HAMAS attacks. President Bush said, 'I strongly condemn them as acts of murder that no person of conscience can tolerate, and no cause can ever justify. Chairman Arafat and the Palestinian Authority must immediately find and arrest those responsible for these hideous murders. They must also act swiftly and decisively against the organizations that support them.'"[504]

The following day, December 3, 2001, "Deputy State Department [spokesperson] Philip Reeker called on [Yasser] Arafat to 'bring violence and terrorism to an end through immediate, comprehensive and sustained action by the Palestinian Authority against both the individuals responsible and the infrastructure of the groups that support them.' He added, 'They need to bring them to justice, but they need to act against the infrastructure of those groups that support those individuals. And there is no excuse for failure to take immediate and thorough action.'"[505]

Agent Vincent and I discussed these HAMAS attacks and President Bush's and Mr. Reeker's above comments. We agreed it was hypocritical of the United States to blame Arafat and insist that he act against the infrastructure of HAMAS when most of the HAMAS financing activities occurred within the United States. Meanwhile, the ITU continued to allow HAMAS and other Middle Eastern terrorist organizations based in the US to continue conducting illegal activity to finance such attacks against Israel.

We agreed that President Bush was doing a great job addressing the new war on terrorism; however, we were confident he and other high-ranking US officials were unaware of the many problems within the FBI. Specifically, the FBI's dereliction of duty for the past fifteen years and beyond to prevent HAMAS from financing terrorism from the US.

During another news conference, President Bush stated,

> Good morning. Today we take another key step in the financial fight against terror. At midnight yesterday, the Treasury Department froze the assets and accounts of the Holy Land Foundation in Richardson, Texas, whose money is used to support the Hamas terror organization. Earlier today, federal agents secured the offices and records of the Holy Land Foundation in Texas, California, New Jersey, and Illinois as a part of an ongoing investigation. We have blocked the accounts of a Hamas-linked bank, and Hamas-linked holding company based in the West Bank. The message is this: Those who do business with terror will do no business with the United States or anywhere else the United States can reach.
>
> Hamas is an extremist group that calls for the total destruction of the State of Israel. It is one of the deadliest terrorist organizations in the world today. Hamas openly claimed

Afterword

responsibility for this past weekend's suicide attacks in Israel that killed twenty-five innocent people, many of them teenagers, and wounded almost 200 other people. Hamas is guilty of hundreds of other deaths over the years, and just in the past 12 months, it killed two Americans. And today we act.

Hamas has obtained much of the money that it pays for murder abroad right here in the United States, money originally raised by the Holy Land Foundation. The Holy Land Foundation is registered with the IRS (Internal Revenue Service) as a tax-exempt charity based in Richardson. It raised thirteen million dollars from people in America last year. The Holy Land Foundation claims that the money it solicits goes to care for needy Palestinians in the West Bank and Gaza. Hamas uses money raised by the Holy Land Foundation to support schools and indoctrinate children to grow up into suicide bombers. Hamas also used money raised by the Holy Land Foundation to recruit suicide bombers and to support their families.

America has called on other nations to suppress the financing of terror. Today we take further steps to suppress it inside our borders. But the facts are clear: the terrorists benefit from the Holy Land Foundation, and we are not going to allow it.

Our action today is another step in the war on terrorism. The net is closing. Today it just got tighter. And now it is my honor to welcome to the podium the Secretary of Treasury, Paul O'Neill.[506]

O'Neill stated the following in response:

> Thank you, Mr. President. In October, we broadened our pursuit of terrorist assets to include all foreign terrorist organizations, including Hamas. We stated very clearly our intent

to pursue the bankers who finance these terrorists. Today, we are advancing on those financiers of terror.

The Hamas terrorist organization has taken the lives of scores of individuals, including American citizens. They have proudly claimed credit for their acts of evil, including the horrific attacks this past Sunday. They raise money in the United States and around the world. Hamas is a terrorist organization of global reach.

Today we are shutting down three Hamas-controlled organizations that finance terror. The Holy Land Foundation masquerades as a charity, while its primary purpose is to fund Hamas. This organization exists to raise money in the United States to promote terror. Last year, Holy Land raised $13 million in the United States.

Similarly, the al Aqsa Bank and the Beit El-Mal Bank (aka BMI) are not just banks that unknowingly administer accounts for terrorists. They are the direct arms of Hamas established and used to [finance] Hamas [terrorism].

We will continue to name the financiers of terrorism to ensure that Hamas and other terrorist organizations have no ability to finance their acts of evil. We will work with every civilized nation around the globe to ensure there is no safe haven for terrorist money. Just as in the ground war, we will win by taking one hill at a time, advancing tirelessly every day, until terrorists and their money have nowhere to hide.[507]

Next, Attorney General Ashcroft approached the podium and said:

Today we have launched another coordinated enforcement action against more organizations that finance terrorism around the world. With this action, we go beyond the al-Qaida network to target groups whose violent actions are designed to destroy the Middle East peace process. The suicide bombings in Israel over the weekend and previous attacks claimed by Hamas leave no doubt about the urgency of stopping terrorism in all its forms, whether the terrorism emanates from Afghanistan or from the West Bank and Gaza.

By freezing the financial apparatus of Hamas, we signal that the United States of America will not be used as a staging ground for the financing of those groups that violently oppose peace as a solution to the Israeli-Palestinian conflict. We will not tolerate it any more than we will tolerate the financing of groups that on September 11 attacked our homeland.

Today's action is a result of the FBI's work with the Treasury Department on a continuing terrorist financing investigation coordinated by the Department of Justice's Terrorist Financing Task Force. This task force's sole mission is to dismantle US-based organizations financing terrorist operations. The task force was created in the aftermath of September 11.

Today's action targets a US-based organization operated by individuals who have been the focus of joint law enforcement action prior to September 11th. The Holy Land Foundation for Relief and Development based in Richardson, Texas, shares employees of an Internet company known as INFOCOM. INFOCOM was raided by the FBI and had its assets frozen by the Treasury Department six days before the World Trade Center and Pentagon attacks and the plane crash in Pennsylvania. INFOCOM, like the Holy Land Foundation, received much of its early money from Mousa Abu Marzook, a top Hamas official who, the US courts have determined, was directly involved in terrorism.

Besides sharing Marzook as an early sponsor, INFOCOM and the Holy Land Foundation were both established in

California and moved to Texas in the same period of time. They are currently located in the same business park and appear to share office space and personnel.[508]

Although it has been common knowledge for many years that the Holy Land Foundation in Richardson, Texas, is one of HAMAS's largest non-profit front organizations operating in the US, many, including President Bush and members of Congress, do not realize the actual size of the HAMAS presence in America. Likewise, they are not aware that the ITU, in the name of job security, has allowed Middle Eastern terrorist groups, such as HAMAS, to thrive in America.

The FBI ITU has intentionally ignored its duty to protect the American public. I can say this since I have seen FBI documents dating back to the '60s and '70s regarding Middle Eastern terrorist organizations. When I saw these documents, I thought, "My God! The FBI could have stopped these guys decades ago and saved many lives." They should have shut down the entire US-based HAMAS network long ago. Shutting down only a few of their criminal enterprises only temporarily inconveniences HAMAS.

The shutdown of a few well-known HAMAS pieces is insufficient against a major international terrorism network. On Tuesday, December 4, 2001, President Bush, Attorney General Ashcroft, and Treasury Secretary O'Neill gave a news conference at the White House addressing a small portion of HAMAS's US-based enterprise. Unfortunately, twenty-five Israelis lost their lives, while another 215 were injured over the preceding weekend before the US finally shut down the Holy Land Foundation, a closure that should have happened at least five to six years earlier.

Following the above news conference, three things stood out to me. First, VB targeted the Holy Land Foundation, INFOCOM, and BMI.

Afterword

Second, there was no sign the FBI had reopened VB or the civil case to assist the United States Attorney's Office in preventing the $1.4 million seized in 1998 from being returned to terrorists Mohammad Salah and Yassin Kadi. Both of whom were designated international terrorists by the US government.

The third concerns BMI. In 1999, the Chicago FBI served the BMI President with a federal grand jury subpoena. The BMI president wanted to meet with Abdel-Hafiz to inquire about the VB investigation and his upcoming Chicago grand jury appearance. Abdel-Hafiz told six of us, three AUSAs and three FBI agents, he would not conduct a secret recording with the BMI president because "A Muslim does not record another Muslim!" The meeting never happened because Abdel-Hafiz refused to perform the recording covertly.

FBI management's cowards failed to investigate Abdel-Hafiz's refusal to secretly record Muslim terrorism subjects of FBI Chicago and Tampa investigations who sought information about FBI cases concerning them. Instead, FBI management, including Dallas SAC Danny Defenbaugh, encouraged Abdel-Hafiz to file an EEO complaint against me. One FBIHQ supervisor, in an email, encouraged Abdel-Hafiz to sue me.

The FBI supervisor's email to Abdel-Hafiz reads:

> Based on what you have told me regarding this issue [Abdel-Hafiz's refusal to secretly record terrorists who reached out to him], if I were you, I would sue Bob Wright individually for slander. I do not think the Department of Justice would defend him against such a lawsuit and even personal liability insurance might be questionable, particularly if you show it was intentional. In such a case, any legal expenses or judgments against him would be out of his [Wright's] pocket. Best wishes to you![509]

Although VB identified most, if not all, of the entire US-based HAMAS criminal enterprise, the US government only shut down three of the dozens of HAMAS-controlled organizations. This cosmetic approach of shutting down a few of the front organizations did nothing. HAMAS would transfer the responsibilities of INFOCOM and the HLF to one or more of their remaining US-based non-profit organizations. They could transfer the responsibilities overseas to another HAMAS front in Canada, France, Great Britain, or elsewhere if required.

The US government should have simultaneously shut down all known HAMAS US-based enterprises. The FBI's haphazard approach to closing down only a couple of them allowed HAMAS to continue operating in America and financing international terrorist attacks. Terrorist attacks that would lead to the deaths of innocent Israeli and American citizens. The continued funding of HAMAS from the US would continue for the foreseeable future. The only way to end HAMAS and all other American-based international terrorism organizations would be for Congress to establish a new federal agency whose sole responsibility is to identify and neutralize international terrorism threats in America to protect the American public.

Following the above press conference, my attorneys requested permission to forward a copy of the thirty-seven-page complaint they filed on my behalf with the DOJ Inspector General to President Bush's staff. The attorneys wanted me to share with the president my knowledge of the problems within the ITU and explain the continued threats HAMAS posed to the US and Israel.

I warned my attorneys that the FBI pre-publication rules prohibited my dissemination of the manuscript and complaint to President Bush or any member of the US Congress before the FBI pre-publication

Afterword

review unit thoroughly reviewed and approved the documents for publication. I advised my attorneys that the pre-publication unit chief guaranteed I would receive information regarding their review of my manuscript and the thirty-seven-page complaint on or around January 2, 2002.

Therefore, unable to forward a copy of the complaint to President Bush, Judicial Watch issued the following press release ahead of the FBI's final decision regarding the review of the manuscript and the November 4 Complaint to the DOJ Inspector General:

> JUDICIAL WATCH PRESS RELEASE
> December 2001
>
> Since August 1999, FBI Special Agent Robert Wright and his attorney, David Schippers, Schippers and Bailey, Chicago, IL 60602 have been working to legally expose the very real and foreseeable Middle Eastern terrorist threats to American citizens at home and abroad. During July 2001, Larry Klayman, Judicial Watch, 501 School Street, S. W., Suite 725, Washington, DC 20024 met with Agent Wright to discuss his concern regarding the FBI International Terrorism Unit's dereliction of duty to protect American citizens from terrorists operating within the United States. Concerned for the public interest of all Americans and the country, Larry Klayman offered the legal assistance of Judicial Watch to aid Agent Wright in legally exposing the FBI's dereliction of duty.
>
> From 1993 to 1999, Agent Wright was assigned to "the Chicago Division Counter-Terrorism Task Force. In this capacity, Agent Wright became familiar with techniques used by international terrorist organizations to surreptitiously move and launder money in and out of the United States; including through use of domestic financial institutions, in support of extortionate terrorist

and paramilitary activities and operations in the United States and abroad, including the State of Israel and elsewhere." Against the wishes of FBI management, in 1995, "when he uncovered criminal violations in several of his cases, Agent Wright promptly initiated corollary 'Act of Terrorism' criminal investigations on the subjects." Agent Wright developed "probable cause to believe that some of these transfers or transmissions have been of money intended for support of domestic and international terrorist activities; the illegal transfers have supported specific terrorist activities involving the extortion, kidnapping and murder of the citizens of the State of Israel."

Agent Wright's successful investigation, "codenamed VULGAR BETRAYAL," led to the June 6, 1998, seizure of $1.4 million of Middle East terrorist funds. This seizure was the first occasion that the US government used the civil forfeiture laws to seize terrorist assets in the United States. The funds were linked directly to Saudi business executive Yassin Kadi. On October 12, 2001, the US Government designated Yassin Al-Qadi as a financial supporter of Osama bin Laden. According to a US Government source, Kadi provided $3 million to Osama bin Laden and his al-Qaida organization.

Despite the unqualified success of Agent Wright's investigation of Middle East terrorists, FBI management failed to take seriously the threat of terrorism in the United States. Specifically, FBI management intentionally and repeatedly thwarted and obstructed Agent Wright's attempts to launch a more comprehensive investigation, which would identify terrorists, their sources, and methods of funding before they attacked additional U. S. interest, killing more American citizens. The FBI's lack of support for Agent Wright's Vulgar Betrayal investigation was obvious to his new supervisor,

Afterword

who after four months wrote in April 1998, "Agent Wright has spearheaded this effort despite an embarrassing lack of investigative resources available to the case such as computers, financial link analysis software, and a team of financial analysts. Although far from being concluded, the success of this investigation so far has been entirely because of the foresight and perseverance of Agent Wright."

Although the Vulgar Betrayal investigation had "been proposed for designation as a major FBI case because of its far-reaching scope," in 1999, Agent Wright in an effort to further the terrorism investigation, purchased much-needed computer software and a scanner with his own money since he could not obtain the necessary funding and support from the FBI. Worse yet, FBI officials retaliated against Agent Wright because, against their wishes, he aggressively continued to pursue the Vulgar Betrayal criminal investigation to prosecute terrorists in the United States. This retaliation evidences a scheme to discredit and, thereby, silence Agent Wright, who has sought to communicate his experience to Congress and others in the public interest.

In retaliation for Agent Wright's internal criticism of the FBI's dereliction of duty, the FBI has dispensed strong medicine to silence him. A threat was even leveled by a Department of Justice (DOJ) official against Agent Wright to his attorneys to prevent him from meeting with members of Congress during the week after September 11. In fact, the following morning, in order to prevent Agent Wright from traveling to Washington, DC, on his own time to meet with members of Congress, the FBI informed Agent Wright he could not travel outside of the Chicago division without permission from the FBI. Moreover, the FBI has established a clear pattern of vindictive retaliation to silence Agent Wright to prevent him from disclosing the incompetence of FBI managers.

Agent Wright's "Exceptional" efforts have always been geared toward neutralizing the terrorist threats focused on taking the lives of American citizens, besides harming the national and economic security of America. However, because of the incompetency and intentional obstruction of justice by FBI management to prevent Agent Wright from bringing the terrorists to justice, Americans have unknowingly been exposed to potential terrorist attacks for years.

Fortunately, because of the foresight of Agent Wright, since 1999, he has been working to legally expose the FBI's incompetence and dereliction of duty in the terrorism arena. Because of Agent Wright's foresight, he has written a single-spaced 500-page manuscript titled, Fatal Betrayals of the Intelligence Mission (aka Vulgar Betrayal), the manuscript outlines the FBI's intentional failure to pursue the terrorists and thereby prevent terrorist attacks such as those of September 11. Ironically, Agent Wright completed the text of this manuscript on the morning of September 11. In addition, on November 5, 2001, Agent Wright through his attorneys filed a 38-page complaint with the United States Department of Justice, Office of Inspector General "FOR DERELICTION OF DUTY BY THE FEDERAL BUREAU OF INVESTIGATION IN FAILING TO INVESTIGATE AND PROSECUTE TERRORISM AND OBSTRUCTION OF JUSTICE IN RETALIATING AGAINST SPECIAL AGENT ROBERT WRIGHT, JR."

In addition, Agent Wright through his attorneys, filed a 118-page complaint with the United States Department of Justice, Office of Inspector General detailing the "WHISTLE

Afterword

BLOWING RETALIATION BY THE FEDERAL BUREAU OF INVESTIGATION AGAINST SPECIAL AGENT ROBERT WRIGHT, JR."

FBI rules and regulations prohibit Agent Wright from disseminating the documents listed above to anyone, including US President Bush and any member of Congress, before submitting the written material to the FBI's Prepublication Review Unit. Therefore, in a good faith effort to legally share the contents of these documents with President Bush, members of Congress and the American people, Agent Wright has abided by the FBI's established rules and submitted the manuscript and complaints to the FBI's Prepublication Review Unit for review.[510]

On December 3, 2001, in response to the 9/11 attacks, FBI Director Mueller announced an FBIHQ reorganization plan. He "implemented a restructuring plan for Headquarters, Federal Bureau of Investigation. The major elements of the first phase of the Headquarters reorganization effort include the creation of four new executive assistant director positions to oversee key FBI functions. The positions and their designated heads include: Executive Assistant Director for Law Enforcement Services—To be headed by 23-year veteran Kathleen L. McChesney."[511]

I was stunned to learn McChesney, fifty-one years old, was likely a step away from becoming the first female FBI director. This was her second promotion within five and a half months. She would never have to answer for her negligent closure of the Vulgar Betrayal investigation.

The following is a brief list of newly promoted McChesney's poor leadership decisions and her fast-track FBI management climb to one step below the FBI director during the past three years:

The FBI's Pre-9/11 Vulgar Betrayal

March 17, 1999: McChesney becomes the SAC of the FBI Chicago Division.

August 4, 1999: McChesney removes me from the Chicago Joint Terrorism Task Force.

October 1999: An FBI communication reads, "The RICO criminal conspiracy relating to the above-captioned investigation VULGAR BETRAYAL is no longer being pursued." Under McChesney's leadership, VB is dead since no further investigation is being pursued.

September 11, 2000: Under the leadership of McChesney, Vulgar Betrayal is officially closed, per Chicago EC to FBIHQ, National Terrorism Unit.

September 2000: The Chicago ASAC told me, "Bob, both the Vulgar Betrayal civil and criminal cases have been officially closed." Since McChesney refused to allow the FBI to assist the US Attorney's Office, her decision to close the civil case means the $1.4 million must be returned to the terrorists.

2000 & 2001: McChesney twice refused written requests by the Chicago US Attorney's Office to reopen the VB civil case and bring me back as the case agent. The requests were sent to prevent the return of the $1.4 million to the terrorist, Mohammad Salah and terrorism financier Yassin Kadi.

June 15, 2001: McChesney is promoted to Assistant Director of the FBI.

September 11, 2001: 9/11 terrorist attacks.

September 25, 2001: McChesney prohibits me from working on any aspect of the FBI's 9/11 investigation. I have no knowledge of any other FBI employee being banned from working on any aspect of the 9/11 criminal investigation.

December 3, 2001: FBI Director Mueller promoted McChesney to FBI Executive Assistant Director, the second-

Afterword

highest leadership position within the FBI. Her second promotion within six months.

To my knowledge, at the time of McChesney's second promotion, the FBI had still not reopened the VB civil case or sent any help to the United States Attorney's Office to prevent the return of the $1.4 million to Salah and Yassin Kadi. Four weeks after the 9/11 attacks, the US government discovered Kadi to be a chief financial supporter of Osama bin Laden and designated him a "Specially Designated Global Terrorist."

After learning about McChesney's promotion to the second-ranking position of the FBI, I thought, "You can't make this stuff up. Nobody will ever believe this story."

It was then that something hit me like a ton of bricks. Her closure of the Vulgar Betrayal case provided an excellent way to help prove my story accurate. I could now legally get copies of actual documents from the VB case files. Since VB was an officially closed FBI case, I could file a Freedom of Information Act (FOIA) request for the VB documents.

After writing the list of documents I needed to back up my story, I filed the FOIA request with the FBI. My concern was how much information they would redact from the VB documents. After receiving the redacted VB documents, I incorporated many of them into this book.

On January 2, 2002, I received exciting news from the FBI. The FBI's pre-publication review unit completed the reviews of both my manuscript and the November 2001 complaint filed with the DOJ Inspector General and OPR. They approved 82 percent of the manuscript and 96 percent of the November 4 complaint for publication. I was relieved that my two-year effort to locate and use public source information to aid in telling my story had paid off. The most critical portions approved were my conversations with all FBI employees, supervisors, ASACs, SACs, and others.

The pre-publication review unit identified only 18 percent of the manuscript as problematic. I addressed these issues and resubmitted the manuscript for further review in two days. Since these issues were easy fixes, I had no problems with the material they had requested I alter. I now had complete confidence and trust in the FBI's pre-publication review process.

I was relieved I could now legally tell my story without fear of being retaliated against and fired by the FBI. After being told I could release the portions of the 82 percent of the manuscript that the pre-publication review unit had already approved, I forwarded some of the FBI-approved material from this manuscript to Judy Miller at *The New York Times*, as I had promised her on the morning of 9/11.

However, all hell broke loose at FBIHQ on Friday, March 8, 2002. The FBI learned Miller intended to use the FBI-approved materials I provided her to write a three-day, front-page story in *The New York Times*. FBIHQ management made plans to prevent her from authoring her story. The story would concern the FBI's terrorism dereliction of duty prior to the 9/11 attacks.

The following day, Saturday, March 9, Mrs. Miller called me at home with some unwelcome yet unsurprising news. She said that FBIHQ had contacted her and offered her a once-in-a-lifetime proposition. If she delayed publishing her story, she could travel to FBIHQ in Washington, DC, to interview FBIHQ officials in person about me and the VB case.

I told her, "Go for it! Everything I have written and spoken is true." I assured her that the FBI could not deny anything within the pages of the book I had given her. I informed her they could not explain away the RICO statute of limitations issue as the reason for closing VB. I wondered how they would try to defend its many mistakes that cost people their lives.

Being offered the rare opportunity to interview high-ranking senior FBIHQ officials at the top law enforcement agency in the land was a reporter's dream, particularly following the 9/11 terrorist attacks. She could not resist the offer.

"Judy, you must go to headquarters and listen to what they say. I am not lying about anything," I told her. I even sent her a copy of all my FBI performance appraisals, which show the rapid progression of the VB investigation and my exceptional performance ratings.

After agreeing to attend the meeting at FBIHQ, she postponed the planned newspaper series until afterward.

On March 20, 2002, Mrs. Miller went to FBIHQ and met with several managers whom I had never met, seen, or spoken with during the VB investigation. The only person I knew who attended this meeting was SSA Tim Gossfeld. The FBI paid to fly him from Chicago to attend the meeting with Miller. It turns out that during the meeting, the FBI agents lied repeatedly to Miller about me and the VB investigation.

To counter their lies, she, Agent John Vincent, and I each sent separate written requests to FBIHQ through our attorneys, seeking permission for John and me to be interviewed by her to address the lies they told Mrs. Miller. The FBI denied all three requests and told John and me we could not speak to her.

Meanwhile, I received a call from the pre-publication review supervisor.

"Bob, something has happened here that has never happened before in the history of the pre-publication review unit," said the supervisor.

"What happened?" I asked.

"The FBIHQ legal unit entered our workspace and seized all of your submissions. Your manuscript, the two complaints, and your and Vincent's responses to the questions of the *New York Times* reporter. They took everything, Bob," said the supervisor.

"I warned you this would happen. I am not surprised," I said.

"Bob, what was in the manuscript? I never read it," she asked.

"Everything is in there. I wish you would have read it. Then you would understand why they have seized everything," I said.

In the future, the above supervisor would deny that the above conversation occurred. At the time of the unit chief's call, realizing the severe gravity of the matter, I wrote her comments down as she made them. As I have said before, I'll take a polygraph test to verify the events and conversations contained within this book.

Next came a letter from John Collingwood, Assistant Director of the FBI's Office of Public and Congressional Affairs, to Judicial Watch President Thomas Fitton. The letter said the FBI employment agreement prohibited John and me from disclosing information obtained in our official capacity as agents. The further letter stated I couldn't release any information from documents I submitted to the FBI for pre-publication review, including the already approved sections. The FBI falsely claimed that I could not release any information in my manuscript and other submitted documents because they deemed the documents to be "so interwoven with both classified and grand jury information."

This FBIHQ statement was an absolute lie. I was careful not to include classified or grand jury information in this book. There was no one outside the FBI to whom we could file an appeal regarding the FBI's intentional lies. FBI management is above the law. Unfortunately,

Afterword

it was clear they had no intention of ever allowing this book to be published or released to any members of the US Congress.

After telling their lies to Mrs. Miller, she had no choice but to hold off on writing her news articles. The FBI was lying to protect their reputation, to prevent Congress from removing their terrorism responsibilities and giving them to another federal agency, to protect ITU managers, and lastly, to protect the gross negligent closing of the VB case by McChesney.

In another letter from AD Collingswood to Mr. Schippers, Collingswood wrote, "Unauthorized disclosure of this type of information could impair national security, place human life in jeopardy, deny subject(s) of FBI investigations due process, or otherwise prevent the FBI from effectively discharging its responsibilities."[512]

After Dave read the above paragraph he exclaimed, "He says your exposing the truth about the FBI's incompetence will 'place human life in jeopardy!' Bob, you are trying to save lives! This crap is nothing more the FBI trying to hide the truth from Congress and the American people! We will not let them get away with this crap!" In the almost three years I had known Dave, I had never seen him get this upset.

Schippers and I had expected FBIHQ would pull a stunt like this to prevent Congress and the American public from ever learning the truth about their negligent intelligence terrorism investigations. Schipper and I then had a conference call with the Judicial Watch attorneys in Washington, DC. We all agreed that the expected second lawsuit against the FBI for violating my First Amendment rights would need to be filed against the FBI.

The reality hit me. The FBI was now forcing me to sue my employer because of FBI management's self-preservation instincts.

Unfortunately, because of the conduct of management toward my First Amendment rights, the decision to follow through on suing them was simultaneously easy and scary. It was terrifying because I did not know how FBI management would react to an active FBI agent suing them. However, their actions left me with no choice. I needed to file the lawsuit so that others could learn the truth about the FBI's international terrorism-related negligence before the 9/11 attacks.

Following the conference call, Schippers and I had a lengthy conversation about what would likely occur.

"Bob, I regret to tell you this, but although we have discussed filing a First Amendment lawsuit against the FBI, I did not believe they would act in this unprofessional manner. Now that they have, they will stop at nothing to take you down. They need to discredit you, and they will say and do whatever it takes. Are you prepared for what is coming?" he asked.

"Dave, I have been ready for this day since the day they removed me from Vulgar Betrayal. I know they are going to do everything they can to fire me. I want to expose everything that happened, and I want terrorism responsibilities removed from the FBI. They're incapable of conducting proper international terrorism investigations," I said.

"That's good. I will call several US senators and tell them about you and your manuscript. These senators will help us protect you," he said. He then added, "Bob, I want you to consider doing two more things."

"What are they?" I asked.

"First, you need to start writing a second book. You completed the first book on 9/11. Add an afterward chapter at the end of the book. Your second book will cover what happens from here on out. The FBI is going to come after you hard, and you need to document everything they are going to do to prevent you from telling your story to Congress

Afterword

and the public. Bob, this is your story and no one can tell this story but you. You need to tell this story," Mr. Schippers said.

"Dave, there is no way, I cannot write a second book. I do not have it in me," I said.

"Listen to me, the FBI will do everything possible to fire you! It would be best if you documented this incredible story in real time," he insisted.

"Please tell me you are not serious, Dave," I said.

"Bob, there will be a lawsuit filed on your behalf against the FBI soon, and you will have US senators helping protect you from their retaliation. At some point, I am confident the FBI director and Attorney General will become involved with your situation. It would be best if you considered documenting your story as it is happening in real time from here on out," he instructed. Then he said, "There is one last thing."

"What is that?" I asked.

"Though it may be difficult for you to comprehend at present, this is based on my years of experience," he stated.

"Okay," I said.

"At some point, likely many points, you will want to quit the FBI. Don't quit!" said Schippers.

"Why not?" I asked.

"I want you to stay with them as long as possible. Stay through your mandatory retirement date. How many years before you are mandatory?" asked Schippers.

"I could end with thirty-one years of service in 2021. That's another nineteen years. Why?" I asked.

"Bob, again, the FBI will do everything they can to prevent the release of your manuscript to Congress and the public. They will do everything in their power to delay the release of your manuscript for years. The day will come when a federal judge rules against the FBI and approves your manuscript for release. Should you publish your manuscript while still employed as an FBI agent, FBI management will make your life a living hell," he said. Then he continued, "Bob, what I'm about to say is crucial. Do not worry about the passage of time when publishing your book. No matter how long it takes, you must tell this story to the American people in the future. With that said, Bob, I want you to stay in the FBI for the full thirty years. Staying in the FBI for 30 years will boost your credibility, given what they have done and will do to you. You are young, and you will outlast everyone who has and who will try to stop you from telling the truth about the FBI's dereliction leading up to the 9/11 attacks. Bob, you wrote a 500-page book about the FBI's negligence before the 9/11 attacks. That's huge."

"You must be kidding. I cannot stay in the FBI for another nineteen years!" I said.

"Try. Trust me, Bob," he said.

"I can promise you one thing, Dave. No matter how many years this mess lasts, I will never quit. I would never give these bastards the satisfaction of letting them believe they were successful in forcing me out," I said.

"Bob, you realize they will try to fire you at some point, right?" he asked.

"Dave, they have no alternative. They must fire me to discredit me. If they fired me, they would claim that I'm a disgruntled former employee who was fired and is not credible. This is the method FBI management pursues to remove unwanted employees. I have always known they are going to try firing me. That's why I hired you two

Afterword

and a half years ago, Dave," I said. I then added, "Dave, to date, the FBI has fired or forced out every FBI street agent Whistleblower; as long as you guys do not abandon me, I know we can beat them at their own game in the end."

On March 14, 2002, US Senator Charles E. Grassley from the US Senate Judiciary Committee, sent the following letter to the FBI and a copy of the letter to Schippers:

> To whom it may concern:
>
> I am writing to you regarding FBI Agent Robert Wright. Mr. Wright is assisting my staff and me with an oversight investigation of the Federal Bureau of Investigation and its counter-terrorism performance both before and after September 11, 2001.
>
> As ranking member of the Subcommittee on Crime and Drugs of the Judiciary Committee, I conduct continual oversight of the FBI and its activities. As a US Senator, I have made protecting whistleblowers a priority, and will not tolerate retaliation against or interference with a whistleblower or a person cooperating with a Congressional investigation.
>
> Federal law provides individuals who are assisting a Congressional investigation protection from retaliation. In addition, Federal law states:
>
> Whoever corruptly, or by threats or force or by any threatening letter or communication influences, obstructs, or impedes or endeavors to influence, obstruct or impede the due and proper administrative of the law under which any pending proceeding is being had before any department or agency of the United States, or the due and proper exercise of the power or inquiry under which any inquiry or investigation is being had by either House, or any committee of

either House or any joint committee of the Congress—Shall be fined under this title or imprisoned not more than five years, or both. See 18 USCS 1505 (partial cite).

I have instructed Mr. Wright and his attorney, David Schippers, to contact me if they have any concerns regarding retaliation. If you have questions regarding this matter, you may contact John Drake on my staff at (202) 224-xxxx.

Cordially yours,
Charles E. Grassley[513]

Also, on March 14, 2001, Senator Grassley sent a second letter to Schippers, which reads in part:

Dear Mr. Schippers:

I am writing to confirm that you and your client, FBI Agent Robert Wright, are cooperating with my staff and in our oversight of the Federal Bureau of Investigation.

I conduct continual oversight of the FBI and its activities. Specifically, I look forward to the assistance of Mr. Wright and yourself as I investigate the FBI's counter-terrorism performance both before and after September 11, 2001.

I request that you or Mr. Wright immediately contact my staff and I if either of you have any concerns regarding retaliation. Your point of contact will be John Drake, of my staff, who can be reached at (202) 224-xxxx.

Cordially yours,
Charles E. Grassley[514]

One morning in early May 2002, after FBIHQ had read my manuscript and prevented me from releasing any information contained within the manuscript, I received calls from several FBIHQ supervisors who knew me. The supervisors asked me, "Bob,

Afterword

is it true that you wrote a book and submitted it to the FBI for a pre-publication review?"

I said, "Yes, it's true."

The next question was, "Did you mention anything about Kathleen McChesney being responsible for closing a major international terrorism investigation in Chicago?"

I said, "Yes."

The supervisors asked me what exactly I wrote about McChesney in the book. I said, "Over two years before 9/11 occurred, McChesney negligently killed the FBI's only AOT criminal case, which may have prevented 9/11. In 1998, we seized $1.4 million from HAMAS and a guy named Yassin Kadi. After McChesney killed the case, she refused two written requests for the FBI Chicago office to reopen the VB investigation. The Chicago US Attorney's Office needed the FBI's help to prevent the return of the money to the terrorists. One million of these funds belonged to Yassin Kadi. After 9/11, Kadi was declared a chief financier of Osama bin Laden and labeled a 'Global International Terrorist Financier.'"

Each supervisor commented about "a rumor spreading like a wildfire throughout FBI headquarters that FBI Director Mueller called McChesney into his office this morning and told her she must retire." The rumor was Director Mueller learned about a book written by a Chicago FBI agent. Allegedly the book contained negative news about a terrorism case McChesney closed while still the Chicago SAC. According to the supervisors, the rumor was that "McChesney's refusing to retire."

I told two of the supervisors, "Of course she is refusing to retire. She does not believe she has done anything wrong. She is clueless. Because of her shutting down VB, a lot of innocent people have died in Palestine and Israel. She even prohibited me from working on any aspect of the 9/11 attacks. I have it in writing. I'm likely the only FBI employee to be banned from working on anything related to the FBI's 9/11 criminal investigation. How pathetic is that?"

Six months had passed since FBIHQ managers told me the rumor about Mueller requesting McChesney retire. On November 8, 2002, FBIHQ issued a national press release that reads:

> FBI Director Robert S. Mueller, III today announced that Executive Assistant Director Kathleen L. McChesney is retiring from the FBI after 24 years as a special agent to accept a position with the US Conference of Catholic Bishops.
>
> Ms. McChesney, 51, began her career with the FBI in August 1978 and rose through the ranks as an investigator, supervisor and manager in both field and headquarters positions. She served as special agent in charge of both the Portland, Oregon and Chicago divisions, and she served as assistant director for FBI training at Quantico, Virginia.[515]

McChesney would never retire on her own at age fifty-one after being promoted to the number two position in the FBI. I believe that in May, the FBI director gave her six months to find a new job.

I had warned McChesney that she could not justify the closing of Vulgar Betrayal. Specifically, on March 8, 2001, I had said, "On July 27, 1999, you requested that National Security designate Vulgar Betrayal as a major case. Two weeks later, you took my case away and shut it down. A lot of innocent people are going to die because of your closing Vulgar Betrayal. How will you ever explain your closing of Vulgar Betrayal in the future? Ma'am, there was no credible or justifiable reason to ever close this successful case."

Afterword

While conducting research for this book, I came across a letter written by a frustrated Muslim. She was upset with Muslim fanatics who used the Muslim religion to justify killing innocent people. Muslim terrorists claim the Muslim religion justifies their killing of innocent people in the name of Islam. However, most Muslims do not support the fanatic Muslims' misinterpretations of their peaceful religion.

Gulf News published the letter from Ayesha Nazar in Riyadh, Saudi Arabia, on August 27, 1998, following the bombings of the US embassies in Kenya and Tanzania. After reading her letter, I believed many Muslims felt the same as she. Therefore, I decided in 1999, I would end this book with her letter. The letter reads as follows:

> I am a Muslim by birth who practices Islam because I like what it teaches and because it makes sense. I don't feel the need to make such announcements but given the prejudiced nature of Muslims today I felt compelled to do so.
>
> I have been reading in your newspaper and in others of the region about how arrogant Americans are by attacking Afghanistan and Sudan. The ones who are arrogant are the so-called Islamic organizations; although what is Islamic about them, I have always failed to understand.
>
> They are so arrogant that they kill Americans, then openly announce intentions of further killings, and expect no retaliation. Then if America retaliates, they get all upset and give fatwa's that it is war against Islam. Which world are they living in, and which Qur'an do they read? The Qur'an I read forbids the killing of innocent civilians, especially women and children.
>
> Arrogant are these Muslims who see nothing wrong in one Islamic state attacking another for the sake of oil and wealth. The Qur'an I read leaves no forgiveness for a Muslim who

kills another Muslim. America came over to help us from such Muslims and all that we do is spit at them.

We suddenly get these warm feelings for Saddam Hussein who throws nerve gas on his own people, who again are Muslims. Where are these saviors of Islam, bin Laden and his cronies when this is happening? Where is Bin Laden when Muslims in Somalia scrape a few crumbs of food from the ground and eat boiled leaves at other times?

We again want America to send food because bin Laden is busy spending his money in thinking up a way to kill 12 Americans. I respect the Americans for they at least tried to keep the human casualties low by attacking at nighttime unlike the very intelligent Muslims who killed 12 Americans and 200 others. The Americans could have killed more but showed restraint and the Muslim terrorist could have killed fewer but did not.

The enemy of Islam is not America but we Muslims who do not stop these terrorists and punish them ourselves. It is our responsibility to keep a list of all organizations suspected of creating terror in the name of Islam and then we should denounce them collectively. Why do we allow a few thousand to blacken the name of millions of us? Because the peace-loving Muslims are cowards and have no confidence in their conviction.

Ayesha Nazar, Riyadh, Saudi Arabia.[516]

Afterword

Regarding Vulgar Betrayal's
Final Two Volumes, 3 & 4

The FBI's Post-9/11 Vulgar Betrayal Volumes 3 and 4 complete the *Vulgar Betrayal* four volume set. Volumes 3 & 4 were written from September 2001 through 2010. They provide a real-time account, with documentation, of the FBI's retaliatory efforts to prevent Agent Robert Wright from warning the US Congress and the American people about the FBI's failures to prevent 9/11.

The FBI did many unethical things to discourage Agent Wright from warning others about the FBI's inability to protect the America people from terrorist attacks. The following are a few of the unethical things the FBI did to Agent Wright.

Following the 9/11 attacks, after reading *Vulgar Betrayal*, FBI Headquarters (FBIHQ) lied to US senators and the media about Agent Wright, his Vulgar Betrayal investigation, and falsely claimed *Vulgar Betrayal* (Volumes 1 & 2), was "so intertwined with both classified and grand-jury information," that no one outside the FBI could view the book.

FBIHQ, in an email, encouraged a Muslim FBI agent to sue Agent Wright. Thereafter, FBI Chicago anonymously sent documents to the Muslim FBI agent's attorney to assist the Muslim agent's efforts to defeat Agent Wright in court.

Both FBIHQ and FBI Chicago pursued media smear campaigns against Agent Wright through *The Washington Post* and *Chicago Tribune*.

An FBIHQ Assistant Director and Deputy Director instructed the FBIHQ OPR Unit Chief to write a communication "in such a way as to deceive" a DOJ official from taking over an FBI investigating of Agent Wright. The Assistant Director claimed if the FBI could prevent the DOJ from taking the investigation, he could "take out" Agent Wright.

FBIHQ tried to fire Agent Wright twice for his legal efforts to expose FBI HQ's failures to prevent 9/11 to the American public and US Congress.

Several US Senators helped to protect Agent Wright from these and many other FBI management retaliations. Agent Wright credits US Senator Charles Grassley for protecting him from being wrongfully fired by the FBI in 2005.

The above are only a few of the many retaliatory efforts by the FBI against Agent Wright. The FBI did these things to cover up the FBI's negligence and incompetence leading up to the morning of the 9/11 attacks.

In May 2002, Agent Wright filed a First Amendment lawsuit against the FBI. The case was heard by US District Court Judge Gladys Kessler. Seven years later, on May 6, 2009, Judge Kessler's MEMORANDUM OPINION, finding in favor of Agent Wright publishing his book (*Vulgar Betrayal* 1&2), reads in part:

> This is a sad and discouraging tale about the determined efforts of the FBI to censor various portions of a 500-page manuscript, written by a long-time FBI agent (Wright), severely criticizing the FBI's conduct of investigating a money laundering scheme in which United States-based members of the Hamas terrorist organization were using non-profit organizations in this country to recruit and train terrorists and fund terrorist activities both here and abroad.

Afterword

In its efforts to suppress this information, the FBI repeatedly changed its position, presented formalistic objections to release of various portions of the documents in question, admitted finally that much of the material it sought to suppress was in fact, in the public domain and had been all along, and now concedes that several of the reasons it originally offered for censorship no longer have any validity.

Unfortunately, the issues of terrorism and of alleged FBI incompetence remain as timely as ever.[517]

AUTHORS BOOK REVIEW REQUEST

"If you enjoyed reading VULGAR BETRAYAL Vol. 2, please leave a book review on Amazon. Your review will help new readers learn the truth of the FBI's PRE-9/11 efforts, to keep this information from all Americans and Congress. I promise to read every review."

—Robert G. Wright, Jr.

For advanced notice of the future release date of 'THE FBI's POST-911 VULGAR BETRAYAL,' send an email to Support@VulgarBetrayal.com.

APPENDIX A

Appendix A-1. 472

Appendix A-2. 473

Appendix A-3. 474

Appendix A-4. 475

Appendix A-5. 476

Appendix A-6. 477

Appendix A-7. 478

Appendix A-8. 479

Appendix A-9. 480

Appendix A-10. 481

Appendix A-11. 482

Appendix A-12. 483

Appendix A-13. 484

Appendix A-14. 485

The FBI's Pre-9/11 Vulgar Betrayal

Appendix A

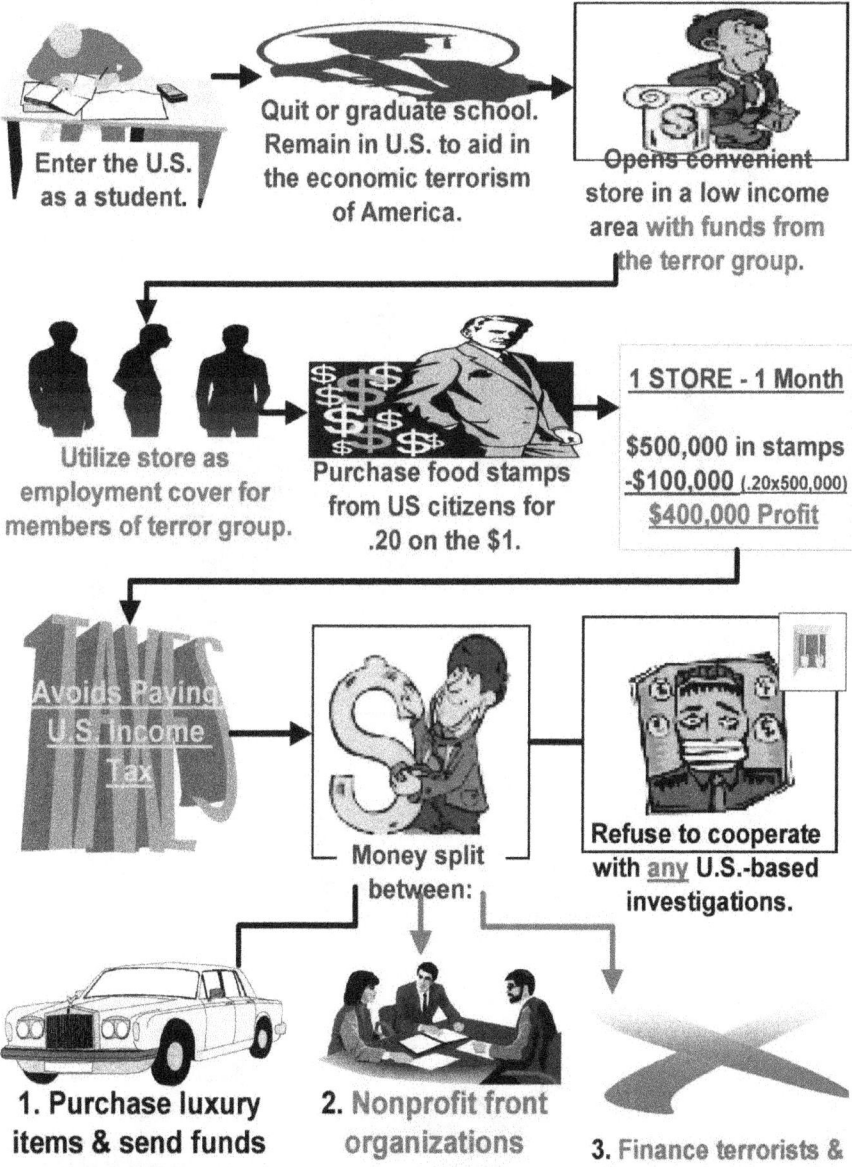

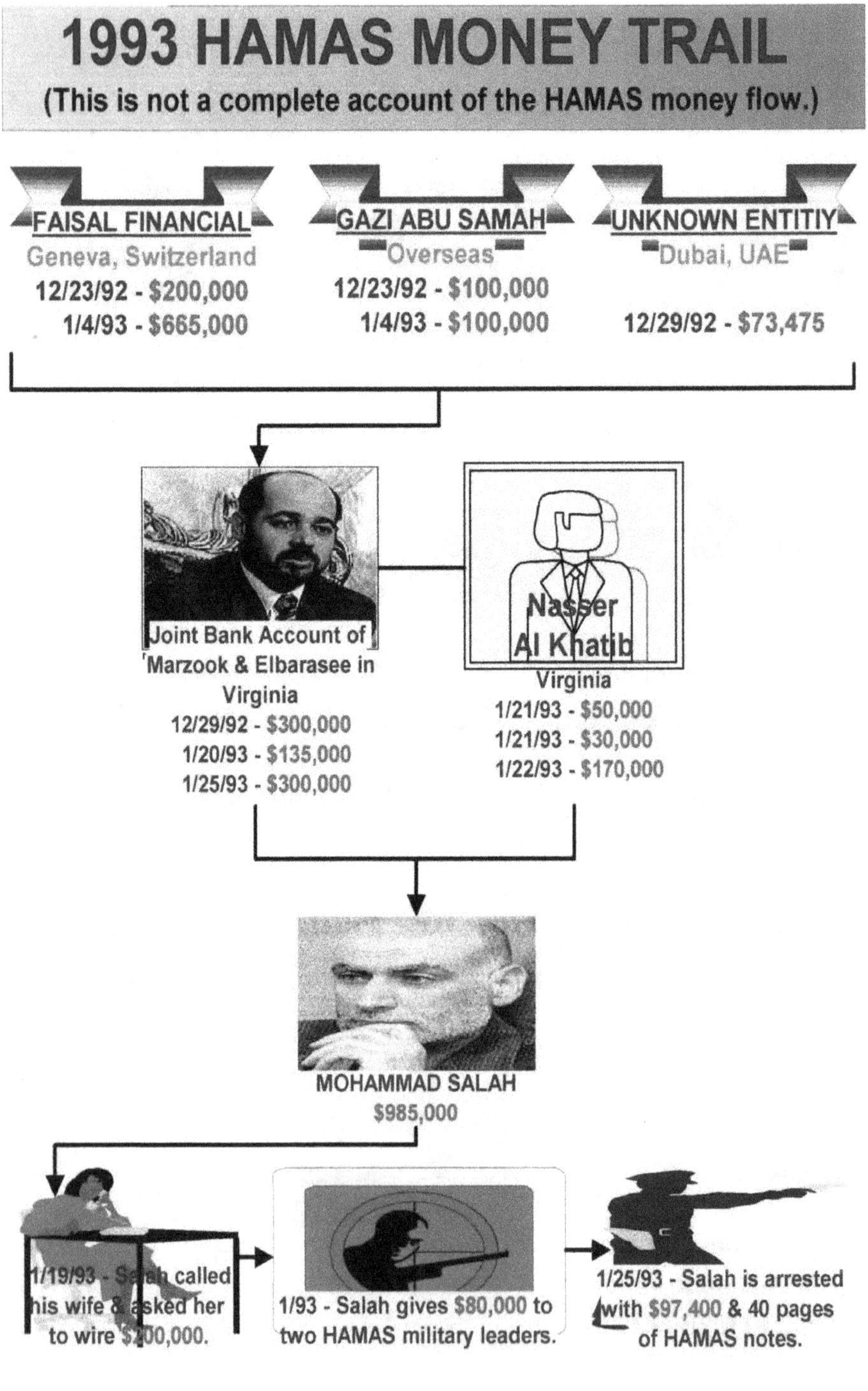

The FBI's Pre-9/11 Vulgar Betrayal

1993 HAMAS MONEY TRAIL
(This is not a complete account of the HAMAS money flow.)

FAISAL FINANCIAL
Geneva, Switzerland
12/23/92 - $200,000
1/4/93 - $665,000

GAZI ABU SAMAH
Overseas
12/23/92 - $100,000
1/4/93 - $100,000

UNKNOWN ENTITIY
Dubai, UAE
12/29/92 - $73,475

Joint Bank Account of Marzook & Elbarasee in Virginia
12/29/92 - $300,000
1/20/93 - $135,000
1/25/93 - $300,000

Nasser Al Khatib
Virginia
1/21/93 - $50,000
1/21/93 - $30,000
1/22/93 - $170,000

MOHAMMAD SALAH
$985,000

1/19/93 - Salah called his wife & asked her to wire $200,000.

1/93 - Salah gives $80,000 to two HAMAS military leaders.

1/25/93 - Salah is arrested with $97,400 & 40 pages of HAMAS notes.

Appendix A

US-BASED TERROR TRAINING
(May 1990 - January 1993)

MARZOOK
U.S. HAMAS LEADER

SALAH
MILITARY COMMADER

7 Additional U.S. based leaders from Virginia, Mississippi, Tennessee, and Illinois assisted Salah in the U.S.-based training of HAMAS terrorists.

TRAINING CAMP #1
May 1990
CHICAGO, ILLINOIS

Attendees:
Sharif Alwan
Rizick Abdelrazick
5 others

Instructors:
Mohammad Salah
1 other

Training:
Explosives
Use of Detonators
Bomb production
Stinger Missles

TRAINING CAMP #2
June 1990
WISCONSIN

Attendees:
Sharif Alwan
Rizick Abdelrazick
Hisham Hidimi
Many others

Instructors:
Mohammad Salah
Mousa Marzook
4 others

Training:
Explosives
Weapons
Car Bombs
HAMAS Ideology

TRAINING CAMP #3
Fall 1990
CHICAGO, ILLINOIS

Attendees:
Sharif Alwan
Rizick Abdelrazick
10 others

Instructors:
Mohammad Salah
2 others

Training:
Explosives
Weapons
Long distance walking

TRAINING CAMP #4
December 1990
KANSAS CITY, MO

Attendees:
Hisham Hidimi
5 others

Instructors:
Mohammad Salah
1 other

Training:
Explosives
Weapons
Car Bombs
HAMAS Ideology

INTERNATIONAL TRAINING CAMP #1
SYRIA - September 1992

Attendees: **Alwan & Abdelrazick**
Trip Ordered & Financed by:
Mousa Marzook & Mohammad Salah
Trained by: **Hizbollah Terrorist Org.**
Training: **Weapons & Explosives**

INTERNATIONAL TRAINING CAMP #2
LEBANON - November 1992 to Jan. 1993

Attendees: **Alwan & Abdelrazick**
Trip Ordered & Financed by:
Mousa Marzook & Mohammad Salah
Trained by: **Hizbollah Terrorist Org.**
Training: **Weapons & Explosives**

The FBI's Pre-9/11 Vulgar Betrayal

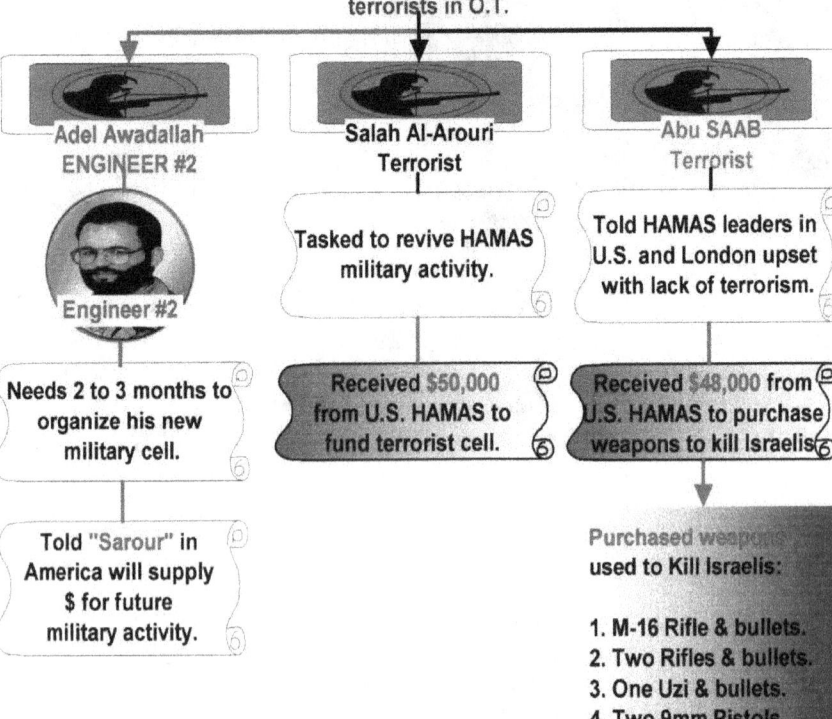

Appendix A

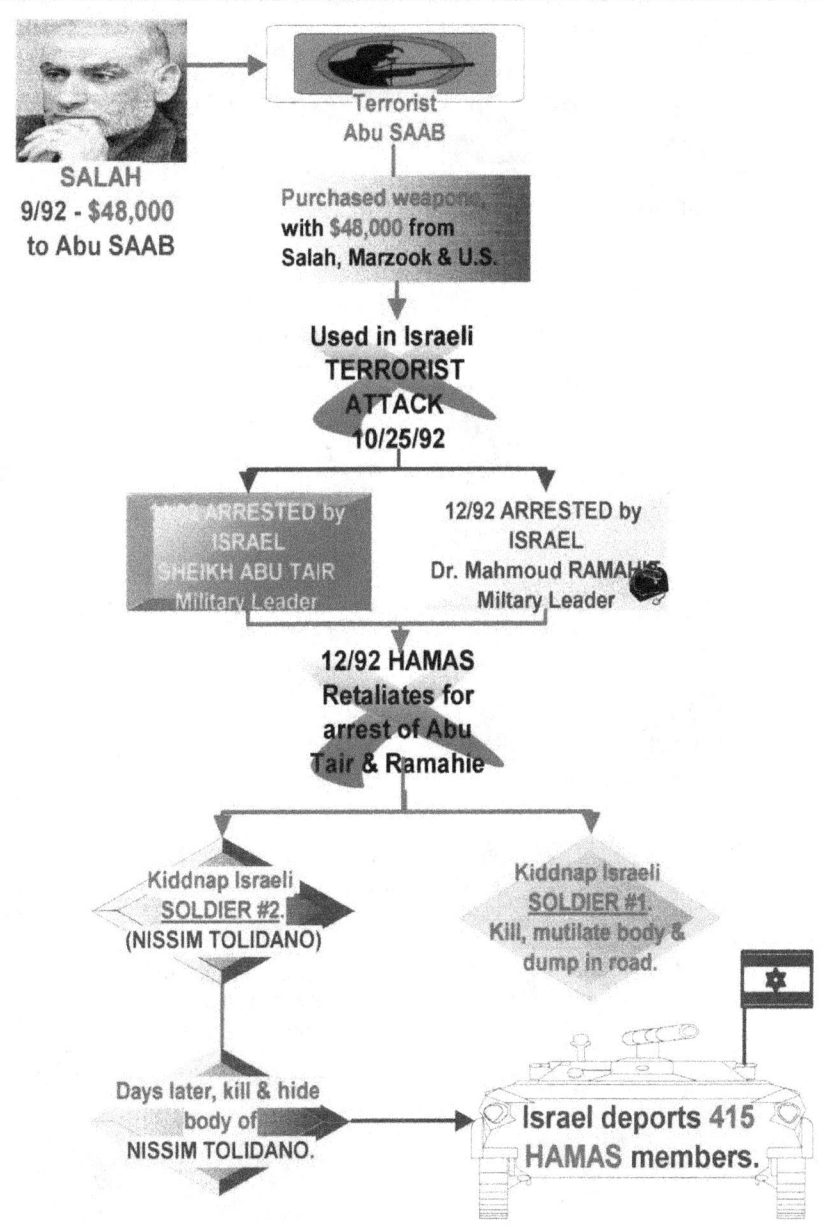

The FBI's Pre-9/11 Vulgar Betrayal

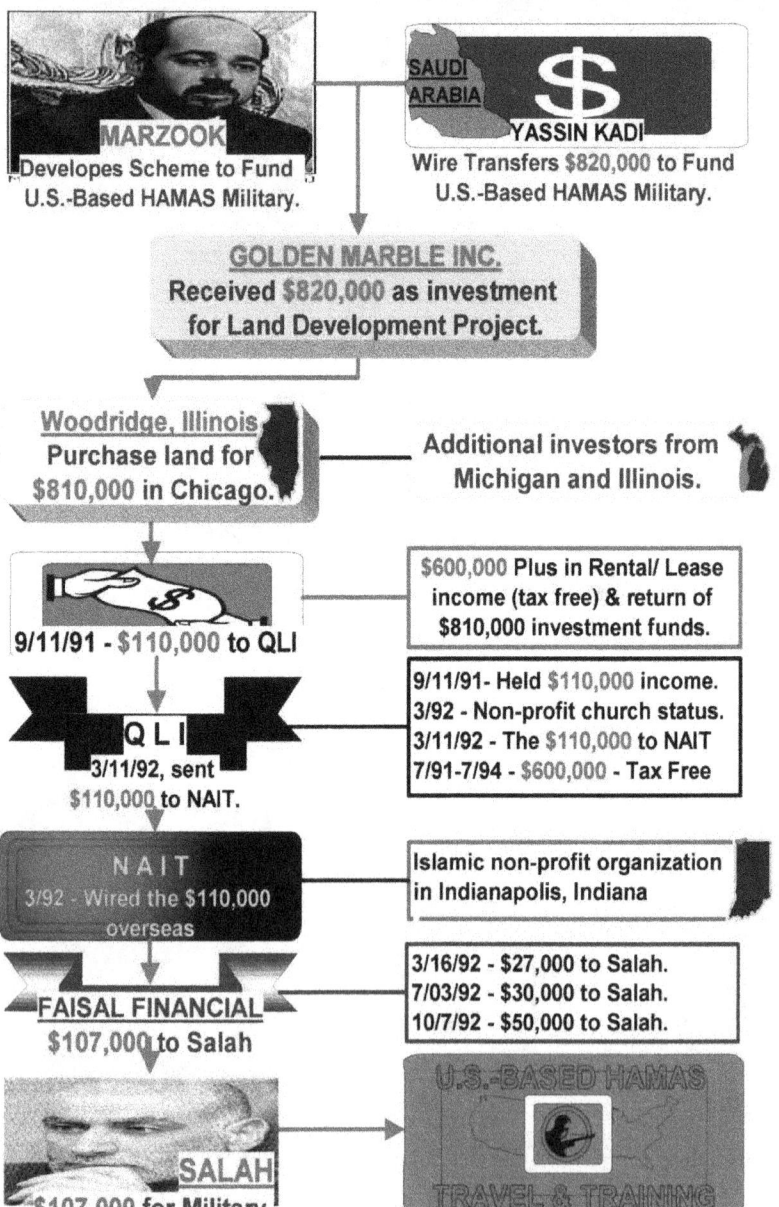

Appendix A

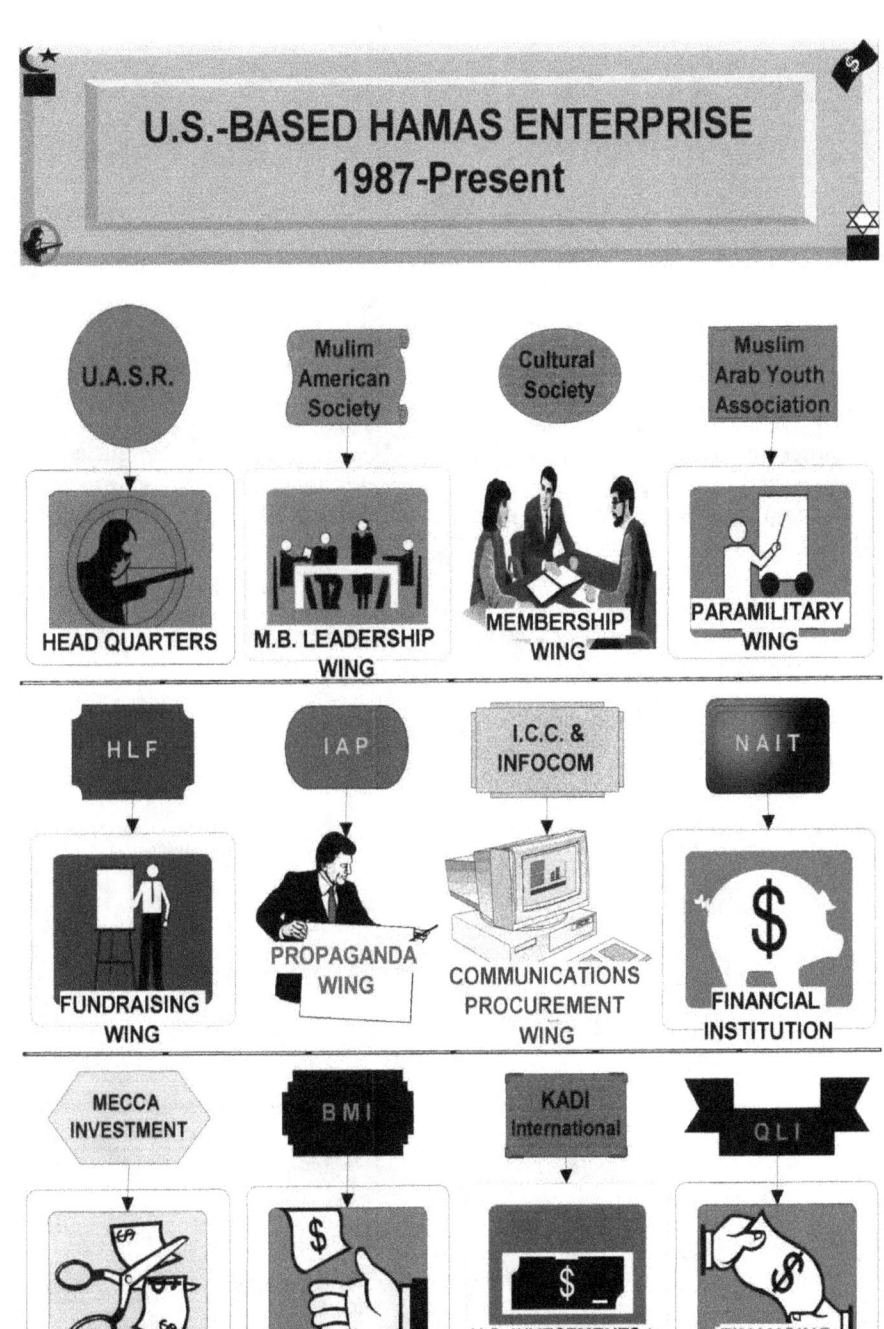

The FBI's Pre-9/11 Vulgar Betrayal

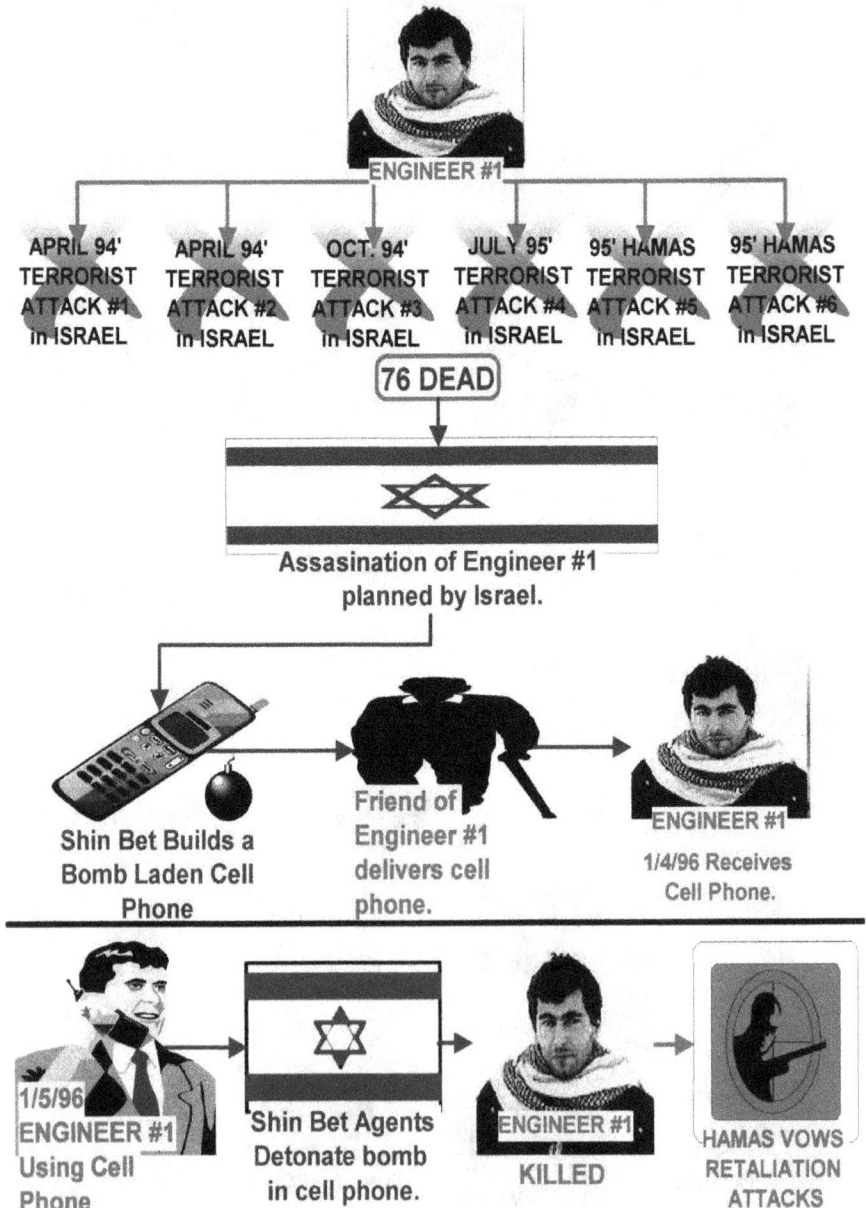

Appendix A

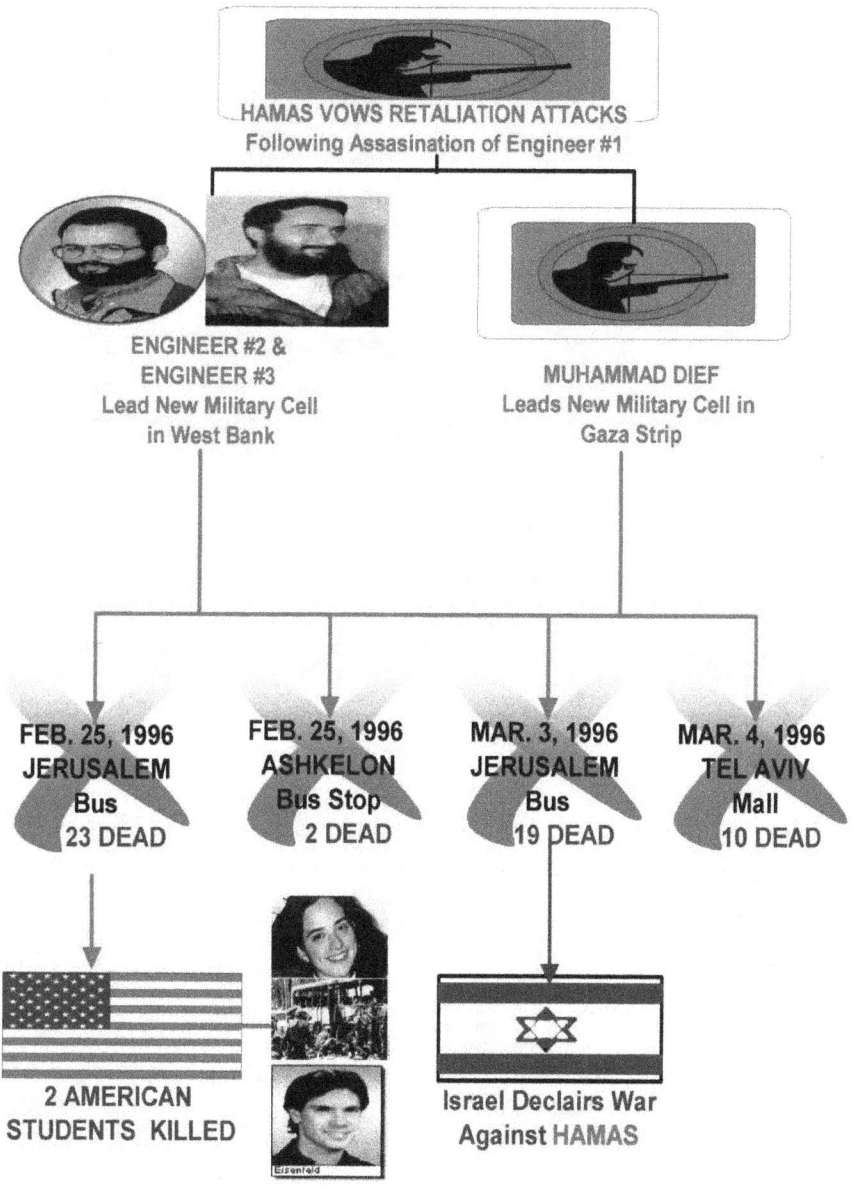

481

The FBI's Pre-9/11 Vulgar Betrayal

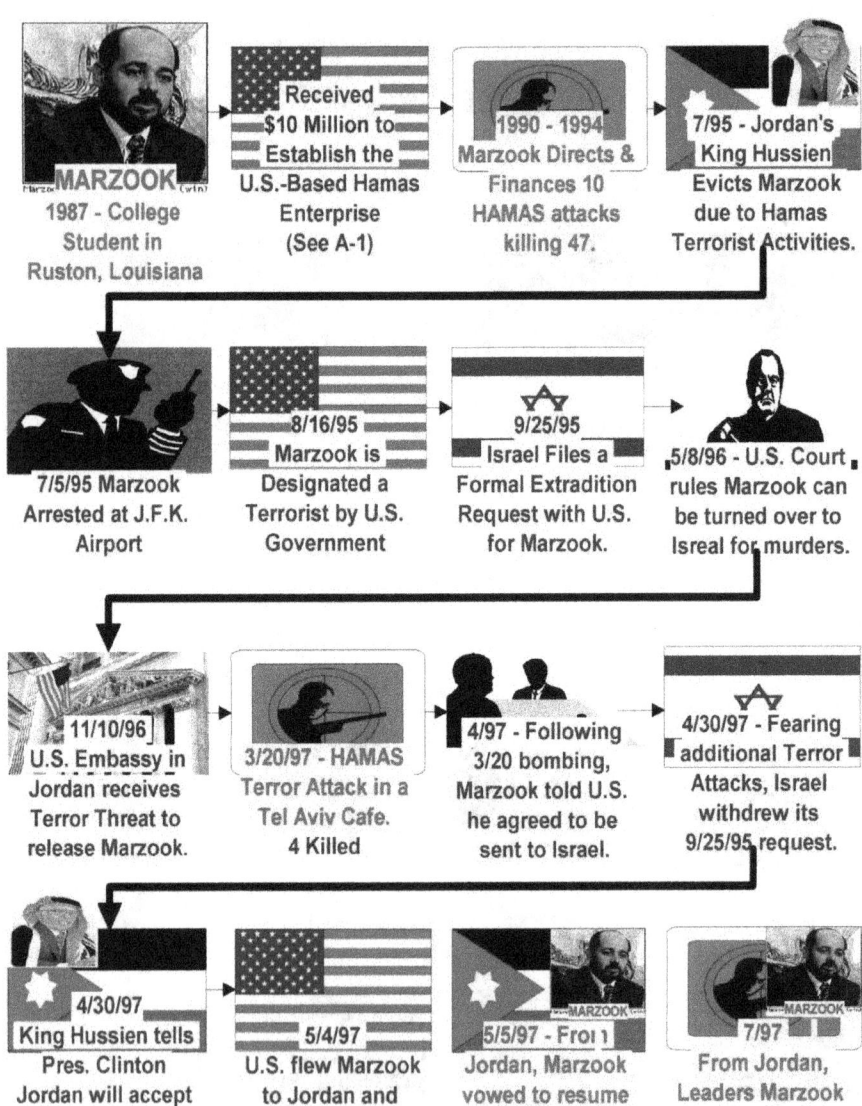

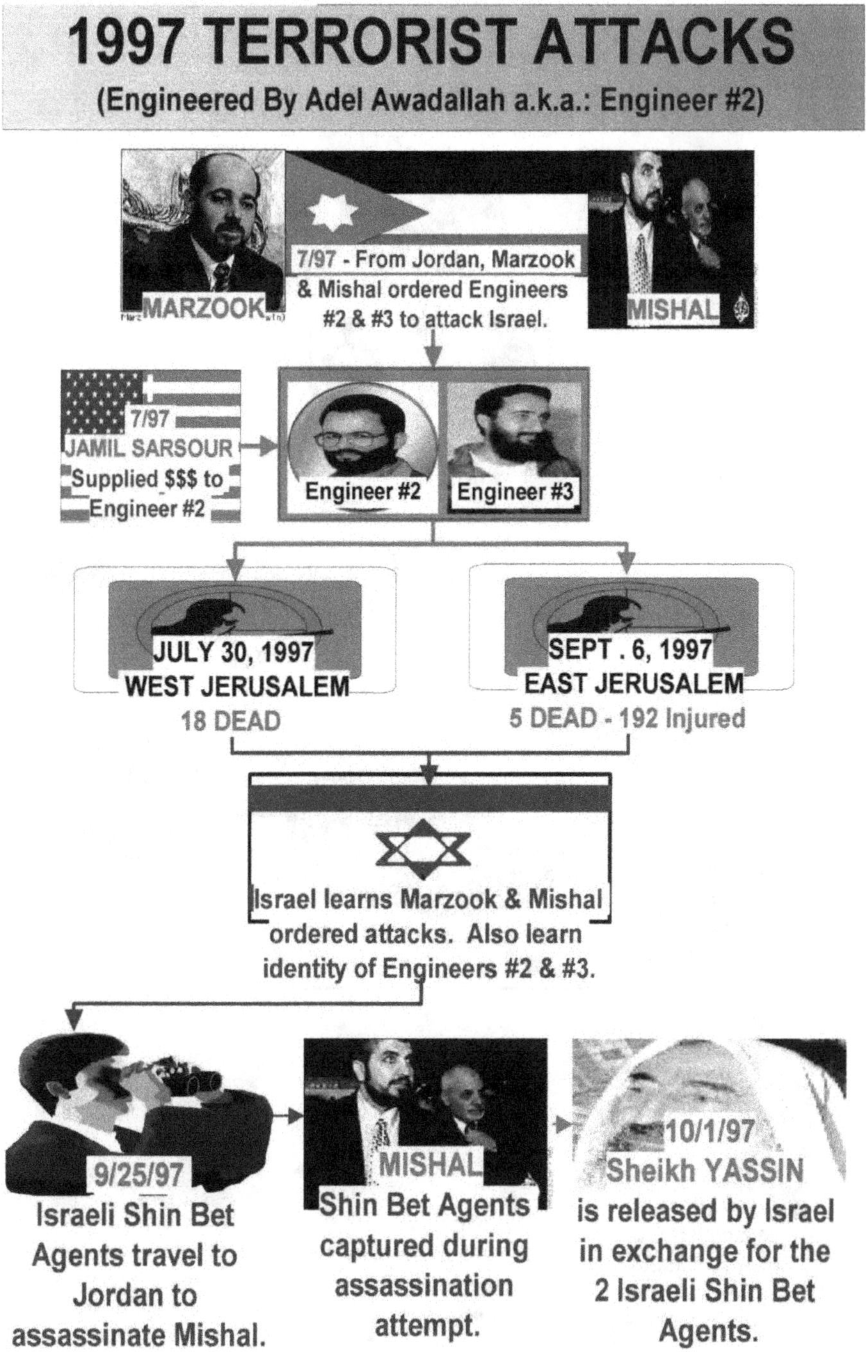

Appendix A

1997 TERRORIST ATTACKS
(Engineered By Adel Awadallah a.k.a.: Engineer #2)

7/97 - From Jordan, Marzook & Mishal ordered Engineers #2 & #3 to attack Israel.

MARZOOK — MISHAL

7/97 JAMIL SARSOUR Supplied $$$ to Engineer #2

Engineer #2 — Engineer #3

JULY 30, 1997 WEST JERUSALEM — 18 DEAD

SEPT. 6, 1997 EAST JERUSALEM — 5 DEAD - 192 Injured

Israel learns Marzook & Mishal ordered attacks. Also learn identity of Engineers #2 & #3.

9/25/97 Israeli Shin Bet Agents travel to Jordan to assassinate Mishal.

MISHAL — Shin Bet Agents captured during assassination attempt.

10/1/97 Sheikh YASSIN is released by Israel in exchange for the 2 Israeli Shin Bet Agents.

The FBI's Pre-9/11 Vulgar Betrayal

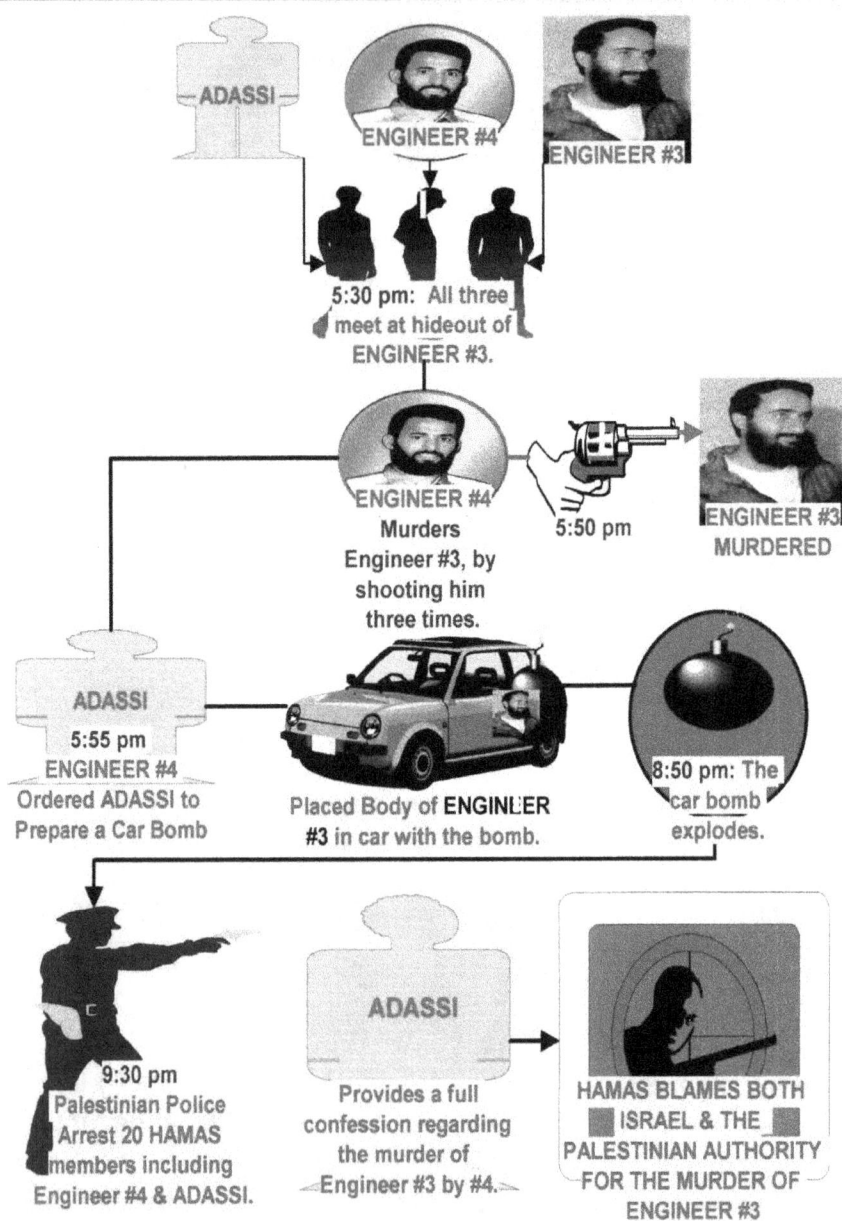

Appendix A

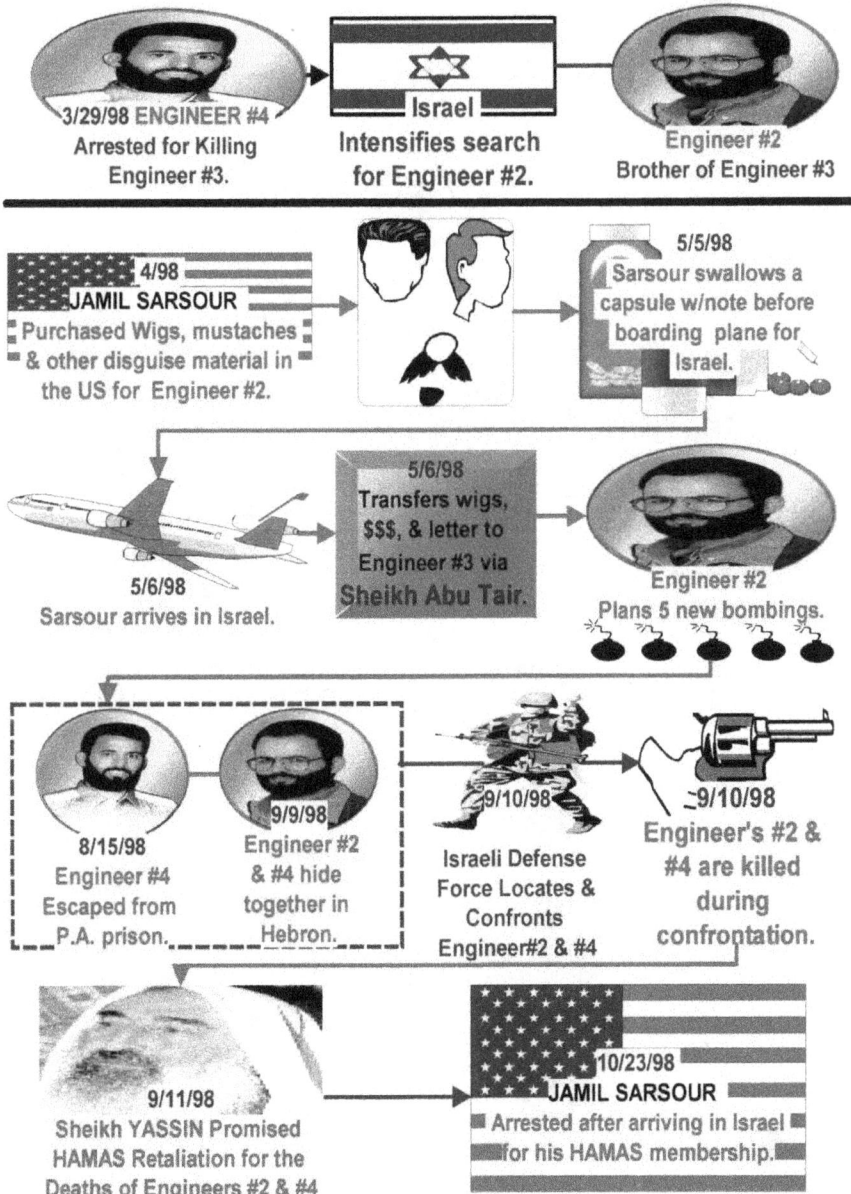

ABOUT THE AUTHOR

Robert G. Wright is a retired FBI Special Agent who spent seven years of his career on the FBI's Joint Terrorism Task Force, based in Chicago.

He grew up in Jasper, Indiana, and graduated from Indiana State University with degrees in Criminology and Business Administration, attended the Indiana University Law School, and passed the Indiana Bar Exam and became an FBI Agent in 1990.

During his thirty-two years with the FBI, retiring in 2022, Wright received two FBI Director Letters of Commendation, an FBI Director Incentive Award, an FBI Director Citation for Special Achievement, and five FBI Director Time Off Awards. Wright also received four FBI 10K gold Fidelity, Bravery and Integrity medals for his years of service to the FBI.

Wright received an FBI commemorative pin for his work on the 9/11 investigation. Wright gave the FBI 9/11 pin to ABC News reporter Brian Ross. "FBI Assistant Director McChesney banned me 'from working on any aspect of the 9/11 investigation.' I gave Brian the FBI 9/11 pin because he was doing more than anyone to help John Vincent and me expose the FBI's pre 9/11 negligence to the American people and Congress," he said.

This book is the culmination of years of work investigating the largest FBI act of terrorism criminal case in the bureau's history before the attacks on 9/11. The investigation was code named Vulgar Betrayal, also the title of this book.

Wright met his wife, Angie, in October 2005 and married in October 2007. They have five children, Beemer (2008), Sabrina (2010), Tabitha (2012), Clarissa (2014), and Priscilla (2016). Wright has coached the kids in basketball, soccer, and football teams.

As a new agent, Wright was told by senior agents that he should focus on retirement plans for his life after the FBI. In 1995, he came up with a business retirement option. In 1999, the FBI allowed Wright to proceed with his business retirement plan. Since 1999 and after his retirement, he and Angie have continued working a successful business together.

www.ingramcontent.com/pod-product-compliance
Lightning Source LLC
Chambersburg PA
CBHW060447030426
42337CB00015B/1515